READING

for the

LOVE OF IT

Michele Landsberg

READING
for the
LOVE OF IT

Best Books for Young Readers

PRENTICE HALL PRESS
New York   London   Toronto   Sydney   Tokyo

For Stephen, my partner in all things that
matter most, including the pleasures of
children's literature

———————

Prentice Hall Press
Gulf + Western Building
One Gulf + Western Plaza
New York, New York 10023

Originally published as MICHELE LANDSBERG'S GUIDE TO
CHILDREN'S BOOKS in Canada by Penguin Books Canada Limited,
1986.

PRENTICE HALL PRESS and colophon are registered trademarks of
Simon & Schuster Inc.

Library of Congress Cataloging in Publication Data

Landsberg, Michele.
  Reading for the love of it.

  Rev. ed. of: Michele Landsberg's guide to children's books. 1985.
  Includes index.
  1. Bibliography—Best books—Children's literature.
2. Children's literature—Bibliography. I. Landsberg,
Michele. Guide to children's books. II. Title.
Z1037.L313 1987   [PN1009.A1]   011'.62   87-9247

ISBN 0-13-579822-1
ISBN 0-13-755125-8 (Pbk.)
Designed by Laurie S. Barnett
Manufactured in the United States of America

10 9 8 7 6 5 4 3 2 1

First Paperback Edition

Acknowledgments

I would like to acknowledge, with pleasure and appreciation, the following people who helped me to see this book through to fruition: My children, Ilana Naomi, Avi David, and Jenny Leah Zlateh, for their wildly various and volubly shared tastes and insights; my editor, David Kilgour, whose tactful criticisms were all the more valued because he believed in this book; Sheila Kieran, for more kindnesses than can be listed; Judy Sarick, owner of the Children's Book Store in Toronto, for generous advice, moral support, and wisdom; Celia Lotteridge, Marion Seary, and the other staff of the Children's Book Store, who were always willing to stop for book talk; Lissa Paul of the Children's Literature Round Table, for her encouragement; Anna and Julian Porter, for their enthusiasm and practical help; my dear friend Ellen Denoon Charney, for listening skeptically; Leslie Coates, who volunteered with unbelievable generosity (and a keener eye than mine) to do painstaking picture research, and Margaret Maloney, Jill Shefrin, and Dana Tenny, librarians of the Osborne Collection in Toronto, for their unstinting assistance; the East York/Scarborough Reading Association, from whose annual conference I took the title for this American edition; the Canadian Children's Book Centre in Toronto; the Children's Book Council in New York; the knowledgeable and forgiving librarians of Toronto's Boys and Girls House; the late librarian of St. Clement's, in my childhood, who made all the difference.

Table of Contents

INTRODUCTION

The moving accident is not my trade;
To freeze the blood I have no ready arts:
'Tis my delight, alone in summer shade,
To pipe a simple song for thinking hearts.

William Wordsworth, "Hart-Leap Well," 1800

Into the narrow, quiet, regular life of a child growing up in Toronto in the 1940s—the overgrown backyard, the alleyway where I bounced my ball against the side of the house, the bus trips to piano lessons—suddenly there thundered a huge caravan of exotic warriors, heroines, and horses, swords flashing, animals bellowing, clouds of dust and incense, the blare of horns calling me to adventure. I did not merely stand and gape: Sitting on the concrete steps of our porch in the long shady afternoons, or trapped in my wooden prison of a desk at public school, I simultaneously leaped astride those sweating horses, swung in a long, stomach-dropping arc on a jungle vine, turned my ship into the teeth of the gale. I was *inside* those children who stepped back through the magic arch into ancient Egypt, shivering their shiver of apprehension and excitement. And nobody knew (except perhaps my librarian) that while I plodded dutifully to school—a new roll-top pencil box was the thrill of second grade—I was secretly living a hundred other lives.

It began quietly enough with Ping, the Yangtze River duck, waddling across my path. Soon enough the Bobbsey Twins came simpering by. The procession swelled; the Eskimo Twins panted along in the turbulence created by Henty's *Armada,* Blind Pew stumped and stalked beside the girl on the garden swing, Nesbit's *Five Children and It* scampered ahead into an arcadian future, the splendor fell on castle walls, and we all galloped from Ghent to Aix, breathless and dazzled.

3

Books were far more than an amusement in my childhood; they were my other lives, and this visible existence I now lead in the workaday world was touched and transformed by them forever. The spell was never broken; all through my adult life, children's literature has given me unabated pleasure. It's like those big blackball candies we used to buy: The longer you rolled one around inside your cheek, the more splendid and various were the colors revealed. As my own children grew, the books I had loved and the books I discovered through and for them took on ever-new colors and shades of meaning, and confirmed my belief that a child's life without books read for pleasure is a child's life deprived.

My hope is that through this book, many more adults will be persuaded to discover, not only how literature can enhance a child's life but what surprising delights await the adult who can unbend enough to read along with the child. Moreover, I hope to show, step by step, how any adult can become a skilled and confident chooser of the best books for the particular child he or she has in mind. I do discuss some approaches to learning how to read, particularly in the "Taking the Plunge" chapter, but this is primarily a book on the "why" and the "what," not the "how," of children's reading.

No list, however extensive, can ever do justice to the wealth of children's literature. As Sheila Egoff, Canada's leading writer on the subject, has pointed out, more than 100,000 children's books have been published in Britain and the United States alone since 1957. That's why a list of titles is the merest beginning. I've tried to be more thoroughly useful in this book by writing about exemplary books in some detail, showing what strengths and beauties to look for in choosing a book, and by discussing the adult's role in encouraging, stimulating, and sustaining the child's interest in reading.

Most adults who pick up a volume about children's books expect or hope for a neat tour-guide of the best books for each age group, like restaurants listed by neighborhood. But how sound can those age gradings be? I know twelve-year-olds who read *Winnie the Pooh* with delight, six-year-olds who zoom through Tolkien, and eight-year-olds who are just cutting their teeth, so to speak, on sophisticated picture books. Reading ability and rigid age groupings do not go hand in hand; furthermore, a child of any age might read widely across the whole range, leap forward, or regress for a while to some simple, comforting book that has just the right balm to soothe a current ache.

For that reason, I've tackled this dauntingly huge subject matter by theme, rather than age group. If you need, right this minute, a thrilling adventure story for a ten-year-old, you may turn to the chapter on adventure and find there a discussion of adventure stories for children in each age group. But remember that themes as well as reading levels overlap, and every child needs a wide variety of books.

Another way to use this book is to consult the guide to recommended reading at the back of the book. You will find there the titles of more than 400 works of fiction for children five to fifteen, arranged according to ages and reading levels. Picture books have been included, but are chosen specifically for their value in encouraging or enabling the child to read. Many spectacular picture books are not mentioned here only because they didn't fall within this narrow definition.

As far as I know, this is the first comprehensive guide to general children's literature that represents an equal balance of books in which boys and girls play active, central roles. For a discussion of the relative importance of this aspect of childhood reading, please see chapter 10.

You may be dismayed to find that some of your own favorite books are not mentioned here. It's chilly comfort, but many of my favorites are missing, too: In choosing boys' and girls' books, a mix of the easy and the demanding, and an ample selection for every age group and interest, I found to my horror that there just wasn't room for a pure distillation of all my most loved books. There are, however, representative best works from the whole of the English-speaking world, and almost all of the stellar authors are present at least in the bibliography.

A further note about selection: I strove for balance, but the guide is also determinedly personal. I have not included any book that I didn't read and enjoy myself, no matter what its claims to popularity or glory. What's the point of a guide that lists everything, to cover every taste? You might as well resort to the library's card index. Instead, I've tried to show as clearly as possible my grounds for selection; readers will certainly not share all of my conclusions, but they will at least know how and why I reached them.

Grounds for nonselection are more ambiguous. Since this book was published in Canada, hundreds of people have asked me, in tones plaintive or accusatory, why I omitted one of their cherished favorites. Some books are not on the list because I don't recommend them; some aren't there because, though I loved them, they are hopelessly unavailable (such as *The Far-Distant Oxus, Escape to Persia,* and *Crowns,* by Katherine Hull and Pamela Whitlock). And some stars in the firmament of children's literature, such as *Alice in Wonderland, Winnie the Pooh,* and *Peter Pan,* are not here because they are so well known that it hardly matters that they glitter rather coldly for me.

This is a critical guide. I've tried to share my enthusiasm for some wonderful books and to show my reasons for disliking or even detesting others. Criticism, however, is not a popular avocation. Along with the democratization of culture has grown up an almost belligerent attitude that negative comment on *any* book, film, or play is a personal attack on those who actually enjoyed it. This seems to be a particular problem in the children's book world. No one would take Harold Bloom, John Updike, or Elizabeth Hardwick to task for failing to give serious consideration to Judith Krantz's latest work, but children's book critics are inevitably accused of elitism, prissiness, or bourgeois smugness if they so much as suggest that there is a difference between good and bad children's books. In part, this is a legacy of the counterculture. An ironic enthusiasm for trash (consider, for example, the zest for cartoons, graffiti, and TV imagery in the art world) is now accepted as the hallmark of a creative and independent individual who defies the norms of bourgeois culture. To encourage children to wallow in popular culture, however, is quite another matter, discussed in chapter 10.

Still, one must confront one of the main arguments advanced by aggressive populists: They say, and they are right, that adults *do* stand between children and books. Adults choose, buy, and convey the books to those too young to act autonomously. Children's advocates often fear that overprotective, narrow, or censorious mother figures (librarians, teachers, or critics like me) will impose their repressive taste on young people, merely by expressing literary opinions. It is interesting (though maybe not conclusive) that, in my experience, it is often men who take this line, and often in terms so personally rancorous that they would seem still to be struggling against some powerful and suffocating Mom. The pop-culture negative image of librarians is, I think, an offshoot of this misplaced misogyny.

Let it be said right here that this book never argues for removing, repressing, or censoring any kind of childhood reading. Adult responsibility, as I see it, is not to deny, but to add, enrich, stimulate, amplify. To turn away with an indifferent shrug from helping children to choose books is not good enough. If anything goes, nothing matters. And children's literature does matter, so intensely, that we adults ought to argue ferociously among ourselves about it. We ought to be willing to examine our own tastes and compare them rigorously with the informed opinions of others.

Over the course of forty years of reading children's literature, I've often been grateful to critics for pointing out hidden treasures or overlooked flaws in books with which I was familiar. I hope, with an amateur's ardor, that my readers will approach my judgments in the same open spirit.

One last word on the practical uses of this book. Many of the works I've written about are now, horribly enough, out of print. Some of them, even recent titles, are going out of print as I'm writing, so that even if I wanted to write a book recommending only current titles, it would be physically impossible to do so.

In the last decade, as the market has been flooded with "commodity" books for children (those based on cartoon, toy, or film characters, with sentiments and vocabulary vilely calculated by market survey), publishers have had to hatchet away at their back lists with appalling savagery. They tell us that they can no longer afford the warehouse space to keep classic children's works—or even the award-winning children's novels from the year before last—in print. It's like letting all of Jane Austen vanish from the world because Sidney Sheldon is more profitable.

The obvious answer is to search the local libraries for some of these gems that may longer be available in bookstores; lobby the bookstore owner to lobby publishers to reprint vanished works; check the children's shelves at library sales, garage sales, and used book stores. I have found all the books in this guide, even those never published in the United States, available in American libraries. Some I have found on bookstore shelves where they had obviously sat, quietly gathering dust, while they went out of print. If your local library or bookseller can't find a title for you, keep your eye open for it in every bookstore you visit. The glee of serendipity, when you spot it in the most unlikely place, will reward your perseverance.

Like any commitment, a devotion to excellence in children's literature is going to cost you money. Once you become familiar with superb authors, you will want to buy their most recent book at once, instead of waiting to see when—or if—your impoverished local library will get round to buying it. Indeed, buying books (and frequently they are available in very cheap paperbacks) is the only way to ensure that they stay in print.

A common complaint is that children's books, especially high-quality picture books, cost so much. All I can say is that they always cost less than a dinner out or a new pair of kids' jeans. The books I read as a child transformed me, gave meaning and perspective to my experiences, and helped to mold whatever imaginative, intellectual, or creative strengths I can lay claim to now. No doll or game had that impact on me; no pair of new jeans ever changed my life.

Chapter 1

TAKING
THE PLUNGE

Like all mothers, I used to ask my son when he was six and seven what he had done in school that day. I misguidedly longed to know what *I* thought was important: the schoolyard adventures, the teacher's comments, the tests and projects. Invariably, he would pause, reflect, and then tell me, with sparkling eyes, whatever story he had heard or read that day. He, at least, knew what had been most important to him.

Imagination is the quality we say we value in children, but in our adult lives we are always in danger of passing it by without a flicker of recognition. To my child, the imaginative life kindled in him by stories was unquestionably the most real and gripping event of his school day, but I would stand metaphorically on one foot, waiting for the *real* stuff of classroom achievement.

"Imagination," wrote Ted Hughes, the English poet, "is the faculty of creating a picture in our heads and holding it there while we think about it." All human endeavors have to begin with just such an exercise of the imagination, he argued, and yet education completely neglects the task of strengthening this vital human faculty. Perhaps Hughes is wrong in saying "completely"; after all, there are classrooms like my son's where stories are told and read. Listen to Dan Yashinsky, a gifted Toronto storyteller, who recently wrote in the *Globe and Mail:*

> I see it in the eyes of children when I go into schools to tell stories: a deep hunger for the world of wonder, a deep satisfaction with the unadorned spoken word, and, most of all, a pride that they too can possess a story to call to their own remembrance.

Most of us recognize imagination at work and pause respectfully for it when a three-year-old stops short on a sidewalk and contemplates a pebble or an ant for what seems, to the hurrying adult, like an endless moment. Beyond that, however, we flounder.

Paula Fox, an outstanding American author writes:

> Goethe wrote that supreme imagining is the effort to grasp truth through imagination. It does not consist in making things different but in trying to discover them as they are. Imagination is random and elusive. We deduce its presence by its effects, just as we deduce that a breeze has sprung up, a breeze we can't see, because we hear and see the rustling of leaves in a tree. It is the guardian spirit that we sense in great stories; we feel its rustling. Imagination can be stillborn; it can be stifled. But it can be awakened. When you read to a child, when you put a book in a child's hands, you are bringing that child news of the infinitely varied nature of life. You are an awakener.

To be an awakener now seems to me the supreme challenge of parenthood. Our North American children are the best nourished, educated, healthiest, and most cherished population of children in history. Yet the single most common cry from the heart I heard from readers when I was a newspaper columnist was this: "Why don't my children seem to have any values?" In the winter of 1985, that dilemma seemed to be crystallized in the news story about a university student who went to Nicaragua. He took a series of pictures, later to be published internationally, of a Nicaraguan peasant who had been captured by the Contras. The pictures showed the peasant digging his own grave at gunpoint, lying down it, and being stabbed in the throat by the Contra guerrillas. The young photographer later told interviewers that he didn't really have any reactions while he took his profitable pictures; he was too busy with the speed and aperture settings on his camera.

The incident wonderfully focused for me my own goals in writing this book. It would, of course, be folly to suggest that the student photographer would not have grown into a morally and emotionally numb bystander to cruelty had he only been raised on good children's literature. Still, his icy self-command, apparently born of a bottomless detachment from the human condition, is the specter that troubles the dreams of civilized parents.

Who can take an honest, dispassionate look at the world in which we raise our children and not be dismayed, not worry that the humane values we cherish will be bludgeoned out of our children by the world's horrors? By now, the mind of every child I know over the age of eight is tinged with nuclear nihilism. No parent can any longer protect the child from dangerous and fearful knowledge. Where will the children get the courage, resilience, and commitment they will need to cope with the future?

We try to raise our children optimistically, but scientific advances and the relentless push of technology have left our conventional moralities lurching far behind: the sale of body organs for transplant or research, global satellite spying, dead lakes, poisoned fish, oil slicks drifting to the silent poles, the march of deserts and starvation across continents, a permanent and growing world population of embittered unemployed youth. . . . Everyone knows the litany; no one has answers.

Cocooned in consumerism, we would like to believe we can draw a magic circle of safety around our families. We concentrate our energies on living well—so far beyond the dreams of our parents— and anesthetize ourselves to the rest. We even have a special term of mock-opprobrium for the rising generation which seems to epitomize this see-no-evil self-centered acquisitiveness: We call them "yuppies." But aren't they, with their stylized consumption, their croissants, jogging clinics, business degrees, and baby aerobics classes, just the latest wave of threatened settlers, circling the wagons to ward off encroaching doom?

They, too, will have to face the task of raising children who may be redundant—or incinerated. They, too, looking in their children's eyes, will wonder what to give them to make them equal to the world's overwhelming challenges. Meanwhile, the children, growing up in a uniquely menacing age, have wired themselves for sound and are doing their best to obliterate thought. They live in a constant din of electronic noise, their eyes glazed with channel-flicking images of fragmentation and visual chaos. Is there any room left for reflection, dream, and curiosity?

From the ages of nine months, when the typical North American infant watches an hour and a half of television a day, to preadolescence, he or she watches 7,000 violent deaths during 15,000 hours of television. That is more time than is spent in play, in school, or in conversation with parents. Our children are being reared by television.

For the past twenty years, the Annenberg School of Communications at the University of Pennsylvania has been studying the impact of television on society. More than ten years ago, I first read their grim conclusion that television is not a *part* of our culture; it *is* our culture. I realized the truth of it as I looked around at cultivated parents with post-literate children whose heroes are "Miami Vice" cops and He-Man, Master of the Universe. The ages-old natural process by which parents transmitted their culture (ideas, values, ways of speech, heroes, myths) to their offspring has been brutally broken off. Now all our children are the children of McLuhan, and their values are shaped by the thousands of hours of cops and robbers shows that they watch.

For the most part, those values are shockingly warped. Parents are aware of this; most make valiant efforts to encourage the watching of excellent programs on public networks. But even the most vigilant adults report that their children seem to slip effortlessly past the restrictions. If they don't soak up hours of commercial television at home, they see it at their friends' houses and listen to inexhaustible verbal replays on the playground.

By now, it is a truism that commercial television shows a false and crazy world in which the rich are worshipped, violence is the way righteous men solve problems, and only a third of the population is female. Heavy viewers of television are, according to the Annenberg School's studies, more racist, sexist, and frightened of the world (hence, more accepting of violent solutions) than nonviewers. Many parents shrug off this danger because they "don't want to make the children feel different from others" by keeping television out of the house. The result is that the children aren't different: They share a common TV culture with other children, no matter how various are the values of the parents.

The typical TV-watching child is impatient, bored with anything but the most immediate and explosive stimuli, and a worshipper of

media fame. Listen to any grou
ground, no matter what their fan
a constant, shrill invocation of m
ing cars, and superheroes. The fa
Go-bots, ingeniously devised sma
formed into weapons. The metaph

In the past five years, we've g
of hanging, shooting, gang rape, an
against other children, all in imitatio
or true. We know that there is a c
amount of violent television watched
of television have a lower rate of su
and a higher rate of violent behavio
controlled by a medium that has no int
of merchandise.

Those who rule our destiny are much more aware than we are of how simple it is to seize and maintain power through media control. The history of the Reagan administration in Washington is a study in overwhelmingly successful media manipulation. A few years ago, the president-as-performer was a figment of the satirical imagination; now it's a reality. A genial performer, elected on the strength of his TV presence, rules the western world. A White House public relations aide explained why the printed word doesn't matter any more: When the president's mistakes are reported in the press, "Maybe 200 people read it, or 2,000, or 200,000," but when he smiles on television, in carefully controlled circumstances, eight million people are watching.

White House public relations staff have invented a whole encyclopedia of media control techniques. TV cameras are allowed to film the president as he boards a helicopter, smiling and waving. The helicopter engines are deliberately revved up ahead of time so that reporters' shouted questions can't be heard. At presidential events, reporters are roped in behind a "shout line" to protect him from questions. The stationing of cameras at public events is carefully managed to prevent unwanted camera angles or politically revealing shots. The American president is not alone in his awareness that television coverage is crucial. In the 1985 hijacking of a TWA airliner from Athens to Beirut, the terrorists quickly displayed a hand-lettered sign to the waiting media: "All coverage is pool coverage."

When the wielders of political power devote such scrupulous care to every TV image, can we any longer doubt that our children who watch are television's mere minions? The effects are profound. The sense of time past, of humanity's continuity, seems to have evap-

teacher in a high school program for the gifted
parent–teacher night, that he didn't know what to do
teenagers; they had no sense of the past, of chronology,
ive: "As far as they're concerned, the Middle Ages and World
probably happened at the same time."

We know all that, and yet we continue to allow the television to flicker away, day and night, in our living rooms. Ted Hughes wrote a brilliant description of the way, in front of a television set

> . . . paralysis overcomes us. What keeps us mesmerized? Why can't we move? Reality has been removed from our participation behind that tough little screen and into another dimension . . . our inner world of natural impulsive response is safely in neutral. Like broiler killers [chickens], we are reduced to a state of pure observation. Everything that passes in front of our eyes is equally important, equally unimportant . . . [We] can only free ourselves from the spell of passivity by a compulsive effort of will . . .

Dorothy and Jerome Singer, leading American researchers into the role of television in children's lives, have added another detail to this pattern. "Children who spend more time watching television tend to have fathers who are heavy television viewers," they reported. On the other hand, mothers' TV viewing, educational level, and employment status "were not significantly related" to the child's success in school or reading attainment. Whether this is because of stereotyped gender roles in our society, or because Freud was right about the father as representative of society's values, this fact implies a heavy cultural responsibility for the father. A father who cares about his child's intellectual and spiritual life cannot afford to spend his leisure hours watching sports on television or to leave bedtime reading to his wife—not unless he is content to let his child grow up imprinted with the values of the commercial mass media.

Only a few years ago, the defenders of television rationalized that television could do no real harm because even very young children were able to distinguish between fact and fantasy. By the age of five, it was argued, children could tell you that commercials are not always true and that the Roadrunner doesn't really get killed when he is dropped over a cliff.

Strangely enough, however, it seems that this superficial cynicism engendered by television is not so much an ability to distinguish clearly between fact and fiction as a diffuse blurring of what is real. The producer of "Gilligan's Island" once marveled, in print, that faithful fans of the program had sent indignant telegrams to the U.S. Coast Guard and the navy, demanding that the castaways be rescued at once. "Who did these viewers think was filming the castaways on that island?" he wondered. "There was even a laugh track on the show. Who (did they think) was laughing . . . ?" He wondered, too, about parents who deny that their children are influenced by television. Sponsors spend more than $2 billion a year on commercials, he wrote, and the more viewers they get, the more money they make. "How can anyone believe that the viewer is influenced by the commercials on a show, and not influenced by the content of the show itself?" His conclusion, after a lifetime in television: Not only do many viewers believe that whatever they see on television is real but things aren't real until they see them on television—"the most believable news medium" according to countless surveys.

Perhaps television's hypnotic power can best be seen in its positive impact. When a picture book is featured on the excellent program, "Reading Rainbow," its sales can leap from a mere 2,000 to a steady 25,000 annually, according to Harper & Row's children's book marketing director, Frank Johnson, quoted in the *New York Times*. Alas, "Reading Rainbow" is just one tiny gleam in the wilderness. The entire children's book market amounts to "$460 million annually . . . about half what people spend on golf clubs," Mr. Johnson said. Just one cartoon show, though—Mattel's He-Man—brought in $350 million in toy sales in one year.

I believe that not only are chronic TV viewers handicapped in their ability to understand what is real and what is important but that those who are print literate will become an increasingly rare and privileged elite. They will be the ones with the power to think, analyze, connect, and create new meanings. But we are long past the time when traditional schooling alone can teach literacy. Television makes a new kind of child, one who is not easily taught by the methods currently available. And only the parent in the home can control how much television is allowed to shape the child's life and mind.

The parent who wishes to make the best use of this book will have to come to terms with television, one way or another. Aside from all other considerations, the child who watches five hours a day of television will simply not have time to ready widely and deeply. Furthermore, as any contemporary publisher can tell you, the TV-influenced child is likely to be an impatient and reluctant reader, demanding instant action and automatically recognizable stereotyped characters in books as in viewing. Most literature will truly be a closed book to him.

Pessimism, however, is not the burden of this book. I began this chapter by quoting Maxim Gorky because he offers one of the most stirring examples in twentieth-century literature of what reading can mean to a child in even the most impoverished and deprived circumstances. In his three-volume autobiography *(My Childhood, My Apprenticeship,* and *My Universities)* Gorky powerfully describes his brutal early childhood. Abandoned by his mother, abused, a witness in his grandparents' home to every kind of savagery and depravity, he nevertheless had one glowing advantage: His grandmother was a storyteller of mesmerizing power. Put out of his grandparents' home at the age of ten, the unschooled child Gorky had to work at the most gruelling and menial of tasks to keep himself alive. His discovery of books opened the world to him and transformed his life. In his impassioned, scatter-shot devouring of books (he had to steal the wax to make crude candles to read in secret, and was more than once beaten into unconsciousness when caught with a book), he gradually pieced together a vision of the possibilities of life that was entirely at odds with his stunted environment.

Gorky's saga is so moving because we see not only the impact of literature on his own genius but also the lesser pleasures—escapism, refreshment—in the way the illiterate peasants around him responded to the popular and mystic tracts he read aloud to them. "He took the book from me and carefully examined it, showering the cover with tears. 'A good book is just like—a holiday!' "

Wordsworth, the source of the other quotation that opens this chapter, had every advantage, but ironically found the same release in his childhood reading: the discovery of other worlds, the forgetfulness of self. Every poet and critic who writes seriously about literature echoes this idea of transcendence. The difference from television is this: The picture of other worlds served up on the screen is passively received by the watcher; in reading, a far greater imaginative effort must be made. The marks on the paper must be translated into words, the words into meaning, the linked meanings into a mental picture of events that is held in the mind while the narrative goes on. Reading demands an active stretch of the mind, and this greater effort, this deeper involvement, yields a far richer and more complex perception of reality than do the flitting and vanishing pictures on the screen.

Books are portable packages of life and meaning, unimaginably diverse. They can be hugged, chewed, carried to bed, or to a secret hideout in a tree, read and reread, and the reader is always in control—skipping, going back, absorbing deeply, or skimming forward. The creative power of reading is as far from the passive watching of television as exploring a wilderness is from browsing through the supermarket. And because the reader virtually creates in his mind the book in his hands, books offer uniquely appropriate rewards to every age group. The toddler listening to a picture book read aloud may be delighted simply to recognize, in two dimensions, objects from his daily three-dimensional world. This, too, is an important part of learning to decipher print. The middle reader is thrilled to embark on adventures and discover worlds more fantastic than any-thing on the screen (because the imagination, unlike the special ef-fects crew, is limitless). Inner exploration, the moral and emotional testing of the child's mettle in folk and fairy tales, is just as exciting at this age. The preadolescent, struggling to form some coherent sense of self, is free to try on in books the feelings and identities of countless others.

Jacques Barzun said that a work of art, unlike mere escapism, carries the individual back to the real world at last. In my experience, heavy viewers of television are dazzled by celebrity; they are help-lessly envious. But bookreaders come back to the real world with an inner ferment of ideas, feelings, and the sense of possibilities.

"Identity" is a moot point in our society: in most films and televi-sion, it's a matter of physical beauty or fashionable clothes, the out-ward surface. (Think of teenagers whose "identity" is a punk costume or the "look" of the latest rock star, mimicked faithfully down to the last spangle and bangle.) In good books, identity is character in ac-tion, interaction, or introspection, the inner self as springingly alive as the outer. The well-read child, like Gorky, knows "he is not alone." He is better equipped to interpret his own experience and measure it against that of others; he has an ample frame of intellectual refer-ence for every new encounter or dilemma in his life; his familiarity with many kinds of prose style makes him more receptive, more alert, to all forms of art and communication. Reading fiction allows the child to know himself better, and endows him with an invaluable store of our culture's symbols and archetypes.

The elemental stories, wrote Ted Hughes, are

> . . . little factories of understanding . . . Stories think for
> themselves, once we know them . . . they continue to light up
> and attract everything relevant in our experience, and
> continually produce new implications and revelations of
> meaning.

The child who comes to school already having experienced the deep satisfactions of listening to stories is, as any teacher can testify, a privileged student, far ahead of the others in literacy skills, attention span, responsiveness to ideas, and capacity for abstraction.

As this book will try to show, school achievement is only a small part of what reading can do for a child, but parents, in their anxiety to do the best for their children, often grasp at the sheer mechanics of reading as both the method and the goal. Early reading schemes and flashcard alphabets have become ubiquitous in the last decade. Conscientious parents, especially those who have only one or two children, are understandably eager to enhance their child's prowess.

Extreme caution is advised. If there is one thing on which most reading experts in the English-speaking world agree, it is that early parental teaching of alphabets or words is counterproductive. If you wanted your child to enjoy athletic activity, would you begin by drilling the baby in the crib with pictures of the different parts of a ski harness? Or would you simply take him along in a backpack, and watch the glow come into his cheeks as you enjoy the exhilaration of skiing on a cross-country trail?

Of course, you would take him along to share your pleasure. And when he was old enough for skis—small ones appropriate for his age—you would encourage him to join you, adjusting your pace to suit his, and laughingly setting him on his feet when he tumbled. The technical knowledge would come to him through the soles of his feet and the seat of his snowsuit; the motivation to learn would arise from his natural desire to imitate his parents, to gain mastery, and to join in the fun.

The reading of books dawns most brightly in just the same atmosphere of mutual delight. How to discover, or rediscover, that delight in reading, and thus to inspire it in your child, makes up a large part of this book. I am aware, for example, that the vast majority of parents have fallen out of the habit of book reading. It's estimated that almost all book reading is done by a mere 10 percent of the population. In Quebec, a community college teacher lamented that, according to an extensive survey, half of all seventeen- and eighteen-year-olds have no interest in reading, one-quarter of first-year students do not open a book outside of class, fewer than 15 percent of students read ten books or more a year, and, when they do read, they are likely to choose "soft romance novels." In England, a leading critic of children's literature reported that a third of all intelligent, middle-class fourteen-year-old boys never read books for pleasure at all.

Despite the frenzied efforts of some libraries in urban centers to lure nonreaders with copies of *Popular Mechanics* and *Penthouse*

("I don't care if they use the books to prop open their windows, so long as the books get off our shelves," one librarian told me), I don't think there is much to be gained in lowering standards and abandoning literary values in order to tempt nonreading adults into the mindless consumption of print for its own sake.

Appealing to children is a more urgent matter. For those of us for whom fiction has fed a vibrant undercurrent in our lives, whose sensibilities have been broadened and emotions deepened by books, it seems senselessly cruel to raise a child without at least trying to instill the love of reading.

Parents who do not try are, I suspect, frustrated by not knowing how to begin. But children's literature offers an almost magical opportunity to nonreading adults to begin again, and to discover the pleasures of reading along with their children. Not only that, but parents who read with or aloud to their children, or at least read some of the books most favored by their children, gain an enriched intimacy and an enlivened field of conversation, debate, and play. The summer my children read the entire *Little House in the Big Woods* series, we all played at pioneers and settlers in the woods around our rented cottage. That imaginative adventure is a more cherished memory, now, in all our lives than any of the birthday presents given or received that summer.

In my experience, the rote exercises in "imaginative work" so often seen in schools have limited use because the much-celebrated imagination of children rarely takes the form of inventing new things to order. The deepest current of a child's imagination runs in private places—interpreting the world, making new links among the varied objects and impressions in the child's experience ("Oh, grass!" exclaimed my two-year-old, stroking the soft fringe on my new dress) and giving narrative expression to the fears, hopes, and fantasies that compose the inner life.

Through fiction, adults can deepen those capacities in the child in the most spontaneous, unforced way. It's a commonplace to hear a mother doing it as she looks over a picture book with her wide-eyed child. "Look, that's just like your ball, only this one has a big blue stripe," she might say, and in the child's mind, newly enriched by words, forms an idea of that ball, its hardness and resilience, its sameness to and difference from the ball in the corner of the playroom. That ball, with its color and three-dimensional shape, *bounces* in her mind, right through to the end of the book and beyond.

She is practicing using her imagination, without being asked to perform an imposed task, and it is all happening without a second thought. If you continue to share the child's world of books, then you are always in a position to stimulate your child's amplifying imagination.

"What would Pa have done *now?*" my children would ask with relish, that summer we played Little House. Pa had become a rounded, real person in their minds, a permanent archetype of the brave, competent, loving man, and they were generously inviting me to participate in their imagined world. It would not have worked for a moment, however, if I had chimed in with condescending joviality. Some child part of me had joined in falling in love with Pa. That was my ticket of admission.

The intimacy established between my children and me through books continues to this day. Even while writing this book, and discussing with my twenty-year-old daughter some of her memories of loved stories, I found we both gained startling insights into the underlying themes of the narrative we make of our lives. Along the way, I was able to help my children develop their imaginative capacities for re-creating the world in their mind's eye, and for seeing new connections and meanings at every turn. I hold this up as one example of the uses of childhood literature, but emphatically not as a tribute to my own virtues: My entrance into this fictional inner world of my children's lives was mostly accidental.

Like many another adult, I became temporarily indifferent to contemporary adult fiction at a point in my life when I most needed reassurance about the purposefulness of life. My babies were young, I was busy and exhausted, and my emotions were unwontedly open and vulnerable. I was as tender and bruisable as a peeled peach. A news flash on television of a distraught mother could reduce me to tears. The violence of most current movies became unbearably painful to me. Contemporary fiction—a surrealistic blur of postnuclear nihilism, chic despair, fragmentation, incoherence, and sexual obsession—left me irritated and sickened. My daily concern was the nurturing of new life; an aesthetically fashionable alienation, or a flippant cynicism about human endeavor, was the last thing I needed or wanted. I tried browsing through the literature that had given me so much enjoyment when I was in university, but, with scarcely ten minutes at a time to myself, I didn't have the sustained intellectual energy necessary for Chaucer, Shakespeare, or even nineteenth-century novels.

It was at that point that I rediscovered Charles Dickens. His tumultuous vitality, his relish for the human comedy, his robust affection, and his engrossing plots, were just the infusion I needed. And rediscovering that primary pleasure of self-forgetfulness in an author's created world of plot and character led me back one step further. I found myself skulking off to the local library and returning laden with all my childhood favorites. A stack of Arthur Ransomes stood on my bedside table. Awake at three or four in the morning to nurse the baby, I lay on my side, propped the book on a pillow, and with the small warm bundle nestled in beside me, I read with childlike pleasure.

My two preschoolers were quick to notice how jealously I guarded that changing pile of library books beside the bed. I had no ulterior motive in telling them those books were for *my* pleasure and not to be carried off, but I had stumbled unwittingly on the secret of motivating my children to read fiction. Listening to picture books read aloud by their father (to his and their immense satisfaction) was already one of their favorite pastimes. Now they were itching to discover what it was I enjoyed so much in those long "chapter books." Within months, they were reading my library books in my wake and eagerly sharing their discoveries with me.

I don't propose that parents should use negative psychology to stimulate their children's interest in books. The salient fact was that mother was seen to value those stories, and not just for the good they might do the children. I'm convinced that if adults could overcome their prejudice against childlike joys, they could gain a great deal of pleasure from children's novels and open the door for their own children's lifelong reading.

Prejudice there is, however, and it is overwhelming. Many adults who remember only stilted, prissy, or moralistic books from their own childhood are unaware that there now exists a vast hoard of children's books of genuine depth, linguistic skill, wit, and absorbing drama. Though novels written for children may have a circumscribed subject matter, there are children's authors today (I think of writers like William Mayne and Philippa Pearce) who tower above most adult bestsellers in mastery of language and insight. The sheer excellence of many children's books is a breathtaking surprise for anyone who has not read the genre since childhood.

Still, there are barriers of pomposity and conceit to overcome. One winter night, my family left for a downtown concert a full hour ahead of time to make sure of getting through the blizzard. Sure enough, we arrived too early and my son, then fifteen or so, began to read the book he had brought along for just that contingency. An elegant gentleman in the seat next to him leaned over and exclaimed *"Riddley Walker!* Excellent book, just read it myself." They got into one of those book-swapping conversations. "Have you read Russell Hoban's other books, like *The Mouse and His Child?"* asked my son enthusiastically. Baffled pause. "It's a children's book," he explained. The man recoiled with the surprised expression of a frozen haddock. "Oh you'd have to ask my *wife* about that," he said at last, condescendingly. "You should really try it," urged my son. "No *thanks,* I'll stick to the grown-up stuff."

Ursula LeGuin has a wonderful passage (in *The Fantasists)* about "adult chauvinist piggery," parodying the conversations she has at cocktail parties. "You're a juvenile writer, aren't you?" Yeth mummy, she says inwardly. "I love your books—the real ones, I mean, I haven't read the ones for children, of course!" Of courth, daddy. "It must be relaxing to write *simple* things for a change." "Sure, it's simple, writing for kids," says LeGuin. "Just as simple as bringing them up. All you do is take all the sex out and use little short words and little dumb ideas, and don't be too scary and make sure there's a happy ending. Right? If you do all that, you might even write *Jonathan Livingstone Seagull* and make twenty billion dollars and have every adult in America reading your book."

LeGuin's spoof is pointedly accurate. Of course, the dismissal of children's books as unimportant and mindless is the same kind of egotism that has for so long dismissed child rearing and women's concerns as trivial. And that conceit leads the patronizer right into the fallacy of assuming that even good children's books are somehow less good, less important, than the trash that often turns into adult bestsellers.

Such condescension can be forgiven in adults whose only familiarity with children's literature comes from the supermarket and chain store shelves, laden now with mass-market commodities disguised as books. Although they may be packaged in shiny flat boards, such market-adjusted products as Care Bears and Cabbage Patch Kids are not books. In fact, they are sugar-laden assembly line products, as detrimental to the intellect as bubble gum is to the teeth.

Countless thousands of parents, misled by their own nostalgia for a mythically perfect childhood, think of children's books as shiny, pretty, cute, and cuddly toys. Cuteness, in fact, is the bubonic plague of children's publishing. Every month, while I was writing a newspaper column, I would receive at least one amateur manuscript from a would-be author, almost invariably featuring fluffy little creatures with names like Snowball and Whimsy—darling wee cuddly-wuddlies who would teach children to be nice to each other, brush their teeth, and do what mommy told them.

Cuteness is a disease of self-conscious falsity that we inflict on children like unwanted damp kisses. Books do give joy, but joy is not a glucose drip for children any more than for adults. And a tacked-on moral lesson has no more place in children's literature than it has in the fiction that adults enjoy.

Real books are to be found in book stories and in libraries, not in groceries, and only rarely in toy shops. Even here, though, there is real danger in the tidal wave of commodity publishing. The bad, the commercial junk, and the exploitative "contemporary" novels, the easy-to-read series and the teenage romances, all heavily advertised, are pushing the more authentic literature right off the shelves. Every time you buy a Strawberry Shortcake book, you are helping to ensure the death of another, better book which simply cannot compete for that shelf space in profitability and quick turnover.

Another danger is the well-meaning proselytizer. It is one thing to laugh out loud at the humor in a children's novel and to share your enthusiasm with your family; it is quite another to come home laden with good books and press them imploringly into the hands of your reluctant reader or teenage recalcitrant. The frontal approach with older children is almost bound to fail: Finding your own good books is, after all, a part of the intoxicating freedom that is gained by fluent reading. In the early years, of course, the children are all yours; the treat of snuggling onto a parent's lap and basking in adult attention is enough to convince a child that books are a reliable source of refreshment and entertainment. If you keep it up, reading aloud from books that you are able to choose with your own child's tastes and inclinations in mind, there is every reason to trust that excellent fiction will hold your child's attention right through primary school.

Today, of course, the child's delight in reading is far more likely to be undermined by an over-ambitious parent than by one who is too prim or restrictive. If I feel alarmed by this turn of events—horrified, in fact, by the thought of an army of determined parents coaching their glaze-eyed toddlers with flashcards—it may be because I remember my own earliest reading with such force. I was allowed to come to it in my own sweet time, at my own will. It was private, and so was the shock of joyful liberty it brought me.

In those days, it was feeding and toileting that were regimented by the experts. Well-meaning mothers, anxious lest their children fall short of accepted standards, held three-month infants over potties and forced their screaming babies to wait the approved four hours between feedings, to their mutual torture. Intellectual ambition had not yet been invented as a fertile field for baby experts. Toddlers were expected to pick dandelions in the back yard, eat nicely with a spoon, build with their blocks, and wait to learn their ABCs when they were old enough for school.

I count myself lucky. That moment when I learned to read, with no adult ego hovering over my accomplishments, is my single clearest memory of being four years old. I was sitting on the floor of the bedroom I shared with my brother Alan, who was nearly two years older than I. His school primer, the ghastly Dick and Jane, was open on my knees. "Don't you see," my brother said just a little impatiently, "every one of those letters I taught you makes a sound and the sounds go together to make words. That *a* right there says 'aah'."

Even though it made no sense that that fat, familiar little *a* should suddenly be saying "aah" on the printed page, I did see, all at once, what he meant. I'll never forget that moment. A shutter opened, light fell on shadowy confusion, pieces sprang magically together to form a whole puzzle. It felt as though my hand had unexpectedly fitted around the great handle that opened all adult mysteries.

That was the second-child syndrome. First-born children are far more likely to prolong the years when their parents have to read aloud to them. They learn to read for themselves, calmly, in the first grades of school. None of the bright first-born children I've known raced toward reading with the same ardor I've seen in the second-born, who are always panting at the heels of an older sibling, desperate to catch up. That's important to remember if you are tempted to compare your child's development with that of little Alfred next door. Is Alfred a second-born, spurred on by imitation of an older sibling? Preschoolers are willing to expend reckless energy to become more autonomous. The role model, the hero to be envied and emulated, is the older child, whose pleasures, privileges, and accomplishments are so much more recognizable to the younger child, so much more tantalizingly within his reach than the remote and godlike attributes of adults. In our older siblings we can see tangible proof that we too will grow and become powerful.

And could a child today, surrounded by dancing pictures, toys that talk, puzzles that are all but alive, "interactive" computers, and cities bursting with commercial entertainments, feel the same thrill of initiation that I did? I doubt it. Reading has not lost its importance to the child's life, but its glamor has faded and its immediate rewards are not as obvious as they once were. The first task of the concerned parent, then, is not to spoil the child's already tenuous flicker of interest in reading by burdening him or her with anxieties about early achievement.

The early reading craze of the 1970s—fed by books like Sidney Ledson's *Teach Your Child to Read in 30 Days,* complete with a system of candy bribes—did a terrible disservice to true literacy, because it shifted the focus from pleasure to performance. It may have been gratifying to parents' egos to have a three-year-old who could belt through Dr. Seuss, but most educators are adamant that early reading confers no special advantage. Many a forced sprout of a reader has wilted in motivation by the time he arrives in the classroom.

The goal is to make reading a lifelong source of delight to the growing child. Any competent teacher can train a child in the mechanical decoding of letters. But the will to read—the most important thing a child can bring to school on the first day—is nurtured, like the will to live, in the child's early emotional experience.

Reading has its roots in play: the verbal and rhythmic play of nursery rhymes, chants, and songs. This old oral culture, alas, has bled almost to death, unnoticed, in the last two generations, mortally wounded by television. Preschoolers chant beer and shampoo commercials now—verbal expressions whose only purpose is to manipulate—while the haunting opacities or breakneck anarchy of nursery rhymes are forgotten. If you dip into a book like Alice Kane's *An Ulster Childhood,* you will be amazed by the verbal richness that bubbled through her childhood and helped to shape one of Canada's best-loved storytellers. And you will perhaps be saddened by the contrast between her times and our own days, when a child may reach kindergarten age without ever hearing a story or rhyme produced from the parent's memory.

To make your child into a reader, forget the flashcards and the alphabet. Concentrate on song, finger play, and the association of loving physical contact with stories told and books read aloud. Create an atmosphere in which verbal jokes are savored, where language is respected and narrative attended to; a home where parents talk about their childhood and the outside world and dip into stories from the common storehouse of tales. Listen to your child's meandering stories and write them down. Make sure yours is a home in which books are freely available and enjoyed by adults too, not just prescribed as medicine for children. I would have stacks of picture books around the house, and would read aloud whenever a moment could be squeezed from the daily routines—not just at bedtime. And I would never teach letters or turn reading into a lesson unless the child herself demanded information.

Does it all sound too easy, too mushy and liberal and unproductive? On the contrary. To create a language-loving home takes far more effort than the rote teaching of the alphabet. I know, because as a true North American, a child of an immigrant generation, just emerging from one culture and not thoroughly blended into the next, I grew up without a large store of fairy tales or nursey games. When my own children were small, I had to learn the finger plays about the two dickie birds on a wall (a guaranteed winner) and the teddy bear going around the garden (tickle under *there!*) from acquaintances and library books. Lullabies came from records. The love of reading was the one secret weapon I could already lay claim to.

All very well, you may say. But what about the child for whom the mechanical skills of reading don't seem to come naturally around the age of six or seven? Ah. That was my hardest lesson of all. My two older children followed the expected pattern: My first daughter learned easily and simply to read when she went to school. My second child, a boy, fell over himself to catch up to her and surprised me by teaching himself to read quite fluently at the age of three. My third, going her own stubborn way, was the one who taught me the most.

Jenny was just as verbally bright as her older brother and sister, and a nonstop storyteller from the moment she could talk. But just like a sturdy, bright-eyed pony trotting up to the gate and refusing to jump, she planted her feet and refused to learn to read.

Our first inkling came in nursery school, when the teachers thought Jenny was ripe for a reading readiness program. Jenny clearly indicated that she did not agree. By kindergarten age, in a pleasant, middle-of-the-road public school, Jenny was one of the very few in her Sesame Street generation who still didn't (or wouldn't) know her alphabet. Knowing how stubbornly self-determining my daughter was even at the age of five, I had asked the teacher not to pressure her into the "prereading" activities she seemed to reject so fiercely. The teacher was bemused. Most of her pupils' parents were pressing for more achievement, not less.

That was the hard part. What if I were making a terrible mistake in not pushing her harder? What if I were sentencing her to a lifetime of academic inferiority? Everything seemed to conspire to increase my fears. At the end of that year, a playmate in the park threw a handful of fine sawdust straight into Jenny's eyes. At the Hospital for Sick Children, a senior ophthalmologist removed the sawdust particles and then insisted on testing Jenny's eyesight by having her read a standard letter chart. "But doctor, she doesn't know her alphabet." "Nonsense! Every five-year-old knows the alphabet." Jenny blithely read the chart, missing half the letters and identifying only the E's which were backward or upside down.

"This child has such poor eyesight that she needs immediate corrective work!" exclaimed the doctor. "She didn't even mention that the E's are backward." I explained again that Jenny hadn't really mastered the alphabet, and normally made her E's upside down or backward. "Nonsense!" he boomed again. "I can tell you right now, this child has such deficient eyesight that she will never make it through primary school."

The next day, we had Jenny tested by an ophthalmologist who was willing to accept that a five-year-old might not know her alphabet. It turned out that her eyesight was perfect.

Halfway through her kindergarten year, I moved Jenny to a small, familylike private school where each child progressed at his or her own pace. Luckily, the school had an extremely literate program for the early grades: Songs, playwriting, artwork combined with narrative, and reading aloud were all part of the daily curriculum. Jenny, her receptivity sharpened by her strictly oral personal culture, was a whiz at listening to stories. She had a phenomenal capacity to concentrate and to absorb oral information whenever a story was being told.

Jenny was nearly eight years old when she came into my workroom at home one day, took down a book from the shelves, sat on the floor, and began to read silently. The book was *The Castle of Yew* by Lucy Boston; subtle, beautifully written, and not an obvious choice for a beginner. The first paragraph reads:

> Joseph and a boy whom he had often seen but did not know
> by name stood together by the high wire fence peering in at
> the garden beyond it. Their fingers clung to the wire mesh as
> they put their eyes against it in order to see through the tangle
> of roses and honeysuckle that grew over it. There was a path
> on the other side, narrow and overgrown and overhung, and
> beyond that, glimpsed between leaves and stalks, the shine of
> water.

That book must have been the right choice for Jenny, because she wouldn't stop at suppertime, or at bedtime, or until she had finished. And she hasn't stopped since. An avid reader, she still goes her own way, leaping from the heights (Shakespeare) to the swampy depths (Harlequin romances) when the mood seizes her. We never knew by what mysterious process she had come to a decision to read, but we did learn that you can't force and control a child's reading. You can only enable and enrich it, and prevent it from being ruined by outside interference.

Once your child is past the age of eight or nine, aside from your occasional tactfully expressed excitement about a book you recently enjoyed, you should concentrate on helping the child make his or her own discoveries. Stock your own shelves with children's books you like; talk to your husband or wife about them; offer to read them aloud while the children plough through some purely physical chore. But make sure also to give them the opportunity to choose books for themselves as well as receiving them as gifts. Since there are approximately 250 specialty children's bookstores in the United States, and perhaps as many as another 200 which have children's departments, it should be possible to arrange solo bookstore visits for your children now and then—gloriously provided with gift certificates.

Children, as parents know all too well, have a built-in resistance to anything forced on them by authority. Dozens of books I might otherwise have loved were permanently spoiled for me this way by school. I have always hated the memory of *A Tale of Two Cities,* for example, though I love the rest of Dickens; I realized the source of my antipathy recently when I unearthed my tenth grade copy of that novel and found that our teacher had required us to look up in the dictionary a dozen words per chapter and write out the definitions. It takes a gifted and unusual teacher to avoid murdering a book's enchantment when it is used as part of the curriculum—all the more reason for parents to instill a love of literature before the children go to school and learn that reading is a task at which you might just fail, rather than one of life's most rewarding pastimes. (There are more and more teachers, I hasten to add, who know the value of silent reading periods in school, when students are free to choose from a wide range of novels and do not have to answer irritating questions on every character and plot device.)

Classics are another pitfall for the unwary parent. There was a time when children had access to very few books written especially for them. For want of anything more appropriate, avid readers naturally turned to so-called family classics *(The Adventures of Tom Sawyer, Robinson Crusoe, Gulliver's Travels),* some of them quite beyond the range or interests of childhood, and gleaned what dramatic scraps of adventure they could, skipping the "boring" descriptions, confused or troubled by the author's ventures into philosophy or satire. Encouraging children to read fondly remembered classics before they are ready for them is a sure way to ruin the book for them, or discourage them from reading altogether.

This book is intended as a guide to the hundreds of genuine classics for children, many of which have been written in the last twenty years and may be unfamiliar to today's parents. There are, of course, grievous omissions in this book; there was, for example, not enough space to write about folk and fairy tales or poetry. The early primary grades are the perfect, ripe time for fairy tales. They have become so popular lately, in many single-story picture book editions, that parents may mistakenly feel that these tales are best suited to preschoolers. There are so many outstanding collections suitable for seven-, eight-, and nine-year-olds, however—such as Isaac Bashevis Singer's tales, or the two-volume set of Grimm's called *The Juniper Tree,* brilliantly translated by Lore Segal and illustrated by Maurice Sendak—that any adult could confidently choose among them with the help of a bookstore clerk or a librarian. Beware of garishly illustrated rereleases of fairy tales; there are fine versions and appalling ones, and a knowledgeable sales clerk (as well as your own developing sense of discrimination) is your best ally.

Poetry is a different conundrum. Children read very little poetry today and practically none is taught in school. What a strange amnesia has crept over us! Read aloud from Tomie dePaola's *Mother Goose,* or the delicious *Faber Book of Nursery Verse,* and observe your children's spontaneous, natural delight in rhythm, rhyme, and the spellbinding fascination of unfamiliar words, madcap nonsense, and lyrical repetition. Most families, though, don't tread much further than these familiar grounds. It's an extraordinary loss, because 99 percent of modern children will never come to poetry by themselves. The immediacy, the shock of a new perception leaping into the reader's mind in one perfect image, the music and deep enthrallment to words—all the passionate experiences of childhood poetry—are jettisoned.

Poetry, with its reverberating words and images, was one of the most intense discoveries of my childhood. The goblin who howled for the green glass beads, Robert Louis Stevenson's dark brown river, "the long light shakes across the lakes . . . Blow, bugles, blow, set the wild echoes flying . . ." from Tennyson—just repeating those phrases sends shivers down to my toes. Poetry was a constant reminder, no matter how dull or disappointing my daily life, that there were other levels of existence, other, more piercing, planes of perception and feeling.

True, it's difficult to know how to bridge that gap between nursery rhyme and more demanding poetry for the middle readers. One of my sadder failures as a parent was my cowardly abandonment of the field with my own children. I tried them on a few poems when they were kindergarten age and then, noting their apathy, abandoned the effort for fear of turning them against poetry altogether. I assumed they would get around to it on their own, but I was wrong, and not one of my three experienced that keen childhood enthrallment to poetry that I had had. I wish now that I'd persisted.

Contemporary parents have the task made easier, thanks to several superb anthologies. The immensely valuable *Riverside Anthol-*

ogy of Children's Literature, edited by Judith Saltman, (sixth edition published in 1985) has—in addition to a treasure-store of picture books, legends, fiction, and nonfiction—168 poems, ranging from nursery rhymes through ballads, riddles, lyrics, and narrative poems, from Eleanor Farjeon to Langston Hughes.

A smaller, but equally thoughtful, collection is the *The New Golden Land Anthology,* originally edited by the poet James Reeves, and updated by Judith Elkin in 1983 to include many of the best modern writers. Poems and finger-play rhymes for all ages are included.

Three indispensable anthologies for older children are so astonishingly rich, varied, surprising, and captivating that I know I will "lose" the whole morning whenever I incautiously flip one of them open. One is *The Rattle Bag* by Ted Hughes and Seamus Heaney, in which more than 400 poems are arranged, quite simply, in alphabetical order by title. Since the poet-anthologists ranged widely and surprisingly through the centuries and the world, this arbitrary arrangement produces jolts and miracles. Another is *A Flock of Words* by David Mackay, an equally fresh and rivetingly original collection, arranged by subtle connections in theme from one poem to the next, regardless of the time or place of the poem's origin. The way these poems "rub shoulders together" (in the editor's words) is a constant stimulus and illumination. A third outstanding anthology—and there are many more to be searched out in libraries—is *Why Am I Grown So Cold? Poems of the Unknowable,* edited by Myra Cohn Livingston, which ranges from Shakespeare's songs to American Indian chants in its effective search for that tingle of the mysterious and the unearthly which is one of poetry's joys.

One last word on reading poetry aloud to children: don't be afraid of sophisticated subject matter. One six-year-old I know was mesmerized by Alfred Noyes's *The Highwayman*—as who isn't?

Difficult books are another category I've not had space to plumb in depth in this volume. William Mayne is particularly unclassifiable; there is no more assured and skillful writer in the whole field of children's literature, and there are few forms he has not tried, all with astonishing success; fantasy, time travel, adventure, preschool stories, adolescent novels, school stories. I've discussed only two *(A Year and a Day* and *Earthfasts),* but parents of talented readers ought to be looking for his books from the time their children are about seven years old. The difficulty lies not in his vocabulary or his plots, but in his elusive, oblique manner of expression. It is extremely condensed and evocative, and perfectly honed to catch the flicker of mood and feeling just below the surface of action. Such accomplished writing provides a complex, distinctly literary pleasure for the advanced reader, but may prove too much of a challenge for the less practiced. *No More School,* for example, is a brilliantly perceptive story about a group of primary school children in an isolated village who run their own school—unbeknownst to all the adults—while their teacher is away. It's a moving and vigorous novel of strong characters engaged in an admirable act of independence, and perfect for a good nine-year-old reader. It (and others of Mayne's works) are to be found among the wholeheartedly recommended books in the treasury at the end of this book.

One of the motives that drove me to write this book was the dismay I felt when I saw literate friends and acquaintances choosing books for their children on pragmatic, nationalist, feminist, or didactic grounds. Though I broach this complicated subject in chapter 10, "Girls' Books, Boys' Books, Bad Books, and Bias," I want to emphasize here that such narrow selectivity does a severe injustice both to the child reader and to children's literature.

Naturally, adults who care about what children read will want to ensure that their children are given a chance to read about their own culture, that ugly biases will not be overwhelmingly present, and that the overall tone of novels will be neither nihilistic nor tasteless.

Still, there seems to me to be only two essential bases for choice: a sensitive awareness of what a particular child enjoys and needs, and an informed judgment about books based on literary merit. "Literary": That's a stumbling block. Most parents and teachers quail before the idea of setting themselves up as literary critics.

In the chapters that follow, I try to show in detail what gives each book I discuss its special quality. Before long, anyone who is not yet familiar with children's literature will begin to see what I mean by literary merit and be able to make his or her own informed judgments. Is the language original, fresh, and interesting? Are the characters wooden, or do they live and breathe on the page? Do they speak in individual voices, so that you can tell who's talking just by the characteristic speech patterns? If the book in question is a picture book, do the illustrations add to the meaning of the words, or overwhelm them? If it's a fantasy, does the author create a believable world, no matter how strange, and abide by the rules of that world so that your belief in it is never shaken, or do you come thudding back to the banal commonplace with maddening regularity? If the story is an adventure, does it convince *you?*

The idea that second-rate, mechanical, mass-produced books are good enough for the kiddies is just another facet of that condescension of which I spoke earlier. And because children's books are usually not so long, complex, or intellectually demanding as the finest "classics" for adults, it is relatively simple to become a competent critic. The point of developing such expertise—an easy and pleasant exercise—is that good books can do so much for children.

At their best, they expand horizons and instill in children a sense of the wonderful complexity of life. Even a book that ends on a mournful note can be encouraging because the child characters do go on, building their lives despite losses or setbacks. Even a book that gives expression to some of children's most haunting fears can be exhilarating, because the reader has had a chance to feel those chills down the spine while sitting safely at home, conqueror of the print she surveys, able to control her imaginative re-creation of the book's horrors to the limits of what is bearable for her personally. The very act of tackling a challenging narrative and winning through to the exciting kernel of the plot reinforces the idea that language and literature can be thrilling. And, of course, by drawing a reader into the inner lives of the characters, good books help her to recognize the all-too-human impulse to cruelty or the radiance of achievement *in herself*. No other pastime available to children is so conducive to empathy and the enlargement of human sympathies. No other pleasure can so richly furnish a child's mind with the symbols, patterns, depths, and possibilities of civilization.

But those rewards can't be gleaned from books that are poorly written or thinly imagined. Bad books may have their uses, and children will unerringly find them—again, consult the last chapter—but in this cluttered and distracting world only caring adults can ensure that children will find the immeasurable rewards of good books. That is why I confidently invite you, in the chapters that follow, to become your own literary critic.

Chapter 2

BOOKS TO ENCOURAGE THE BEGINNING READER

I know nothing of myself till I was five or six. I do not know how I learnt to read. I only remember my first books and their effects upon me; it is from my earliest reading that I date the unbroken consciousness of my own existence.

Jean-Jacques Rousseau, *The Confessions,* 1781

At the beginning of the summer holidays when our city street drowsed under its overhanging maple trees, I would sit on the tiny concrete porch of the duplex where we lived with a sense of luxurious pleasure that would not have been out of place in a Venetian palazzo. In summer, we were allowed to take six books at once, not the usual three, from the local children's library. And so, beside me on the porch, was a treasure heap that was sure not to run out too soon. I would open the first page of the first book, smooth down the page (those tough green library bindings always made the covers want to snap shut), and, with a keen sense of anticipatory magic, dive down beneath the summer surface of my world into somewhere else.

Look at a child reading: sprawled immobile, all that restless energy dissipated somehow or gone up into the mind where it is unseen, holding a collection of paper, glue, and print in front of her eyes. She is there but not there; she inhabits another world that has mysteriously been created by the words on the page and now lives inside her head, and she is moving invisibly through palaces or shanties that are more real to her at this moment than the living room rug where she is lying or the dinner waiting to be served. Call to her, and you can watch her self come back slowly, from far away, into her eyes.

Children's reading should mesmerize, transport; reading ought to be a free-flowing stream of pleasure and consolation that runs beneath their daily lives like an underground spring. But how to begin? How can we ensure that the mechanical process of reading becomes such second nature to our children that it turns transparent like a window? We should consult our own experiences for a start. Try to remember how and why you learned to read; ask friends who are ardent readers; ask, especially, the ones who never pick up a book.

The experience of my daughter Jenny—her surprising choice of *The Castle of Yew* for her very first book—ought to stand as an epigraph for this chapter. For one thing, any category called "beginners' books" can be taken only as a very arbitrary selection. There really is no predicting what will be the right first book for any given child. He may, in the course of a single day, listen enraptured while *The Hobbit* is read aloud, dip into a classroom encyclopedia, browse through a Superman comic behind the couch, and be ready for a favorite fairy tale at bedtime.

How, then, can you choose the beginner books that will most stimulate the child to want to read for herself? Look for themes that spring from the common emotional experiences of the beginning reader's age group, roughly four through eight years old. The child is growing more independent. She separates from mother to go to school and enjoys the experience (after the first dreadful pangs of cutting loose) and yet she greets with a rush of relief that moment of reunion at the end of the day. At school, the child meets for the first time an impartial and sometimes incomprehensible authority from above. Questions of justice and fairness, therefore, loom large. Friendship, and how to achieve it, is an anxious priority. And since many children will not find a best friend in the first year or two of school, loneliness is an important theme, too. Helplessness (think of those schoolyard bullies) and its delicious opposite, competence, are crucial matters for the beginning reader.

The passionate dependencies of the preschool years are over, but think how close a first-grade child often is to losing control over newly conquered functions: crying, forgetting how to tie shoe laces, or wetting one's pants are major humiliations. Humor, therefore (from the raucous guffaw to pointed wordplay), is a welcome tool to keep the emotional temperature down and enable a child to feel in control. Getting a joke is a splendid way to assert one's knowingness, one's worthiness to belong to the group.

Luckily, this age group is blessed with an abundance of picture books of such splendor of color and design that the only difficulty is to choose wisely. Illustrations provide both a stimulus and a prop for a reader still struggling to decode printed words. In many less obvious ways, as I hope to show in more detailed descriptions of some particularly apt choices, good picture books encourage reading skills and reinforce rewards that may turn a beginning reader into an eager one.

The spate of I-Can-Read books published in the last decade has greatly enriched the available selection, but you would still have to search hard for better beginner books than the now-classic *Little Bear* series by Else Holmelund Minarik, with illustrations by Maurice Sendak. They are just the right grown-up book shape and size, with chapters, yet enlivened and made more accessible by pictures on every page. Sendak's early style of rounded, expressive crosshatching achieves the perfect balance: surely, no ursine family ever had more bearlike claws or convincingly long snouts. But how human are their tender looks of amused affection, glances that weave the strands of the story from page to page, and knit the family members together in a web of tolerant attachment.

The subject matter is really the way in which Mother Bear tacitly supports the pretend play of Little Bear and his friends. In "Birthday Soup," the story with the strongest element of suspense, Little Bear fears that his mother has forgotten his birthday. Resourcefully, and not forgetting the duties of hospitality, he makes a vegetable soup to serve to his friends who arrive to help him celebrate. When mother gets home just at the crucial moment, bringing a beautiful cake, Little Bear is no less grateful for the surprise, even though he has coped remarkably well on his own as host and chef. And the story ends with a sentence of resonating maternal reassurance ("I never did forget your birthday and I never will") that is matched in picture books only by the emotional roundedness of Maurice Sendak's last line in the famous *Where the Wild Things Are:* Max journeys back from the land of wild things, after all his adventures, to find that "supper was still hot."

Not all beginner books are aesthetic masterpieces. When my husband first brought home to our three preschoolers a book called *Are You My Mother?* by P.D. Eastman, I dismissed it. It looked cartoonish, starring a gawky bird and a gaggle of bulldozers and steamshovels. The story, I thought, seemed trite. How wrong I was!

Torn between terror at the little bird's separation from his mother and superior laughter at his awkward mistakes in interpreting the world, the children sat riveted. They loved the building tension of the search, the repeated question ("Are you my mother?") and the overwhelming relief of the mother-and-child reunion at the end.

Are You My Mother? is a perfect example of a book that may lack aesthetic appeal to the educated adult eye, and yet has an emotional validity that is immediately irresistible to the child. H.A. Rey's *Curious George* books, the often repetitious adventures of a too-lively monkey, seem to get the same double response: ho-hum from adults, spontaneous loyalty from children.

A child of prereading age will usually sit still for almost any story that an adult will take time to read aloud; the closeness of sitting on a lap will make up for almost any lack of depth or interest in the book. But a parent who is sensitive to a child's responses will quickly learn to tell when the child has been well and truly engaged by a story and when he is simply listening politely. The story that grips is almost certainly one that will tempt the listener to try to read for himself.

The Bunyip of Berkeley's Creek by Jenny Wagner, with its golden-hazed, mysterious drawings of a dark night, snares the interest at first with its gentle spookiness, its innocent version of the horror movie's opening gambit: "Late one night, for no particular reason, something stirred in the black mud at the bottom of Berkeley's Creek." But with the Bunyip's very first waking words— "What am I?"—the reader is seized by the intrinsic interest of the Bunyip's identity crisis. One great emotional task of the school-age child is to determine "what am I . . . aside from my parents' child?" No wonder that the Bunyip's plight (unhandsome, unrecognized, unloved) arouses such a sympathetic rush of fellow feeling. With its flat-footed posture and short arms, the Bunyip has the endearingly defenseless look of a kindergarten child on the first day of school. In the face of an unkind world, he maintains a lugubrious optimism. (If only for its correct use of the adverb *hopefully,* this book justifies its purchase price.) The message is one of acceptance, of self-realization through love—a measure of the large themes that can be tackled unpretentiously and well in a picture book of artistic strength.

Robust, extroverted humor is beloved of preschoolers, and one of the best early readers in the Cat in the Hat series from Random House is another P.D. Eastman book, *Go, Dog, Go.* Though there's no plot, only a succession of ridiculous episodes (a greeting on a mountaintop, dogs driving cars, a dog party in a tree), the terse captions and energetic pictures sweep you along. It's impossible not to laugh out loud, in fact, at these wiry red and yellow dogs with their expressions of crazed eagerness and wild joy—you can practically hear their yelps of enthusiasm.

At the purely mechanical level of reading, the book is a valuable tool. What nonreading child could fail to recognize the words *go* and *dog* after just one of two read-alouds of this madcap endeavor, with its rhythmic repetitions and racy pictures? Like all good illustrations, whether they are as painterly as the *Little Bear* pictures or as Disneyesque as the ones in *Are You My Mother?*, these show more than the words alone indicate. One double-spread picture in *Go, Dog, Go* brings the breakneck action to a sudden halt. All the dogs are asleep in one huge bed, companionably snuggled together. Children love this enormous bed and never fail to notice that one dog is lying stark awake, eyes wide open in the dark. Why? No reason given. The unexplained detail gives the young reader something to ponder, to talk about, in the midst of pell-mell activity.

The child beginning to read is just about to embark on the long voyage to self-reliance. It's not surprising that some of the most loved and enduring books for this age group deal with the struggle between autonomy and the rules of group life. As always, and just as we expect in adult literature, the themes are not baldly stated. You can, of course, if you wish to encourage your child in crude and shallow thinking, buy mass-produced kitsch like the Mr. Man series, sold nearly everywhere, with its simple-minded prescriptions for "proper" behavior. These books are worse than useless since they teach the child a sort of insincere lip service to convention, without respect for the child's inner drive toward growth and mastery over impulse.

To illustrate the difference between the commercial moralistic books and one that looks at a central dilemma of child life through the child's eyes, consider *The Story about Ping*, by Marjorie Flack, which has been in print continuously for more than fifty years. It was, as I've said, the first book I ever read for myself. When I picked it up again, exactly forty years later, I recognized every line in every picture so well that I could actually spot some sloppy changes and color distortions in a recent Puffin edition (avoid that one and buy the accurate hardback or the earlier Viking paperback, if you can find it).

Ping is a handsome young duck who lives, along with a flock of aunts and cousins, in a "wise-eyed" boat on the Yangtze River. Every night, as the ducks walk back up the gangplank after a day of diving and feeding on the water, their keeper lightly slaps the hindmost duck with a long switch. It's an offhand, almost benign ritual, but one so resented by Ping that he runs away. Instead of returning to the boat one evening, he hides on an island of reeds. Few readers will ever forget the wistful back view of Ping as he watches the wise-eyed boat sail into the distance. The duck is so small and stretches so yearningly for one last look against that serenely wide river vista. Kurt Wiese's softly grayed blues and yellows, and the sinuous black outline with which he highlights his simple shapes, breathe emotional life into the scene.

Ping does survive alone on the river, but not without hunger and difficulty. One of the most memorable pictures in the book is of Ping's startled encounter with a flock of cormorants: We see him back-paddle furiously in astonishment at the sight of these frightening, hook-beaked birds, with iron rings around their necks to prevent them from eating their catch. I recall my own uneasy mix of fear and compassion when I first saw those menacing, enslaved cormorants diving for their master.

Maybe I loved *The Story about Ping* because it matched my own growing complexity of perception. Family life, I was just beginning to realize, was warm, secure, the only imaginable way to exist in the threatening wide river of life. But along with the safety, one had to endure its small stings and balks. Because the child reader's sense of injustice has been deeply acknowledged through artistic representation, the moment of reconciliation, the acceptance of order at the book's finale, rings true.

The attractiveness of order is part of the appeal of the classic favorite, *Madeline,* and the subsequent Madeline books by Ludwig Bemelmans. Those twelve little girls live in two such straight lines in the cloistered security of Miss Clavel's school in Paris. On their walks around familiar Paris landmarks, we see them "smile at the good and frown at the bad." Perhaps it is this grave decorum that enables them to take part in the life of such an adult city, sparkling with the sophisticated gaiety of Bemelman's drawings.

Of course, infant insurgency is given its due: Madeline is not only the smallest and bravest of the girls, she is also the cheekiest. In *Madeline and the Bad Hat,* Miss Clavel is taken in by the company manners of the naughty boy next door—Pepito, the son of the Spanish ambassador. Maybe there's just a hint of social snobbery, too, in Miss Clavel's doting admiration of the elegant boy. But Madeline isn't fooled for a minute. She is severe. She knows what Pepito is doing with that tool kit Miss Clavel gave him: He's building a guillotine for chickens.

Several levels of awareness are working here. The reader knows that Pepito's badness is as skin deep as his company manners for adults. We know it by the cherubic grin under his preposterously villainous black hat, and we know it by the sheer comic gusto of the verse: He ate those chickens " . . . roasted, grilled, and frito, / O what a horror was Pepito!" Not to overburden a delicately witty vehicle with too heavy a freight of meaning, part of this story's charm is the ingenious vigor with which the children are working out their own moral order, right under the noses of the adults.

Picture books that have strong appeal for a beginning reader are often based on deep-sprung fantasies that remain as vivid at age thirty-five as at five. *Zoom at Sea,* by Tim Wynne-Jones, with illustrations by Ken Nutt, has that quality. You recognize it by the lift of pleased gratification you feel at the climactic moment, when Zoom, the softly drawn kitten who has longed for the ocean, prances ecstatically on his homemade raft in a magical sea, calling out "More sun! More fish!" to Maria, the enigmatic, motherly woman who has summoned the whole ocean for him out of jars, bottles, and secret drawers.

One Canadian reviewer, Sandra Martin, suggested only half-jokingly that Maria is a prostitute figure. After all, Zoom finds her address in his uncle's old diary, and there's more than a hint of post-erotic lassitude in the way Zoom and Maria drink tea after the magical sea voyage, Maria with her hair tumbling loose and the hem of her skirt bedraggled. I couldn't help but notice that there's a rising sun (remember the House of the Rising Sun in the folk ballad?) engraved on the glass over Maria's door. Not to mention the dreamy suggestiveness—almost as though Maria's house is a public facility—in the last line, when the departing Zoom asks if he may return and Maria murmurs, "I'm sure you will."

Comic speculation aside, if there is an erotic element in this fantasy, it is an appropriately oblique, tender, and childlike dream eroticism, a fulfilling of oceanic wishes by a richly evocative maternal figure. The drawings expertly capture this mixed tone of tenderness and wit: Note Zoom's perfectly feline, though perfectly impossible, pose as he straps wooden spoons to his feet so he can paddle in the sink.

Whose Mouse Are You? by Robert Kraus, with pictures by Jose Aruego, is one of my favorite books about sibling rage, precisely because it takes a sidelong approach to its subject without in the least pulling its punches. A vividly colored, sparely drawn book, with cartoonlike figures filling up red and orange pages, it leaps straight into the action with the question "Whose mouse are you?" asked by an unidentified voice-of-authority. "Nobody's mouse," answers the sulky little hero. "Where is your mother?" "Inside the cat." And so goes the catechism, with each answer disposing of one more family member. The father is caught in a trap, the sister is far away on a mountain. The brother? "I have none."

This is the first clue that the story is about the mouse's rebellious tantrum over an imminent new baby in the family. Then comes the question: "What will you do?" For the answer, there's a completely blank page, a pause while both the mouse and the reader may consider what alternatives there are to getting along with a new sibling, particularly if you decide symbolically to annihilate the whole family and are left alone in the world. Then, with gathering momentum, the little mouse reverses the action. He shakes the mother out of the cat, rescues all his family, wishes for a baby brother, and when at last he is asked again *"Now* whose mouse are you?" he is ready, and happy, to acknowledge his whole family. Restitution has been made.

Whose Mouse Are You? shows the beauty of metaphor, humor, and understatement in dealing with direct emotional conflict. With the rage comfortably projected onto the mouse (and eventually diffused, without a new baby ever being mentioned directly), the reader can put his own feelings into perspective. That, indeed, is one of the functions of art. A mass-market book, on the other hand, with its trite, treacly clichés about proper attitudes to new babies in the family, denies the child's true feelings and cannot possibly provide the consolation achieved here.

Books with strong emotional impact are sometimes all the better for being read aloud by a parent. Though *Whose Mouse Are You?* is ideal, at the mechanical level, for private reading by a beginner, it is emotionally perfect for a shared snuggle and read-aloud when the participation of the parent is a tacit reassurance that the child's anger about a new sibling is recognized and accepted.

Other picture books are challenging enough for an accomplished reader to tackle alone, and yet are deeply satisfying to a reader at the age of six or seven if mediated by an adult. I'm thinking of the extraordinary series of six Homeric hymns, translated from the Greek poetry of the seventh century B.C. by Penelope Proddow, and illustrated by the gifted American artist Barbara Cooney, who went to Greece to soak up the light and colors that radiate through these retellings of the ancient hymns sung by wandering bards. I can't imagine a more electrifying introduction to the Greek myths than these six books, all of which, unforgivably, have been allowed to lapse out of print. They are timeless classics and ought to be hunted down in libraries if they cannot be found in the bookstore.

The language of the books is strong, rhythmic, incantatory, and filled with Homer's imagery—a revelation for a child who may be more accustomed to the mumbled monosyllables and thin quackings of the television voice. "Now I will sing of golden-haired Demeter," begins the poet, in *Demeter and Persephone.* You can practically see him strumming the first chords on his lyre in some long-vanished banquet hall: "Demeter the awe-inspiring goddess, and her trim-ankled daughter, Persephone, who was frolicking on a grassy meadow."

Calm and wise, with the strong profile of the classical period, Demeter in her deep blue shawl gazes into the heart of a poppy. Behind her, fresh and innocent in diaphanous robes, Persephone plays with a butterfly. On the next page we see Persephone with the daughters of Ocean, gathering spring flowers in a meadow above the blue Aegean. These opening pictures strike the reader with a thrill of freshness: not just the sun-washed clarity of the pure, lyrical colors, not just the lovely girls in gossamer with their arms full of flowers, not just the delicacy of the irises and violets wound around their tendrils of curls, but the whole vision of spring, and the startling depiction of female beauty without the customary sickly overlay of self-conscious sexiness.

Suddenly Persephone is abducted by a darkly handsome king of the underworld. While in Hades, she eats some of the crimson seeds of the pomegranate he strews around her. Demeter, meanwhile, ravages the earth in her grief-stricken loss. This, of course, is a myth of imperishable power. And this version of the story has great resonance because it includes so much: the many ambiguous names for the mysteriously attractive Hades, for example; provocative details like those ruby-red pomegranate seeds, and the futility of Demeter's attempt to fill up her loss by raising another woman's baby as an immortal.

Demeter and Persephone is almost irreplaceable in any collection for another reason, too: It is one of the very rare depictions in children's literature of strong love between mother and grown daughter. Our popular culture abounds in Edith Bunkers and Playmates and other shaming travesties of womanhood. But womanly dignity like Demeter's is so rare as to be almost shocking in its novelty. Juvenile literature is loud with the exploits of male heroes, and today there is a conscious effort to give equal roles to brave or athletic girls, but you would have to go far to find such a gripping portrait of female power and love as this one. It is an interpretation that is equally important for boys and girls, and is all the more potent for being so visually beautiful and unmarred by propagandist motive. The same series of books offers a parallel affirmation of a boy:

Hermes, Lord of the Robbers is enchanting in the delicate wit and beauty of its illustrations and in its story of a boy leaping into manhood in a single day.

Before you read any of this series aloud to your child, read it to yourself to note some of the subtleties of the pictures. (See, for instance, how Hermes in his leafy wood sandals is making the cows walk backward to deceive pursuers.) A book so far off the beaten track needs adult guidance. Your enthusiasm, your willingness to read with greater clarity and cadence than is usually called for, your pointing out details in the story, will make these superb examples of pictorial and verbal art even more memorable. They are worth the effort.

Naturally, most books for this age group won't have the scope or lyricism of Homeric hymns. But even at the most mundane level, picture books can illumine the themes of everyday life. Anyone who has ever watched the excitement of a six-year-old entrusted with an important grown-up task (helping to wash the car or fold laundry) will know how much satisfaction the child gains from making a real contribution to the family. In typical middle-class life, there are few real tasks left for a small child to perform. He may have no role to play other than that of a junior consumer of toys and cereals. With our labor-saving devices and smaller families than in earlier years, we seem to require less and less from our children. Yet nothing is more undermining of self-worth than to feel useless and unneeded.

An early reading book that warmly conveys a sense of children's participation (realistically enough, the characters first complain about working when they'd rather go swimming) is *Six Darn Cows* by Margaret Laurence. The format, with its pastoral watercolors by Ann Blades and short but adult-style real chapters with titles, is well calculated for the beginning reader, to whom such ego-bolstering details are important.

When Jen and Todd Bean discover that they have inadvertently left the pasture gate open and let the cows wander away, they decide to tackle the problem on their own. Mother rescues them with a flashlight just when things are getting spooky in the darkening woods; I like the ironic tone when the children confide to their mother, "We thought you'd be mad" and she replies, "You have a point." But she goes on to say, "I'm proud of you. You did what you thought was best." Like so many peak moments of satisfaction in children's literature, the final scene takes place around the family dinner table, where both parents help give shape and meaning to the children's experience by joking and even singing about the day's small adventure.

Herman the Helper by Robert Kraus, illustrated by Jose Aruego and Ariane Dewey with huge, almost fluorescently bright pictures, is a lighthearted testament to a child's need to be resourceful and self-reliant: Herman, a sprightly little octopus, dashes through the bright blue water, all eight tiny legs streaming neatly behind him as he rushes to the aid of friends and relatives.

Much of the humor lies in Herman's unflagging and kindly ingenuity, always shown in the pictures rather than mentioned in the text: He ties balloons to tired old turtles, for example, to help them swim, and darts into a glass bottle to help his uncle build a miniature ship. Not only does the child "read" the pictures for much of the action but he's lured into reading the good-humored snippets of dialogue that are hand lettered right on the pictures, like the speech bubbles in comic strips.

That, of course, is one of the beauties of books that are most suited for beginning readers: They initiate the child into the art, not merely the mechanics, of reading. The jaunty bits of dialogue from the fishy characters in *Herman the Helper* ("Thanks, Herm!" they exclaim breezily) are written in a distinctly more speechlike tone of voice than the text of the story itself. It is a first experience in catching the feel of naturally written dialogue, and in hearing the shift in the author's tone. The gentle wordplay serves the same purpose: When the baby seahorses spin around on Herman's carousel and their exclamations ("Whee!") come out upside down, the child is being invited to play with the possibilities and tricks of language. Herman has the very last joke in the book. At dinnertime, Herman's dad offers to help him to some mashed potatoes. "No thanks," grins Herman. "I'll help myself."

Rosie's Walk by Pat Hutchins is famous for this same quality of a joke shared by author and reader. An adult reader is constantly engaged in the play of the author's mind and several levels of awareness are always at work: what the author knows, what the characters know, and what the reader perceives of both. A child who doesn't learn to read at these different levels simultaneously will miss most of the pleasures and rewards of literacy in adult life. And the process of understanding may begin early and naturally when a five-year-old child can see a whole plot being enacted in the pictures that is not even mentioned in the text. This is what happens in the story of Rosie, the hen. What the words tell us is that Rosie is going for a walk across the yard, around the pond, past the haystack, and home in time for dinner. What we see in the pictures is a sly fox chasing Rosie across each double page, and coming to woeful, predictable grief every time he makes an ill-timed pounce. The deadpan slapstick of the action and the stylized bright red and yellow illustrations perfectly enhance the child's crowing delight in being an insider, in getting the joke shared with the author.

Even a wordless book can help the child in the first lessons of reading closely, noticing details, linking them together in sequence and holding them all together in the mind for lightning cross references as the story progresses. *Moonlight* by Jan Ormerod is justly recognized for the charm of its realistic and touching watercolors depicting an evening in the life of a young, modern, middle-class family. The book begins with a family dinner scene that we "read" horizontally from left to right: the mother looking informal and capable with her short-cropped hair and casually crossed legs beneath the table; the four- or five-year-old daughter, relaxed and loved, glancing perkily up at her mother (and she really is a preschooler, as the litter of crumbs and dropped cutlery beneath her chair tells us); then the father, his curly beard and youthful face letting us know that he is gentle and playful.

The great skill of the narrative in *Moonlight* lies in the way the child reader must make the connections, though all the clues to the story are provided in correct sequence. On pages where four or five separate panels tell the story, they lead from left to right with continuing action, and sometimes the little girl even walks from one frame to another, leading the reader's eye visually and the mind temporally. When the child makes two little boats from a melon rind and a triangle of orange peel, we are reminded that the food scraps and other makings (toothpicks, a fallen leaf, red paper napkins) have been in the pictures from the beginning. That's an example of the forward and backward cross referencing I mentioned earlier. Incidentally, the fate of the little boats provides another strand in the continuing story. We see them being sailed in the bath, gradually coming apart, and then being abandoned as the action goes on.

Just as in older fiction, we must read motivation and character from the sequence of events. The father washes the dishes; where is mother? The question is left hanging, like a small subplot in a novel, until it becomes clear, a few pictures later, that she was in the bathroom running the bedtime bath for the little girl. The shower cap and the neatly hung roll of toilet paper become the tags that carry us to the next picture, where the once-tidy bathroom is strewn with the child's clothes. The toilet paper roll is on the floor (a clue to the unstated intervening action which the reader must infer) and the shower cap, just visible above the rim of the tub, tells us where the little girl is.

Action leads to consequence: Not only is the child's bathtub play deliciously drawn but the reader can anticipate what might come next when the shower cap drifts away, and the girl's hair gets more wet and bedraggled by the minute. When the mother comes back, her hands-on-hip stance clearly spells out her exasperation; the last frame of the bath sequence shows mother (whose face wears a "Well, it's your own fault" expression) combing out the wet tangles, while the child squawks in protest.

The bedtime scene—its rituals, its tenderness, its fears—is just as sensitively narrated. In every frame, the reader is called upon to remember previous details, make connections, deduce causes and consequences, and identify emotionally with the characters. Humor, surprise, comfort, and family love are all there. All count on the reader's active imaginative involvement to make the story live. Without words, the drama of nuance and character are fully present: the father's amused affection, for example, and the mother's more down-to-earth personality, in which the child greatly resembles her. The beauty of *Moonlight* (and its companion volume, *Sunlight)* is that all this is drawn from the reader without any strain. The reader's work is unconscious, just as it is in an engrossing but complex adult work of fiction.

This is the priceless lesson of beginner books: how to read with an awakened imagination. The ABCs of reading, the mechanical mastery, are mere eye exercises compared to this. As long ago as 1880, Randolph Caldecott, the great English illustrator, showed the way. His *Hey Diddle Diddle,* now reprinted in a Godine paperback for less than one dollar, is just an old familiar nursery rhyme, but the way Caldecott spun out its meaning is like a blueprint for the reader's inner eye. Nearly every phrase in the rhyme has its own full-page illustration, and these pictures show how the reader's imagination must work to bring the written text into abundant life. The phrase "Hey diddle diddle," for example, introduces us to a children's party, with a cat as music master leading a dance. "The cat" shows us a proud papa cat, stuffed into his best jacket before the admiring eyes of his demure wife and kittens. This scene, we realize, takes place just before the first party scene, and shows us the cat getting ready to perform. "And the fiddle" is also a prior action; we see the fiddle left on a table by a milquetoast music teacher; then we see the cat, having "liberated" the instrument, fiddling manically on a garden wall while animals cavort, the cow nearly transported by the gaiety of the music. When the cow "leaps over the moon," she is really kicking over the milk bucket, and her flying heels frame the new moon low on the horizon.

Best of all is the conception of the dish who elopes with the spoon. The demonic cat is fiddling so madly that ordinary objects are beside themselves; the vinegar cruet has sprouted breeches-clad legs, and even the plates on the shelf kick their heels while a dish steals away with a simpering spoon. Even when the rhyme finishes, Caldecott's wit does not: An end page shows the dish lying shattered on the ground while the other plates weep, and the errant spoon is marched off between a grimly upright fork and a stern knife.

The parent who reads aloud can help the child to notice these humorous details by taking time to speculate aloud about them. Otherwise, much of the complexity will simply be overlooked, especially by the modern child accustomed to the crude shapes and one-dimensional meanings of Disney books and Saturday cartoons.

I've tried to show, in some detail, how to "read" the pictures because this is one of the primary goals in sharing a picture book with your child: to encourage the youngster to form detailed and coherent pictures in his own mind rather than letting the words slip across the surface of his consciousness. Reading on his own, an older child will often be content to "skip" descriptions and gulp down the plot, but if this habit of active imagining has been instilled early on, he may well go back over the book and gain twice as much from it at a more leisurely pace.

In selecting only a few picture books that have particular reading value for the beginner, I'm doing a conscious injustice to the whole field of picture book art, which could well command an entire volume of its own. Today, there is such a profuse flowering of this form of children's literature that more and more adults have realized what a sophisticated resource it can be for the older reader as well. Thousands of picture books have subtle and complex stories, with content geared to a higher level of maturity. Elaine Moss, a British writer who has worked to encourage reading among inner city children, once described how she put challenging picture books on a top shelf in a library to signal the older children that the books were meant for them, not for the floor-level preschoolers. In the next chapter and in the treasury, I've mentioned some examples that may prove particularly enticing to a reader who is not yet comfortable with densely printed text.

Picture books are a garden of delight for all age groups. Wisely chosen by parents, they can make an enormous difference in preparing the child to become the best kind of reader, the one who creates whole worlds of images in the mind, who is the author's active collaborator, questioner, and fellow explorer.

Chapter 3

FIRST NOVELS

. . . to surrender to a novel is not necessarily weak, any more than falling in love is necessarily weak. That, too, involves not merely surrender but some long-term sinking of one's own consciousness in another person's. One of the symptoms of being in love, which does not mark any other form of love or lust, is that you want to hear everything the other person can or will tell you, not primarily for the information it may give you about life or even about the person concerned, but for the preciousness of seeing the world through his eyes— just as you see *a* world through the novelist's eyes, and want to hear everything he is prepared to tell you . . . With the novel, you might as well surrender wholly or not at all.

Brigid Brophy, "The Novel as a Takeover Bid," in
Don't Never Forget, 1966

Your child can read—and he can do it without too many agonizing hesitations, without the limping sing-song he used when he could only decipher letters rather than whole sentences full of meaning. Now he pauses only occasionally when he stumbles over a totally unfamiliar word. Most often, he can read right through the print on the page to the meaning beyond, as if he were looking through a clear stream to the colored pebbles on the sandy bed. That first great barrier has been leaped. Now what?

This is a critical time. If the child has learned to read at four or five, not from internal passion but from parental prodding, the first glamorous glow of achievement may have worn off by the time he is seven or eight. In fact, in the new excitement of independence, reading for pleasure may be rejected along with the bottle and the blanket and other cherished objects of early childhood, particularly if reading has always been a mechanical process of decoding, and has never grown into a thoroughly assimilated skill. And if the child learns to read only when he reaches school age, silent reading may seem a pallid attraction indeed amid the heady welter of distractions available to his age group. Television—action dramas and sports—may become an important topic of conversation in the peer group, especially among boys; video parlors, two-wheeled bicycles, active street play, organized sports teams, and activities like scouting all offer the allure of peer group acceptance and new bases of friendship. Ironically, just when a child's decoding skills are good enough so that he can begin reading novels, all his motivation to read may evaporate overnight.

Unless there is an active effort by the parent to establish reading as a prime source of pleasure, it is more than likely that, at this age, boys especially will fall by the wayside as readers of books. Most book-world professionals and many classroom teachers acknowledge that boys read for entertainment far less than girls do, and experience more mechanical difficulties in reading. Boys may also develop reading proficiency later than girls because of a difference in brain development. Or it may be that girls read more because, even now, they have less opportunity and less pressure to excel in athletics. In any case, girls seem to have more time and more motivation to escape into books, and it is probably at this early primary school age that the patterns are formed which make women the greater readers and buyers of literature.

Pleasure is the word to remember. You may be eager to encourage your child to read, but unless you can find ways to do it through subtle encouragement rather than pressure, it might be better to leave well enough alone. At this age, more than any other, it is useful for you to be familiar with the most interesting books available. But remember, a new reader does not automatically fall with cries of ecstasy on a shiny new stack of books offered by the parent; you can make the difference by your unfeigned enthusiasm for a book or a poem.

Don't give up reading aloud. Just because a youngster can now plough through a school primer (and, by the way, there are few stronger deterrents to reading pleasure than a school primer), it doesn't mean that read-aloud times at home should come to an end. It does take ingenuity to find the right time in your own family's life to share stories. You can take a new book on a family picnic, to the doctor's office to while away the wait (don't rely on the tattered cast-offs too often found on the waiting room table), or to the supermarket to beat the checkout line doldrums. Don't worry about funny looks from bystanders. They'll just be straining to hear the story themselves.

You will, certainly, be wrestling with the habits of our culture, in which electronic amusement accompanies the child everywhere and effectively closes out all other forms of human discourse. I remember the folk song marathons our children invented to while away the time on long car trips; the singing was started by their father, longing for some peace while at the wheel, and his animated renditions were eagerly imitated by the back-seat crew. If our car radio had worked more efficiently, the children may never have developed the repertoire that enabled them to sing from the beginning to the end of a two-hundred-mile trip, with no repeats.

Boredom is a great resource. Trap your children at a cottage without television, and watch them rediscover arts and crafts, swimming, games, and reading. Refuse their requests for computerized games, and watch them fall back on other wellsprings of invention. The intrinsic fidgety fascination of the machines will easily drive out other interests the way English sparrows drove out the bluebirds. The child who reaches teenage years as a computer whiz kid, but who never had the chance to become a reader in early childhood, probably never will.

What are the right books, then, to lure early readers into the "falling in love" experience of fiction reading? The child opening her first novel may be as young as six or seven or as old as eight or nine; obviously, "first novels" will have a wide range of difficulty. They should be long enough to yield the true rewards of the novel: sustained involvement with unfolding characters, and the detailed recreation of another world in which the reader can live and move. Yet if they bog down in detail at the expense of story, they may daunt the young child.

Simplicity is one attraction of the "lowest common denominator" books, such as Enid Blyton's *Noddy* series or spinoffs from popular films like *Star Wars*. I can remember racing through all of *The Bobbsey Twins*, the impossibly saccharine *Five Little Peppers and How They Grew*, and even the complete Twin series, including, most memorably, *The Eskimo Twins* and *The Japanese Twins*. All those series were commercial, badly written, thinly plotted—and devoured by my generation for the exhilaration of being able to read and the easy diversion of their simple, predictable plots and undemanding characters.

Another thing those books had in common was that they were family stories. And young readers today, whatever their surface sophistication—however much they know from television about alcoholism, divorce, or anorexia nervosa—still love and need those stories that breathe an atmosphere of safety, warmth, and family solidarity. It is true that older children, ready to confront painful realities, may want to read about the darker undertones of traditional family life. But that comes later. Despair and cynicism are utterly inappropriate for eight-year-olds; no matter what their life circumstances, the earliest readers yearn for stories about the loved and accepted child who moves in a secure world. Though curiosity is at a peak, introspection is not: Action, comedy, or adventure, in real or imagined worlds, are far more alluring than the tortured problem novels that are considered so attractive for prepubescents.

Simplicity and extroversion, however, are not synonyms for poverty of character and skimpiness of plot. The richer the stories are in truth and feeling, the more satisfying they will be to the reader.

Fortunate, then, is the child who comes across *Hello, Aurora!* and *Aurora and the Little Blue Car* by Anne-Catharina Vestly. These stories may have seemed gently radical in the 1960s when they were first written in socially progressive Norway: Preschooler Aurora and her newborn brother, Socrates, are being brought up by one of literature's first and most endearing house husbands. Aurora's father, Edward, is a doctoral student in classics and history who cooks, bakes, and does laundry while mother works full time as a legal secretary. If *Aurora* sounds like a feminist fable with about as much aesthetic appeal as poached parsnips, then my synopsis does an injustice to the sweetness and individuality of tone in this series.

The story is told from Aurora's viewpoint, no easy feat when the heroine is at most five years old. Yet without condescension, and with an uncanny feeling for the indirect way in which preschoolers often communicate their most intense anxieties, Vestly makes the reader feel the lively affection of a close family and the sensitivity with which the parents respond to each other and to their children. Particularly satisfying to the reader is the way in which the sturdily practical Aurora, with her sharp powers of observation and memory, helps her befuddled father to cope with supermarket protocol, driving lessons, or ruined laundry. Father's competence with the baby and his authority as a caring adult are not questioned; the shrewd balance of skill between Aurora and her father is one of this book's strongest assets, along with its tolerant and gentle humor.

It is always a trap to judge a book by its worthy content (that way lies the Sunday school tract), but when a novel with a "relevant" theme has ample and well-selected detail, when its characters are drawn with enough depth that they seem to have a complex life of their own, and when the density of human experience is felt through prose simple enough for a seven-year-old, we can be fairly sure that the book rises above mere contemporaneity. Aurora and her family have that kind of individuality; Aurora herself is an appealingly brave, vulnerable, natural child, light years away from the smart-aleck, knowingly urbane kid who haunts the sterile prose of many current mass-market books.

The first- and second-grade child, reading about Aurora's snide neighbors who disapprove of working mothers, will almost certainly recognize the feeling of those first piercing revelations that outsiders may be critical of one's family values or style. The surprised hurt of this, the first doubts and perplexities about what always seemed inevitable and immutable, are perfectly mirrored in Aurora's stubborn, wounded defensiveness. And the way her parents deal with Aurora's worry is realistic, simple, and comforting.

Comfort, highlighted by danger and challenge, is the hallmark of another family story that ought to be snatched back from the jaws of television. The television series, "The Little House on the Prairie," did a disservice to the books on which it was loosely based. For one thing, Pa—the rosy, robust, blackly bearded giant in the books—was damped down into the smarmy, close-shaven Michael Landon, a psychologizing 1970s dad who was untrue, physically and emotionally, in every detail to the original story. Landon might have been *nice,* but that's not the point; the viewer of the series gets a transposed, pioneer-costume soap opera that is contemporary in tone and values, and misses the discovery of real frontier life in all its rigor and sensuous immediacy.

Children should be given the chance to read the stories before their mental image of the characters is spoiled forever by Hollywood's pallid imitation. (Librarians sometimes argue, correctly, I'm sure, that many children are stimulated to read a given book because it has been televised. But I wonder if that works both ways—I know a good many children who can't be bothered to read a book if they've already seen it on television.)

The Little House in the Big Woods, the first book in the autobiographical ten-volume series by pioneer Laura Ingalls Wilder, is perfect for the beginning novel reader. A large-print paperback with affectionately detailed drawings by Garth Williams, it's a book as deeply engaging to boys as to girls. (In chapter 10, you'll find a more detailed discussion of boys' books and girls' books, and the dangers of restricting a child's range of empathy on the basis of gender.)

The family of the Little House books, living in the great woods of Wisconsin, is all action and resourcefulness. From the first page, the reader is caught up in the family's thrilling, challenging isolation. Wolves howl outside, the snow drifts up to the windows, but inside is safety and purpose: Pa makes lead bullets by the fire with his two young daughters to help him, while Ma grates a carrot into the pale winter milk to color it yellow.

So absorbing are these physical details of pioneer life that two university students recently told me with keen pleasure how they read the books at ages six and seven, and could still remember the way Pa smoked the deer meat in a hollow log, and the fragrance of the hickory chips with which Laura fuelled the smoke-fire.

Pa, not incidentally, is an attractive male figure with whom small boys might delight to associate. Not only does he play boisterous games with his little girls but he's also a skilled huntsman and protector, a stern but just father, and a merry fiddle player. And any child, male or female, can identify with Laura's realistic fears and the courage she derives from the solid mutual support of the family.

Family stories have petered out in recent years. Modern authors can't seem to help but inject a note of chaos, despair, or bleak cynicism into their accounts of the modern nuclear family. (Perhaps that word *nuclear* is a tip-off to the source of disenchantment.) But young children are disturbed enough by the intimations of family doom they hear all around them. The enduring popularity of family stories written as far back as the 1930s, such as the imperishable *The Moffats* by Eleanor Estes, or the 1950s, such as *Henry Huggins* by Beverly Cleary, shows us how much children still want to live, imaginatively, in a world where family love is the unquestioned basis of existence.

"Letters reveal that children want to love and be loved by two parents in a united family," author Cleary said when accepting the 1984 Newbery Medal for her book *Dear Mr. Henshaw.* Cleary is an earthy and pragmatic author who, as a children's librarian in the 1940s, sympathized with the nonreaders who wanted books they could understand, "books in which they do not get lost in the first chapter and can't tell what the author is talking about."

Henry Huggins, published in 1950, was her response to this need, and teachers tell me that the book is just as popular as ever with first- and second-graders, despite its dated view of small-town life and narrow gender stereotypes. In a kindly universe, Henry struggles with the small dilemmas of childhood: How is he to get home on the bus, where no pets are allowed, with his starved foundling puppy in a paper bag that threatens to burst open? How might he repalce another boy's deliciously new football which Henry has—O horrors!—accidentally thrown into the open window of a passing car? Which of his million guppies, in a triple row of jars ranging around his bedroom, can he bear to part with, now that he has rashly promised to give one away? Children are won over by the wry humor, the accurate and unsentimental observation of child life, and by Henry's guileless character.

Even more popular, however, is the little terror Ramona Quimby, also created by Beverly Cleary. There's more bite, more surprise, in this series of books about another middle-American family, probably because Ramona is a much more original character than Henry. Ramona is a force of nature: a ferociously determined, imaginative, energetic tyke of four when we first meet her, in *Beezus and Ramona,* driving her nine-year-old sister mad by riding round and round the living room on her tricycle, breathing in and out on the same two repeated notes on the harmonica. Clear, unaffected, with a sharp ear for naturalistic dialogue and a shrewd though forgiving eye for children's secret motivations, Cleary manages to be realistic and accepting at the same time. Her descriptions of Ramona's violent temper tantrum in *Ramona and Her Mother* is one of the best I've read—from the inside out—of a child's torrential rage, self-pity, guilt, and egotism in the midst of a lie-on-the-bed-and-kick-the-wall outburst. It has just enough distance in it to enable a child to see herself with a rueful eye, even while she revels in the reconciliation with mother at the end of the book.

An even more sensitive and evocative writer for the same age group is Eleanor Estes. Her story *The Hundred Dresses* dates from World War II, and, like Henry Huggins and the Ramona books, is set in small-town America, where the two-parent family is rarely questioned and school is strict but kind. It still reads swiftly, delicately, and hauntingly. More tautly organized and pointed than the Cleary books, it tells of a troubling incident in the lives of two young schoolgirls.

Maddie, the central character, can't help but go along when her friend Peggy, the prettiest and most popular girl in class, begins to tease the awkward, shabby Wanda Petrowski. (Fredelle Maynard, the Canadian writer, tells of a similar incident of schoolgirl racism in *Raisins and Almonds,* her memoir of a prairie girlhood. In a phrase I've never forgotten, she recalls her troubled conscience as "a needle of glass that pierced my heart.")

Maddie is not spared that "needle of glass"; later, when the damage has been done, when Wanda has moved away and it is too late for reparations, Maddie wonders "if she were going to be unhappy about Wanda . . . forever." The muted, bittersweet ending is not too difficult for child readers to bear; it may arouse in them a recognition that they are not the only ones to have indulged in cruelty, and that an uneasy conscience is both their punishment and their guide to a solution.

Gentle, impressionistic watercolors by Louis Slobodkin decorate the chapter headings and the edges of the pages; their effect is so unobtrusive as to be almost subliminal—perfect for this age group, for whom the printed word takes precedence over the picture; and perfect for this story, too, because they evoke the ambiguous quality of happy schooldays—bright autumns, tingling evergreen-scented Christmases, and a melancholy tinge of wronged innocence.

The excellence of *The Hundred Dresses* is reflected in its language. Estes uses imagery that is perfectly suited to the early reader. On the bleak and remorse-haunted autumn day when the two girls trudge in the rain to Wanda's shack to make amends, they find that the family has moved away: "Wisps of old grass stuck up here and there along the pathway like thin wet kittens."

Richness of language is always a clue to excellence for the beginning reader as for any other age group. Of course, "richness" does not always refer to imagery, and never to mere ornateness. An example is the lovely pared-down ironic humor of *Ellen's Lion* by Crockett Johnson. Ellen is a buoyant, imaginative child who talks to her stuffed lion. One day, he answers back. "You talked! You said something!" exclaims Ellen, jumping up and down on her bed in delight. "It wasn't anything that important," says the lion, in the fine crotchety tradition of Eeyore. "And watch where you're jumping." Part of the reader's pleasure in these twelve linked humorous stories comes from participating in Ellen's imaginative play while at the same time rising to an ironic awareness—shared with the author—that it is Ellen who makes up the lion's dialogue. Somehow, while remaining childlike herself, Ellen projects an adult awareness through the lion.

Few authors lavish more expressive, demanding language on their child readers than the author-illustrator William Steig. In themes and narrative suggestiveness, his picture books really qualify as first novels. The format of *The Amazing Bone*, for example—with its lyrical, impressionistic, and color-drenched paintings—is that of the traditional picture book, but its language is extraordinarily exuberant and varied, and the plot touches on themes of deep interest to the older child.

Pearl is a young pig who loiters in the springtime woods on her way home from school. The world dazzles with its colors:

The warm air touched her so tenderly she could almost feel herself changing into a flower. Her light dress felt like petals.

"I love everything," she heard herself say. "So do I," answered a voice.

A bone (what a strange object for Steig to choose—one whose symbolism, perhaps, doesn't bear too much thought) is lying in the grass and speaking to Pearl. And, as is characteristic of Steig's energetic, overflowing delight in words, the bone speaks several languages, indulges in flights of rhetoric by turns courtly and gleeful, and, in a magical incantation designed to rescue Pearl from a foxy kidnapper, voices some of the most inspired gibberish I've ever read.

On a hidden level, the story seems to be about romantic love and marriage. It disappoints me that one of the only two books the brilliant Steig has written with a female central character (another is *Brave Irene)* presents her as a passively rescued and enraptured "princess." But Pearl's generous soul and poetic sensibility make her something more individual than the standard rescuee.

It's not surprising, either, that a book with such strong appeal to young children elliptically portrays a romantic match, ending with the bone being accepted and loved by Pearl's parents, sharing Pearl's bed every night, and making "beautiful music." For though the family story is a tremendous source of affirmation and reassurance to young readers, every child also longs to try out, in fantasy or in fiction, the pleasures of adult autonomy. (See Steig's magnificent *Caleb and Kate* for a fablelike tale of love, anger, and reconciliation in marriage.)

For some of the same reasons, as the English author Joan Aiken has wittily said, there is hardly a child alive who doesn't like to fancy himself or herself as an orphan. The orphan, after all, can savor the joys or terrors of independence without feeling guilty toward a hindering parent. This first novel group includes many rewarding independence fantasies. The time-honored resource is the fairy tale, and age seven or eight is certainly the right time for these often frightening but also profoundly reassuring tales of children (youngest sons, youngest daughters) struggling to overcome enchantments, evil parents, or monsters.

Of modern orphan fables for this age group, *Goldie the Dollmaker* by M.B. Goffstein is one of the most touching, strange, and enduring. Goffstein's astonishing line drawings, wiry and spare, yet as distinctly individual as a signature, greatly enhance the fairy tale feel of the story: They are universal, yet intensely particular.

Goldie lives alone in a forest, in her parents' little house, carrying on the doll-making work they did when they were alive. In her babushka and wooden clogs, she looks as unassuming as a peasant; in her quiet routines of sleep, carving, painting, and carrying the finished dolls to town, we sense the self-contained artist. Note the process by which Goldie paints her dolls' faces: She paints

> . . . a little gleaming black eye on either side of the doll's nose and finally, holding it firmly around the waist with one hand, Goldie smiled and smiled into the doll's eyes in the friendliest, sweetest way, and she painted a smile right back to herself on the little doll's face . . . They said that if you looked at a Goldie Rosenzweig doll you bought her, even if you weren't going to buy any doll in the first place. Because the truth about that smile was that it was heartbreaking.

Goldie is crushed when her friend Omus laughs at her dedication. But she is strengthened, in a luminous dream, by the universal fellowship of artists. She has just bought a ravishingly beautiful Chinese lamp, splurging a whole month's wages on it. In her dream, the maker of the lamp comes to her, showing her why she works as she does, and why the lonely life of the artist is finally worthwhile. In an understated, satisfying ending, Goldie looks around the softly lit room where she works, and she knows that it is her house, her tools, her work, that give her life meaning.

A parallel story by Goffstein is *Two Piano Tuners*, the story of Debbie who lives with her loving grandpa, Reuben, a piano tuner for famous virtuosi. He wants her to be a great pianist; she wants to be a piano tuner. In a story told as limpidly as *Goldie the Dollmaker*, Goffstein shows us how both the adult and the child have to change to allow Debbie to grow into her own person. Goffstein has a rare quality of making all the small gestures of daily life reverberate with meaning. To watch Debbie's grandfather move quietly about the kitchen, making coffee in the old yellow coffee pot and setting out the blue and orange plates on the table, is to sense, deeper than words, the almost sacral quality of daily life, and how the simplest actions can resonate with affirmation through our care and attention.

The well-loved Tim stories by Edward Ardizzone feature what might be called a "pseudo-orphan," since Tim's parents stay well in the background and seem to accept his fantastically daring adventures with benign resignation. Ardizzone's illustrations are his glory: Quick, sketchy, intimate, they are always gratifyingly detailed when it comes to things nautical, and satisfyingly vague about the faces of the young heroes—a perfect screen, as Ardizzone himself says, for the projections of the daydreaming young readers.

Fairy tales, the original orphan stories, (told in "a tone licked clean over the centuries by mild old tongues, grandam to cub, serene, anonymous," as poet James Merrill says) still seize the young imagination. They combine a yearning for freedom, the urge to test oneself against adult realities, the terror of being left alone and helpless, and the itch to know who one might become if loosed from family bonds. Since children's literature serves in part to provide dream answers to these unspoken questions, the most popular and esteemed children's books have often placed children in at least a quasi-orphan role, with parents absent, distracted, or otherwise rendered harmless. It's something of a cheat, in modern mass-market books, to discover that young people no longer enjoy this immunity from the burden of adults. Supposedly in the name of realism, pre-pubescents in today's novels often have to struggle with malign, inadequate, or hurtful parent figures who are the focus for the child's disillusionment or bitterness. The child becomes the victim, preoccupied with oppressors, rather than an adventurer striking out on his or her own, filled with excitement, fear, and resolution at the beginning of a new life.

That "realism" of many modern novels, in any case, is like the realism of televised soap opera: Despite the studied banality of the dialogue, the painstakingly reconstructed living rooms of middle-class America, and the surface resemblance to things in the real world, the naturalism of the soap opera is instantly identifiable as fake. The reason, I think, that the speech and plots of soap opera fall so flat on our ears (you could recognize that fake-real speech pattern as soap operatic if you heard it in the middle of a sandstorm in the Gobi desert) is that there is nothing real in the realism. There is no person under the screen personality, no character under the mannerisms, no tangled junk in the kitchen drawers on the set, no underlayer of perception or resonance of lived lives in the clichés exchanged by the characters.

So it is all the more distressing to read, in a newspaper article about a group of Toronto children at a theater school, that the eight-year-olds scorn fairy tales and express an interest in "more realistic stories." You just know that when these precocious urban youngsters talk of realism, they mean TV realism, with its clutter of life-mimicking details. A TV drama about child abuse, with its blatant manipulation and control of the viewers' emotions, is more "realistic" to them (more familiar, perhaps, and undemanding?) than the surrealistic horror of a fairy tale like *The Juniper Tree*. Yet an important dimension of human feeling and an artistically valuable literary form have been abandoned.

Alert parents will want to make sure that every child—particularly the one beginning school and a new life of literacy—will have access to the more invigorating sort of stories, the adventurous and imaginative rather than the reductively realistic; stories in which children go past their parents rather than remaining morbidly preoccupied with them.

The "wish to be an orphan" is in part a wish for joyful anarchy, and the quintessential orphan of modern fiction is surely Pippi Longstocking, the nine-year-old girl who lives alone, climbs on the furniture, and scrubs floors by tying brushes on to her shoes—though not always before rolling out her cookie dough on the linoleum. I have noticed that children's eyes light up when they remember reading Astrid Lindgren's Pippi books: The playful wish fulfillment is so strong that the glee lingers on in memory.

Pippi is the strongest girl in the world; her mother is an angel in heaven (far more liberating, as any Victorian daughter could have testified, than an Angel in the House) and her father is a marooned cannibal king on a desert island. She lives in her own secluded house with a horse on the porch, a monkey called Mr. Nilsson, and a suitcase full of gold coins. Pippi's marvelously breezy style ("So long, boys," she says to the sailors who have brought her home after her father was lost at sea) is a bracing antidote to the sentimentality with which children's vulnerability is so often treated. Leaving the sailors, she strides into her new life without looking back . . . and it's clear that her physical strength is a metaphor for her emotional indomitability.

But Pippi offers more than just a fantasy of omnipotence. Even more wonderful than her physical power is the freeing of imagination she brings to play with the rather conventional and stereotyped children who live next door. Pippi is a namer. She delights in explosively expansive language ("My name is Pippilotta Delicatessa Windowshade Mackrelmint Efraim's Daughter Longstocking, daughter of Captain Efraim Longstocking, formerly the Terror of the Sea, now a cannibal king"); linguistic ridicule ("I have got along without any pluttifikation tables for nine years," she says in a dreary math class); and the creation of magic through words. One of her favorite games is finding things: An old rusty can becomes a delightful JAR WITH COOKIES if you put cookies in it, or JAR WITHOUT COOKIES if you don't.

There is an enriching dimension of poignancy to the Pippi story. Headstrong Pippi, in her willful defiance of convention, does not have it all her way. She may sabotage her neighbor's well-meaning tea party by her unrestrained greed and her *reductio ad absurdum* of adult chit-chat, but there is a price to pay for anarchy. Pippi is left out in the cold, socially and at school.

Not too much is made of Pippi's isolation. The tone of the story, after all, is not emotional realism but liberating tomfoolery. Nevertheless, this slight shading of the book's high spirits tends to deepen its color and integrity. To see how fresh, how inspiriting a book *Pippi Longstocking* is, compare it to any one of a thousand mass-circulation books for young children in which wayward choo-choo trains or discontented flowers who want to be butterflies finally learn to accept their fate and buckle under to conformity. Pippi never buckles; she may wilt momentarily in the cold draught of society's disapproval, but, more characteristically, she bounces away to a new, ever more outrageously naive plan of adventure.

For some strange reason, fantasies that feature boys in this age group most often weave themselves around themes not of power and anarchy but of deep intimate relationships with the unattainable other. Or perhaps the reason is not so mysterious: Fantasies give the child what is most keenly missing in real life. And still, even now, girls miss courage, autonomy, and the chance to be tested on grounds of intelligence and moral strength, rather than mere prettiness. And boys miss intimacy, physical and emotional, which girls can still receive nonchalantly from their mothers and teachers, but which boys seek or accept only at peril of their manly reputations and self-images.

Significantly, the boys in these fantasies long for closeness not with a female figure (though there are rare exceptions, like the boy in *The Midnight Fox)* but with a male, usually an animal, a robot, or an imaginary hero. What boys dream of, to judge by their chosen fantasies, is the warmth and acceptance of a loving, all-powerful father without the competitiveness, the authoritarianism, and the harsh judging to which so many fathers are prone. In some versions, it is not the real-life father who is rejecting or inadequate, but society, in the guise of school authorities.

Wingman, by Daniel Manus Pinkwater, seems to me to rank among the most beautiful and satisfying of all these fantasies, all the more remarkable because it uses a terse contemporary idiom. "At school he was Donald Chen, but at home he was Chen Chi-Wing or Ah-Wing," we are told. Donald is the poorest kid in his class in a run-down New York neighborhood; he lives with his father and sister in two crowded rooms behind his father's laundry.

Sparely and swiftly, with a few vivid details, Pinkwater evokes for us the whole texture of Donald's life. The illustrations are just as selective and as forcefully modern—thick black magic marker drawings that resemble a cross between Superman and a Roy Lichtenstein. Each full-page illustration is divided into four comiclike panels, but the pictures themselves use cinematic zoom and close-up techniques. On the first full page, we are offered a series of symbols that give us essential clues to the important things in Donald's life: his father's face, an iron, a stack of comic books (Donald's most precious possessions—he has 2,000 of them), and a middle-distance view of Donald's father, standing with his arm affectionately around Donald's shoulders while the boy reads a comic.

One of the great pleasures of Pinkwater is the way he can write obliquely, but with complete clarity of meaning. When he tells us that Donald goes to school every day, even in the coldest weather, without a coat but with a fresh white shirt, we know two things without being told: that his father anxiously looks after him in the only ways available to him (the clean white shirt is lovingly washed and ironed, of course, by the exhausted father), and that Donald is impervious to cold because he is numb with misery. Where lesser authors might have hammered home these perceptions in flat, declarative sentences, a true writer of fiction like Pinkwater tells us all by telling us practically nothing and letting it reverberate.

Reading about Captain Marvel and Hawkman helps Donald "not to worry about things, like being thrown out by the landlords." Rarely has children's escape reading had a more succint or sympathetic defense. When Donald is driven to truancy by an inexcusably obtuse and clumsy teacher, he takes refuge by climbing the giddy heights of the George Washington Bridge, where he crouches on a beam and daydreams away the hours surrounded by the rumble of cars overhead, the flurry of seagulls, and his stacks of comic books.

The arrival of Wingman, a Chinese superhero, is a masterful blend of fantasy and acute observation: Just as pigeons seem to take flight the moment Donald turns his head to look at them boldly, Wingman vanishes when stared at too directly. So Donald learns to discipline his eagerness. He learns that only when he sinks himself into his comics, losing all self-awareness, is he granted a sight of Wingman landing on the beam beside him. With pounding heart, he steals sidelong glimpses of his feather-caped hero.

Later, Donald has another lesson in vision, when a new, more humane teacher takes his class to the Metropolitan Museum of Art on its first-ever field trip. By now, Donald has surged ahead in confidence because of his incredible journeys with Wingman and his triumphs in teaching the class to read through comic books. When the class sees its first Chinese paintings "full of mist and space," they fall silent "not because it was scary like the Egyptian tomb stuff, but because there was something about these pictures that was like a little bird perched on your finger." Donald, already self-taught in coaxing an elusive bird to reveal itself to him, stays alone with the picture until it comes alive for him. This passage is one of the simplest and most affecting descriptions I've found in children's literature about the self-forgetfulness you must bring to art, and the transcendence with which you may be rewarded.

The Iron Man is better known than *Wingman,* perhaps because of its author, England's poet laureate, Ted Hughes, or perhaps because its language is so grippingly intense that teachers have found it a never-fail magnet for the attention of even the most fidgety eight-year-old boy.

> The Iron Man came to the top of the cliff.
> How far had he walked? Nobody knows. Where had he come from? Nobody knows. How was he made? Nobody knows.

Hughes's language is as polished, spare, and powerful as that of the best poetry; the rhythm, repetition, and assonance are enough to assure our rapt attention. Read it aloud and see how the vowel patterns alone force you to speak it at a measured, emphatic pace, full of the immense, ponderous menace of the Iron Man himself. Note the startling simplicity of the images: ". . . his great iron head, shaped like a dustbin but as big as a bedroom." Hughes does not forget that his book is "A Story in Five Nights," a bedtime story, and the images ("a foot as big as a single bed") are arrowed straight at the child sitting bolt upright in bed, listening.

Hughes's verbal pyrotechnics, in fact, are a wonderful introduction to the ways in which a reader must create mental images in order to create the novel. He sets the words out on the page in patterns that force us to pause, hear silences and echoes and meanings. He sets the scene so carefully that only a spectacularly lazy reader would not be compelled to see the rocky beach, hear the sound of the sea "chewing away at the edge," "boiling and booming" while the stars wheel overhead, or see the dawn when the darkness "grew blue and the shapes of the rocks separated from each other."

The Iron Man has crashed over the edge of the cliff, flying into dozens of separate pieces: "Only one of the iron hands, lying beside an old, sand-logged, washed-up seaman's boot, waved its fingers for a minute, like a crab on its back. Then it lay still." The ghoulish scene in which the hand scuttles about, finding the other parts and reassembling them, is brought to a stunning climax when the Iron Man, whole again, red eyes blazing, walks into the sea—deeper, deeper, deeper—until the waves have covered him and "the gulls circled low over the line of bubbles that went on moving slowly out into the deep sea."

Of course, it is a young boy, Hogarth, who becomes the intermediary when the Iron Man returns and terrorizes the neighborhood. It is Hogarth who dares to ask the Iron Man what he wants—leading to the happy scene in which the monster at last retires to a scrap-metal dump, content to gobble old rusty chains (better than any spaghetti), his "eyes crackling with joy" as he licks the delicious crumbs of chrome off a greasy black stove. Hughes's dramatic phrasing and cadences sweep the beginning reader along, the many stops and repetitions reinforcing the images but scarcely slowing the pace.

The Iron Man is only occasionally comic, but many books treat this passion for a "secret sharer" with the lightest of touches. In *Thing* by Australian Robin Klein, Emily Forbes longs for a pet. Her mother is sympathetic but her landlady is ogreish on the subject. Emily settles for an attractively oval "pet rock" turned up by bulldozers making a new sports field. When it hatches into an amiable young stegosaurus, Emily and her mother are delighted. The humor of the book derives from the matter-of-fact, though ingenious, accommodations made by both the prehistoric animal and the very contemporary single-parent family. Emily pretends, when the censorious landlady asks, that Thing's startling footprints on the hall stairs are caused by her new swim flippers, and she wraps Thing's enthusiastically thumping tail in newspaper so he won't betray his presence.

Thing, in turn, cleverly contrives concealment by disguising himself, at various moments of emergency, as a piece of modern sculpture, a length of pebbled patio, a cactus, and a coffee table. His eventual triumph derives in part from his fanatic attachment to TV cooking and aerobics shows.

Of course, the archetypal lighthearted story about unusual pets is *Mr. Popper's Penguins,* a prewar favorite that still holds low-key comic charm for young readers. Mr. Popper, a house painter and daydreamer who loves to read of polar explorations, strikes us as very much a boy at heart: innocent, impractical, unflaggingly enthusiastic. His devotion to his unusual pets goes to remarkable lengths—in one of the most hilarious scenes, the family obligingly huddles in mittens and overcoats, with the living room windows open to let in the snow and cold, so the penguins can slide about on the iced floor "gorking" happily. This unquestioning care and consideration eventually leads to fame and fortune for all the Poppers.

Even more riotous as a spoof of the boy-loves-pet genre is *The Hoboken Chicken Emergency* by D. Manus Pinkwater (yes, the same one—he shuffles his first names around with each new book). Pinkwater is probably the most sophisticated and surrealistic of American humorists for the young. The deadpan narrative style of *Mr. Popper's Penguins* is taken to outrageous lengths here: When Arthur brings home a 260 pound live chicken with a tenor cluck, his parents' most severe reaction is a mild scolding at the dinner table when Arthur sneaks some mashed potato to the gigantically hungry Henrietta. "I don't want this chicken to get in the habit of begging," Poppa warns, though he is also pleased about Henrietta because "every boy should have a chicken."

Perhaps the vast sociological shifts of this century account for the gradual disappearance of the anthropomorphic animal story and its replacement by the animal friend story. Where stifled and well-behaved children once wept sentimentally over the plight of victimized animals like Beautiful Joe, their hearts now beat faster to stories in which lonely children make mystical contact with another species.

In *Stig of the Dump,* by Clive King, eight-year-old Barney meets not an animal but a shaggy-haired cave man living in a local dump. The two become fast friends. The unreal is made utterly plausible by this talented author because we see the whole story though the eyes of the lively, curious, but unsophisticated boy, whose childlike preoccupations are mirrored in the brisk, sturdy prose. Barney completely accepts the existence of his fur-clad prehistoric friend. In fact, much of the humor is derived from the fact that Barney never has to lie to hide Stig's secret life—he simply, calmly, tells the truth and the grown-ups blindly refuse to hear it because it doesn't fit in with their previous version of reality. What child won't recognize that experience?

After Barney's first visit to the dump, for example, he enthusiastically tells his grandmother and his sister Lou about Stig's improvised living arrangements. He's "a sort of a boy. He just wears rabbit skins and lives in a cave. He gets his water from a vacuum cleaner, and puts chalk in his bath. He's my friend." Lou blandly translates for the grandmother: "He means he's been playing cave man."

There are two enduring charms about *Stig of the Dump.* One is the way in which Stig becomes Barney's playmate and protector, always there to engage in some fascinating new project of spear sharpening or thief nabbing, and suddenly appearing in all his startling muscularity just when Barney is being bullied by the ruffianish Snargett brothers. Second is the marvelous clarity with which King describes the physical world as Stig and Barney reinvent it together. In fact, Stig's patient, wondering exploration of the junk in the dump (he decides that an umbrella is a turnip spit) exactly parallels the way a young child looks freshly at the world, fascinated by physical manifestations that adults have long since taken for granted and forgotten to notice. A highlight of the book is the midsummer night scene when Barney and his sister Lou are carried back in time to Stig's Stone Age settlement. What is unforgettable is not so much the time-shift fantasy, but the high-spirited description (eeeeyooo*thump*) of just how and why prehistoric men hauled and levered and chanted those giant stones to their remote sites.

The animal (or primordial man) as friend-protector surfaces again in *Stone Fox,* by John Reynolds Gardiner, a Rocky Mountains legend that is told with a swift intensity usually foreign to this folksy genre. Willy, only ten years old, is left in cruel isolation when his grandfather suddenly "gives up on life," takes to his bed and refuses to speak. Willy has only his faithful dog, Searchlight, to help harvest the crops and save the farm. The climax of the brief novel is a heartbreaker: Willy and Searchlight take part in a breathlessly exciting sled race across the snowy countryside, competing with a mysterious giant Indian, Stone Fox, and his magnificent team of Samoyeds for prize money that may save the farm. Willy wins—but Searchlight pays the ultimate price. Only the reticent but moving tribute paid by Stone Fox to the boy and the dog make the ending bearable. Stone Fox—his name and his monumentality place him among the forces of nature—helps Willy to triumph over adversity.

In a completely different tone and style, two gerbils help to draw together a painfully fractured British working-class family. *The Battle of Bubble and Squeak,* by Philippa Pearce, is really the battle of unhappy and resentful Sid with his preoccupied mother, Alice, and her new husband, the affable Bill. The gerbils are never portrayed as anything but themselves; the author uses the dramatic reactions of the family members to the vicissitudes of gerbil rearing in order to weave a gentle and perceptive story about Sid's growth to greater responsibility.

Young children of early school age have a well-known affinity for animals, and it's not hard to think of the reasons why. A first- or second-grade student is at the bottom of his school's hierarchy, uncertain of his ability to cope in the larger world, increasingly private about his feelings, and, in today's smaller families, quite likely to be lonely. It is the right age at which to enjoy the feelings of competence and affection earned by caring for a dependent pet. But there is another factor, too. Just as children at puberty may feel a powerful nostalgic tug for the childhood from which they are rapidly departing, the school-age child may be pulled toward the abundant, richly unknowable world of nature and the affinity the preliterate child has with the animal kingdom.

Two powerful stories, *The Sea Egg* by Lucy Boston, and *The*

Midnight Fox by Betsy Byars, convey a sense of nature rewarding the alert, sensitive child with a precious gift of secret knowledge and communion. In *The Sea Egg,* two English brothers on a seaside holiday with their parents are observant and imaginative enough to notice a particular beauty and egglike promise about a "stone" found by a beachcomber. They buy it from him and put it carefully in a tidal pool, isolated from the public beach by chalk cliffs and tunnels.

Boston's style is hypnotically poetic; her precise observation and lyrical description almost envelop the reader in the ocean world of heat, infinite blueness, sand, and salt. Seals floating upright in the sea are "like half-sunk bottles"; seen through the binoculars from a boat, they are like "a secret vision" that disappears when the boat rocks; they are "slow balloons" moving on the rocky coast.

From the boat, the boys glimpse something up by their rock pool where they have left the mysterious egg. Stunned, they realize it is a triton—an impish boy with a seal's tail. The next day, despite pelting rain ("The fish-gray waves when they broke sounded heavier for being cold"), they dash along the shore amid "an orchestra of sounds" to see this seal-boy who, they know, has hatched from their egg.

The boys drench themselves in the life of the sea; they play with the triton, drape themselves in seaweed, learn to swim with the tide through the frightening tunnel, and finally, one moonlit night, answer the triton's horn and swim out through the "gilded glinting" sea with him, to discover a gathering of seals in an island cave. After their midnight adventure, they must part with the triton, who leads the seals on their annual migration just before a furious storm breaks. The boys have dipped into an enchanted world from which their parents are excluded. They've gained confidence and skill, but most important is their sense of carrying back with them, to the prosaic world of school, a sea memory of magic.

There are some false notes; Boston verges on the mawkish whenever she draws back and comments on the boys from the outside, as when their mother sees them swim through the tunnel: " 'Oh boys!' she said, thinking they looked confident and beautiful and splendid, 'you are too provoking . . .' " or when the narrator makes a few embarassing, almost groveling, references to the lordly "young authority" of the triton. Nevertheless, this is an enriching book for a skillful young reader who can cope with the vocabulary.

More contemporary in tone, more realistic, laced with the wry humor of the modern sensibility but no less haunting than *The Sea Egg,* is *The Midnight Fox* by Betsy Byars. The story is narrated by Tommy, thinking back four years to the summer he was eight, when he was sent to Aunt Millie and Uncle Fred's farm while his parents bicycled through France. Tommy hates anything new, and he hates spending the summer apart from his more outgoing best friend, Petie. Comic scenarios run through Tommy's fertile mind, filled with up-roarious reversals: When his mother tries to convince him of the charm of watching lambs at play or collecting eggs in the henhouse, Tommy glumly imagines himself as the first boy in the world to be trampled to death by baby lambs or run down by vengeful chickens.

Any tendency to the maudlin is neatly undercut by Tommy's self-deflating humor. Perhaps he is more imaginative, more self-aware, than we could reasonably expect of any eight-year-old. Yet the tone never falters; few children's books told in the first person manage to achieve such a touching and three-dimensional persona for the narrator. Byars uses an inspired child version of adult narra-tive irony: It is through Tommy's inner monologue of slapstick com-edies, TV dramas, newspaper headlines, and parodied interviews that he gains a perspective on himself and his situation, and that we come to know him so much better than the flat, self-conscious "I" of so many lesser children's novels.

Tommy's fantasies are wonderfully, surprisingly, poetically alive. They make Tommy real in our eyes, and they lend a welcome legit-imacy to any child's private world of self-justifying daydreams. He dreams of fulfillment (he will discover a brand-new color and, for a moment, the whole world will fall silent), of loss (an old hermit ar-rives at a lonely airfield to announce that he has invented a flying machine; when the young people laugh at him, he quietly presses a button on his knapsack and softly flies away), and of brotherhood (a magical Indian word, when blurted out in emergency, will automat-ically bring help).

Tommy spends his first few weeks at the farm being wary, un-comfortable, and at loose ends. It is only in his private reflections that we see his tender sensibilities. Aunt Millie, fussing kindly over her young guest, offers him a favorite book of her now-grown sons, *The Lamb Who Wanted to Be a Cat.* Tommy greets it with polite enthusiasm, but in truth it only adds to his depression—it makes him feel awful to think about "someone who was trying to be something he could never, ever be."

The summer mood, languid and hot, is shocked into vibrancy one day when across the crest of a hill a magnificent black fox with pale golden eyes leaps into Tommy's line of vision. The fox becomes his secret sharer, wild and tantalizing with its high clear bark in the distance. Tommy tracks it through the woods for long days at a time. Finally he finds its den and realizes it is the mother of a lone cub, an enchanting, woolly little ball of fur. The tender relationship of the watchful mother and her tiny warrior of a cub is all the more riveting because of Tommy's separation from his parents—and because of his unspoken fears that he can't live up to their expectations of him.

The tenuous bond of trust between Tommy and the fox is threatened when Aunt Millie chivvies Uncle Fred into hunting the marauder who stole her turkey. But because Tommy is too wary for his own good, he can't bring himself to say the word to Uncle Fred that might call off the dreaded hunt.

Wretched and ashamed of his own timidity, he stands by when Uncle Fred finds the den and digs out the baby fox to use as a lure to entrap the mother. At first, Tommy thinks the cub is dead. "He's just play-acting," says Uncle Fred. "His ma taught him to do that." Tommy thinks that "if I lived to be a hundred, I would never see anything that would make me feel any worse than the sight of that little fox pretending to be dead when his heart was beating so hard it looked like it was going to burst out of his chest."

The torpor of the heat wave and Tommy's paralysis both break that night in a tremendous thunderstorm when, in the driving rain, he rescues the little fox. In the moment when he gives up to freedom what he most cherishes, Tommy comforts himself with the consolation of art: Someday in an art gallery, he thinks, he'll see a painting called "Fox with Baby at Midnight," the fox and her baby running beneath the wet ghostly apple trees toward a patch of light in the distance . . . and his heart will stop beating.

At a superficial level, you could say that *The Midnight Fox* is "about" a young boy's growing self-awareness and confidence. But that would be like saying that *Macbeth* is about troubled family life in the suburbs. In truth, the book is as many-layered, as deeply tolerant of human nature, as rich in incident, character, and humor, as any excellent novel for adults. And the surprise is that it is not even the best known or most widely admired of its kind. I can't even find a reference to it in the usual works of criticism.

There are, in other words, so many hundreds of such fine books available that even a splendid example of its kind can be overlooked. That argues well, actually, for the abundance and variety we enjoy. Not every child, of course, will be thrilled by *The Midnight Fox* or *The Sea Egg* or *Wingman*. But, with an empathetic adult's help, every youngster can surely find a few captivating novels to love in those early reading years.

Love is not too strong a word. Nearly every literate adult can remember, with an unreasonable surge of emotion and loyalty, one or two books from childhood that had special meaning. They might have been comics; they might have been from the Nancy Drew series; all the better when they were books by authors like E. Nesbit or Philippa Pearce, which led on to other literary discoveries.

The key is that the beloved book spoke with a clear voice to that individual child. Escape was part of the pleasure; so was wish fulfillment, the satisfaction of inarticulate yearnings. But even more, there is the deep satisfaction of narrative. From the picture book stage, the reader of early novels has stepped into the temporal world of the school buzzers, timetables, and hobbling of freedom as well as the impending knowledge of evil and decay. But narrative is the orderly pyramiding of a story that builds in time; narrative is the transformation of chaotic and sometimes painful experience into something *made,* something desired and good. Because the reader collaborates actively in imagining that written narrative into an inner landscape, it has a more profound and potentially valuable impact than the electronic entertainments that wash over the passive viewer, twitching the right cry-and-laugh electrodes as they surge past.

The child I've been writing about in this chapter, the child of seven, eight, or nine, who experiences the grip of narrative, will likely keep the reading habit alive until the competing claims of other entertainments can be considered from a more mature perspective. But if children are completely lost to television at this vulnerable age, it seems unlikely that they will ever find their way back to the world of books.

Chapter 4

L-C S N X-T-C.

LIBERATING
LAUGHTER

"How's that new baby brother of yours?" said Grandpa.

"Willy?" said Louie. "No fun."

"Not cute," said Mary Ann.

"All he can do is eat and sleep." said Louie.

"Or cry," said Mary Ann.

"That bad, eh?" said Grandpa. "Your parents must feel awful."

James Stevenson, *Worse than Willy!*

One morning there was a moose in Mr. Breton's yard. It was a blue moose. When Mr. Breton went out his back door, the moose was there, looking at him. After a while, Mr. Breton went back in, closed the door, and made a pot of coffee while he waited for the moose to go away. It didn't go away; it just stood in Mr. Breton's yard, looking at his back door. Mr. Breton drank a cup of coffee. The moose stood in the yard. Mr. Breton opened the door again. "Shoo! Go away!"

"Do you mind if I come in and get warm?" the moose said. "I'm just about frozen."

Manus Pinkwater, *Blue Moose*

Children's books are, of course, drenched in humor. It could hardly be otherwise, since any sane adult tries to raise children in an atmosphere of optimism—and hope, even of the most rueful kind, is the expression on comedy's face. Children, like all the powerless, find their best release and choicest weapon in humor; they are always ready to drop an armload of tension or anger to indulge in a liberating shout of laughter. And, as teachers are well aware, laughter is the reward that lures the most reluctant reader.

Writers for older children, especially mediocre writers, may pick away gloomily at the sores of the pubescent soul the way their adolescent subjects pick at their complexions, but the characteristic mood of the writer for younger children is one of a summoner to glee: Hilarity, slyness, and the chuckle lie on every hand. But humor, as well as being the richest vein of invention in children's literature, is also the form most open to abuse, exploitation, and even, as I shall try to show later, to some rather sinister manipulation.

Some of the finest humorous writing for children is in the tone of James Stevenson's Grandpa, quoted above. The wit is deadpan and droll, but the underlying sensibility is one of tender acceptance of the child's foibles. Stevenson, a celebrated cartoonist for *The New Yorker* magazine, gives his young readers some credit for sophistication: Though the unstated theme of *Worse than Willy!* is the children's resentment of a new baby brother, he never stoops to glib reassurances or the usual head-patting condescension. Instead, a poker-faced Grandpa, his straw hat sitting on the end table beside his wicker chair on the porch, treats Louie and Mary Ann to a wild story about the antics of his own "awful" brother Wainey. And, most delicious of all, in the cartoonlike, irresistibly funny panel illustrations of Grandpa and Wainey in their infancy, we see them exactly as the listening children visualize them: junior editions of their grown selves, complete with a brush moustache tucked under the infant Grandpa's button nose.

That tenderness is what makes Arnold Lobel's *Frog and Toad Together* so winning a comedy. An I-Can-Read beginner book, it is a model of simplicity. Little Toad and the more mature Frog are best friends. In five short stories, Toad exhibits all the impatience, self-indulgence, and self-aggrandizement of a typical preschooler. "Toad will now dance and he will be wonderful," announces a master of ceremonies in Toad's dream, while Frog, in the audience, shrinks smaller and smaller. The dream turns into a nightmare as Frog seems to vanish entirely. Waking, Toad is intensely relieved to find a normal-size Frog at his bedside. "Frog, I am so glad that you came over." "I always do," says Frog. No matter how laughably Toad behaves—and every child will laugh at his all-too-recognizable impetuosity and conceit—the kindly friendship of Frog endures.

Manus Pinkwater's gourmandizing *Blue Moose* is a more urbane kind of friend for a slightly older reader; he makes us laugh out loud by the sheer incongruity of his sophistication in the north woods of

Maine. Children's humor thrives on role reversal, and here a shy and insecure restaurateur, the good-hearted little Mr. Breton, blooms into prosperity after the moose moves in and takes on the job of head-waiter, bullying the customers with time-honored headwaiter hau-teur. (The way the townsfolk brag about being on good terms with the moose is a typically sly Pinkwater joke, this time about compet-itive dining out.) The style may be terse and jaunty in the best mod-ern manner, but the solid base of the story, what touches and engages us, is the mutual kindness of man and moose and their odd but richly reverberant friendship.

When you stop to analyze why a funny book provokes laughter from many children of very different tastes, you almost always find that there's an unstated theme in the book that is common to the deepest experience of childhood. *Mary Alice, Operator Number Nine* is the heroine of the popular picture book by Jeffrey Allen and illus-trator James Marshall. Mary Alice, a duck with a head cold, has to take a few days off from her job as a local telephone operator who gives the exact time to the public.

"Don't worry," says Boss Chicken, "I'll find someone to take your place. It's an easy job." This, naturally, makes Mary Alice feel even worse. What kindergarten child hasn't been made to feel that someone else could set the table, make beds, or wash the car faster and better than he? And so we rejoice as Mary Alice's series of sub-stitutes all prove comically inept. That's the obvious message. But there's a subtler one, too. Consider that the five- or six-year-old reader at whom this book is aimed often has a new baby brother or sister at home, and the dread of being superseded becomes sharply rele-vant. Or think about time and all the anxieties of clock watching and schedules that drop on the shoulders of the first-grade child, who has lived in a timeless dream world until the first day of school.

Anxiety, as the author Selma Lane has astutely pointed out (in *Down the Rabbit Hole),* is the engine that powers *The Cat in the Hat,* possibly the best-known beginner book in North America. As the mysterious Cat visitor wreaks mayhem and chaos in the children's house, their horror mounts: Mother will soon come back and find "this big mess." Uncontrollable mess is a source of panic to more people than just schoolchildren; I confess that when I first read *The Cat in the Hat,* I could find very little jollity in the spectacle of an uninvited demon-cat and a house knee-deep in smashed cake, broken lamps, and spilled milk. Even the ugly drawings are nervous, edgy, and tense: The children are bug-eyed with consternation, walls seem to tilt, tables teeter, and the horizon line wobbles, upends itself and disappears in the whirlwind of activity. The laughter that accompanies the end of this book is, I would wager, the laughter of semihysterical relief.

There is a place for that, certainly. And since funnybones are as individual as fingerprints, some children will find Cat in the Hat humor worth revisiting many times. Others may find a subtler, and funnier, recognition of child realities in a book like *The Judge,* by Harve and Margot Zemach. Every child alive has had the wormwood-and-gall experience of telling the truth and not being believed. In this book, a boorishly peremptory judge refuses to give a moment's credence to a series of hapless witnesses who are dragged before the bench.

The verse, with its internal assonance and urgency, is perfectly pitched to the mounting suspense and hilarity. "Please let me go, Judge / I didn't know, Judge, / That what I said was against the law / I just said what I saw / A horrible thing is coming this way, creeping closer day by day / Its eyes are scary, its tail is hairy / I tell you, Judge, we all better pray." And each defendant—beribboned simperer, cringing boy, woebegone cripple—adds to the litany of description in a perfect cumulative tale. How delicious, how surprising, how perfectly *deserved* it is when a horrible monster face appears in the window behind the back of the spluttering ("Ninnyhammer! Dimwit! Dunce! To jail at once!") Judge. How mild and deeply satisfying are the smiles of the freed prisoners as they stroll away, vindicated.

Clumsy adults get their comeuppance in scores of humorous children's books. The success of *Jacob Two-Two Meets the Hooded Fang,* Mordecai Richler's bestseller, is testament to the allure of this theme. The book has real liabilities—an overload of belabored jokes, cliché, and sagging plotlines. Worse, it has moments of embarassing sentimentality and falseness. The villains of Slimers' Island, we are told, shroud the place in fog because they can't stand sunshine. Why? Because "any big person who cannot stand little ones also fears the sun" (also pets, flowers, and laughter). The ending is a bit of a cheat, too. After all the hoopla and the uproariously gothic plot, Jacob awakens on a park bench, and we are left to decide whether the entire story wasn't just a dream.

Still, in addition to occasional flights of inspired verbal tomfoolery, the book has another basic strength, and that is the accurate perception of how it feels to be the youngest in the family, the one who always gets teased, tricked, put-upon, left out, and drowned out by ebullient older siblings. If Jacob Two-Two cannot ride a bike or cut a straight slice of bread, he can nevertheless enjoy a comic triumph by seeing clearly through the hypocrisies of adults, judge and jailer alike.

Humor is as intensely individual a taste in children as it is in adults. I know a little girl who sat stonyfaced through all the boisterous shenanigans of Jacob Two-Two, but burst into peals of delighted laughter at the mere sight of the little squirrel in the hat, in M.B. Goffstein's *A Little Squirrel Went Walking.* That minute animal, smaller on the page than a baby's fingernail, a mere laconic squiggle of ink, with two dot eyes and an incongruous brimmed hat, is somehow the essence of affection—the sprightly way it walks (on two legs), the way it snuggles in the shelter of a girl's arms, its jaunty pose on the tree branch. All this could be dangerously, sickeningly cute. That it succeeds in being touchingly funny instead is due to the wit, restraint, and accuracy of the drawings.

A very different author, Beverly Cleary, evokes a similar outburst of affectionate recognition with her series of shrewd, loving portraits of *Ramona the Pest,* already described in chapter 3. The books are such a sympathetic evocation of a child's inmost feelings that both parent and child, reading them, laugh out loud in surprised recognition. There are dozens of such piercingly observed moments in each Ramona book: the way four-year-old Ramona tells an adult questioner that her eyes "are brown and white"; her agonizing introduction to kindergarten, when the teacher tells her to "sit here for the present" and she proudly refuses to budge all morning, waiting for the "present" to be given to her alone; the moment when Ramona savors the first bite of every apple in the basket and, when caught, quickly uses a nursery school catch phrase to excuse herself: "I want to share the apples"; the keen disappointment of discovering that there is no tricycle license plate that says "Ramona," though there are Jimmys and Joans aplenty.

Linguistic invention is another form of humor that wears equally well. Indeed, the earliest forms of humor in children's literature are nursery rhymes, with their absurd juxtapositions and delight in patterns of rhythm, sound, and rhyme.

For young children, folk tales are another good source of strong, repetitive, and oddly resonant language. *Tikki Tikki Tembo,* the well-loved Chinese folk tale, retold by Arlene Mosel with subtle Blair Lent illustrations that add a third dimension, is a story of sibling rivalry. The mother has lavished the fanciest possible name, Tikki tikki tembo-no sa rembo-chari bari ruchi-pip peri pembo, on her older son, and bestowed a negligent monosyllable, Chang, on the younger. And just because of this unfairness, the older nearly drowns in the well. But the reason the story has lasted so well is its wonderfully memorable mouthful of nonsense syllables. The comic punch of the story comes at the moment when a breathless, frantic little Chang garbles the message—"Chari bari rembo tikki tikki pip pip has fallen in the well!"

The Vigananee and the Tree Toad, by Verna Aardema, uses onomatopoeia, a familiar device of African folk tales. The effects are almost magical if read boldly aloud: The story leaps into auditory life when the tree toad sits in a deep starry window to sing her friends to sleep, taw-aw-aw-awt, or when the bushy monster comes up the walk, pusu pusu pusu, and rudely gulps the savory stew, yatua yatua yatua. Rat, who is sweeping the walk, fras fras fras, hits him with the broom—ZAK!

The purest verbal comedy for older children is *The Phantom Tollbooth,* written in 1961 by Norton Juster, and still going strong. You would think that an entire novel based on wordplay would become as tiresome as a birthday party that goes on too long—nothing is more exhausting than forced jollity. But because the story is so elemental (the boy Milo goes on a life-or-death quest through a strange wonderland), the narrative urges us along through showers, fountains, and ambushes of verbal play.

Even better than the triumphant climax when Milo rescues the "fair" princesses, Rhyme and Reason, is the banquet in Dictionopolis when, it turns out, everyone has to eat his words. Since Milo had neglected to bellow out the names of some favorite foods before the meal, King Azaz the Unabridged consoles him with some scraps—rigamarole, somersault, and ragamuffin—while they all wait for their just desserts. Though readers of nine and ten may miss some of the endless, dizzying wordplay, there are jokes enough, broad and narrow, to keep everyone amused right to the end.

Inspired wordplay, of course, accounts for the spectacular success of *Alligator Pie,* by Dennis Lee, the first poetry for children to adapt the rhythms of nursery rhymes to a Canadian context. Though everyone knows the compulsively chantable "Alligator pie, alligator pie / If I don't get some, / I think I'm gonna die," equally memorable are the Seussian tonguetwisters like the Sitter and the Butter and the Better Batter Fritter, or the cumulative rhymes that contain chaos within a tight frame ("My dad got snarky and barked at the shark") as well as poems that simply peel a word and make a child see its insides ("Skyscraper, skyscraper, scrape me some sky").

Alligator Pie works so well because it plays off a literary form that is familiar to even the youngest child. It may surprise adults to know that there is a large body of humorous work for children springing from the idea of literary parody. These books count on a basic literacy among their young readers—not just the ability to decode letters, but an easy familiarity with the enduring literary forms of our culture. *The Paperbag Princess* by Robert Munsch is a running gag that depends on the child recognizing the anachronisms, tricks, and discordancies that are slipped into the basic fairy tale. The prince and princess have modern names, Elizabeth and Ronald, and are shown in 1980s preppy style with tennis rackets and "expensive" clothes—a deliberately jarring word in the fairy tale context, since kings may have ordered costly clothes for their daughters, but nothing was ever expensive for them. The emancipated ending, in which Elizabeth carries the day without Ronald's help, is a twist on the familiar pattern. So basic is the fairy tale structure to our civilization, so ingrained is its accustomed tone and style, that there can hardly be a child in the country who doesn't get the joke.

Literary satire exists at all levels. Seven-year-olds recognize and delight in the turned tables of *Clever Polly and the Stupid Wolf* by Catherine Storr, a witty series of linked stories in which brave and ingenious Polly outwits the babyish wolf at every turn. Even within the book there's a good sprinkling of literary satire: The wolf consciously tries to imitate the tricks that worked for the wolf in *Three Little Pigs, The Seven Kids,* and *Little Red Riding Hood,* but is always stymied by a combination of modern life (busses and the family car instead of the path through the woods, for example) and Polly's knowingness. The child reader is buoyed by being one step ahead of the wolf all the way, thanks to shared knowledge of the fairy tales.

E. Nesbit used the convention of the heroic narrator to add comedic spice to *The Story of the Treasure Seekers* in 1899, and, curiously enough, the trick still works as well today. We owe our pleasure to her skill in building the character of Oswald, the ostensible narrator of the book. Filled with romantic daydreams, conceit, and a fitful dedication to noble ideals, Oswald is an unwitting comedian, and despite his bossiness, an oddly endearing boy. He has energy, ideas, and largeness of soul. "It is one of us that tells this story—but I shall not tell you which," writes the narrator. The delicious joke is that by the bottom of page one, Oswald has utterly given himself away, and continues to do so at frequent moments of high excitement during the book. All the way through the high-spirited adventures and amusing scrapes that make up the episodic plots of the book, the author lets the reader in on the joke. Adult hypocrisy or child preposterousness, we are allowed to see through it all. At the same time, the pleasure and suspense of the stories is not spoiled by Olympian omniscience; it's one of the most successful balancing acts in children's literature, and it works, I think, because Nesbit never fails to treat her characters with affectionate respect. You can see that she loves these imaginative, absurd, brave, squabbling, but loyal children as much as we do.

Readers in the middle age-range can be remarkably sophisticated in their capacity to enjoy an adult form, such as the thriller or detective story, when it has been tailored to their interests. One example that seems to have universal appeal is Ellen Raskin's *The Mysterious Disappearance of Leon (I Mean Noel)*. While it lay open on my desk for the writing of this chapter, each of my three teenagers— all with widely differing tastes in books—wandered in at different times, noticed the book and lit up with enthusiastic nostalgia: "Oh, I *loved* that book!"

Raskin has surgically dissected the adult detective novel and used the parts to make up a highly original kit: Assemble and solve your own mystery, clues and instructions included. She does it with wit and hectic invention, and somehow keeps the whole concoction both coherent and appealing. The mystery revolves around the obsessive search by Mrs. Caroline Carillon, née Little Dumpling Fish, for her missing husband Leon, who vanished after their childhood marriage of convenience. Her two adopted children, Tony and Tina, help solve the puzzle, which requires them to decipher an obscure message delivered by a drowning man: "Noel glub C blub all . . . I glub new. . ."

What helps to knit together the zany plot, with its clever black-and-white drawings that serve as clues, is a firm underlying message: All mysteries are solved when the names of things are made clear and true. By the end of the story, everyone comes into his or her own true name, and everyone is freed from the prison of false identity. But the reader need barely be aware of this unstated message to enjoy the comedy of errors and detection.

One English cops-and-robbers story for children that stays closer to the traditional chase pattern, along with some of the "caper" elements that remind one of *The Lavender Hill Mob*, is *Me and My Million* by Clive King. It's hard to think of a more engaging hero than Ringo, the undersized Cockney waif, illiterate, naive, and cynical, who is an unwitting participant in a major art heist. Ringo, who has never seen a painting before, is suddenly on the lam in London with a "Pestalotsy" painting of "a mum and a kid" stuffed in a laundry bag. The fast-paced plot has humor of its own, with Ringo keeping one step ahead of rich but venal art dealers, pretentious art experts, decent cops, hippies, lunatic terrorists who turn out to be animal liberationists, and even his own big step-brother, Elvis, the original thief of the painting. The subtler humor lies in the way clear-eyed

Ringo begins to love and value the painting. He and a genial art forger, who gives him refuge on a canal boat, may be the only true art lovers in the book. I can't think of a children's thriller with a more gripping plot or more sympathetic humor.

Gaiety and high spirits, with no dark undertones or foreshadowings of adult irony, used to be the unique voice of children's humor. That innocence of tone is long-gone now. Even Farley Mowat's well-known *Owls in the Family* or *The Dog Who Wouldn't Be* might not be written with the same carefree openness today, when animal rights activists are on the alert for every transgression against nature wild and free. But children still enjoy the lovable antics of Wol and Weeps, the two Mowat owls, and the clownish clumsiness of Mutt the dog. These two family stories are still masterpieces of sharp observation and droll, good-hearted comedy.

Examples of that kind of humor are far more common among the picture books; one that springs to mind is *Three Strong Women,* a Japanese folk tale that probably predates women's liberation by a few thousand years. It is a tall tale, an imaginative stretching of reality that has no ulterior motive, no barb in its tail, no moral to press home but the pleasure of laughter.

We catch the mood at once as the story begins, with lovely, delicately funny drawings by Kazue Mizumura. A famous wrestler strolls along toward the capital, where he will wrestle before the Emperor. He is strong, healthy, pleased with himself—just a little too pleased with himself—and we are invited to smile at the way he enjoys the sound of his own voice as he saunters and hums. Then he is distracted by the sight of "a round little girl with red cheeks and nose like a friendly button. Her eyes looked as though she were thinking of ten thousand funny stories at once." He longs to tickle her (kochokochokocho) to hear her giggle. But no sooner does he try, than this cheerful girl casually traps him in an armhold.

Maru-me, the girl, takes the wrestler along to Forever Mountain, where her mother and wizened little grandmother turn out be as chucklingly, self-deprecatingly strong as she is. The lessons he learns from them stand him in good stead in the capital, but in even better stead in his life, which takes a new, more serene, and fulfilling path.

Those life-affirming comedies, very much like those well-loved early Hollywood movies that had no quarrrel with the world, are rare nowadays. It would be hard to write one without falling into a sickeningly sweet Norman Rockwell tone of voice. Nevertheless, there are a few humanistic gems that veer toward slapstick to avoid sentimentality and succeed with a flourish. *Freaky Friday* by Mary Rodgers is a comedy of transformation: Thirteen-year-old Annabel

Andrews, unhappy possessor of a mouthful of braces, a knobbly figure, a perfect little brother, a messy room, and failing grades, wakes
up one morning in the curvaceous body of her mother.

Annabel is overjoyed to be an adult, with all the supposed pleasures and freedoms of adulthood at her command. Although her exhausting, tense, and hilarious day disabuses of her of those dreams,
it does bring her an almost endless supply of balm for her soul. By
the next morning, Annabel has turned into a pretty teenager with
her braces off. She has learned that her secret crush, Boris, now
thinks she is "some beautiful chick," that her teachers believe she is
highly gifted ("I admire and love your little girl," says one teacher
somewhat wildly to Annabel-disguised-as-mother), and that even her
kid brother, the maligned Ape Face, adores her so much that he
hopes one day to have braces just like hers. Blatant teenage wish
fulfillment combines delectably with the sardonic Manhattan wise-
crack.

The best English writers for children seem to have a matchless
verbal brilliance at their command. Joan Aiken, one of the funniest
authors alive, dazzles us in *Arabel's Raven,* a sort of working class,
surrealist *Owls in the Family.* "Oh my stars, look at that creature's
toe-nails, if nails they can be called," remarks Arabel's mother, when
she finds Mortimer, the raven, sitting in her fridge surrounded by the
remains of the family's food supply. Aiken is the complete master of
throwaway lines: In the midst of Mortimer's squalid mayhem at the
dinner table the narrator dryly observes: "Mortimer enjoyed the
baked beans, but his table manners were very lighthearted."

Physical chaos, of *The Cat in the Hat* variety, is the hallmark of
this kind of humor. But Aiken doesn't leave it there. Like a pianist
playing riffs, she spoofs the speech patterns of her characters, pushing the dour, the official, the laconic, the crazed, and the Cockney
to their comic extremes. "If birds had fingerprints, I wouldn't mind
taking the dabs of that shifty-looking fowl," observes a disgruntled
policeman, called to the site of one Mortimer-inspired shambles.
"Thoughtless our Mortimer may be," retorts Mrs. Jones at her most
haughty, "untidy at times, but honest as a Bath bun, I'll have you
know." And there are wonderful spoofs of flower-child song lyrics,
mad modern technology (viz. the vending machines for olive oil, foot
massage, or cheerful poems), and even of tough-talking American
gangster films. "You'd better cooperate, Coal-face," snarls a thug to
Mortimer, "this is a flyjack." A parent who dares to try a few different
voices and accents could enjoy doing a star turn when reading this
book aloud.

Another artist in slap-happy chaos, of course, is Helen Cresswell, inventor of the remarkably obnoxious Bagthorpe family, a collection of trendy, upwardly mobile achievers and their offspring, all of whom have more than one String to Their Bow, except for poor *Ordinary Jack*, the hero of the first Bagthorpe book. When kindly Uncle Parker decides to help Jack win his own little share of immortality by pulling off a ridiculous scam on the rest of the family, the confusion mounts to an almost hysterical climax. Jack's sheepdog, Zero, is second perhaps only to Mowat's Mutt in the sheer, ardent, disastrous clunkiness of his efforts to be loyally helpful.

Slapstick is bearable only because all those dreadfully physical things keep happening pell-mell to people who aren't quite flesh and blood. If we thought for one moment that the characters felt the same shock, pain, and humiliation we would feel in similar circumstances, the entire effect would be ruined. The comically horrid adult Bagthorpes, nearly all of whom are as greedy, self-centered, egotistical, and stubbornly irrational as very small children, richly deserve their comeuppances. Even so, Cresswell manages to avoid extremes of malice in these portraits. The "bad guys" are childlike, not evil, and physical harm is not often part of the action. Though there's an edge to the humor all the way through (some competitively ambitious middle-class families may squirm), the mood is upbeat, not grim.

A uniquely Canadian voice in this style of humor is that of Brian Doyle. In *Up to Low,* and more recently, in *Angel Square,* he manages to combine a sort of Celtic plangency with Ottawa Valley tall tale, Canadian colloquialism, and working-class deadpan. It's an original mixture that proves particularly rewarding in *Angel Square,* a story of postwar bigotry in Ottawa's Lowertown. Roving packs of "Dogans," "Pea Soups," and Jews (Doyle doesn't quite have the courage to name them "kikes" in the real slang of those days) beat each other up in the ironically named Angel Square, the junction all must cross on their way to their various parochial schools. Tommy is the young hero who, together with his friend Coco Laframboise, confronts anti-Semitism and tracks down the brutal assailant of Sammy Rosenberg's father. Tommy himself is the epitome of Canadian seat-of-the-breeks pragmatic ecumenism: To earn money for Christmas presents, he waxes floors at the Talmud Torah, sings in the choir at St. Albany's, serves as altar boy at St. Brigit's, and works as stock boy at Woolworth's after school.

The names are wonderful: Toe-Jam Laframboise, Killer Bodnoff, Fleurette Fetherstone Fitchell. So is the evocation of urban winters a generation ago—Flat Fifties given to Dad for Christmas, the smell of cheap chocolates, perfume, and melting snow on wool mitts in Woolworth's, the muffled approach of streetcars in thick snowdrifts.

There's plenty of Irish blarney, an unfortunate predilection on Doyle's part for comic drunks, and a touch of romanticism beautifully carried off. Tommy's favorite teacher (and there's a wickedly funny spoof of the bad ones) is Mr. Maynard, who moves Tommy's imagination in science class one day by talking about the utter eternal lifelessness of the moon. If one leaf falls on earth, he says, it's more change than may occur on the moon in a hundred autumns. The words echo in Tommy's mind as he watches the eclipse of the moon one snowy night, and serve as a guide for individual action on earth, too.

One form of humor that doesn't seem to have survived the Victorian era, luckily, is the ghoulish admonitory tale, such as *Struwelpeter,* in which cruel mutilations and other asorted punishments are visited upon naughty children. The only two contemporary examples that come to mind are both transmogrified into something curiously satisfactory. "Pierre," one of the tiny tales in Maurice Sendak's *Nutshell Library,* is a gem. It is a virtuoso use of the miniature size; not only do the blue and yellow pictures perfectly exploit the space available in terse expressiveness but the typography and the use of white space also make a comic statement. Pierre, who doesn't care—not about anything—is taught a sharp lesson at last by a placid lion. Along the way, there are some memorable lines. I'm particularly fond of the father's coaxing blandishment, "I'll let you fold the folding chair," because it pinpoints so adroitly the kind of excitement small children find in the most ordinary actions.

The other example of admonitory literature in which the children emerge unscathed is the series of books about *Nurse Matilda* by Christianna Brand, illustrated by her famous artist cousin Edward Ardizzone. To capture the Victorian flavor of the stories, the books are richly produced, small in size, with gold-tooled green leatherette bindings, and even a red ribbon to mark the reader's place. *Nurse Matilda* deserves such attention to detail, because it is a bizarrely original story of a huge, almost numberless, and certainly ungovernable Victorian family of children and their unusual nanny, Nurse Matilda, who has eyes like black beads and a nose "like two potatoes." Nurse Matilda has unsuspected magical powers. She was apparently not inspired by the earlier Mary Poppins; the author tells us that Nurse Matilda is based on a family story handed down through several generations. I find her a more humane and amusing invention than the egomaniacal and emotionally icy Poppins. The magical adventures she creates are not for herself, as Mary Poppins's almost always are, but for the children, to teach them the seven lessons they must learn before Nurse Matilda moves on.

This book has its cake and eats it, too: The children's inventive cussedness becomes its own punishment, but what wayward fun it can be while it lasts! On Matilda's day off, the children are warned to do *precisely* what they are told. Ordered to put on their hated best clothes for a surprise visit from an auntie (and there is a marvelous description of Victorian children's newly laundered clothes, all starched so that the sleeves and legs come apart with a lovely tearing-apart noise) the children obey to the letter. They put them on, all right—on the piano, on the pig, on the donkey, and on the chickens. The chaos that ensues when a dim-sighted great aunt arrives to adopt one of the children is as wild as anything invented by Helen Cresswell, but with an added charm of merriment at a distance of time.

This book, although it would seem on the surface to be stuffily preoccupied with children's naughtiness and how to cure it, actually responds to something rooted in children's nature. A universal experience of childhood is that fevered, itchy desperation of being in a foul mood, being very very bad, and *not being able to stop.* Nurse Matilda's "lessons" evoke that feeling with horrid clarity. Her comforts and consolations, too, have all the soft coolness of mother's forgiving hand on the throbbing post-tantrum brow.

This is comedy of a fairly demanding kind, despite its occasional slapstick. It asks the young reader to identify both with the naughty children and with their governess, and to picture a world that has long vanished. Does it make children laugh? Not all of them; not all children are sophisticated enough in their literary tastes to enjoy a spoof of Victorian family stories, though Ardizzone's lively drawings do make the story more accessible. Still, it has an eccentrically memorable flavor.

Stories of rebellion in which adults, not children, are naughty, are far more the modern mode. *The Shrinking of Treehorn,* the wittiest and most trenchant book produced so far by the American Florence Parry Heide, is often recommended in England for the very youngest readers, perhaps because of its small, picture book format and simple, straightforward text. But deadpan satire and mordant humor at the expense of insensitive, distracted adults is hardly the most rib-tickling fare for kindergarten kids.

Poor Treehorn. He has begun, inexorably and inexplicably, to shrink. However patiently he deals with his predicament, the adults are relentlessly obtuse. His parents wonder if he is deliberately trying to be difficult; his principal gives him a stunningly banal pep talk; his teacher scolds him in timeworn school clichés. "We don't shrink in this class." Even his friend the bus driver doesn't recognize the shrunken Treehorn and doesn't listen to explanations.

"Nobody gets smaller," said the bus driver. "You must be Treehorn's kid brother. What's your name?"

"Treehorn," said Treehorn.

"First time I ever heard of a family naming two boys the same name," said the bus driver. "Guess they couldn't think of any other name, once they thought of Treehorn."

It's a devastatingly funny book, but only for those old enough to recognize, and survive, the inadequacies of adults.

Perhaps this is a good place to look at another, wildly popular school of recent humor which I believe should be approached with some caution. There is no other name for it: "anal humor" it is and must be called. Most parents are familiar enough with Freudian cliché to recognize, and be tolerant of, that phase in a child's life when a mere shout of "Poopy!" is enough to send a preschooler into fits of wild giggles and hysterical silliness. The shrillness and obsessiveness of the jokes ought to alert us that terrible anxiety—anxiety about losing control—lies just beneath the surface.

Nothing could be easier for an author with matching obsessions and an eye for commercial gain, than to exploit that vein of bathroom compulsiveness that is universal in early childhood. What surprises me is that adults condone it so eagerly, as though unwilling to be thought prudish or unhip. Raymond Briggs, the English artist, is in my view one of the worst offenders. An extravagant anality and a snidely derogatory portrayal of women are present in many of his books, most disturbingly in the well-received *When the Winds Blow*, a horrific comic-style admonitory book about nuclear war. Crude, music hall misogyny is also evident in his popular *Fungus the Bogeyman* books, though here it is anality that takes pride (if you can call it that) of place. Unlike its elaborately, even laboriously, witty hardback predecessor, *Fungus the Bogeyman,* the pop-up version, *Fungus the Bogeyman's Plop-up Book,* has little redeeming satirical merit. In shades of bilious green, puce, and magenta, it goes about as far as humanly possible in wallowing in bodily disgust. It revels in slime, stinking feet, and reeking underwear, rotten socks, pop-up strings of snot, mouths full of toads, people sniffing at the crotch of dirty trousers—and, *piece de resistance,* the Bogey Umbilical Cord, a weird appendage through which Bogeys "discharge noxious stomach gases" into the bedrooms of sleeping people.

Is there any harm in all this? It certainly panders to the child's most primitive instincts. I don't know many parents who would think it helpful to join in, with shrieks of "poo-poo!" and "tinkle!" when the toddlers get manic. But giving them this sort of book amounts to the same thing. Far from being supportive or life affirming, as its authors probably think, the adult approval implicit in writing, buying, and giving the book may ultimately disturb and unsettle the very children to whom it appeals. My instinct is to let children discover and enjoy such illicit, rebellious pleasures on their own, with neither encouragement nor censorship.

Dennis Lee seems to have sensed this dilemma, though perhaps not followed it through, when he told *Books in Canada* (December 1983) that his poem about Georgie, the one with smelly ears, is "morally corrupt ... you can be an absolute slob, a real pig, and tell Georgie off while feeling you're on the side of the angels." Lee admits, in the course of the same interview, that "Sometimes I feel like the Jack the Ripper of poetry, enticing kids to take off their pants. With their parents, well, it's as if the kids and I are looking at dirty pictures together."

Lee is probably referring to his poems in *Jelly Belly* and *Garbage Delight,* an astounding number of which dwell on ruddy bums, muddy bums, bloody crud, smelly snouts, smelly bellies, nosepicking, and various other forms of grossness. I think Lee is right to feel a little uneasy. These are cheap laughs; he's playing to the pit with a vengeance. Body dirt and anal aggression are legitimate preoccupations of childhood, but simple repetition does not an affirmation make.

While uncontrollable laughter is no great disaster, most parents recognize it as a symptom of uncomfortable tension, rather than literary appreciation or even liberation from repression. Children will discover and celebrate flatulence and excretion all by themselves, among themselves, without any need for adult cheerleaders. While we have their attention with a book in our hands, why strike a Jack the Ripper posture?

It could be argued that humane subversion, in this case the rebellion of the child against adult authority, is a worthy function of literature. Certainly, one of the most enduring themes of children's books is the celebration of the humanity of children, and the dignity of their own concerns, not just "enticing them to take off their pants." One laid-back rebel who deserves immortality, especially among the ranks of six- and seven-year-old boys, is Tom, the fooling-around artist and hero of *How Tom Beat Captain Najork and His Hired Sportsmen* by Russell Hoban.

Patrick Blake, who can't draw a picture that doesn't brim with edgy wit and loopy humor, helps immortalize this slouchy boy with the amiable smile who is somehow unfazed by his bustle-bottomed Aunt Fidget Wonkam-Strong, she with the dreadfully vivid name and the iron hat. When Tom simply won't stop his fooling around and messing around and playing around with bits of string and mud and alley rubbish, Aunt calls in her perennial threat: the moustachioed, debonair Captain Najork, a knee-jerk hearty jock if ever there was one. Tom's triumph at womble, muck, and sneedball against all the unfair odds stacked against him is a comic hymn of praise to the ingenuity and resilience of kids. Part of the fun, of course, is that Tom gets to chug away in his newly won pedal boat to a new town, where he promptly advertises for, and hires, a new aunt, Bundlejoy Cosysweet.

It is no accident that Tom's new aunt sounds something like a cross between a burlesque queen, a flower child, and a soft porn star; he even lays down "his terms" to her in the fine high-handed style of the most old-fashioned chauvinist husband: "No greasy bloaters, no mutton . . . And I do lots of fooling around. Those are my conditions." We are not told what's in it for Bundlejoy, but that hardly matters in this story, which is Tom's. And in Tom's world, there are two kinds of female figures, those in authority, like Aunt Wonkam-Strong who withers nature ("Where she walked the flowers drooped, and when she sang the trees all shivered") and those not in authority, who are as sensually alluring as Bundlejoy.

Tom's story is poetically true; like it or not, this is how young males, at some point and with some parts of their psyche, see the women who bear, raise, and teach them. The innate misogyny is well within acceptable limits. Besides, though the aunt is stern and demanding beyond all reason, she is not malicious, and she gets her own happy ending within the story—marriage to Captain Najork, who is smitten by her opaque charms.

The same is generally true of another classic boy's story, the strongly written *Soup* by Robert Newton Peck. The mother, the aunt, the school nurse, and the teacher are all the kind of narrow, sex-hating, repressed, prudish, religion-prating dominatrixes made into a national American stereotype by Philip Wylie in the 1950s. Woman is the implacable Other in Peck's work; though the female reader may find this disturbing, the writing is good enough to convince us that this is an honest account of reality as perceived by at least one small-town boy. "The wind was as ripe as apples, so full of fall that you could almost bite every breath," Peck writes, and the atmosphere of tough, small-town boyhood, with its poverty and exhilaration, its cruelties and bigotries, has moments of high farce and moral insight that are relished by generation after generation of schoolchildren.

While Oedipal conflict is a main wellspring of humor for male authors, I can't think of a single example that works back in the other direction, with daughters humorously exposing fathers as laughable or despicable characters. Of course, it is mothers who still do most of the intimate, daily work of child rearing and who are therefore still fated, alas, to take the brunt of children's rebellious anger.

Since every child's needs are different, I would hesitate to say that these books have no place on the shelf. One author's books that I would definitely not recommend, however, are those of Roald Dahl. The children who so eagerly read these stories of spite, vengeance, and unbridled aggression must sometimes pause for an astonished moment to wonder why adults press Dahl's books into their hands. His huge popularity among children, however, is not perplexing; the prose is swift and lively and the plots are incredibly violent, of a style much encouraged by our culture. But why have adult purchasers made Dahl an international best seller? Perhaps they are seduced by the sugar coating of his themes, so familiar from the movie version of Dahl's most popular book, *Charlie and the Chocolate Factory.* Those vats of bubbling chocolate almost guarantee annual Christmas reruns (and book sales). Adults assume that candy and children have a powerful affinity, and Christmas is an indulgent time. (A convincing alternate reading of *Charlie and the Chocolate Factory,* by Hamida Bosmajian in the periodical, *The Lion and the Unicorn,* suggests that it is an extended "excremental vision" of an inferno, with the factory as a giant digestive system.)

Perhaps the immense adult acceptance of *Charlie and the Chocolate Factory* also owes something to the voguish adult taste for sadism and black humor, tinged by an unadmitted animosity toward modern children. For though the book seems to sympathize with children as underdogs, it is really a *Struwelpeter* in disguise; one of those gleefully punitive nineteenth-century diatribes written to scare little children into better behavior. Charlie, the hero and the only worthy child in the book, is, like all of Dahl's heroes, an extraordinarily passive, obedient, and compliant little boy. His impoverished family is starving, right in the shadow of Willy Wonka's huge chocolate factory, but Charlie—fading away into a ghostly thin little presence—wearily, uncomplainingly, meekly, the very model of the deserving poor, prepares to starve to death without protest, without struggle, and without any effort to save himself.

When Charlie's grandfather helps him to win a contest that will admit him to the mysterious chocolate factory, Charlie's life is saved. At the factory, though, he meets four other children who are to be severely, even gruesomely, punished during the course of the factory tour. Veruca Salt, for example, ("She needs a good kick in the pants," says Grandpa Joe—an example of the book's linguistic fineness) is the spoiled-brat daughter of a rich American-sounding capitalist. Her father smokes cigars, tries to buy everything he sees, and her mother is grossly fat. To my ears, this characterization comes uncomfortably close to a common anti-Jewish stereotype.

The humor of the book consists of the ghastly punishments inflicted on the four children by the Oompa Loompas, the little jungle pygmies who work virtually as slaves in Wonka's factory. In the original edition, these pygmies were fuzzy-headed Africans; Dahl had to change this detail after protest.

Willy Wonka, the factory owner, is presented as a weirdly capering, shrill, hyperactive little leprechaun, a malign dwarf who seems to be the modern opposite of a fairy tale pixie. At one point, he threatens to make a beard and mustache grow on Veruca—a vengeance on girls that is strangely echoed in a Dennis Lee poem. Finally, Veruca Salt is dropped down a garbage chute, where she will now, as the Oompa Loompas gloat, have to associate with garbage like herself, instead of her fancy friends. But where will she go?

"Why, to the furnace," Mr. Wonka said. "To the incinerator." The scene in itself is distasteful enough, with its approving images of punishment by fire. But parents may be even more disconcerted when they learn of Roald Dahl's anti-Semitic comments to the British weekly newspaper, the *New Statesman:* ". . . there is a trait in the Jewish character that does provoke animosity . . . I mean Hitler, I mean there's always a reason why anti-anything crops up anywhere; even a stinker like Hitler didn't just pick on them for no reason." The *New Statesman* had interviewed Dahl after he published an article in a literary magazine in which he speculated that "the American president and Senate and the Congress [are] utterly dominated by the great Jewish financial institutions. . ."

Holocaust hints and images run through the book, chief among them the sinister factory itself, with its "huge iron gates . . . and smoke belching from its chimneys," a factory sealed to the townspeople. Willie Wonka's chief competitor, Dahl tells us, is Fickelgruber—unmistakably reminiscent of Hitler's birth name, Schickelgruber.

When the Oompa Loompas watch Veruca's parents follow her down the garbage chute "to the furnace," they chant victoriously: ". . . we very rightly thought / That in a case like this we ought / To see the thing completely through / We've polished off her parents, too." The Final Solution, so to speak—though these characters do reappear at the end of the book, not dead but covered in garbage. Surely we must question the appropriateness of a children's story in which scenes of "justified" violence have a parallel with the Holocaust.

Misogyny is another distressing motif in Dahl's work. Many of his numerous books rehash the same tired plot: A meek small boy finally turns on his adult female tormentors and kills them. In *James and the Giant Peach,* the noble small boy is treated cruelly by his wicked aunts; he squashes them flat with the giant peach. In *George's Marvelous Medicine,* the noble small boy is tormented by his "old hag . . . grizzly old grunion . . . miserable old pig" of a grandmother. She is a "filthy old woman"; she has "a small puckered-up mouth like a dog's bottom." One of her worst crimes is that she is a castrator: She tells George that it is a crime to grow. "Daddy says it's fine for a man to be tall," George bravely defies her. (Fathers are usually wonderful, as self-servingly portrayed by Dahl, and one is reminded that when *Charlie and the Chocolate Factory* was criticized in *The Horn Book* magazine, Dahl angrily defended the book on the grounds that he wrote it for his injured son, to whom he was a devoted father.)

George gets his own back: He mixes a potion of liquids scrounged from kitchen, bathroom, and barn (some of the details are explosive with explicit sexual disgust and rage) and detonates his grandmother. Her ghastly physical sufferings, which include an electric shock goosing, go on for a day or two ("There's squigglers in my belly! There's bangers in my bottom!" she shrieks, in a parody of a rape) until she finally is destroyed utterly. "George . . . felt quite trembly," the narrator says as the book ends. "He knew something tremendous had taken place that morning. For a few brief moments he had touched with the very tips of his fingers the edge of a magic world." This tremulous orgasmic moment of pleasure seems obscene, to say the least, in light of what has gone before.

The depiction of woman as evil is even more explicit in *The Witches,* which is presented as children's humor but which, to an adult reader, seems shot through with a chilling vein of hatred and fear. This time, the kindly adult figure is, for once, a woman, the boy's grandmother. An introductory note starts off the book. "Listen very carefully. Never forget what is coming next. REAL WITCHES *dress in ordinary clothes and look very much like ordinary women. They live in ordinary houses and work in* ORDINARY JOBS . . . a REAL WITCH hates children with a red-hot sizzling hatred . . . " (emphasis is Dahl's). Witches, it turns out, hate children and plot to kill them all because, to witchy nostrils, children smell like fresh dog excrement. Dahl creates a very real atmosphere of horror and fear in this book; the witches are genuinely loathsome. At the end of the book, they have managed to transform the hero into a mouse. Still, he has learned the secret of how to destroy them, and we leave the mouse and his grandmother at a peak of excitement: They have just vowed to spend the rest of their lives crisscrossing the globe, seeking out and exterminating witches.

Children's literature is so rich in humor of the genuine, humane, affirmative kind. There are so many books for every age level that do not reek of dog excrement or "red-hot sizzling hatred." It is a shame that commercial exploitation has spread this ugly form of comedy so widely across the English-speaking world. An informed parent or teacher, however, who is alerted to some of the more destructive content of Dahl's writing, does not need to buy it or promote it to children. Humor can splutter with indignation and rage, and often does, but hatred is not funny.

Chapter 5

THE QUEST
FOR IDENTITY

We read books to find out who we are. What other
people, real or imaginary, do and think and feel . . . is
an essential guide to our understanding of what we
ourselves are and may become . . . a person who had
never listened to nor read a tale or myth or parable or
story, would remain ignorant of his own emotional and
spiritual heights and depths, would not know quite fully
what it is to be human . . . There have been societies
that did not use the wheel, but there have been no
societies that did not tell stories.

Ursula K. LeGuin, *The Language of the Night,* 1979

As I read for and mulled over this chapter on the theme
of a child's quest for identity, a funny little nursery rhyme rhythm
kept tapping away at the door of my consciousness. "When the hum
was hum-hum, / The hum began to hum."

"What *is* that rhyme?" I finally asked my youngest daughter,
hum-humming it out for her.

"When the pie was opened," she said at once, "the birds began
to sing." Of course! There is the king, counting his money; the queen
busy with her honey; and if we count the little blackbirds tucked up
in their pie, we have the whole archetypal nuclear family in its cozy
nest. Those blackbirds, bursting forth with such verve, must have
pecked at my subconscious because they embody the energy of the
emerging child—the child who must break the tight bounds of the
family circle and learn to sing a new song.

Books have a special place in this task. Some children, of course,
never read and still manage very nicely to become individuals. In
my own childhood, though, books were an essential adjunct: I would
walk for blocks unconscious of my surroundings, engrossed by the

strangeness, the sheer surprising difference, of the way someone in a book spoke or thought or acted.

The otherness I met in books helped me to define myself; once I was past the quick dazzled gulping of stories for the sheer magic of being transported, I came more and more to value books that let me into some other world that was tangibly real but spiced with strangeness. The one thing I hated was false goodness. When Jo in *Little Women* stopped putting her hands in her pockets, quit whistling, curbed her temper, and learned to be demure, I lost all interest. There was nothing to learn from someone who had started out with such promise, only to capitulate to the same stultifying standards that were being imposed on me.

There's nothing in books so likely to make a child mean-tempered and uncivil as a story of saccharine goodness and light; Pollyanna, when I met her, made me savage with cynicism. When she cooed over the crutches in her Christmas barrel (now the barrel interested me; what *was* a Christmas barrel?), I wanted to throw them at her head. I don't know how modern children can tolerate the pap of Holly Hobby and Miss Cheerful, those commercially bland damsels who inhabit cardboard meadows starred with tomato-colored flowers. The best fantasies, the ones that summoned our delight and commanded our loyalty, were always those that had the solid feel of three dimensions.

Among the charms of Beatrix Potter's *The Tale of Peter Rabbit,* for example, is its delicious frankness: Peter is naughty, Mrs. Rabbit is loving but stern, Mr. McGregor is emphatically an enemy. He *ate* Father Rabbit. Even small children appreciate the delicate interplay between Peter Rabbit-as-lovable-child (is there any more instantly recognizable childhood gesture of discomfort than that pose of Peter Rabbit's, when he must hold his chin up while mother fastens his top button?) and Peter Rabbit as indelibly rabbitlike, dashing frantically around the garden when he forgets the path to the gate, or hiding in a watering can with his quivering ear-tips betraying his rabbity presence.

In the falsely sentimental toddler books that clog our chain book stores, a rabbit could only be an adorable bunny. In Beatrix Potter's hands, Peter is sometimes silly, definitely greedy, but without question lovable, if only because of the subtle and endearing watercolors in which he appears, and the story's precise, intelligent prose.

The best works always seem to radiate an acknowledgment of children's nature as it really is. Without that deep, sure acceptance by the adult world, no child can be self-accepting. That is why the commercial flatteries of Smurfettes and Care Bears are so irrelevant to children's development: They encourage a simpering niceness that is incongruously imposed on a child's nature, like a crust of caramelized sugar on top of an interesting stew.

Books can be forthright about children's characters at the same time as they are loving. Both my daughters were devoted to *Don't You Remember?* by Lucille Clifton, the pink and brown picture book about four-year-old Desire Mary Tate, a little girl who "remembered everything" and suffered, as all children must, from the ardor of her wishes and the maddening carelessness of adults who seem to take forever to keep their promises. Desire pouts, whines, and even takes furiously to her bed with an indignant curse ("Dag double dag!"—an expressive oath taken up enthusiastically by my own children). The kindness with which her family helps Desire to overcome her frustration is the strong foundation of this book's appeal.

Tell Me a Mitzi by Lore Segal was another favorite. My children loved the homely, rumpled, affectionately portrayed New York family and the wry, observant wit of both author and illustrator. One morning, Mitzi decides to take baby brother Jacob and go to visit her grandparents before her parents wake up. Mitzi patiently wrestles with the physical reality of a baby—climbing into his crib, taking off his pajamas, changing his diaper, putting on his clothes, filling a bottle, struggling with a stroller, dealing with an elevator, hailing a taxi— only to meet with defeat when the taxi driver asks her, "Where to?" and she can only reply, "Grandma's house."

It's one of those shaggy dog jokes: After Mitzi retraces all her steps, dragging heavy, homely Jacob back upstairs, getting him undressed and putting him back to bed, Mother wakes up, comes in, and asks her to be a big girl and get out of her pajamas all by herself this morning. "You do it," says Mitzi, "I'm exhausted."

Still, she makes sure to ask for grandma's address. "Why?" asks mother. "Because," says Mitzi. There's an acceptance here of Mitzi's ongoing private life, her stubborn resolve, and the fact that children have capacities far beyond what parents often assume.

One reason, certainly, that my own family doted on the Mitzi stories was that the family is recognizably Jewish; they also loved Desire Mary Tate, who was brown, and Peter Rabbit, who was furry, but it was an added pleasure to see their own identity mirrored and confirmed in an engagingly warm and humorous story. Ian Wallace's *The Sandwich* is important for the same reason. Vincenzo Ferrante, who is in grade two at a downtown Toronto school, tastes the mingled bitterness and triumph of an archetypal Canadian schoolchild experience. His peanut butter-loving friends are at first revolted by Vincenzo's "stinky" mortadella and provolone lunch sandwiches; later (though not, to my mind, entirely convincingly) they seem to accept the idea of *chacun à son gout*. Vincenzo wins by sticking to his guns and not trying to imitate his non-Italian friends.

Friendship is the first bridge a child builds out to the larger world. In a friend's house you first notice how the kitchens of different families smell different; you first sense the different shadings of harshness or jocularity in the way other men and women talk to each other and to their children; in the offhand swapping of stories between friends, you first catch yourself in small betrayals of family secrets, family loyalties; in the first fallings-out, you learn the hurt fury of rejection, and the first stinging recognition that your own values and behavior are not universal or universally approved.

Stories of friendship can comfort the lonely child, for whom friendship in the book is a rewarding substitute, but they can also illuminate the painful shocks and surprises that are inevitable in those first, intense real-life bondings. *The Secret Language* by Ursula Nordstrom is particularly sensitive in the way it captures the clinging together of two lonely children at a boarding school. The heroine is the timid and sheltered ten-year-old Victoria; her friend is the tough little school rebel, Martha. Martha is more worldly than Victoria, more imaginative and more troubled. She rescues the tearful Victoria from dreadful homesickness by drawing her into an exclusive comradeship which defies the mores of the rest of the school, a defiance symbolized by their use of a private language ("ick-en-spik" is Martha's invented phrase of scorn for the goody-goodies).

True to the play of children and the world-opening energies of friendship, the two girls invent fantasy houses for themselves, first with tiny dolls in a drawer, and later in a real hut they build in the woods, with considerable effort and ingenuity. But the little shelter of their friendship is often threatened. At one point, mutual resentments smolder when Martha scoffs at Victoria for believing in the tooth fairy. And Victoria, who is, after all, the rather prim daughter of a priggish mother, is pained when she realizes that her mother disapproves of the outspoken Martha. Vicky, though, is staunchly loyal, and Martha eases the way with a generous gesture, an apology for "being a dope in front of your mother."

They may seem like tiny dramas indeed, but these small events trigger, for the girls, significant experiences of loyalty and betrayal, dismay and reconciliation. Nordstrom handles them believably and precisely, always through the children's play and conversation. *The Secret Language* is an emotionally true and sensitive story for girls between the ages of six and ten about how two children can enrich each other's lives, even while in the process of growing past each other.

More sophisticated, witty, glancing, and contemporary is *Thunder and Lightnings*, a fine book by Jan Mark about the friendship of two boys in rural Norfolk. Mark, like the outstanding English author William Mayne, knows how to extract sly humor from everyday sensory perception and incident, and she is superb at evoking physical sensation. Andrew, about ten or eleven years old, is the town boy whose warm, chaotic middle-class family has just moved into the ramshackle Tiler's Cottage. He is befriended by Victor, a working-class boy who lives nearby in a harsh, compulsively waxed and polished household. Mark is wickedly funny about the way the boys have to negotiate the floors and rugs in Victor's house: They sidle around the linoleum bordering the living room rug "like ancient Egyptians" and go up the stairs bowlegged, with their feet "on the wooden bits" on each side of the newly vacuumed stair carpet.

Victor and Andrew base their friendship on a fascination with the old-fashioned Lightning jets and World War II Spitfires at a nearby airbase. The crash of sound barriers breaking, the howl and whine of engines, the thrills and thunder of the modern era, are cheerfully present on every page. Behind the excitement of plane watching is a more subtle kind of observation, as the two boys warily sniff out the cultural differences between them, their different ways of defending themselves from hurt, their different ways of being clever or kind. Andrew, who is superficially so much more sophisticated, is actually (as his mother notices) more childishly naive, and it is only after clumsily bruising Victor's feelings several times that Andrew begins to acquire some of his friend's native tact.

Thunder and Lightnings is so sharply perceptive that it can be read with pleasure on several levels. *Dawn of Fear*, a similar story of comradeship between two English boys, is actually less complex in its writing, and deals with younger boys, but its sheer emotional wallop is so much more intense that it is best suited to a slightly older child, perhaps of eleven or twelve. Susan Cooper is known for her excellent series, *The Dark Is Rising*, but this semiautobiographical realistic story about the London blitz is as good as, if not superior to, her better-known fantasies.

As in *The Secret Language*, the children—Derek, the central character, his sunny-tempered friend Peter, and Geoff, who is not quite accepted by the two best friends—are wholeheartedly engaged in building a hut. North American children would call it a "fort"; Derek calls it a "camp," but its ritual meaning as the first home away from home, the first tasting of independence and self-reliance, is the same everywhere. While the boys, who are rather middle class and vulnerable, try to defend their camp from their rougher, tougher working-class enemies, the White Road gang, they are also coping with nightly treks to air raid shelters, fatigue, and a pallid, skimpy rationed diet for which their parents keep apologizing but which is all the children have ever known.

True to the strange intensities of child life, it is the war and the air raids, with their deafening noises and tracer-lit skies, that seem dreamily unreal to the boys, a spectacular sort of game or show, while the planning, building, and defense of their camp is desperately real and arouses fierce and even frightening emotions in them.

Dawn of Fear is a scrupulously honest and tautly written book. We watch one week unfold through Derek's eyes; we see him draw new insights from Peter's generous nature; we share his bursting grief on a grim Wednesday morning when Peter's house is gone, all but the front gate.

> The misery and fright were growing inside him like a great swelling balloon. Yesterday the world had begun going badly wrong, but it was to have been better again when today came; the bits of nightmare could have been forgotten. But instead today had brought a change that would need more than forgetting. His world had stopped and the world he would live in from now on would be a different world. The old one with Pete in it would never come back again.

The dawn that teaches Derek real fear and pain also heralds a growing up that begins with loss. Yet *Dawn of Fear*, though powerful, is not a depressing book; the constructive strength of friendship carries the reader right past the grief of the last scene.

The same is true of another wartime story, *Alan and Naomi* by Myron Levoy. The main plot seems rather melodramatic at first: Twelve-year-old Alan Silverman, a sensitive only child growing up in Brooklyn during World War II, is asked to befriend a profoundly distressed French Jewish refugee child, Naomi, who saw her father being murdered by the Gestapo.

"Not me," protests Alan at first. "She's a girl, she's crazy and I *won't!*" Levoy is particularly skillful at catching the different ways that youngsters talk with different people: the genuinely funny banter and screwball comedy between Alan and his best friend, Shaun Kelly, who has all the toughness and street smarts that Alan lacks; the nervous, defensive, and finally tender dialogue between Alan and Naomi; the rough jeering of the stickball players at dusk in the streets; the embarrassed formality of Alan talking to a teacher; his fond impatience when he fends off his affectionate, demanding parents; the secret, tentatively sexual voice of Alan, fantasizing about Naomi as his girlfriend.

In the end, though the author clearly intends the relationship with Naomi and her final devastating breakdown to carry the emotional weight of the novel, it is a minor theme that seems fresher, less forced, more genuinely touching. Alan has ruptured his friendship with Shaun because he failed to trust him with the secret of his relationship with Naomi. Alan feared, perhaps pardonably, that rough-tough Shaun might share the macho and xenophobic sentiments of their street pals. It is Alan's suspiciousness (springing, one feels, from his own initial ambivalence about Naomi), that leads, in part, to Naomi's tragedy. At the end, only the reconciliation of Alan and Shaun helps to balance the painful loss of Naomi.

All these stories of friendship carry a sense of risk and strain along with their pleasures; undoubtedly, their authors are remembering accurately the hazards that had to be skirted in those first ventures outside the circle of the family. Another kind of book in which children define themselves seems to hark back to an earlier, more comforting mode of self-definition: the strong identification with place.

There are some books, most loved by girls (and I'll come back to that in a moment), that invite a swooning rapture over landscape. Years afterward, one remembers not so much the characters as the colors of things, the heightened emotionalism that seemed to rise like a dizzying perfume from the grass, the trees, the flowers drowsing in hot sunshine. *Anne of Green Gables, Heidi,* and *The Secret Garden* are three that seem curiously linked in this way. As the English psychologist Nicholas Tucker points out, all three share a basic plot with heavily Oedipal overtones: A clever, spunky little girl with more ardor than beauty to recommend her wins over a gruff, remote older man by the sheer power of personality. I wonder if the overwhelming seductiveness of the landscape in these novels is the result of an awakening sensuality, unconsciously displaced onto the birds and the bees.

Years later, I remembered the setting of these three novels better than I did their plots. From Johanna Spyri's *Heidi* I remembered the bracing mountain air, the charming simplicity of milk drunk from bowls, meals of fresh cheese and bread, a bed of hay, pastures starred with primroses, and snowy peaks flushed with sunset reflections. Re-reading it, I see the charm of that early Swiss pastoral (first published in 1880) which endorsed all the most vigorously progressive views of its day. We first see Heidi at the age of five, struggling up the mountainside in the summer heat, wearing all the clothes she owns to spare her aunt the trouble of carrying them. Sensibly, Heidi rebels, strips down to her underwear and goes capering up the mountainside in splendid barefoot freedom. Furthermore, no one is shocked and no one scolds; indeed, the gruff old "Alm-Uncle" with whom she is to live merely smiles when he sees the eager little girl clambering up toward him. I can hardly imagine a generation of little girls since 1880, including my own, to whom this would not have represented the most unimaginably heady freedom.

Within hours, Heidi's cleverness and the ingenuousness of her prattle have won over the flinty old man who is feared by everyone. Anne of Green Gables (nearly all of Lucy Maud Montgomery's hero-ines are named by the houses they inhabit) is another such. Her story, too, begins at the moment when she makes a startlingly un-conventional impression on a crusty old man.

In Anne's case, it's her "imagination" that beguiles the patholog-ically shy bachelor, Matthew Cuthbert. Anne's imagination is ar-dently attuned to the landscape: She first tells Matthew that she thought of spending the night in a nearby cherry tree, "all white with bloom like marble halls"; by the time the two of them arrive at Green Gables, Anne has rhapsodized about "a painted sunset like a great rose window at the end of a cathedral aisle," named an unlikely avenue of apple trees "The White Way of Delight," and utterly won over the woman-fearing Matthew by "the rapt light in her eye."

It's as though the child's heated response to natural beauty has kindled some long-frozen kindred emotion in the cold adult; remote, withdrawn fathers must be all too common, judging by the long-lived popularity of this daydream.

Anne and Heidi share another quality, that of an entirely unnat-ural artlessness. Both are given to gleeful leaping, singing, and sprite-like dancing. But no matter how extreme their response to the landscape, no matter how poetic or exalted, they are never tortured by self-conscious embarrassment. This, of course, is because they are written from outside, seen through the sentimentalizing eyes of an adult. Though Anne and Heidi (and Mary Lennox in her secret gar-den and Jo of *Little Women*) are loved by girl readers, there is a half-suppressed guilty twinge of envy and alienation that accompanies one's admiration of these idealized heroines.

Was Anne Shirley never ashamed of her outrageous showing

off? Did the poison of self-consciousness never cloud Heidi's sunlit days as she lisped to the trees? Nevertheless, the author's sensuous evocation of house and landscape is unforgettable; so is the secret Eden discovered by Mary Lennox, the cross little orphan girl who was healed by nature on those romantic windswept moors so loved by the Brontes.

The Secret Garden, written by Frances Hodgson Burnett in 1911, still works its magic, even more strongly than *Heidi* or *Anne,* because Mary is not automatically adored. Before she can win over her stubborn old man, she must forge a new character for herself, and she is helped in this difficult task by a wonderful Pan-boy, Dickon. He is as soft-spoken, sweet, and nurturing as no true adolescent boy who has existed ever before or since, and not only speaks in an enchantingly rustic Yorkshire dialect, but also can charm the birds and the animals with his pan pipes.

Mary brings the long-neglected garden back to life, and in return, the garden bestows on her a serene and giving temperament, a healthy appetite, and a new delight in life. It is this possibility of transformation that takes hold of the reader's imagination—a wholesome growth, nurtured and applauded by a whole chorus of earthily wise, rosy-cheeked peasants who know the virtues of hard work and self-sufficiency.

To reread *The Secret Garden* as an adult is to discover with a nasty shock, however, that though the spell of the garden remains intact, the book goes seriously off the rails toward the end, when Mary sets out to heal her hypochondriac cousin, Colin.

This boy is crippled and bedridden by sheer hysterical dread of death. Helping him, Mary learns new reserves of patience and generosity. Once Colin begins to regain his health, though, Mary disappointingly disappears from the story. The moment of her eclipse is even marked by the author: As Mary's crotchety uncle Archibald returns to his Yorkshire mansion, he is amazed to see his hated, sickly son all healed, racing toward him. "I can beat Mary in a race," Colin yells, and, in a fever of omnipotence, "I'm going to live forever and ever!" Colin has developed into an arrogant, high-strung little minister of pantheism. He actually leads the forelock-tugging servants (the gardener, Ben Weatherstaff, blinks away tears of admiration) in singing the Doxology in the garden. If Burnett had a weakness for Christlike little boys, she was more realistic and surer of touch in depicting Mary, a flawed soul who courageously healed herself. It is for that transformation that the book is remembered and loved.

Blue Willow by Doris Gates, which won the Newbery Medal in 1940, is another powerful story of rural seeking, aimed at an under-twelve audience. Janey Larkin, ten, is the child of migrant workers, dustbowl refugees from Texas in the years of the Great Depression. Rarely has an author created such a rawboned picture of stark poverty without for one moment reducing her characters to sentimental caricatures. Janey Larkin, too thin, too small, guarded and wary beyond her years, is one of the most believably brave girls in children's fiction, old or new.

Like Anne and like Heidi, Janey triumphs (she gains a home and security for her family) by winning the friendship and admiration of an older, powerful man. And, just like these other stories of Oedipal triumph, *Blue Willow* conveys a sharp impression of place—the heat-dazzled cotton fields of the San Joaquin Valley—along with the heroine's passionate desire to belong, to attach herself permanently to an adopted landscape. But Janey is no sparkler. We know her not through the doting avuncular descriptions (why isn't there a word for auntular?) of the narrator, but from the inside, through her convincingly childlike hopes, fears, hesitations, and wellings of excitement.

Perhaps Janey is such a moving character because she has so little. Her only book and her portable school is the New Testament, which her father makes her read daily. She mines it for meaning and for beauty; the moment when she feels love for her stepmother is the moment when that weary, silent, defeated woman suddenly says, about a stand of willows along a slough: "Rivers of water in a dry land."

Janey is deeply attached to the only thing she owns, a blue willow plate, her sole remaining link to an earlier life when she had her natural mother and a real home. For her, living in a dry, harsh, and hungry world, the scene on the plate expresses a world of romantic beauty and cool enchantment. Her courage—in defense of the plate against a crude bully, and in grievingly giving it up when money is desperately needed—is what changes the family's luck at last. Though the dusty landscape of *Blue Willow* is not nearly so seductive as the lush beauties of Green Gables, Alpine meadows, or Yorkshire Edens, Janey is a more realistic—and more inspiriting—heroine than Anne, Heidi, or Mary.

Naturally, a sense of place is a vital element in many novels, but in some it predominates. The Israeli novelist Amos Oz, for example, has written a sparklingly witty and poignant day-in-the-life of an eleven-year-old daydreaming scamp. *Soumchi* (the name of the book and of the scamp) is redolent of a typically mixed, chaotic Jerusalem neighborhood in the days of the British mandate. Arched doorways, derelict courtyards, cobbled lanes, evenings scented with pomegranate, all breathe from the page. *Soumchi* is worth reading just for the depth of the boy's reactions as he drinks in the exotically unfamiliar atmosphere in the varying homes of his friends.

Place, as a shaper of identity, is the focus of *Hold Fast,* by Kevin Major, a 1978 novel that marked a breakthrough for the unapologetic use of the Newfoundland dialect in fiction. When both his parents are killed in an accident, Michael, fourteen, is forced to leave the village of Marten and move to a larger town, St. Albert, to live with a tyrannical uncle and his cowed wife.

Mike hates to leave what he knows and loves best: running a trapline, riding a skidoo, fixing lobster traps. "Squiddin is a lot o fun, idn't it?" he wistfully asks his loved grandad before he leaves and the grandfather replies, "Yes b'y, it is so." The whole story is told in Mike's language and from his limited, belligerent perspective. Angry, grieving, and stubborn, he is shipped off, hates town, and finds his way back. Mike does not learn much or change during his painful odyssey; in fact, the whole of his accomplishment is to "hold fast" to his own rough-and-ready viewpoint, his outport individualism, against the sneers of the townies and the bullying of his uncle.

The problem with this kind of nostalgic stubborness is that identity doesn't come to a youth as a static inheritance; because Mike modifies nothing of his own behavior or character (pugnacious, self-justifying, semidelinquent, hot-tempered) we never see him learn or change. He exploits a town girlfriend who is willing to hold his hand and listen to his endless talk of himself ("I did get a few great kisses out of it, too"), steals a car from an old lady who befriends and feeds him, and finds an excuse for his every action, including knocking another boy unconscious "by accident" when he punches him.

Major is celebrating Newfoundland dialect and defending Newfoundland working-class values against smug "brainer" (bookish) townies, and he does forcefully convey the fierce loyalty of an outport boy to his local way of life. What might have strengthened the portrait was a flicker of conflict within Mike himself; any hesitation, doubt, or questioning that might have grounded his final choice more solidly. As I'll discuss later, in connection with more powerful works like *The Slave Dancer,* moral ambiguities are a truer and more disturbing truth about the inward life of humans than the brash certainties of a boy like Mike.

Inwardness is the hallmark of these books in which young people are seen sorting through their experiences and trying to forge some sense of who they are, or even find out if they *are* anyone identifiable. Anne of Green Gables voiced a familiar worry when she lamented that there seemed to be so many Annes inside her—if only she knew which one was the real Anne, life would be so much simpler.

The most extreme version of this self-seeking in adolescence is what I think of as the "lonely vigil" genre: modern Robinson Crusoes who must survive alone in complete isolation. When I first read *Island of the Blue Dolphins* by Scott O'Dell, I was astounded by the popularity of such a bleak story. What could be more depressing than the plight of a young Indian girl, left isolated from all her tribe, surviving on a rocky, windswept island for eighteen years with no companion but a wild dog she has tamed?

But of course preadolescents are mesmerized by this account of survival. Aren't they, too, teetering on the perilous brink of adult life, facing challenges that they must meet all alone? Yet these readers are still not far past the age of total dependency on parents, when the fear of being abandoned is the most bone-shaking of terrors.

Survival stories usually involve a lone youth, who is stripped of parents, friends, possessions, shelter, tools, and sustenance, and yet who manages through skill and courage to endure. These stories serve as a bracing fantasy reassurance with a comfortingly familiar pattern. The marooned soul is terrified at first, longs for rescue, nearly perishes through ignorant mistakes, and then, because he or she doggedly learns from those mistakes and tries again, begins to adapt to the environment. At the midpoint of the story, we almost always see the survivor reconciled to, even enchanted by, the formerly threatening isolation. At the end, the choice is always to rejoin civilization, a painful compromise made possible because the survivor is strengthened and at peace, having wrested from danger a sure sense of competence, courage, and identity.

In *Island of the Blue Dolphins,* Karana begins to thrive when she gives up her numb grieving for her lost people and considers breaking the fearsome tribal taboo against a woman making weapons. Throughout, the narrative is remarkable for showing us, without benefit of human characters with whom Karana could interact and with little inward reverie to break the flow of the action, how she changes and grows.

O'Dell tells the story with a clarity of detail and a restrained, unpoetic narrative style, perfectly reflective of Karana's contained character, which slowly builds a rock-ribbed feeling of reality. So fully imagined is the Island of the Blue Dolphins itself that we feel we know every hummock and ravine. Karana's deepening maturity and her love of her animals are revealed in lively and often touching incidents.

Perhaps because Karana was a real person, and her story is true (the Lost Woman of San Nicolas lived on that island alone from 1835 to 1853), O'Dell was able tell it with complete conviction. The handling of time is noteworthily skillful, too; O'Dell makes us feel the slow rhythmic passage of those eighteen years by keeping track of Karana's repeated seasonal tasks and pleasures, yet he never becomes tediously repetitive. Seamlessly, he balances immediate action and emotion with the lengthy passing of months and years.

Few other stories of lonely vigil can match the power of *Island of the Blue Dolphins,* but *My Side of the Mountain,* by Jean Craighead George, comes close in popularity, and even more successful is *Julie of the Wolves,* written eight years later by the same author.

In *My Side of the Mountain,* teenaged Sam Gribley calmly runs away from his overcrowded family apartment in New York because he wants to try living on the land, specifically, on land once owned by the Gribleys on a Catskill mountain. "I am on my mountain in a tree home that people have passed without ever knowing that I am here," begins the narrative in classic Crusoe style. Though much of the book reads like a plodding but worthy naturalist's guide to eating wild foods, there's an intrinsic fascination in seeing how Sam will cope with each succeeding difficulty, from capturing and training a wild hawk to catch game for him, to sewing deerskin clothes.

Perhaps these survival stories are more convincing when they concern native people, or perhaps George simply increased her literary skills by the time she wrote *Julie of the Wolves.* Julie—Miyax, in her native Inuit language—is a thirteen-year-old who has run away from her home in Barrow because she has been molested by her slow-witted teenage husband in a marriage of convenience. Lost on the tundra, Julie survives by studying the ways and language of a nearby wolf pack. So well does she imitate wolf pup behavior that she is adopted by the pack leader. The wolves feed her (at first regurgitating swallowed meat as they would for their own pups) and take her under their protection; months later, as she treks toward Point Hope on the Alaska coast, the wolf pack is still running near her, protecting her, and bringing her food.

The idea is preposterously romantic but George makes it believable, mostly by showing us the workings of Julie's mind as she desperately recalls and uses every trick of survival known to the Inuit peoples. *Julie of the Wolves* works so well, too, because the Arctic is exotically beautiful and strange, a landscape as desolate and challenging, yet as teeming with hidden possibilities of life as Karana's windswept rocks.

Nkwala by Edith Lambert Sharp is a 1958 Canadian story of lonely vigil that holds up well in this distinguished company. Nkwala, a twelve-year-old Salish Indian boy, undergoes his ceremonial trials of hardship in order to become a man. He must wait alone in the wilderness until Day Dawn, the god of children, sends him his own name, song, and protecting spirit.

The lonely terrors of Nkwala's vigil ("The night that flows into the empty spaces, and crowds close to the shoulder; the night that is breathed in and out through the nostrils and beats on the drum of the pulse. . .") and how he conquers them make a compelling story, vividly told. For once, we are made to experience the fear and anxiety ("uneasiness prickled over his skin like a cold breeze") as well as the triumphant overcoming; furthermore, Nkwala's solitary trials teach him extraordinary skills that later save his people from attack as they go on a dangerous journey away from the drought lands of the prairie.

Middle childhood is the season of possibilities, the time when questions arise and roads stretch into the future. After the first books that open doors into new worlds, and before the single-minded narcissism of so much adolescent reading, there are the two quests: the quest for identity and the quest for adventure. The two overlap, of course (there are no simple labels in all of literature) but a book that helps children explore inwardly is a useful one to keep in mind, when so much is available that provides only the relief of escape into action and adventure.

Nor is the search always in deadly earnest. Rightly, there is often a playful, venturesome spirit, a feeling of wonderful rebellious possibilities. *Harry the Dirty Dog* is one of the loved examples among picture books. It deals with identity at the reassuring basic level of the coherence of the individual: Even when naughty Harry is unrecognizably covered with dirt, he is still Harry, he is still treated lovingly by the family, and they uncover his real self in short order. Just how important a point this is, though it seems so crashingly obvious, is known to every parent who has seen a three-year-old try on an older child's Halloween mask and then panic when everyone pretends not to recognize him.

Cannonball Simp by John Burningham is more serious, though still in picture book form. Nobody wants Simp. She is small and fat, a homely little black dog whom we see being cruelly abandoned near a garbage dump by a raincoated anonymous owner. In one dramatic sweep of a picture, with the menacing black pit of the dump opening beneath the helpless feet of the tossed Simp, Burningham sums up the trembling void of abandonment that is every child's worst nightmare. But Simp does not despair. Hungry and cold, she nevertheless scrabbles for a living. She forges on. And when a yellow path of light lays down its shining ribbon through the woods, leading away through the dark to a shimmering white circus tent, we know Simp is on the road to salvation. Indeed, she saves the hapless clown who befriends her, by inventing a dog-shot-from-cannon stunt. Then we see Simp Resplendent, landing on a drum in the circus ring, star of the show and still her homely self, graceless claws spreading at the end of gangly legs under her tubby little body, tiny eyes gleaming in delight.

The Bee-Man of Orn by Frank Stockton, the inventive nine-teenth-century fabulist, is another comical and endearing twist on the search for identity. The Bee-Man, as illustrated by Maurice Sendak, is a contented, rumpled, wildly homely eccentric, with a huge bristly chin, a foolishly happy smile, a flapping leather coat, and hives full of bees who are his best friends.

When a Junior Sorcerer tells the Bee-Man that he was surely transformed from something or someone else, the Bee-Man is troubled. He feels it is only right to discover his original identity "even if it's horrid, because no one has a right to keep a form that is not his own." His adventures are engaging because he plays the role of the fairy tale innocent, the naive truthsayer whose honesty shames the pretentious and the phony. At the very end, a sorcerer grants the Bee-Man's wish and transforms him into his original self—a marvelously funny baby, with his same ugly mug, grinning with delight in a baby's nightie, snug on his Mama's lap, and surrounded by doting sorcerers! As though that were not a strong enough reassurance about the continuance of identity, the Bee-Man (who now has the option to grow up into anything at all) chooses to grow back into the same happy, sloppy Bee-Man, now that he knows he's entitled to that form. The ending is so satisfying because it is the true ending of all transformation tales: We are what we are.

Ninny's Boat, by Clive King, is a sparkling, witty, and marvelously well written quest for a boy's true name and identity. "They call me Ninny. Yes, they think it's a funny name. But they say it's mine. Anyway, it's the only one I know," the story begins. The narrator's voice is rueful, humorous, alive with intelligence and spunk. Ninny is a thrall of a savage northern tribe, and, as the story opens, we are swiftly and almost miraculously drawn into the mind of a shaggy boy, sleepily waking in a hayloft to discover that he's been abandoned by the farmer's family to sink or swim in a rising flood. King has never been better than in this adventure, which we experience through the person of a boy with more shrewdness than knowledge. Ninny is an archetypal survivor, with the survivor's rough-and-ready fellow feeling for other misfits. Spinning helplessly in an old milk tub, Ninny makes jokes with himself, enjoys the craziness of his plight, and sturdily, unquestioningly sets about rescuing the poor dumb creatures left behind, including a dog, a cat, a cow, and a witchy old woman marooned in a tree. It's hard, without quoting at length, to convey the quality of merriment and sheer joy-in-being-alive in Ninny's interior monologue. That jokey resignation, the readiness for whatever comes next, never really deserts Ninny in his long search to solve the riddle of his origins.

King makes the most of showing us the world through the eyes of a Dark Ages boy; since we are never allowed to know more than Ninny knows, everything seems fresh, amazing, an age of continual wonders. And, of course, Ninny is a kind of Huck Finn of the North. His innocently faithful recording of events lets even the child reader enjoy the deadpan satire of human foibles.

When the tribe faces a crisis, a wondering Ninny overhears his first council meeting. "We want nothing but peas . . . we must keep the candles out," Ninny thinks he hears. "Sandals? Vandals?" wonders Ninny, and the young reader is delighted to catch on before Ninny does. The spoof of Dark Ages manners verges on the Monty Pythonesque at times: "Grrr, Vandals! Myrgings! Gar!" boos a crowd of thick-witted Angles. King is never a dull writer, but in *Ninny's Boat* he seems to take particular pleasure in playing with language. There's a casual reference to the "bone-fire" when a Viking king is being created—an offhand etymological tidbit about the origins of our word *bonfire*. And familiar nursery rhymes sometimes pop up, in plausibly distorted form, as part of some Dark Ages event, so that we're half convinced we're seeing the true beginnings of a rhyme we met later in time but earlier in our lives.

But this is a quest, and for all the high good humor, Ninny wins through, after daring adventures, to learn at last that he is a long-lost Pictish prince from Britain. By the time he has found his true name (Ninius) he has grown into it, no longer a shaggy, endearing yokel but a weathered and resourceful adventurer who has braved oceans, lived with the "little people," and seen King Arthur die.

Ninny's quest ends with finding his beginnings, but many a quest novel follows a youngster who is trying to disentangle from family roots. *Josh* by Australian novelist Ivan Southall is widely admired for its stream-of-consciousness narrative style. Histrionic, poetry-writing fourteen-year-old Josh visits his Aunt Clara in a back country village and runs smack into a hostile gang of Snopesian local kids. The price the reader must pay for the intensity of Josh's narrative is a certain monotone hysterical quality to his observations, and a muddy confusion of events: Not until the end do we begin to realize why the locals are so implacably resentful of Josh. Some readers, of course, relish the puzzlelike quality of this kind of elliptical narrative, and certainly, seeing events from Josh's narrow perspective lets us see directly into his adolescent soul as he moves from self-consciousness, self-pity, and fear to a bolder assertiveness at the end.

Family stories are often chronicles of a child's moving away from the family's perception of character to a greater degree of self-definition. One of the strongest examples is *From Anna* by Jean Little. Anna is the youngest and homeliest of five children in a solid German family in 1933; she is clumsy, awkward, and a failure at school. Little is frank about Anna's physical unattractiveness and her frequently sullen demeanor, and yet, because she takes us so sympathetically into Anna's feelings, we are always on Anna's side.

One of Little's finest accomplishments in this book, aimed at the middle reader, is to suggest, clearly but subtly, how a child can feel lonely and angry in the midst of a loving family. Anna's family is stable and affectionate, yet Anna feels isolated; her mother is insensitive, and the older brothers and sisters just a bit heartless in their teasing. Anna knows she isn't stupid, and longs to please her beloved Papa, yet she often manages to do just what will most frustrate him, such as refusing to learn English when he decides that the whole family must learn quickly before fleeing to Canada.

"Awkward Anna," her athletic, blond extroverted brothers and sisters call her. In Toronto, the reason for her chronic ineptitude is finally discovered: Anna is nearly blind. Fitted with proper glasses, introduced into a kindly and welcoming special class at school, Anna is suspicious and slow to thaw. Her gradual adjustment to Canada is superbly handled; it rings with honesty and close observation, and so does the stubborn, unforgiving way that Anna hugs her new happiness to herself, refusing for months to let her family know how she is beginning to blossom at school.

From Anna is different from the slick, contemporary novels in which children suffering from acne, small breasts, premature ejaculation, or nasty parents solve their problems strictly within the peer group. Anna's character is as important as her blindness; her family, their patterns of behavior and belief, are significantly shaped by their own time and place, and not seen in the falsely narrow personal perspective that is so familiar from soap operas and situation comedies. As Anna moves out from her preoccupation with sadness, as she dares to try to belong in her class at school, as she discovers poetry and weaving and friendship, she loses the self-consciousness that spoiled her family relationships in the beginning. At the end, having given herself wholly to making a splendid family Christmas in the new country, Anna is singing carols in her living room and not noticing that she has achieved her goal of being Mama's favorite for tonight—not noticing, in fact, that for once she is special to everyone in the room: "In her heart it was Christmas, and she was busy singing."

When children begin to winnow out the true from false in their family's opinion of them, and to find that they are sometimes more truly themselves in contexts outside the family, they are also in the process of testing and sometimes rejecting their families' values. One of the boldest assaults on received values in all of children's literature must be the lonely battle waged by twelve-year-old Patty Bergen in *Summer of My German Soldier* by Bette Greene. Patty, the daughter of a Jewish storekeeper and his wife in small-town Arkansas in the early 1940s, is a knotted, anxious child. She can't stop herself from telling sly, self-aggrandizing lies, and from compulsive attention-grabbing behavior with her parents, even though she knows that to draw their attention is to invite put-downs from her lazy, narcissistic mother and vicious abuse from her tense, embittered, neurotic father.

The only one who loves Patty, and who is wholeheartedly loved by her in return, is the family's black maid, Ruth. In fact, Patty sets herself against all the standards of her family and her community: She values the ease and warmth of black life above the status-conscious hypocrisies of the white townfolk; worse, she finds herself giving shelter to an escaped German prisoner of war, Anton Reiker, in careless defiance of her Jewish family's loathing of the Nazis. More than that, she loves the gentle, literate, decent, and caring Anton.

Summer of My German Soldier is a powerful book; it's been continually in print since it was published in 1973 and has surfaced as a television drama. Emotionally, it is devastating; the atmosphere of heat and petty malice in the bigoted little town is stiflingly vivid. Rereading it ten years after it first appeared, though, I realized that parts of it made me extremely uneasy: There is a sickly taste of masochistic relish in the way Patty, the narrator of her own story, describes in detail how her crazed father beats her with flailing fists and his leather belt.

It rings absolutely true, of course; neurotic families do fall into compulsive patterns, goading each other into the most feared reactions which they then perversely savor. But this is too raw to be illuminating. It almost exploits the sexual edge, the horror of the beatings, to keep the reader fascinated. And then, the gentleness and nobility of Anton beggars belief; not even Greene's vigorous prose can really make us believe in a German soldier on the run in the southern United States who would linger for days to cosset a disturbed twelve-year-old and give her lessons in literature.

The true strength of the story is in the side issue of Ruth's love for Patty; in the melodramatically bleak finale to Patty's escapade, when she is sentenced to reform school and her disgraced parents don't bother to visit her, there is an affecting scene in which Ruth arrives on the bus with a sack full of her fried chicken. Ruth has the power to make Patty believe, if only for a moment, that she is a worthwhile person. Patty has defied all her family's and her culture's values, but perhaps her gesture was too colored by neurotic neediness to signify true independence. At the end, she is only more isolated than ever, and with little more faith in herself or her future than at the beginning.

A more understated family novel—and somehow more realistic even though it includes a murder, a missing father, and a mysterious tombstone—is *The Way to Sattin Shore* by Philippa Pearce, one of the finest novelists writing for children today.

When the story begins, we see ten-year-old Kate Tranter coming home from school alone; she is beginning to be troubled and haunted by the secrets that eddy beneath the calm, working-class patterns of her family's life. It's curiously difficult to summon up the feeling and plot of *The Way to Sattin Shore;* the tone is oblique, matter-of-fact, but sensitive to the most glancing of impressions and the most fleeting ripples of disturbance in Kate's consciousness. A "beam of darkness" lies across her path: It is in fact her grandmother's malicious overseeing of the family's affairs—her meddling—that has laid this beam, literally and figuratively, in the way.

What is clear at the first is that Kate shies away from intimacy, except with her wonderfully true-to-life ginger cat, Syrup, and that the working out of the family mystery makes life open for her again. When her supposedly dead father is rediscovered and reunited with her mother (through Kate's frantic, last-minute effort) the completed family is like an arch through which Kate is finally free to walk out into the world.

Unlike Patty Bergen, Kate seems on the verge of solving the Oedipal triangle without ever having been conscious of it to begin with. *The Way to Sattin Shore* is a beautifully rounded, complete story. Though Kate was the agent, she is not the focus of the married couple's reunion; she is content that they should be caught up in one another, and her own concerns have moved from immediate gratifications to expectations of the future.

Yet none of this is stated explicitly; Pearce's control of dialogue and description is so masterful, the meanings so carefully dovetailed into the smallest incidents of plot, that a semicolon can speak volumes, even to an inexperienced reader.

A book like this gives the reader a feeling of quiet satisfaction because the movement of mind and heart go on beneath the surface of the action. We never feel pushed or manipulated by the author. The story is so thoroughly thought out that all actions and consequences seem to flow as naturally and unpremeditatedly as in daily life, yet with a more satisfying coherence.

Most of us are familiar with purely escapist reading in which we know we will be worked on by the author; in fact, we welcome the pumping up of tension or sexual excitement and their mechanical release through predictable plot devices, because that is precisely the stimulating diversion we sought. Less welcome is the sense of letdown and faint disquiet when we have finished the book—like the vague guilt we feel when we come blinking out of a second-rate movie on a sunny afternoon, having indulged our taste for trash at the expense of something more wholesome.

Books that work on a subtle, more challenging level like *The Way to Sattin Shore,* never leave the reader with that restless unease; while they satisfy the taste for excitement with the plot, they are also engaging the whole mind and attention of the reader with unstated moral complexities. The reader is led to notice the ways, however small, in which words, deeds, secrets, and intentions affect the lives of everyone in the story.

A story that has seized our attention this way leaves us feeling somehow lightened. Our compassion has been stirred; our sense of empathy stretched; our powers of observation honed. Good novels are wonderful because they give us so much easy emotional reward while at the same time letting us feel the natural pleasure of the workings of the mind.

And as every parent knows from those searching questions and earnest frowns, children are morally serious beings. At a certain stage of intellectual development, they insist on working out the rights and wrongs of the world for themselves. At that point, the novels that confront moral perplexities are among the most rewarding that a child can read.

The Indian in the Cupboard by Lynne Reid Banks is a good example of a story so captivating, so exciting, that the moral choices facing the main character seem to be just a more wrenching part of the action. Omri is the youngest of three brothers in an ordinary London family; we are catapulted into the action from the first line, when Omri's best friend, Patrick, gives him a disappointing birthday present—a used plastic Indian figurine, just like the dozens of plastic figures Omri already owns. His older brother gives him a tin medicine cabinet that he found in an alley. And that night, when Omri puts the Indian in the cupboard and locks it with an old curly-topped key given him by his mother, the Indian comes to life.

Of course, it is an old fantasy—the nursery toys coming alive—but Banks gives it a wonderful fresh immediacy by using a modern toy, and one that turns into a real person, though admittedly stereotyped. The transformation makes your pulse leap:

> He was crouching in the darkest corner . . . And he was alive
> . . . though he was trying to keep still, he was breathing
> heavily. His bare bronze shoulders rose and fell, and were
> shiny with sweat. The single feather sticking out of the back of
> his headband quivered, as if the Indian were trembling . . . As
> Omri peered close, and his breath fell on the tiny huddled
> figure, he saw it jump to its feet; its minute hand made a
> sudden, darting movement toward its belt and came to rest
> clutching the handle of a knife smaller than the shaft of a
> drawing pin.

The medicine cupboard is a true Pandora's box. Even before Omri can savor the miracle to its full, he finds himself caught up in the difficulties of having created life. The Indian is imperious, demanding: He asks for a horse, a long-house, a fire, food, and tools, and Omri must use all his wits to keep an Iroquois brave properly equipped from the scroungings of a modern suburban house. Almost at once, Omri is made to realize that a live person, no matter how small or powerless, can't be a toy. When he picks up Little Bull against his will ("his body was heavier now, warm and firm and full of life . . . through Omri's thumb, on the Indian's left side, he could feel his heart beating wildly, like a bird's") he senses Little Bull's humanity—and in the same instant, is struck by the insulting cruelty of handling him.

Life gets more complicated when Patrick insists on being let into the secret. Horses, a cowboy, and an old chief are brought to life, sometimes with disastrous consequences. The small creatures weep, fight, wound each other, stab Omri, shoot at Patrick. The pony, a wonderful creation, has to be taken outside for exercise and real grass; Omri desperately warns Little Bull against "mountain lions big enough to swallow the pony." He has learned to see the world, and the neighbor's cat, through Little Bull's eyes.

Children, who are the bottom of the pecking order, are naturally fascinated with miniatures; all the more enthralling when the miniatures breathe and ride horses; all the more shocking and sobering when they assume a life of their own, and small as they are, are no longer totally in the child's power. There is humor in *The Indian in the Cupboard,* and excitement to spare, but it has another, more difficult but enriching dimension that makes Omri a changed person.

Even more high-spirited is *Tuck Everlasting* by Natalie Babbit, an adventure that leads the overprotected ten-year-old Winnie Foster to discover the burgeoning world outside her gate and forces her to make a choice between mortality and eternal life. The narrative has the warm, amused tone of the rural tall tale: The meandering road that led to the village of Treegap, the narrator tells us, "was trod out long before by a herd of cows who were, to say the least, relaxed."

But there's a sophistication in the telling that makes us sit up and pay attention. Strong images crop up in every paragraph and the perspectives keep changing. The prim Foster family, for example, owns a forest with a magic ash tree hidden at its heart. The narrator wonders how deeply one can own any land—does one own a slice that goes down in ever narrowing dimensions to where it meets all the other pieces at the center of the earth? Or just a thin crust "under which the friendly worms have never heard of trespassing"?

The most startling perspective occurs to Winnie after she has been kidnapped by the delightfully rustic Tuck family. Winnie meets the charming and handsome seventeen-year-old Tuck son and explores the wood for the first time, discovering the deliciousness of life outside her fenced front yard ("The sweet earth opened out its wide four corners to her like the petals of a flower ready to be picked, and it shimmered with light and possibility until she was dizzy with it"). At this moment of rapture, the Tucks have to explain to her, reluctantly, how awful it is to drink from the magic spring, become immortal, and be excluded from the ripening circle of growth and decay. And just when Winnie realizes with horror that she too will die—"just go out, like the flame of a candle, and no use protesting"— she must listen to Pa Tuck explaining that the opposite is no good, either: "Us Tucks are stuck. We ain't part of the wheel no more. Dropped off, Winnie. Left behind."

Not all books of moral dilemma are as life-affirming and invigorating as *Tuck Everlasting.* Some, written with persuasive force and conviction, are deeply equivocal about the value of human life. A novel of total cynicism is so rare in juvenile literature that it forces one to stop and reconsider. Is there a place for stories of "grim realism"?

Robert Cormier's *The Chocolate War* won instant critical praise and wide popularity among teenage readers. Its nihilism seems to echo and satisfy the defiant rage of adolescents against the adult world's genteel hypocrisies. It's part of adolescence's task, after all, to repudiate authority, tear down simpering sanctimonies and smash the clay idols. Many responded hungrily to *The Chocolate War*'s emotional extremism, especially satisfying because its target is a classically repressive high school. We live in an increasingly totalitarian and fundamentalist world; exposure of massive corruption and official lying goes hand in hand with pious rhetoric. For an alert and critical teenager, Cormier's corruption-riddled Catholic high school must seem an apt and courageously chosen symbol of institutional evil.

Still, I am made uneasy by the monotone voice, the patterns of imagery, and underlying philosophy in *The Chocolate War*. In another context, Ursula K. LeGuin wrote:

> Novels of despair are intended, most often, to be admonitory, but I think they are, like pornography, most often escapist, in that they provide a substitute for action, a draining-off of tension. That is why they sell well. They provide an excuse to scream, for writer and reader . . . a mindless response. When you start screaming, you have stopped asking questions.

In a sense, *The Chocolate War* is one long scream. Jerry Renault is a lonely teenager at a Catholic boys' high school. His mother has recently died, his father is a repressed pharmacist incapable of communication, and the school is run by an unholy alliance of sadistic, manipulative priests and a powerful secret student society, called the Vigil. Jerry is afraid to become a cipher, a nobody like his father. He wants to "make a difference in the universe," and that's why he holds out against the annual money-raising chocolate sale and refuses to sell his share. In the end, the priests and the even more monstrously cruel boys of the Vigil punish him for daring to take a stand; utterly alone and beaten into a pulp ("he collapsed like a hunk of meat cut loose from a butcher's hook"), Jerry is defeated.

The overall effect of the book's language and imagery is a tone of near-hysteria, an unremitting, sickened revulsion. Jerry's own values are no humanistic beacon shining out in the murk. Quite the contrary. "Jacking off" makes him queasy with shame, and the girl he admires from afar ends by disgusting him when she uses the word "crap." He despises his father for what seems to the reader, after all, to be a normal human response—the father has taken the phone off the hook in the middle of the night to stop a persistent obscene caller.

Jerry sees this as humiliatingly weak, "giving in" "letting them win." Only one thing gives Jerry pleasure, and that is the "clean" thrill of playing football. On the field, "bruised and battered or grimy and dirty," Jerry feels "part of something." Only when the coach gives him the supreme accolade of calling him "a skinny little son-of-a-bitch" does Jerry feel "absolute bliss, absolute happiness."

We've met this Hemingway ethos before in modern fiction; it is the predominant tone of many thrillers, and Jerry's macho individualism (standing alone and making himself heard in the universe is his one goal) is an echo of Ayn Rand. Even the depiction of the school as rotted through with evil feels unconvincingly melodramatic; there's more than a touch of the B-movie, with its stock villains, about the Satanic priests and the cool, sneering, criminally conscienceless members of the Vigil.

No, the energy of the book, the force and conviction of it, spring from something that runs below the surface: a powerful revulsion from the tainted human body and soul. Much of the prose jogs along at the level of overheated cliché; at Mrs. Renault's funeral, for example, father and son "weep without shame, out of a nameless need" and Jerry feels "anger . . . so deep and sharp in him that it drove out sorrow. He wanted to bellow at the world . . . topple buildings, split the earth open, tear down trees." The overstatement feels mechanical and emotionally hollow.

But elsewhere, when it comes to bodily functions, Cormier has a piledriver energy. Sweat crawls like bugs on foreheads; cruelty and beatings constantly make boys vomit "like geysers"; breath always reeks of bacon or pizza; a poor couple's apartment "smells like pee . . . What the hell were they living for?"; a bully (he "gets horny" when he beats someone up); likes to leave the toilet unflushed so the next boy will have to look at his mess; an obscene caller hangs up and the dial tone is "a fart in Jerry's ear." Physical disgust serves a Swiftian purpose as an expression of spiritual horror.

This thoroughgoing rage with humanity is rare in juvenile fiction, and many reviewers see it as a wholesome antidote to the maudlin manipulations and glib solutions of too much teenage mass-market fiction. Setting aside my own personal dislike of the book, I can see that *The Chocolate War* is provocative, and that it boldly reflects at least one little-discussed truth about adolescence—the wincing revulsion from adult bodily functions. Children and prepubescents are often upset and repelled by adult secretions, bad breath, astonishing amounts of urine—harbingers all of the body's surge into physical sexuality, and its inexorable march toward death and decay.

What disturbs me about these recognitions in *The Chocolate War* is that there is no authorial distance, no calmer or more accepting voice to lend perspective. (Undoubtedly, this lack of a moderating "adult perspective" is one of the attractions for some young readers.) As a result, it seems to me that books like *The Chocolate War* masquerade as profound analyses of moral choice; in fact, there is no moral choice to be made, no possibility of meaningful action or redemption. In all of Jerry Renault's lonely heroics, physical violence is seen as his only recourse, and even that is futile; if he achieves any victory over the always exterior evil he tries to confront, it is only in accepting vicious brutality as inevitable.

The question of evil is certainly not taboo for children's literature; as usual, the real issue is not specific content, but the skill, depth, and subtlety of its literary treatment. In the hands of a talented author, evil can be legitimately presented with the anguishing immediacy and inwardness it deserves. Paula Fox's *The Slave Dancer* stands as one of the most truthful accounts of evil in children's fiction, and yet the final message is far from the ugly, bleak despair of Cormier. Indeed, what makes *The Slave Dancer* so exceptional, so haunting and important, is that there is no final message.

The story tells of thirteen-year-old Jesse Bollier, who is press-ganged from the streets of New Orleans to serve as a fife player on a slave ship, the *Moonlight*. At first, after his brutal introduction to shipboard life, Jesse is comforted by a kindly seeming steward, Benjamin Stout: "You'll see some bad things, but if you didn't see them, they'd still be happening, so you might as well," is Stout's resonantly familiar self-justification for participating in a criminal trade in human beings.

Jesse's new life on board the ship, on its way to the Bight of Benin, is a carefully detailed confusion of the grotesque, the frightening, the uncomfortable, and the exhilarating. He learns a strange new vocabulary ("I especially liked the words skysail and moonsail and turned them over in my mouth as though I was licking honey"), and comes to realize that the "coarse, bawling" Purvis, who kidnapped him, is a friend and that the smooth-tongued Stout is a deadly enemy. And he watches helplessly when Purvis is savagely beaten, in the tender golden light of a radiant sunset, for a crime committed by Stout.

All this moral confusion and anxiety is a fit preparation for the worse that is to come, because when the slaves are brought on board, everything Jesse is told is at war with his immediate perceptions. The crew rationalize that "blacks ain't like us, and that's the truth," that they're "mad and bite their own flesh" or "can will themselves to die." Jesse must reject the beliefs of his closest friends and protectors on board the *Moonlight*.

Still, the boy's compassionate horror fights with his own revulsion at the stench of the holds, whose excrement buckets he must empty. He once yearned to peep through New Orleans windows at women getting dressed; now that he is free to stare at men, women, and children chained naked and helpless, he is appalled at their vulnerability and deeply shaken with shame. The torment, the cries, the music he must pipe while the slaves are forced to exercise their shackled limbs in a ghastly, shuffling dance—at first this horror drives him into a rage of hatred against the victims. And this is a more terrible and profound truth than anything in Cormier's good-versus-bad world, and a more important one, too.

Then Jesse throws down his fife and refuses to play; when he is beaten for his small rebellion, his own salt tears bring him back to himself, to a recognition that he is as vulnerable and as captive as the slaves. The mounting horror of the voyage, with disease, death, and cruelty vividly evoked for us, is made bearable because we see it through Jesse's eyes as he grows more and more deeply alienated from the ship and its morally corrupt crew.

Fox is courageous enough not to settle for an easy upbeat ending to such an appalling story. Jesse does make his amends in the only way open to him by saving a slave boy's life when the ship goes down, but there is no absolution of the kind he yearns for, for him or any of his countrymen. A particularly poignant episode is one in which a black runaway slave, living secretly in the bush, rescues the two shipwrecked boys and tenderly cares for the African youth. Jesse yearns to be part of their powerful communion; his whiteness, his participation in the slave trade—however unwillingly—excludes him. He is treated with grave dignity, but cannot be part of their heart-whole intimacy. His sense of grievous, permanent loss strikes me as a true, if often submerged, note in American history.

Jesse takes up his life once more, supports his widowed mother, learns a healing trade (pharmacy), and moves to the North. He is not exempt from his nation's guilt, but neither is the value of life utterly negated. *The Slave Dancer* is an unforgettable book; it is, in a curious way, uplifting, because it takes its young readers seriously enough to make them feel how thoroughly corrupt and corrupting an evil slavery was—without wallowing in the lurid—and does not shirk the moral complexity of the issues.

Paula Fox has a particular genius for depicting the troubled conscience. In a recent novel, *The One-Eyed Cat*, she takes an unlikely and unpromising cast of characters and a plot that sounds positively soporific in summary, and yet makes them not only illuminating but gripping. A sensitive eleven-year-old boy, Ned, whose father is an overbearingly saintly minister in rural upstate New York, commits a tiny crime: He takes a forbidden Daisy air rifle, tries shooting it outside in the dark one night, and hits—perhaps?—a moving shadow. Later, an injured cat with only one eye and dried blood on its cheek turns up in the yard of a neighbor.

Add to this scenario a sweet-natured mother who leads a shadowy existence in a wheelchair upstairs, crippled by rheumatoid arthritis; an insinuating horror of a housekeeper, Mrs. Scallop, who smugly preens herself ("That's just the way I am, I hate to see anyone hurt") just after she has hooked a poisoned barb into the flesh of her conversational victim; and a lonely, aged neighbor for whom Ned does chores. It all sounds lethally dispiriting.

But the characters are a triumph of roundedness. They constantly develop, turn, change, and surprise us, and Ned's prickly conscience is the motor that drives forward a plot that deepens and becomes more absorbing with each page.

Unlike Jesse, Ned does have a way to expiate his crime, and though he, too, comes to hate the victim—the cat whom he so obsessively keeps alive during the long winter after the shooting—he is rewarded, in the slow course of his penitential labors, with several sweet kinds of love. If children can get past the rather drab opening, *The One-Eyed Cat*, is a beautifully, subtly elaborated story of a boy's coming to terms with his own losses and gaining believably in depth and strength.

Children do not "catch" morals, good or bad, from books, and it would be a shame if parents began to pop books down their children's throats like pills. But books can be a thrilling adjunct to that long journey one makes from about the ages of seven to fourteen, the years when "Who am I? Can I be different? What do other families believe?" are urgent questions. Books let us see how other people grow towards conclusions and solve dilemmas. More than that, they make us *feel* every step of the way; it's as though we could live a dozen lives simultaneously, and draw on the wealth of all of them to help shape our own selves. The literary choices we help our children make are, therefore, important in more ways than one.

I don't mind if my children experience Jerry Renault's nauseated loathing of the world. But I'm glad they have a chance to put that in perspective, that they can confront true evil (slavery was evil; are mean teachers in the same league?) along with Jesse Bonnier and, like him, still taste the freshness of the sea air and know it is good.

Chapter 6

ADVENTURE: THE GREAT GAME

Men say he does magic, but that should not touch thee. Go up the hill and ask. Here begins the Great Game.

Rudyard Kipling, Mahbub Ali to Kim, in *Kim*

The Great Game. What Mahbub Ali meant was Kim's participation in the British spy network in Imperial India, but, as Kipling wrote, Kim would have called it an adventure "if he had known the word." Adult life, independent life, "real" life as seen from the perspective of the child who is waiting for everything to begin, is Great Game and adventure enough.

There were times, when I had grown just old enough to think beyond the cave-coziness of the family, that my heart skipped and lurched with excitement at the mere thought of the possibilities of life. Adventure stories for the young are surrogate journeys into the wonderful world; a child too young to ride the subway alone can bucket across stormy seas of the imagination, always with those mute questions at the back of the mind: Could I be this brave? what would it be like? will I ever ...? Adults, too, read adventure stories, but because the realms of possibility have dwindled for them, the adrenalin has to be stimulated with substitute drugs—sex and violence (detective thrillers) or nostalgia (Agatha Christie). And although adult book lovers may savor deeper and more complex literary pleasures, child readers are luckier in this: Their adventure stories still have the potent promise of Christopher Columbus's world, when half the map was still blank.

The kindergarten child's adventures are usually on the small and intimate scale, close to home, where drama is found in familiar small conflicts or mishaps or in the fears of what may be underneath the bed. The popularity of *Little Tim and the Brave Sea Captain* by Ed-

131

ward Ardizzone, however, points to the allure of the Great Game even for a seven- or eight-year-old. It is a fantasy, but a touchingly earnest one, that a small boy should stow away on a great ship, work his passage home, survive a wreck and a lifeboat rescue, and calmly send a telegram to let his parents know he'll be arriving by train.

Unlike the James Bond fantasies of grown boys, these are dreams of competence, hardships endured, and sensible heroism: Those are real workmanlike knots that Tim learns on the beach from his old friend Captain McFee, and later, when the the ship is storm-tossed in a raging sea, the Captain minces no words. "Come, stop crying and be a brave boy. We are bound for Davey Jones's locker and tears won't help." And what delicious adult license and anarchy is earned: There may be seasickness and hard sloppy work in the galley for Tim, but comforting cocoa waits at the end of the day—and he gets to sleep in his clothes!

Alas, almost all adventures, for the youngest children as for the oldest, pit boys against hardship, boys against danger, boys against every kind of villainy. It is the rare author, male or female, Victorian or postmodern, who can envision the heroism or grit of a girl. Perhaps for that reason as well as for its own rousing merits, I cherish a picture book called *The Funny Little Woman*, an old Japanese tale retold by Arlene Mosel and illustrated gleefully—and with delicate, abundant detail—by Blair Lent.

For no better reason, it seems, than her lighthearted character, the funny little woman who loves to laugh chases a rollaway dumpling down into the fearsome underworld, where she is captured by the wicked Oni, a kind of spirit monster. Her silly but endearing laughter as she careers headlong into danger makes her seem childlike but also invincible. Nothing could be more satisfying than the way she makes good her escape at last, carrying with her the magic paddle that enables her to open a dumpling store and become the richest woman in Japan.

As in the very best adventure stories, the narrative is buttressed by rich details—grinning Oni, ghoulish statues, fascinating trivia of Japanese rural life, like the cottage cooking arrangements—inventively conveyed through pictures rather than words. And, both physically and metaphorically, there are several levels of action. While full-page colored illustrations show the laughing little woman working as a dumpling chef for the Oni, we see a whole year passing aboveground in small black-and-white sketches at the top of the page. An old man comes vainly to look for his friend as autumn leaves fall; then the winter winds blow around her empty little house, and no smoke rises from her hearth. When, finally, spring comes, and flowers sprout from the neglected thatch roof, the old man hopefully returns, and is there to lend her a hand as she climbs up from the hole in the ground. It's a lovely wordless counterplot to her adventures, and lends an extra dimension of emotion to her disappearance and return.

A cozy, rural warmth fairly radiates from the adventure of *Cliptail*, but this beginner's book by the noted French-Canadian author Gabrielle Roy has no mushy center; indeed, there's a streak of agrarian ruthlessness in the story that makes it all the more tantalizing. When old Berthe makes "a sad decision" about the latest litter of barn kittens, the young female cat Cliptail takes the lesson to heart. She carefully hides her next litter far from the house. Cliptail is wily, resourceful, and fierce—her courage is emphasized more than her motherliness—and is magnificent when she leads her kittens to safety during a dramatic snowstorm. There is a distinctively French-Canadian voice in this story, too, a kind of story-teller-by-the-stove tone, that at first seems to intrude on the drama and then seems part of its individual flavor.

Emotional depth is rare and has a worth far beyond rubies when it comes to modern adventure stories written for children; typically, they provide an experience more like taking snuff than reading a fine novel. First they create a pleasurable tension and then move right along to a satisfyingly convulsive resolution. The outstanding exception, and the innovative standard by which all others were to be measured, was, of course, the *Swallows and Amazons* series by Arthur Ransome, which made its debut in 1930.

The stories are almost too well known to need description: They concern a family of middle-class children who spend their vacations in England's Lake District, where they sail a small dinghy and are allowed to camp out on an island. The Swallows—John, Susan, Titty, and Roger Walker who name themselves after their boat—join forces with the Amazons, Nancy and Peggy Blackett, in a summer-long adventure of pretend piracy and castaway island life. Eleven other books in the series introduce new characters and locations; there are two notable fantasy adventures *(Missee Lee* and *Peter Duck)* and two that involve some engaging working-class boys in the Norfolk Broads.

It's hard now, when so many other pleasures have blurred the sharp immediacy of the fictional life, to imagine the impact of these stories on those of us who read them for the first time as children in the 1940s. Passionate involvement is not too strong a phrase for the feelings that still echo when I pick up those sturdy books with their spacious type face, leisurely chapters, inky and vigorously primitive drawings by Ransome himself, and the indispensable maps on the end-papers.

Here were whole families of children who played the pretend games for which I never could find a partner: No one on my street wanted to leave secret code messages under a boulder or understood the thrill of transforming our tiny backyards into the pitching deck of a galleon. That was the particular magic of the books. Though Robert Louis Stevenson's *Treasure Island* is richer in scope, drama, language, and moral complexity, and stands as an unparalleled voyage of adventure, it was too distanced from me by time and place and its relentlessly all-male cast to exert the same spell of possibility. Here were children not so different from me (or the thousands of other devotees) as to be inimitable. Their adventures were all the more heady because they were only one step away from my own daydreams.

We first meet this enviable family as Roger, age seven, and the youngest of the expedition, tacks like a sailing ship up the hill to the farmhouse, where his mother has just received a telegram from their naval captain father in response to their request to go camping on Wild Cat Island. BETTER DROWNED THAN DUFFERS IF NOT DUFFERS WON'T DROWN read that cryptic message, committed to heart by hundreds and thousands of Swallows and Amazons followers. At first I was baffled, then deliciously shocked, and the message has never lost its punch. What a breathtaking mixture of parental insouciance and confidence! I was hooked.

In my own childhood reading experience, only Edith Nesbit's fantasy-adventures rivaled the intense pleasure offered by these sympathetic portraits of child life. How obligingly those kindly or gruff adults stood back at a distance that allowed freedom but guaranteed safety. And yet how forbearingly they entered into the game, content to play the role of friendly natives who would regularly supply the adventurers with pemmican and ginger-beer "grog."

Ransome was an outstanding journalist of his day, a prose writer of pellucid technical clarity. He could make you know in your fingers and toes how to sail a dinghy, rig a leading light, invent an electric alarm bell, or smelt copper. And he could invest all these vigorous practical pursuits with an intoxicating sense of romance.

Modern critics have sometimes huffed that Ransome's appeal was limited by his middle-class cast of characters. That is a dreadfully mistaken view of fiction. Some of Ransome's most endearing characters were boatmen and working-class Norfolk children, but even that is beside the point: Fiction transcends boundaries, and, as a lower-middle-class urban Canadian child who had never seen a sailboat or even been allowed to play outside after dusk, my world was immeasurably enlarged by reading Ransome.

Ardently, I learned to sail and to sempahore from the Swallows and the Amazons. Thirty years later, when I finally had a chance to sit at the tiller of a dinghy, I knew the heft, the feel, and the arcane language as though I were a secret inhabitant of a nautical world. As indeed I was.

Though Ransome was hailed by his contemporaries, more recent critics have commented slightingly about his powers of characterization. Sheila Egoff, for example, thinks that Ivan Southall's anxious adolescents are more three-dimensional than Ransome's solid citizens. It is true that the Swallows and the Amazons were sexually latent far longer than one might have expected. But for ten- and eleven-year-old readers, that seems eminently appropriate. Furthermore, one measure of the successful creation of a character is whether he or she takes on a rounded, independent existence in the reader's mind long after the book is replaced on the shelf. Here I am not a fair judge: Perhaps Ransome's people are still so warmly familiar to me because I met them when I was an impressionable child. Still, I would bet that many young readers today, freshly encountering Southall's cast of characters, find as I do that they blur into one another and slip out of memory.

The Walkers, the Blacketts, and the *D*'s (and even the little brown-sailed, gaff-rigged *Swallow,* a character in her own right) have staying power, not because Ransome drew them with correctly up-to-date psychological verisimilitude, complete with Oedipal complexes and difficult parents, but because they were so real to him, and there was so much of himself in them. John's dogged, conscientious, earnest character was an illumination to me—the youngest and least responsible of my own family; his sense of deep obligation to a moral code, part naval and part familial, was expressed so compellingly in his speech and actions that until my midteens he was a sort of internalized exemplar for me. I think some adult reviewers may have overlooked the touching quality that John's character holds for children. At an age when self-absorption is the rule, John's thoroughly believable idealism is a weighty counterpoise. The personalities of the others carried equal force: Titty's imagination and courage and Dorothea's authorial passions confirmed my own worth, literary landlubber that I was; Nancy's galumphing hoydenism inspired me to greater liberties, and fierce, wayward little Bridget, the youngest, spoke straight to my impatient soul.

The emotional impact is at its most intense in the gripping *We*

Didn't Mean to Go to Sea, in which the four Walkers suffer extremes of seasickness, fear, and exhaustion when their boat is swept out to sea and they must cross the North Sea in a gale. The climax is Ransome's most moving. Safe in Holland, exhausted, but triumphant, the Walkers meet their father and brace themselves for the worst reprimand of their lives. Captain Walker listens to their story, puts a hand on John's shoulder, and says "You'll make a seaman yet, my son." I didn't know until I read Ransome's autobiography that he had a humiliating childhood, the disappointingly clumsy son of a heartily athletic father. He must have put all his childhood yearning into that one moment; its insight and depth of feeling flow straight into the child reader's heart.

Another of Ransome's attractions is the gentle quality of his humor; one of my favorites (then and now), was *Missee Lee,* possibly because she was the first female pirate, not to mention the first pirate who yearned to attend Cambridge, whom I had ever met, and possibly because of the delicious humor and poignancy of her situation. I hope that the pidgin English spoken by the Chinese pirates doesn't ban *Missee Lee* from current book lists; so dogmatic have we become about culturally correct attitudes that even a master storyteller like Kipling has been allowed to drift away to that special oblivion reserved for jingoists. Mild stereotyping is not always malign; Missee Lee, for example, may say "velly pleased" and "Camblidge," but her portrait is drawn with so much life and affection that no one could carry away a warped impression, as one might from a racially contemptuous author like Enid Blyton (see chapter 10, on bad books).

I would make the same plea, even more strongly, for Kipling's *Kim.* The author was an empire booster and a chauvinist of the silliest sort in his conscious opinions, but *Kim* breathes out a different air entirely, an air of wide tolerance, made palpable by Kim's devotion to his Indian, Persian, Afghan, and Tibetan friends.

Kim is not a book for the halting reader, but for older children unafraid of challenge, it is mesmerizing. This is the quintessence of adventure: a free spirit who defies the prison of identity, a chameleon, master by the age of nine of a dozen disguises and as many dialects, able to vanish in a twinkling through the teeming crowds of the bazaar—the ultimate privileged insider and knower of secrets. He has no parents (he is a gifted survivor by his wits) but is watched over by several admiring mentors, men of special and mysterious skills themselves.

Because Kim is spotted by these men as perfect spy material, he is made an initiate of several worlds—educated in a British-style boarding school, trained by a Persian "healer of sick pearls" and an

Afghan horse dealer, and yet, during school vacations, allowed the freedom of the road to follow his saintly Tibetan holy man.

Only against the background of nineteenth-century India, with its beauty, squalor, spirituality, and chaotic variety of people and cultures, could Kipling have made believable such a protean child. Of course, he has language on his side: the rolling, rhythmic, highly artificial but enchantingly colored speech he creates for his mythical India. There is no lack of excitement—thefts, disguises, secret messages, murders, desperate escapes, slyly comic contretemps—all leading up to the humor of a classic "sting" that forms the climax and setpiece of the novel. But what makes it all so hypnotic, aside from Kim's cleverness and the exotic language, is atmosphere. We are ready to believe anything once Kipling has drawn us into that world of smoky dusks, lantern-lit bazaars, perfumed brothels, oxcarts, temples, and the high thin icy air of the Himalayas.

Against such a dazzling variety of sensual riches, North America is positively underprivileged as a background for adventure; we have nothing to compare with Kim's ability to enter other people's worlds. Typically (and especially in Canada) our adventure stories link two teenage boys, one white and one native, against the challenge of the frontier. Almost always, the native boy, seen through the white boy's eyes, is romanticized as the teacher of lessons: He is wise in the lore of the wilds, patient, stoic, in tune with nature. The white boy, made vulnerable by the threatening wilderness, learns to be less impulsive or greedy, and to absorb some (but never all) of the native wisdom of the earth.

These stories are eagerly read by youngsters seeking a straightforward, energetic plot. All, however, are marred by bad or hasty writing, a crude sense of character development, and a flatly exterior view of North American natives.

Farley Mowat's *Lost in the Barrens* avoids condescension but shows signs of hasty writing; some excruciating clichés ("fairly stuttering with excitement") are repeated twice or more, and there are constant jarring lacunae in the time structure of the narrative. Jamie MacNair, seventeen, is eating dinner with his Cree friend Awasin when someone rushes in with the news that a party of Chipewayans has been sighted an hour's distance away. Awasin "bolts his dinner" and runs outside to meet "the Chips," who seem to have miraculously arrived on the instant.

Perhaps adventure stories of this ilk are written at the same furious clip at which they are meant to be devoured ("It took a moment for the idea to register on Jamie's mind, then it registered. A wave of excitement swept over him. Here was the possibility of a real adventure"). Clichés speed the action along with no need for the reader to linger over details or atmosphere. The point, in any case, is not to enter into the characters or their world—the depth isn't there—but to learn something of the survival techniques that keep the boys alive in the harsh landscape of the barrens.

The same lessons are taught in *Frozen Fire* by James Houston, with the added *Treasure Island* fillip that the white man's greed for gold is a threat to survival, not only in its depradations of nature but more immediately in the adventure of the two boys, Matthew Morgan and Kayak, who are lost in the white wilderness beyond Frobisher Bay. Again, we have the flattering physical description so familiar from adult thrillers and detective novels: Matthew is "tall . . . with grey watchful eyes . . . sandy hair, slim with narrow hips, a flair to his shoulders that made you know he would be strong. He was the fastest runner in his school . . ."

These descriptions are a lazy shorthand: They tell the reader whom to admire, and absolve him from the imaginative work of learning about the hero's character. However, like Mowat, Houston offers a convincing friendship between the two boys, who overcome the cultural gulf that divides them, with the added pleasure of their growing skill and competence as they defy all odds to survive. Compared to the formula pap now being churned out to exploit the young teenage market, these books, despite their literary deficiencies, do express an honest commitment on the part of their authors.

For true adventure, though, they can't begin to compare to the shocking immediacy of a native-written survival story, *Harpoon of the Hunter* by Markoosie. The voice of the narrator is so fresh, so startlingly different, that it makes one realize the tragic loss we suffer in not having more native fiction. Here, for the first time, we are inside the Inuit mind. The story reminds me of *Nkwala*, in which Edith Sharp made a valiant effort to show us the inner development of an Indian boy's courage and resilience, but even that cannot equal the vibrant truth of Markoosie, scraped bare of all the sentiment and false glamor with which natives are usually drawn.

Ironically, when authors like Houston or Mowat show us Indian youths through the eyes of white boys, the natives' skills are so unquestioned they are curiously diminished; courage seems less impressive when it is a birthright conferred along with skin color. Markoosie's hero, sixteen-year-old Kamik, is three-dimensional; we don't need to be told what he looks like—no athletic shoulders or slim hips necessary—because we learn to know him through his speech and his actions.

And we see him fully in context. His mother Ooramik, father

Suluk, friends, and tribe all have vital roles to play. When a rabid polar bear menaces the stormbound settlement, Suluk, accompanied by Kamik, leads a hunting party to track and kill the rogue bear. We follow the hunters in their perilous trek, but the narrative leaps back and forth, in rapid vignettes, between the settlement and the hunt. This technique gives us a powerful sense of the fragility of the widely scattered human life in the Arctic wastes, and of the urgent bonds that link these vulnerable humans. Even the usually mushy idea that hunter and the hunted are mystically connected—two forms of hot-blooded life dwarfed by the frozen immensity—has honest immediacy here.

Ooramik, the mother, does not drop out of sight when the hunters leave. She heartens herself with the close friendship of another hunter's wife, and, when the days drag out, she persuades the others to seek help to rescue the now missing hunting party. Ooramik herself volunteers to undertake the crossing of a river on treacherous, swiftly moving ice floes. It is a rare record of native life that gives us so vivid a sense of the conversation of the Inuit, the mutual dependence and dignity of men and women, their ways of argument and courtesy, the pared-to-the-bone directness of lives played out in such harsh surroundings. Factual accounts exist, of course, but here the truth springs to life under the shaping hands of an artist.

Kamik's growth into manliness is seen minute-by-minute as he anxiously asks his older companions in the hunting party if they think all will survive; "There is always a chance as long as we are alive," one replies. "We have two chances—to make it on foot or to be found by others if they decide to search for us." When they face the necessity to eat their dogs, and Kamik balks, a hunter tells him that they have all been forced to conquer a similar revulsion.

The reader is made to feel how desperately earned is Inuit expertise and stoicism. Every mistake made by Kamik and his comrades has painful results. It's astonishing how abundant is the sense of life in this slender, eighty-one page book. Not only do we share Kamik's suffering as he struggles back alone and without food, but we are also given a charming picture of young and lively Putooktee, helping her father lead the perilous river-crossing rescue party, "jumping expertly from one piece of ice to another" with such verve that she brings a smile to the face of one of the young men.

Swiftly, with the urgency imposed by Arctic life, Putooktee and the rescued Kamik fall in love. Their coming together—the exhausted, emotion-racked Kamik and the confident girl—is as frankly simple as all the rest of the story. "This is the first time I ever saw a really pretty girl." "Thank you," Putooktee said. "And I like you,

Kamik." The end of the story is heartbreaking, but as unforgettably honest as all that gone before.

Heroism of this almost mythic quality has all but vanished from modern children's literature but that, of course, does not mean that it is not missed; note the adoration of small children for cartoon "superheroes." It is worth searching the library shelves for heroes just as alluring but less shallow than Mr. T. Why not Robin Hood, for example, instead of Rocket Robin Hood or Batman and his version of Robin? Granted, it's hard to find a completely satisfactory retelling of the Robin Hood story; no prose version that I know of has that sweet wild note of Alfred Noyes's poem, "A Song of Sherwood," with its sun-dappled arcadian longing for the greenwood life.

Antonia Fraser's modern retelling is done in brief episodic fashion, simple enough for young readers, but lacking enchantment and gallantry. Howard Pyle's Victorian version, filled with right good ale and gray goose feathers, has the spirit of the leafy glades intact, but is so awash in forsoothery and inverted sentences that it is all but unreadable today. Between these two extremes is the naive but exciting first novel by the excellent historical novelist Geoffrey Trease; his *Bows Against the Barons* dismisses the struggle between Saxons and Normans as irrelevant (it's the peasants versus the aristocrats instead) and makes Robin Hood's merry band into a sort of medieval International Brigade. At least it captures some of the subversive energy that makes Robin Hood so compelling a legend.

The fullest and fairest retelling of them all is by Roger Lancelyn Green, in *The Adventures of Robin Hood*. Green has gone back to the original sources, enriched his tale with scraps of ballad and medieval song, and faithfully recorded all the incidents (including the triumphant return of Richard Coeur de Lion) missing from many other versions. His sturdy prose does justice to all the characters, not overlooking Maid Marian as brave archer and venturesome spirit. Some readers may feel he has been too thorough: Before the exciting stories begin, the reader must wade through a rather wordy historical scene setting, and the prose never reaches great emotional or poetic intensity. Perhaps, after all, there can never be a completely perfect version of this elementally important story, one that would draw together all its essential threads of mystery, pastoral, anarchic freedom, and the thirst for social justice.

Green at least avoids anachronism splendidly, and anachronism is the great stumbling block of historical novels. Historic settings are ideal for the child's adventure tale, since they offer so many more possibilities for heroic and significant action than prosaic modernity, but how to evoke a period flavor without lapsing into mere "By our faith!" quaintness? And without the decorative trappings, how to avoid a sterile contemporary tone?

Leon Garfield, one of the most energetically imaginative of modern authors, does it by creating a crowded eighteenth-century London, reeking of smog and skulduggery, and giving his quick-witted characters a cockney dialect that wryly undercuts any period pomposities. Here is *Smith* himself, age twelve:

> Smith had a turn of speed that was remarkable, and a neatness in nipping down an alley or vanishing in a court that had to be seen to be believed. Not that it was often seen, for Smith was rather a sooty spirit of the violent and ramshackle town, and inhabited the tumbledown mazes about fat St. Paul's like the subtle air itself.

Smith, like many of Garfield's characters, is an amoral urchin with grubby face and quick fingers. It is his curiosity and compassion—innate human goodness as opposed to conventional morality—that lead him into his Gothic adventures and that set in motion the breathlessly convoluted plot. Typically of Garfield, Smith is keen on the trail of a hidden treasure, but his warmheartedness waylays him. He gets his treasure at the end, but only after forsaking the hunt to save his intended victim's life. Garfield's fantastical facility with language, and his ghoulishly gleeful humor ("Ere's my 'and, you blind old Justice, you!" Smith offers to a sightless magistrate) lend an extraordinary vivacity to his characters.

Smith, determined to learn to read (for the most mercenary of motives) first approaches the dignitary best known to him: Mr. Jones, the Newgate hangman. "Mind your Ps and Qs" snarls the gent, chasing him away. "Bleeding scholars!" thinks Smith. "Want to keep everything to themselves!"

The treasure is even more illusory in Garfield's *John Diamond*, in which a properly brought up young country boy runs away to London and falls into that murky "maze" of back streets that is Garfield's favorite locale. William Jones, the twelve-year-old hero, takes the *Treasure Island* moral one step further. Not only is the supposed treasure an unending source of grief and violence, but it turns out never to have existed. The real treasure discovered, inadvertently, is the friendship of the ragamuffin Shot-in-the-Head, one of Garfield's most engaging creations. He looks like a large rat in his flapping black coat, with his ragged teeth, sharp little tongue, and tufts of orangeish hair "as though someone had set out to burn him down, for health reasons, and left him smouldering."

Shot-in-the-Head is a solemn little roof-dweller, the strangest babysitter in the universe, and a true heart. His occupation, as he explains to the baffled William, is "snick-an-lurk" . . . pickpocketing. His outlaw perceptions, expressed in terse cockney, are a marvel of humor. When the terrified William asks if it's true that people are cut to pieces in one fearsome alley, Shot-in-the-Head replies, seriously, "Yus. But allus very small."

More strictly historical than Garfield, whose Dickensian London seems to float in some mirthful mist of nontime, is the prolific Rosemary Sutcliff. She is unparalleled in her mastery of the form: In each of her novels, particularly those of Saxon and Roman Britain, she brings alive a complete and spacious world, richly and startlingly detailed, in which the reader can move about, observe, sense, and participate in another time and place. Her power lies not only in making us intimate with the daily life of a Bronze Age boy or a Roman centurion, but in letting us see the world through their eyes.

In *Warrior Scarlet,* one of her most emotionally vivid works, the boy Drem must win his place among the warriors of his age group. But he has a paralyzed right arm, which makes it impossible for him to hold simultaneously the traditional weapons of his people, a bronze shield and a dagger.

Sutcliff's prose is lyrical, plangent, almost dangerously romantic, but she certainly makes us see and sense the rolling downs and black night forests of primeval Britain. The landscape is always lit by flaring sunsets or cool gray dawns; when hunters return from the marshes to the huts in the blue summer dusk "a stain of light came to meet them thick and golden like honey trickling from a tipped jar"; there are the flickering illuminations of mutton-fat lanterns, torches, Beltane fires, and shafts of dusty sunlight when the turf roof is rolled back.

It is a complete sensory world, populated by the hard-working shepherds, (the Little Dark People who are the more ancient conquered tribe of the place); by wandering Irish bronzesmiths; by priests who orchestrate the exotically detailed, hypnotic secret rites of initiation; by chieftains and kings. They command our total belief because we see their grip on Drem. We are never taken outside his knowledge of this world and his acceptance of its ways. All the more dreadful and desolating when Drem fails his ritual wolf slaying and becomes an outcast. Without his rigid role of warrior, without his prescribed place in the tribe, he is nothing. "A boy who failed in his Wolf Slaying and did not die was dead to the Tribe. It was the custom." Drem is exiled and must go to live with the despised shepherds on the hill. And his redemption, at last, is also true to the ethos of the tribe; only by stoic endurance and individual heroism does he regain his identity, now enriched by a deeper, gentler resignation learned from his work with the shepherds.

In the portrait of Drem, there is a forcefulness of empathy that is almost unbearable. When my own son, a precocious reader, read *Warrior Scarlet* at the age of five, I found him in anguished tears over the opened book. "I can't go on," he explained between gasping sobs. "Drem has failed his wolf slaying." I had to hold him on my lap to comfort him and read the next chapter aloud before he could bear to go on by himself.

Perhaps he already sensed how different he was and would be from his peers, set aside and "outcast" not only by his giftedness but also by a lateral lisp which, with his sunny and outgoing character, he seemed outwardly to ignore. Three years later, when he undertook on his own to work with a speech therapist, he concentrated with such ferocious self-discipline that his speech defect, commonly held to be almost incurable, was totally overcome within three weeks.

I was astonished and moved, both by his dedication and his triumph, achieved so independently. I asked him (as parents so often ask unanswerable questions) how he had found the will and the courage to tackle his problem and to overcome it. "I remembered Drem," he said after a soul-searching pause. "He was handicapped like me."

No one who knew this intelligent, strong, athletic child, so unfailingly funny and generous, could have guessed that in the secret prison of his heart he felt that he was crippled. Whenever I speak to audiences of teachers and librarians, many of them devoted to the practice of "bibliotherapy"—prescribing "problem novels" to children with matching problems—I tell them this story. I ask them if they would have thought of prescribing *Warrior Scarlet* to a five-year-old boy with a lateral lisp.

The whole force and mystery of literature is that it speaks to us privately, one mind reaching to another, its "therapeutic" power dependent not on mean-spirited calculations of problems and how to solve them, but on the depth of the author's intuition and the strength of her literary imagination and skill. Hundreds of contemporary novelists for children have tackled this theme of the young boy's agonized desperation to prove his virility and to be accepted as worthy by his "warrior clan." It is a solitary trial, apparently, as ancient as prehistory. That Sutcliff's Bronze Age version could reach so unpredictably into a boy's life, and profoundly change it, is both a testament to the strength of Sutcliff's writing and a brisk rebuttal to the reductive and presumptuous tinkerings of bibliotherapy.

A defender of teenage mass-market novels once accused me of

being "against pimples and lust." But a novel's contentious or problematic subject is almost beside the point; what matters is the depth of its treatment, and it is through the author's language that we can most clearly see whether an artist or a mechanic is at work.

In *Warrior Scarlet*, Sutcliff developed a movingly evocative language to create her Bronze Age world. Every image, drawn from the vegetation and animal life surrounding the tribe, deepens the sensory hold the novel exerts on the reader. She makes particularly good use of starkly simple dialogue ("Na, this time there will be no coming back"), as well as a peculiar trick in using the gerund that somehow evokes the primitive mentality: their last hunting, a hard waiting, a long-drawn hushing of wind across open snow.

This elegiac tone is particularly effective in *The Lantern Bearers*, Sutcliff's novel about the departure of the last Roman Legions from Britain. The Jutes and Angles raid, pillage, and loot in their pouncing forays down from the North; already they have begun to make alliances with British warlords and to settle on conquered farms along the coast. Britain teeters on the edge of the Dark Ages. We see the coming chaos through the eyes of the British-born centurion Aquila, who deserts his departing legion because at the last moment he realizes that Britain, not Rome, is his true home. Here the language is crisper, more Latinate, and the repeated images of beacons and failing lights strongly suggest the struggle to "hold back the dark."

Although she never steps outside Aquila's perception that Rome is synonymous with civilization and that the "sea wolves" are barbarians, Sutcliff allows us to see, out of the corner of our eye, how the Saxons, Picts, and Romans have already begun their long, fertile intertwining. She is able to imagine each of these cultures from within, fully and cohesively. Her world view is capacious enough that there are antagonists but no villains.

One-sidedness is a sore temptation for a novelist, and usually a fatal one. Canada, unlike the United States, has a growing tradition of politically "dissenting" novels, which pointedly diverge from the smothering national complacency. Perhaps it is that monstrous, clammy acceptance of the status quo which provokes dissenters to insist too loudly on their point of view. Two stirring and empathetic novels about historic labor conflicts—*The Baitchopper* by Silver Donald Cameron, and *One Proud Summer* by Marsha Hewitt and Claire Mackay—suffer from the authors' eagerness to promote the cause of the underdog strikers. Hewitt and Mackay especially slip into purple prose whenever they describe their saintly proletarian strike leaders: "Pride swelled in her as she recalled her mother's words . . . How fierce she had been! How brave and shining!" or "Fear slunk into her belly like a whipped dog, circled, then settled in to stay."

I would share the authors' opinions about the rights and wrongs of both strikes, but the writers' fixed viewpoints rob their young characters of the opportunity to come to these conclusions themselves. Ironically, the drama of that inner struggle would have been far more effective in winning over the reader. All propagandistic motive in fiction seems to lead the writer to heavy-handed prose: when inner conflict is muted or absent, inflated adjectives and engorged verbs must substitute for the tension of psychological drama. The private inward voice that is the soul of the novel—even in action-oriented adventure—is drowned out.

Mystery and detection are favorite forms of adventure for both adult and children; the lesser varieties (like John D. Fitzgerald's The Great Brain series) are popular enough—and slight enough—not to need discussion here. Generally, the more important the puzzle factor, the less demanding and the less rewarding the book will be as a work of literature.

John Bellairs is an American writer of Gothic mysteries with overtones of the supernatural who is worth noting for the warmth of his characterization. His most popular, and still, I think, his best novel, is *The House with a Clock in Its Walls,* which is enlivened by the humorous, affectionate tone of the relationships between pudgy Lewis Barnavelt, his Uncle Jonathan, and Mrs. Florence Zimmerman, the uncle's friend and neighbor.

The orphaned Lewis comes to live in Uncle Jonathan's turreted mansion, which, he discovers, is haunted by a mysterious ticking noise. The particularly engaging tone of the book springs from the comical clash between appearances of cozy normalcy and matter-of-fact relevations of the supernatural: Uncle Jonathan and Mrs. Zimmerman, for example, are sympathetic poker-playing buddies—and nonchalant practitioners of witchcraft.

There are some chilly moments of real fearfulness in the book, and one wonderful scene in which Uncle Jonathan casts a moon-eclipsing spell, which fills the garden with sudden magic. Lewis, putting his ear to the ground, can hear the earthworms and sense the slow collapse of "the delicate ivory skeleton" of a cat. Lewis has coaxed his uncle to this unwonted display of prowess in order to win over a school sports hero as a friend. But the swaggering Tarby sneers at the spell the moment the enchantment is over, and by this token we know he is no true friend. It is indicative of the jaunty humor and offbeat eclecticism of the story that, at the end, Lewis has made a new friend, Rose Rita Pottinger, who knows the names of all the different kinds of cannon: "Saker, mimion, falconet, demi-culverin . . ." recites Lewis. "Aah," screams Uncle Jonathan in exaggerated protest, "That's all I need! An expert in Elizabethan ordnance!"

Two other styles of adventure story are worth consideration in this chapter. I began by deploring the lack of adventure stories which depict girls acting with skill and courage. The one general exception, aside from Arthur Ransome, is historical fiction. It's as though the crises of recent historical events give authors the license to write about girls as agents rather than bystanders. The Second World War is a most fertile source of such stories, perhaps because that terrible convulsion of history involved the female authors themselves in dramatic events.

Wildcat Under Glass by Alki Zei (translated superbly by Edward Fenton) is a favorite of mine because it so richly conveys, through the eyes of its young narrator, the whole life of a Greek family, village, and culture under the fascist puppet regime in 1936. Melia and her older, prettier sister Myrto exist, like Sutcliff's characters, in a fully realized world. They have a patriarchal grandpa who feeds them walnuts and honey, tells them Greek legends, and teaches them to count in Byzantine; they have their own secret language, as siblings often do, and counting rhymes and games played with the local children; they have a pusillanimous father who wants to toady to the fascists in order to keep his job in the bank; their terse and salty maid, Stamatina, has a tragic history and political convictions of her own; and they idolize their teenage cousin, Niko, because he plays with them and tells them stories.

The looming war introduces sinister new tensions into this already rich constellation of family ties and undercurrents. We see political events entirely through the first small ripples they create in the family, and through the children's own confused perceptions of these disturbances. They know, for example, that they instictively dislike the Bishop who comes to play cards with their royalist aunt, because they must kiss his hand which is "soft and limp, like a slice of bread." The pro-fascists of their acquaintance make them uneasy. But then the school principal invites bossy Myrto to become "a leader" in a new youth corps at school, Myrto succumbs to the flattery, and the girls are headed down diverging paths.

Myrto is drawn further and further into fascism, dazzled by her gold stars, her uniform, and her new importance in the youth group. We see how naturally her political seduction follows from her character: her eagerness for the approval of authority figures, her preadolescent excitement at belonging to a gang that insists on blind allegiance—even beyond the claims of family.

Melia, meanwhile, at once more childlike and more self-directed, is stubbornly loyal to the adored Niko, who becomes a freedom fighter. When Niko is pursued by the police, Melia serves as a courier to take him food and messages. Gradually, the family is painfully wrenched apart by the political forces of the time. It takes a dangerously close call for the fugitive Niko to snap Myrto out of her trance.

Zei has clear convictions about Nazism, but that does not make her story into a political tract. It is a human drama, and shows us how evil forces can subvert good people through their own human vulnerabilities. Children's need for moral clarity has encouraged authors for the young to split the complex human atom; heroes are good, villains are bad, and never the twain shall meet or greet. But the older reader, above the age of ten or eleven, can easily comprehend a deeper level of complexity, especially when the moral struggle is waged and won by a child, against such understandably attractive temptations.

Similarly, the contemporary reader can cope with a story's sadness if the characters are not crushed by evil. One favorite adventure I remember from childhood, and which is still popular enough to remain in print, is Mary Treadgold's *We Couldn't Leave Dinah*. To the impulsive thirteen-year-old Caroline, the Nazi occupation at first means nothing more than the hateful necessity of leaving the family's beloved home on a picturesque Channel Island—and just in the middle of the summer holidays, too, when the Pony Club is in full swing. The book has some of the dreadful clubbiness of English horse books—"You couldn't really believe in awful things like Hitler when you were out in sun and wind and sea spray and with people as marvelous as the pony club"—but it rises above that dated upperclass gush when Caroline and her fourteen-year-old brother Mick are accidentally left behind during the tumultuous nighttime evacuation of the island.

Alone with their beloved ponies, some Island residents who might just be collaborators, and hordes of comic-book Nazis ("My little Nannerl . . . has long to ride wished"), the children are exhausted, frightened, and beginning to realize the seriousness of their situation. When Mick insists on spying on the Germans to help foil their plan to invade England, Caroline protests furiously: "We're only children. Nobody expects us to help like that . . . we only have to collect money and knit and collect scrap iron and things." But stay they do, and the pony club airs and mannerisms fall away as Caroline conquers her fear and joins resolutely in the escapade.

We Couldn't Leave Dinah is a perfect example of the fast-paced, undemanding adventure novel that might appeal to a reader who is not in the mood for complexity—or simply one who is mad for horse stories—and yet is a book that yields rewards well above the average.

A Pocketful of Seeds by Marilyn Sachs is a darker story, shadowed with the horror of the Holocaust but made bearable by the tenacious survival of Nicole Nieman. It is a fictionalized first person account of a true story, told in flashback by fifteen-year-old Nicole, who is waiting out the last days of the war in boarding school in Aix-les-Bains in Vichy France. Our sympathy is immediately caught by Nicole's spiky resistance of the spirit, despite her hunger, the cold, and her desperate fears for her family who were deported the year before. She has just slammed her book shut in the frigid study hall of the school: "I know how to get warm!" she shouts. "Everybody up—up—up!" and she gets all the girls doing the jitterbug "like the American movies." Headmistress Mlle Legrand bursts into the room where the girls are wildly clapping, laughing, and gyrating. "I cannot understand this display of levity," she says icily. "Nicole, the last person in the world who should be dancing is you. What kind of feelings do you have for your parents? For your sister? . . . You must be heartless."

But Nicole dances to silence the pain and to defy the Nazis the only way she can: by clenching her misery in private rage, refusing to let her Petainiste teachers see how she suffers. The book gains its impact from this kind of gritty honesty, and from the picture of Nicole's family life before they are deported. The parents are poor—sellers of sweaters in the local open-air markets—and willful Nicole constantly clashes with the emotionally expressive Mama whom she loves so much.

It is an touchingly believable portrait of the tensions between the argumentative oldest daughter, her weary but devoted parents, and the cute little sister who gets all the attention. The climax of the story is the moment when Nicole comes home from school to find the tiny flat ransacked and her family gone, taken by the Nazis. She snatches the family picture album and flees on her bicycle, sure of finding refuge with friends and neighbors. But her relatives are gone, too, taken in the roundup; as for the neighbors, some are tearfully regretful as they close their doors against her; at some houses, only the curtains twitch as Nicole pounds frantically at the door. Sachs describes all this without bitterness or judgment. It is a true picture of Vichy France, and the facts of Nicole's abandonment—and the cold refuge offered finally by her school—speak for themselves. What the reader carries away from the book is an unforgettable impression of Nicole's battered but defiant spirit.

An equal dignity suffuses the story of Julilly, a runaway slave and the twelve-year-old hero of *Runaway to Freedom* (originally titled *Underground to Canada*) by Barbara Smucker. Of all the Canadian historical adventures I have read, this one has the most compellingly simple and vivid story line. We follow Julilly from the moment she is sold away from her mother on a Virginia plantation until the poignant moment when the two are reunited in Canada, thanks to the Quaker abolitionists who organized their escape.

Smucker successfully re-creates the steamy heat of the Mississippi plantation to which Julilly is sold—the mosquitoes, the bone-cracking labor, the filthy shacks where the slaves collapse in numb exhaustion at night, and the vileness of their treatment by overseers: At "feeding time" a man ladles corn meal mush into a trough in the yard and the slave children "push and shove on their hands and knees, dipping, and sucking with their hands" to get their meager food. Through all this degradation, the tall, strong Julilly holds on to the secret dream of the northern star, which her mother whispered to her before they parted. When she escapes, she takes with her the thirteen-year-old Liza, hunched and crippled from brutal beatings, embittered but determined to be free.

The story of their desperate journey is remarkable. It hardly seems possible that such an epic—and such an honorable chapter in Canada's history—has not been dealt with in children's literature before. So stark are the facts that Smucker nowhere has to belabor a moral; so convincing is Julilly's strength and longing to be free that the story is a joyful one, rather than a horror.

The ultimate adventure for children who are not caught up in the great events of history is not one of overcoming hardship, but of learning how to "read" the world. The mystery, that is, is not who-dunnit, but whom to believe, whom to trust, and how to know. This is the subtext, of course, of *Treasure Island,* as Jim Hawkins learns that even his enemies can be kind, and even his friends can be tainted.

We see the same working out of perplexity in two Canadian historical novels: *Death over Montreal* by Geoffrey Bilson, and *The Journey of the Shadow Bairns* by Margaret Anderson. In both of these books, the young heroes take their chances on an adult who is reviled by other adults as a charlatan, but whom the youngsters intuitively guess to be trustworthy.

In *Death over Montreal*, Jamie Douglas's Scottish emigrant family arrives in Montreal at the height of a cholera epidemic. The ravages of the disease, and the disorganization and squalor of the city, are made horrifyingly real; this atmosphere, even more than Jamie's rather facile volunteering to work with a popular healer, is the backbone of the story.

The dilemma of trust is more fully worked through in *The Journey of the Shadow Bairns*. This time, the Scottish emigrant is twelve-year-old Elspeth MacDonald. Her parents have planned to follow a charismatic leader, the Rev. Moses Barr, to a land grant on the North Saskatchewan River. After both parents die suddenly in an unwholesome Glasgow slum, Eslpeth decides to run away and join the Reverend Barr's ship before welfare authorities can separate her from her four-year-old brother Robbie. She invents a game ("the shadow bairns") to keep her uncomprehending little brother silent and obedient during the long, risky journey.

It is Elspeth's strong sense of "we two alone together" that keeps the story humming along, but an interesting and provocative minor theme is her compassionate sympathy for the Reverend Barr, as the other settlers gradually suspect and then denounce him as a greedy manipulator. In the end, having found her niche in the Canadian wilderness, Elspeth helps Barr to escape the settler's wrath. "No matter what people said about Mr. Barr, she knew he had not failed. He had a part in everything the settlers did here, because it had been his dream."

Two British books, though, tower above all the others in tackling this problem of "how to know"—which is, after all, one of the central tasks of any novel. The first, *No Way of Telling* by Emma Smith, is a thriller that poses the question: How is a child to know about strangers who might be dangerous? What resources can a defenseless child marshall against an armed and sinister adult?

No Way of Telling is a minor work of art, a tense heart-thumper written with precision, intensity, and a sensibility so tuned to the inner workings of the child's mind that it quivers on target as truly as the needle of a compass.

Amy Bowen, who seems to be about ten or eleven years old, gets off the school bus in a whirling, blinding blizzard. Climbing the hill to the isolated Welsh hill cottage where she lives alone with her grandmother, Amy is caught up in the mysterious excitement of a snowstorm: "Snow was a marvel . . . it was like nothing else; it changed the world, the whole of life, in a matter of moments. Not only the shapes of trees and grasses were changed but daily habits— even laws lost their power and had no meaning when snow fell." Everyone has felt the delight tinged with fear of this kind of snow-change, and Smith uses it to marvelous effect to wipe out the Bowens's normal daily ties to the outside and to muffle them in a strange, isolated, and transformed world.

That night, as Amy and her grandmother enjoy the enchanced coziness of their usual quiet tasks by the fire, a monstrous figure suddenly crashes open their door: "In an instant the storm had rushed inside, filling the room, destroying its peaceful inviolability . . . a turmoil of Mick barking and barking, the lamp guttering, the tablecloth lifting, and snow blowing across the floor . . ."

He's a giant of a man, wild and silent, covered with snow, who lurches across the room, grabs some of their food, stuffs it into a sack, and vanishes back into the blizzard. After an anxious night, Amy goes out to the woodpile in the lean-to and notices, after a while, that there are signs that the man sheltered there for night. And their "hacker" (hatchet) is gone. One of the keenest pleasures of the book is the precision with which Smith captures the way people notice things—obliquely, confusedly at first, merely a sensory impression that slowly clicks into place in the mind with, finally, a sudden shock of understanding. Later, for example, Amy sees that a man to whom she has been talking has something black in his hand. At first, her mind unconsciously seeks the nearest explanation, that it is a flashlight. Only seconds later does it dawn on her that it is a gun. Very few suspense stories, whether for adults or children, take the trouble to track the movements of perception so exactly. Very few, therefore, carry the same emotional punch.

Amy and her grandmother are ensnared in a mystery. Soon, hot on the trail of the first man, come two graceful skiers, assumed by the Bowens to be police in pursuit of the huge intruder. By hunch, intuition, minute but telling clues, and the exchange of silent signals between the old woman and the girl, a frightening truth is patched together: The two elegant skiers are murderous.

The story works up to breathtakingly suspenseful climax and a deeply satisfying conclusion. Amy has been worried about not having enough courage to deal with their crisis. "I'd say brave isn't mostly what people are, Amy, it's what they decide to be," says her Granny, a prime exemplar of her own words. "Don't fret . . . you'll find yourself brave enough whenever the time comes that you've got to be." And she is, and believably so, since Smith has taken such care to fill in all the living details and the rounded characterizations that make cause and effect seem so inexorable in a well-crafted story.

Furthermore, Amy, who at first felt helplessly that there was "no way of telling" which man to trust and which to fear, learns by the end that there is indeed no certainty, but that complete perception is a mesh of compassion, swift intuition, experience, shared knowledge, and alert intelligence. The important things can be known.

A complex and impressive variation on this theme is found in *The Emperor's Winding Sheet,* a story about the medieval fall of Byzantium by the distinguished British author Jill Paton Walsh. Piers Barber, wrecked on an English merchant ship and a fugitive from Turkish pirates who rescued and then brutalized him, tumbles from an orange tree into the garden of the Emperor Constantine. At first, he assumes he has fallen in with another lot of incomprehensible barbarians.

The Emperor has just heard a prophecy that he will be safe from the gathering storm so long as he keeps a little bird of good omen with him. Piers is dubbed "Vrethiki," the lucky find, and is promptly washed, clothed, and made the ceremonial companion of the Emperor.

Walsh is a masterful writer, and Byzantium with its shimmering domes, marble walls, and fragrant gardens arises like a mirage before the dazzled eyes of Vrethiki—and the reader. At first, rebellious and mystified, he submits resentfully to the buckets of water in the courtyard of the bath house: "Gray shining snakes and slopping goblets of water struck him and glazed his goosey skin. The cold seized and bit him and cut off his breath in gasps."

Walsh's vibrant prose brings the ceremonies and war councils of the Empire into racing immediacy; she can move us, and Vrethiki, with the Emperor's gentle, grave, spartan demeanor amid the pomp of his court and the gilded splendor of banquets. She can make us sympathize with Vrethiki while exposing to us his narrow condescension toward his Byzantine captors. At first, Vrethiki hates the idea of Byzantium ("There's no accounting for barbarians," shrugs the Emperor's cupbearer) and boasts of his crusader ancestors to a horrified court eunuch who promptly tells him what savage despoilers the crusaders really were. ("You barbarian whelp ... is there *nothing* you know?")

At length, as the Turks beseige the city and the reek of death lies over them all, Vrethiki knows what is most to be loved and admired. "Effendi Mou, my true lord," he cries, kneeling to pledge allegiance to the doomed Constantine. Walsh has solved the problem of historic language; all the characters speak believable English, with the colloquialisms or formality appropriate to their nationality or class. The sense of a distant time is conveyed delicately by a slight strangeness of cadence or diction. This barely noticeable tilt into a foreign voice serves to deepen our empathy for Vrethiki's sense of dislocation; as it begins to fall more familiarly on our ear, it draws us into Vrethiki's own slow growth into wisdom. Unwillingly free at last, wretched at leaving behind the dead Constantine and the ruined Byzantium, he sails home. "In the very house I was born in I shall carry an exile's heart, thinking of that immortal city, and how it passed away. And nothing will be simple for me, ever again."

Worlds and centuries apart, another journey of the innocent heart toward true understanding is *Huckleberry Finn*. To anyone old enough to cope with the spiralling satirical layers of meaning, Huck's raft ride down the Mississippi River with the runaway slave, Jim, is pure deliciousness.

I remember first reading *Huckleberry Finn* as a fairly naive twelve-year-old; earnestness and emotion were more natural to me than irony. Still, the book filled me with a swelling, almost painful mix of elation, bafflement, and wonder. I can still taste that disturbing flavor, the intoxicating strangeness, of Twain's humor. All the way through, I stepped as cautiously as a walker in a quicksand bog, not knowing at any moment whom to take seriously, whom to believe.

As a literary perception, that was somewhat crude but still of the essence: The book is an amazing lexicon, an encyclopedia of religious, social, and racial hypocrisy. There is the gross, in the person of Huck's drunken, reprobate father: "Look at it, gentlemen, and ladies all; take ahold of it; shake it. There's a hand that was the hand of a hog; but it ain't so no more . . ." he swears. It is the very voice of the TV evangelist, transported in a vulgar excess of fake piety. There is the riotously sanctimonious in the person of the salivatingly morbid Emmeline Graingerford, who paints portraits of the dear departed with titles like "I Shall Never Hear Thy Sweet Chirrup More Alas" and "Art Thou Gone Yes Gone Alas." He knew he ought to like such splendid art, Huck confesses, but "I somehow didn't seem to take to them because if I was ever down a little, they always give me the fan-tods."

Then there is the undertaker in his black gloves, mutely ushering in latecomers to a funeral, squeezing people into place and "getting them all shipshape and comfortable" says Huck, admiring his "softy soothering ways . . . he was the softest, glidingest, stealthiest man I ever see; and there warn't no more smile to him than there is to a ham."

Huck's pre–Civil War south is a rogue's gallery, a feast of every form of bombast and fakery, the sentimental, the rapacious, the high-toned, and the ludicrous. Through it all runs the earnest voice of Huck, spouting the revolting conventional morality he has been taught by the Widow Douglas and Miss Watson, even while acting according to the instincts of his anarchic heart. When he sees the ruthless charlatans, the Royal Nonesuch con men, tarred and feathered, he can't help but feel sorry for them. "It don't make no difference whether you do right or wrong," he concludes ruefully, "a person's conscience ain't got no sense, and just goes for him anyway. If I had a yaller dog that didn't know no more than a person's conscience does, I would poison him."

But it is precisely Huck's real conscience, his inner promptings, that lead him right, and it is the imposed voice of received morality that is so shockingly wrong. When the loyal, tender Jim confides to Huck that he dreams of buying back—or even stealing—his own children out of slavery, Huck reacts "properly" according to the morally stunted teachings of the slave-owning South. "It most froze me to hear such talk," says Huck. "Here was this nigger which I had as good as helped to run away, coming right out flat-footed and saying he would steal his children—children that belonged to a man I didn't even know, a man that hadn't ever done me no harm . . . I was sorry to hear Jim say that, it was such a lowering of him."

Minutes later, Jim and Huck are nearly caught by a pair of armed strangers in a skiff; instantly, Huck is spinning one of his fantastically cunning and elaborate lies (always tailored with uncanny psychological shrewdness to trap his listeners) to save Jim's life. His spontaneous actions constantly betray what he takes to be his "conscience." In fact, Huck finally gives up the dictates of morality completely and resigns himself to being damned to hell for remaining loyal to Jim. "I knowed very well I had done wrong, and I see it warn't no use for me to try to learn to do right; a body that don't get started right when he's little ain't got no show."

At the beginning of *Huckleberry Finn* Twain mockingly posted a "Notice" of threatened prosecution against anyone attempting to find a moral in the story; of course, the book is a deeply moral comedy of human error and a devastating satire of hypocrisy. It's interesting that, nevertheless, groups as divergent as black parents and right-wing fundamentalists repeatedly try to have the book banished from public schools and libraries; blacks because their children are wounded by Twain's use of the demotic "nigger" and by what they feel is the demeaning stereotype of the slave Jim; southern fundamentalists because they are infuriated by Twain's mockery of conventional morality.

In chapter 10, I argue for increased sensitivity in the books chosen for school curricula. Minority youngsters, already on the defensive in school settings in which they feel themselves outsiders, cannot possibly open themselves to Twain's humane message. Members of the white majority may argue, with literary and lofty purpose, that

Twain shows us one of the most loving portraits of black-white friendship in all of literature, and they would be right—at least from a white point of view. But they can't know how it feels to be black, to sit in class and to hear the word "nigger" over and over. To force the classroom study of *Huckleberry Finn* in cases in which black parents and students resist is to admit inadvertently (no matter how disinterested the stated educational goal) that one is unmoved by black suffering and indifferent to how little the student really can learn in such circumstances.

Huckleberry Finn is not the only classic work of literature to misfire in the classroom. In one Canadian city, where the school board insisted on teaching *The Merchant of Venice* in the seventh grade, the few Jewish students were later pelted with coins by sneering classmates.

Perhaps these painful incidents are the best possible argument for reading literature at home as an education in true knowing. Books, all by themselves, can't banish bigotry. But any youngster who is well read in adventure stories of high merit would be less likely to misinterpret the meanings of great works of literature, and better able to translate humor, irony, and metaphor into generosity of spirit.

Chapter 7

FANTASY

A genuine work of art must mean many things; the truer its art, the more things it will mean . . . It is not there so much to convey a meaning as to wake a meaning . . . The best thing you can do for your fellow is . . . . not to give him things to think about, but to wake things up that are in him . . .

George MacDonald, on "The Fantastic Imagination," 1893

[The task of poetry is to create] imaginary gardens with real toads in them.

Marianne Moore, 1921

As a child I had what I thought was a fixed dislike of fantasy. It was a long trek, once or twice a week, to the library, and we were limited in those dim days to only three borrowed library books per visit. I would spend hours making sure that not one of my precious three choices would turn out to be fantasy.

Now I realize with amusement that most of what I read and loved best was, indeed, fantasy; it's just that I didn't call it that because, to me, it was grippingly alive and real. I didn't, in fact, hate magic, but its opposite: that sneaky cheat of a writer who would compel my whole quivering attention and make my heart pound faster, only to sneer on the last page, with insufferable adult condescension, that "it was all a dream" or "who knows whether it really happened?" A child who gives herself to a story, who lets herself be seduced by the author into believing in another world, who goes to the effort of imaginatively submitting to its rules and customs, is rightly enraged when the author turns out to have been mocking her naiveté all along.

The other kind of fantasy I loathed was the "talking bunny" type (not, I hasten to add, *Peter Rabbit),* which trotted the young reader through an allegorical zoo of right-thinking animals who existed only to chirp—false lisping little beasts—the author's moral message. Allegory, I resentfully intuited, was trying to get at me with underhand purposes of its own, and I wanted none of it.

The best fantasies, even if they resound with high humor, are morally serious. The author believes in his imaginary garden, has taken pains to make sure that roses do not bloom there at the same time as trilliums—that there is inner coherence and a natural order in the garden—and he leads us by the hand there not to lose ourselves but to find something true. Ursula K. LeGuin, probably the finest fantasist writing in North America today, puts it better than I could when she compares Elfland, the world of fantasy, to a vast and beautiful national park where a person goes alone to get "in touch with reality in a special, private, profound fashion. But what happens when it is considered merely as a 'place to get away to'? Well, you know what has happened to Yosemite. Everybody comes, not with an axe and a box of matches, but in a trailer with a motorbike on the back and a motorboat on top and a butane stove, five aluminum folding chairs, and transistor radio . . . They arrive totally encapsulated in a secondhand reality." To accommodate the tourists, says LeGuin, some fantasy writers are building "six-lane highways and trailer parks with drive-in movies, so that the tourists can feel at home just as if they were back in Poughkeepsie. But the point about Elfland is that you are not at home there. It's not Poughkeepsie. It's different."

This chapter assumes that you do not want your children (or the children you teach or hope to inspire) to travel through literature in a bubble-pack of portable Poughkeepsie. Even without the mushrooming popularity of fantasy-as-teenage-escapism—sword-and-sorcery sagas with flinty-eyed heroes, a liberated woman or two, and a brace of laser guns to give the whole enterprise a gloss of modernity—even without this whole new category of fakery, the reach of the fantasy form in children's literature is immense. Half the books in earlier chapters about humor, beginning readers, quest, or adventure could just as easily slip in under the fantasy label, since children's authors have traditionally enjoyed a greater freedom to stretch the borders of reality.

Faced with this unmanageable torrent, I decided to narrow the field drastically. I began my reading surrounded by a mountain of currently popular fantasy: dragon epics, space epics, trilogies, and quadriologies, and quintologies of popular paperbacks. Some authors are more competent than others, but almost all the recent crop are leadenly derivative of J.R. Tolkien's *Lord of the Rings* trilogy. Worse, they are no more magical than guided tours in which travelers eat hamburgers on the Champs Elysées; the plot ingredients, in other words, are the familiar modern heroes and villians of television, tricked out in medieval finery. Their dragons, not to mention their unicorns, are all too often no more than disguised horses, noble steeds sentimentally loved by teenage girls. Their plots are typically escapist, and whether the enemy is a leathery-skinned monster toad or a beautiful witch, it is always an exterior enemy. Escapist reading, be it the adult thriller or the detective story, depends on the basic good-guy-beats-bad-guy mechanism. Moral ambiguity, in which the good guys (and, by implication, the readers) must painfully recognize the evil as a part of their human selves, both asks more of the reader and gives more.

It is this deeper dimension of complexity which distinguishes the fantasy written for older children from those aimed at the prepubescent; at eight or nine, children may be distressed by a story in which villains are attractive and heroes flawed, but by eleven or so, they are surely ready for the more discriminating task of literature, ready to grapple with the central dilemma of human life, the struggle in our own souls to distinguish and control our most destructive impulses.

So it's sad to see that the new teenage thirst for fantasy (and what could be more natural, and potentially useful, in this traumatic and threatening era?) should be slaked by so much bilge. Beware then, of the meretricious "fantasies" that are no more fantastical than transposed video games, where cynical and violent heroes defeat "evil" with a magic ring, and "heroines" are borrowed from "Charlie's Angels." It takes more than burlap costumes, papier-mâché monsters, and pseudomedievalisms ("I'faith, my lord") to disguise the accents of Poughkeepsie—or to make them worth listening to.

All this dross, therefore, I whittled away from my stack of books. They offer no genuine shocks or surprises, no twists of sharp new perceptions which are the essence of the literary experience. There are no real toads in those gardens.

Tolkien, too, I've omitted from this chapter. His *The Hobbit* and the Middle Earth trilogy are so well-known, deservedly, that I scarcely need remind readers of their existence. But perhaps my selected short list of fantasy may serve as an inoculation against Tolkien fever, that unpleasantly pseudoreligious fanaticism that I first encountered when I was in university in the 1960s and which made me shun Tolkien until my own children read him years later. Tolkien cultists of university age, in full retreat from adult realities, named their cars Gandalf, claimed to have furry feet like Hobbits, and swapped Elvish runes and Shire geneologies like kids swapping bubble gum baseball cards. I think this fey frenzy mostly afflicted those who had never read fantasy before; they were like dazzled tourists to Elfland bringing back native hats and a self-conscious smattering of foreign phrases to impress the suburban neighbors.

Children who are better-traveled in the realms of fairy tale and fantasy are not so likely to bring back cheap souvenirs. Anyone who has, for example, read *The Wind in the Willows* in childhood knows that that is a charmed country, a world you keep whole in your mind and revisit at will. *The Wind in the Willows,* in fact, is a good place to begin in discussing fantasy; it has all the most satisfying ingredients, though the recipe has been passed around among subsequent authors until it is tattered and grubby. There is rural bliss, the glint and ripple of the river, the summertime freedom of messing about in boats or spanking new caravans "with all the little fitments," the comfort of firelit parlors, or wicker picnic baskets bulging with good food. It is a reverie of home, a childhood home whose snugness is all "clear of the clash of sex," as Grahame himself wrote.

But half the charm of those kitchen feasts and expansive fireside evenings lies in their contrast with the tingling excitement of adventure: glorious, wild, irresponsible adventure, reckless speed and mad self-indulgence, all embodied in the lovable person of Toad. Toad is, as the English critic Nicholas Tucker has astutely observed, the children's Falstaff. Unrepentant to the end, grandiose, boastful, sly, rich enough to gratify every impulse, Toad is still generous enough of soul to keep the undying loyalty of Ratty, Mole, and Badger (those kindly Edwardian gents) and of child readers everywhere. Their prudence, their cozy bustle, their sturdy and sometimes stern affection, is the anchor against which Toad's balloon irrepressibly tugs. Who can forget, or resist, the allure of that first motor car: "a small cloud of dust, with a dark center of energy, advancing on them at incredible speed, while from out the dust a faint 'Poop-poop' wailed like an uneasy animal in pain."

Grahame's prose is so spacious and rich that it begs to be read aloud; remember the descriptions of the river "as sleek, sinuous, and full-bodied as an animal" or the moment when a tingling scent reaches Mole's nose—"a fine filament, the telegraphic current . . . home!" An adult reading aloud might judiciously choose to omit the central chapter with its vision of Pan, a passage whose religious effulgence tips the book's delicate balance of ironic humor and calm affections; I remember skipping past those intensely embarrassing pages when I was a child.

The pull between home and adventure, the cozy burrow and the Wild Wood, is a natural theme of younger children's fantasy. One of the most brilliant workings of that idea is in *The Borrowers* by Mary Norton, a book that, as I discovered to my surprise on rereading it, is perfect. The writing is lucid, precise, and lithe enough to stretch effortlessly from the minute observation of the under-the-floorboards miniature world of the Borrowers to the sudden shift to gargantuan scale. By the time Arietty, the Borrower child, has her first glimpse of the human world, we are so steeped in her perspective that we are as shocked as she is to look across the "immense plain" of the gleaming hall floor to the monster stairs, rising into the distance to "worlds upon worlds" that shimmer just out of sight.

Arietty is thirteen years old, one of the little people who live secretly by "borrowing" tiny objects (all those lost safety pins and crochet hooks) from the inhabitants of a well-regulated home. "Even their names were borrowed and not quite right" and it is a mark of Norton's skill that those names echo in our minds, chimingly perfect for their characters and just a little hallucinatory, a little bent from the norm, like a spoon in a glass: Pod and Homily Clock and their child Arietty, the snooty Overmantles, Uncle Hendreary, the gardener Crampfurl, the harridan cook Mrs. Driver, and, in the sequel, the marvelous wild boy Spiller.

The home of the borrowers has all the charm of a doll's house, but is more real. Homily grumbles ("Really, Arietty! Not on your clean jersey") when Arietty, helping to prepare dinner, lightly slings an onion ring round her shoulders. Arietty nods off to sleep in a cigar box bedroom, where lovely ladies in wispy chiffon bedeck the ceiling. And Pod comes back from a foraging expedition with his hatpin (used for climbing) looking queer: "I been seen." Fateful words in this secretive civilization; being seen by humans is supremely dangerous. When three laconic words can carry such foreboding, we know we are not in a dollhouse.

Indeed, it is a complete world, wholly imagined, with its customs, family history, livelihood, greeds, and envies, even a demonology (cats) of its own, and all of it revealed swiftly and with the utmost vivacity through conversation. Sword-and-sorcery fantasies, by contrast, pile on details in the strained effort to create credibility, but they read as excitingly as a hardware catalog, and dialogue is typically sparse and wooden.

The plot of *The Borrowers* builds to the climactic moment when a visiting human-size boy, in his clumsy efforts to befriend the Clock family, pries up a floorboard to lower dollhouse furniture into their bedroom. The jolt to the reader is tremendous: So thoroughly have we entered the Borrowers' world that the crashing invasion via the ceiling is as terrifying as though monsters stepped casually through our own roofs. Mrs. Clock, houseproud and acquisitive, is indignant at the violation and yet greedy for more of the useless but sumptuous dollhouse furnishings. Norton captures her ambivalence in a characteristically economical and revealing snatch of dialogue: The looming boy offers to nail back the floorboards if the Clock family doesn't want any more dollhouse treasures. "Tell him to nail us down lightly," Homily whispers to Pod.

It is Arietty, the impulsive and daring adolescent, who has brought this havoc into the family by secretly breaking a first rule of borrowers: She made friends with the boy. This friendship, and the dreaded exposure to the adult world of authority to which it inexorably leads, causes the final expulsion of the Clock family from their tight, dark, secure—and claustrophobic—underground home. They are forced to "emigrate" into the great outdoor world.

But even before this ultimate upheaval, Arietty's world and the boy's have clashed, to their mutual delight and dismay. One of the finest comic scenes in the book is their meeting under a blossoming cherry tree during Arietty's first ecstatic venture into the outdoors. Boldly, Arietty confronts the speaking giant who casts a cold flick of shadow over her when he moves; she is scornfully certain that the world was made for borrowers and that there can be very few of these giants alive: "Surely you don't think there are many people in the world your size? . . . Honestly . . . I mean, whatever sort of world would it be? Those great chairs . . . Fancy if you had to make chairs that size for everyone? And the stuff for their clothes . . . miles and miles of it . . . tents of it . . . and the sewing! . . . their great beds . . . the *food* they eat . . . great smoking mountains of it, huge bogs of stew . . ."

The boy is younger and more timid; when he first sees Arietty, he can only perceive her as some kind of rodent: "Don't move! Or I'll hit you with my ash stick," he threatens, trembling, "in case you came and scrabbled at me with your nasty little hands." It is a perfect paradigm of the way children make friends, warily, with initial hostility and shaky bravado. But he, too, like Arietty, learns to abandon his smugly egocentric view of the world and take other human realities into account.

This, despite the book's constant bubble of wit and humor, and the author's consummately skillful play of perspectives between the two worlds, is moral seriousness. (*Charlotte's Web* by E.B. White, an American classic for a slightly younger age group, is another example of a superbly written fantasy with deep moral overtones.) Not all fantasy has this serious purpose, nor need it have—I'll discuss the humorist Joan Aiken later in this chapter, as one example—but clarity of intention, coherence of tone, and a respect for the child reader are essential. When E. Nesbit satirizes Victorian society, she speaks directly to the intelligent child, not over her shoulder to some imaginary and smirking adult eavesdroopers.

A book I heartily loathed as a child, and loathe even more now that I've reread it as an adult, is *Mary Poppins* by P.L. Travers, whose heroine was recently beatified by an American critic as "a combination fairy godmother, guardian angel, shamaness, priestess, witch, and guru . . . like Mary Magdalene, she speaks as a woman who knows the All." There speaks a man who in all likelihood did not read the book when he was young.

P.L. Travers is constantly playing to the adult audience, with an air of coy whimsy that can only be described as bloodcurdling. She digresses from her story to pretend that Mr. Banks "makes money" by snipping coins out of gold paper to bring home in a little black bag; she toys with the servant problem, indulges in a little byplay, utterly meaningless to a child, about Royal Academy art, and throws in two or three episodes of stardust and star fairies that seem to have derived from J.M. Barrie via the treacle vats.

Worst of all is the persona of Mary Poppins, the nanny with magical powers. Beady-eyed, peremptory, hardhearted, her most characteristic (and repulsive) utterance is a contemptuous sniff. She keeps the children in perpetual agonies of suspense about whether she will abandon them or not. In fact, she is extraordinarily vindictive, with the disconcerting megalomania of a baby. Her magic is inconsistent and perverse: She takes them to see an amusing uncle for a jaunty airborne tea party, and then righteously denies that the whole episode has taken place. Prim, conceited, and greedy, she self-satisfiedly flaunts all the petty sins for which she reproves the children, teases the children with promises of magic, and snaps at them when they respond with excitement, jeers at their most natural emotions, and saves the best adventures for herself.

The most unpleasant event in the book is the celebration of Mary Poppins's birthday, in honor of which the animals at the zoo brutally humiliate elderly women and pin-striped gents. Mary preens herself over this display like a veritable Nero at the circus. The second most unpleasant episode is the magical circumnavigation of the globe, when the children are introduced to black natives at the South

Pole (the geography is as inconsistent as the magic) who welcome them obsequiously—"Youse mighty welcome. You bring dem chillun dere into ma l'il house"—and offer them watermelon; then there are the Indians in the West who offer hospitality: "My wigwam awaits you; we are just frying a reindeer for supper." Even this racist journey is coherent compared to a bizarre episode in a bakery, where a malignant old crone snaps off the babies' fingers and makes them into gingerbread, breaks into menacing and berserk cackles of laughter, and is then deemed by the children to be "very nice after all." Mary Poppins, as usual, fails to explain things to the children or to protect them. Some fairy godmother, some guru.

Travers's writing is shallow and self-indulgent; her helter-skelter plot, with its utter lack of inner logic or character development, is casually and mistakenly accepted by adults as "magic" appropriate for children just because it involves some hocus-pocus. I can't help but think that many children, lured to the book by its Walt Disney movie version, are rattled and privately puzzled by this meaningless and even sinister concoction.

In all fairness, though, I must say that I have met many adults who did read *Mary Poppins* in their childhood and who tell me they reveled in her infantile character. Here we run smack into one of those difficulties of assessing children's literature: Because children have so little intellectual distance from the books they read, their reactions can be a tangle of personal and extraliterary. Two of my own most anxious concerns in childhood were fear of abandonment and adults who didn't believe me when I told the truth. Perhaps other children could accept Mary Poppins's quixotic and hostile behavior with equanimity, or enjoy it as a sort of vengeful satire on their own less-than-perfect guardians, whereas I felt angered and threatened beyond endurance.

Even allowing for such individual responses, though, I still feel that the Poppins fantasy is too sloppy and unworked-out. As LeGuin says, "Fantasy is a journey. It is a journey into the subconscious mind, just as psychoanalysis is. Like psychoanalysis, it can be dangerous; and *it will change you.*" E. Nesbit's fantasies, written at the turn of the century, changed *my* life, so I know firsthand that LeGuin is right. You can't, of course, prescribe or dictate which book will change a child's life; one of the profound powers of literature is, as MacDonald intimates in the passage I quoted at the head of this chapter, that each reader plumbs a different depth and carries away a uniquely private treasure. The most you can do is make available and accessible the books that you believe to be rich enough to afford this kind of serendipity, and let the child's mind do the rest.

I had librarians who were knowledgeable and tactful enough to recommend Nesbit's books to me at precisely the right moment of my life. On the surface, they are comedies of Victorian family life. In *Five Children and It,* the five children (Robert, Anthea, Jane, Cyril, and the baby, called the Lamb because its first word was "Baa") discover a crotchety sand fairy, the Psammead, who can grant wishes. Their adventures are classic variations on the old "foolish wish" theme of fairy tales, amusingly modernized to include the pony carts, snobbish aristocrats, gypsies, servants, and townspeople who normally populate the worlds of Victorian children's stories. Nesbit's genius was to give these adventures to a realistically grubby, quarrelsome, and thoroughly decent family of youngsters whose conversation reads as freshly today as it did when it was written.

The same children appear in *The Phoenix and the Carpet* and finally *The Story of the Amulet,* both of them inspired works of humor and adventure. It was *The Story of the Amulet* in particular that sent a shiver of wild surmise into my nine-year-old soul. I can still recall the moment when the five children, now traveling in time thanks to the powers of an ancient Egyptian amulet, go forward into the London of the future. Nesbit, a Fabian socialist, draws a vision of a green world, a world without poverty or cruelty, through which the Thames runs sparkling clear and school is so fascinating that children cry when they are expelled for a day. There the children meet a boy named Wells (after H.G. Wells, "The Great Reformer") and his mother, a gentle woman who tells them stories of the horrid Dark Ages when coal smoke darkened the London sky and says "the suffering of the people hardly bears thinking of."

This contrast of two societies—one cruelly workaday, and one a green utopia influenced by William Morris's *News from Nowhere*—changed me by giving me my first, astounding intimation that *the world could be different, and that people could change it;* it was a primitive perception, perhaps, but an earth-shaking one for a child utterly, unthinkingly wrapped in the cocoon of unchanging family life in Toronto of the late 1940s. From that moment on, a gleam of rebellion glowed in me; I knew that my life mustn't pass without my trying to make some difference in the world. (From the point of view of a conservative, of course, this proves LeGuin's point that fantasy can be dangerous.) It's a sidelight on the power of childhood reading that when, in university, I read *News from Nowhere,* it went straight to my heart—even though I didn't realize then that I had visited that land before, in *The Story of the Amulet.*

With Grahame, Norton, White, and Nesbit we are still in the

world of the middle reader, where home and parents are a loved and loving counterpoise to the tug of adventure. In *A Year and a Day*, a haunting book for the middle age-group by the prolific and lavishly gifted author William Mayne, the pull is all toward home and hearth. Two little girls, Rebecca and Sara, living in a working-class cottage in a nineteenth-century Cornish village, draw the eeriness and strangeness into their own family when they find a "wild boy" and bring him home.

It is worth quoting the beginning passage of the book as a sample of Mayne's prose:

> Rebecca sat with her feet in the water and her head in the ground. That was what she thought she was doing. Her feet were in the sea, feeling a soft mud. The top of the water came up and down slowly in her legs, warm as it came up, and cold as it went down. The rest of her was lying in some grass, and she was looking with her head upside down toward the church behind her. The tower went up very steeply into the blue sky. Something seemed to walk across her face. She put her hand to her eyes to push it away, and sat up. She kicked the sea, getting up so fast. The sea kissed the back of her knee, very wet. The thing that had crossed her face was only a horse and a cart and a man, not touching her at all, but dropping a shadow on her, and coming between her and the church . . .

Mayne conveys minute physical sensations with such intense clarity and precision, in the same order as they are felt and then understood by his characters, that it draws us almost physically into the character's mind and sensory world. As Rebecca goes up the pasture lane in search of her sister, on the brink of that strange moment when they find the naked and speechless boy, the sand on her legs dries to sparkling pottery, and then to dust, in the baking heat of the day. We feel not only the sea's kiss and then the heat, but Rebecca's quick reflex of fear and then her flicker of annoyance when she calls her sister in the silent woods, and a cow startles her with a "long bellowing message that sounded rather stupid. Some cows will shout senseless messages."

Sara crashes out of the woods (Becca, the more sensitive and imaginative of the two, likes to stay at the edge and imagine herself in it) shouting, "See what I have found." Sitting in a grassy tangle like a nest, it is a little boy with dark hair and dark eyes and skin pale as milk. He looks at them. He has no clothes on. Their conversation, as always in Mayne, is teasingly tangential and totally revealing. "No clothes. Sacred," says Becca. "Naked," says Sara. "That's the word. Like Adam and Eve." Becca replies—and here we are left to imagine her surprise and earthy realism—"Like but only Adam."

(True, a North American reader may have to puzzle for a moment or two over that unfamiliar locution, "Like but only Adam"—that is, "like Adam only." Many British books are rejected for the North American market because they contain such minor difficulties of idiom, expression, and custom. My belief is that when we protect children from the unfamiliar, rinse their books of any linguistic strangeness, and muffle them up in the security blanket of the mundane, we are depriving them of all that reading stands for. As a child, reading British books, I had to struggle to unravel the mysteries of elevenses, prefects, petrol, lifts, Mars bars, brollies, and Wellingtons; I remember piecing together the clues from the context, and savoring the richly exotic feel of such words as though I had just hauled treasures home from an eastern bazaar. To purge all foreignness from children's reading matter is to diminish their intellectual skills and narrow their empathy—to make them parochial and limited.)

Janey Tregose, a local "wise woman" and midwife, comes to see the strange foundling, and insists that it's a fairy child: "And since you kept him across a candleteening, why, he's here a year and a day, and then he'll be here no more, one way and another. A year and a day. You remember that." This enigmatic speech, the longest so far in the book, gains all the more force from that one strange word "candleteening." All the dialogue in the book, in fact, is rich in overtone, color, and humor; the girls' parents don't have to be described because, through their tersely affectionate and colloquial speech, almost poetic in its evocation of country beliefs and ways, a kind of elemental solid goodness shines through.

Mayne has an uncanny feel for childhood perceptions, thoughts, and emotions, and the artistic genius to express them in the most movingly oblique moments of gesture and speech. Through the simple events of a country year—the arrival of the laden fishing boats and the salting of the winter's fish, the winter fox hunt, the ripening of the blackcurrants—he shows us also the tender ripening of the children's awareness. The story is beautifully rounded out, with poignant loss balanced by the birth of mother's new baby.

A Year and a Day has little to do with conventional ideas of magic or fantasy, but it is so densely packed with a complete social structure (all this in ninety-six pages), and so vibrant with character, drama, sensory vividness, and sly humor, that it is as haunting as any story ever written. Yet all the nuance and depth of emotion is accessible to a careful reader of ten or eleven, for whom the passionate family drama is still at the magical center of being.

Joan Aiken, the ebullient English humorist, aims at the same age group with her linked stories of *Black Hearts in Battersea, Nightbirds on Nantucket,* and *The Cuckoo Tree,* but she takes her readers a jaunty leap sideways: Home is where the rogues are. All the adults are eccentric, hapless dreamers or villainous schemers, and her exuberant young heroes do very nicely on their own. They live in a mythical England where King James the Third is on the throne and the dastardly Twite family, abetted later by the Slighcarps, are involved in a series of lunatic Hanoverian conspiracies to overthrow him.

Aiken is closest to Leon Garfield in her virtuoso use of language. Dido Twite in *Black Hearts in Battersea,* who nearly runs away with the story by sheer brash, scrawny vitality, speaks a cheerfully invented version of cockney: "Brush on, cullies," she urges her comrades in derring-do on a listing ship, "The ship's betwaddled . . . you *are* a loblolly." Dido, with her rowdy appreciation of "ripsmasher" and "slumdigger" moments of excitement, is softened by the friendship offered by fifteen-year-old Simon, the sturdy, sensible, goodhearted sort of hero who is most at home in a fairy tale.

And these are fairy tales, breathlessly exaggerated and fondly parodied to be sure; complete with lost princes, switched identities, silver bracelets, and frantic plot reversals. Though there are villains and wolves and pirates and gunpowder plots, there is no true horror. It is the spunk, natural goodness, and high spirits of the heroes which are in the foreground, overcoming the most daunting difficulties.

In *Nightbirds on Nantucket,* perhaps the most tightly and sparklingly written of the three Simon and Dido books, Aiken goes so far as to spoof Moby Dick—but friendship, not slaughter, is the finale of Captain Casket's lifelong pursuit of the pink whale, Rosie. Dido is at her best as she rescues the captain's daughter, Dutiful Penitence Casket, from a life of pious repression ("Oh, *scrape* ladylike behavior!").

Scattering colorful oaths around her like confetti—"Croopus!" and "Lor love a lily-white duck!" and "Great Snakes! I'm crabbish hungry"—the resourceful Dido is sharp as a tack in puncturing yet another Hanoverian plot. This time, the plot involves a lovable dupe, Professor Breadno, who is constructing a giant cannon (in his weird Scando-German dialect, the professor dotingly calls it a "monstershoot grosseboom") to fire all the way from Nantucket to St. James Palace. ("Is cleverness, not? Will be magnifibang!")

Through all the slapdash merriment, Aiken keeps tight control of her plot, makes the improbable characters come alive through their language, and weaves in some bright threads of convincing friendship and kindness. It is sentimentality, not emotion, that is briskly undercut by Dido's salty practicality. And almost imperceptibly, we have seen friendship change Dido from an impetuously self-centered urchin to a self-assured and compassionate girl.

Most fantasies, in fact, beyond those for the earliest age groups, are journeys of self-discovery and coming of age. While the so-called problem novelists have battened joyously onto the growth market for adolescent novels, they seem to have mistaken the symptoms for the dis-ease: relentlessly, they write about acne, masturbation, divorce, abortion, stupid teachers, witless parents. The best fantasy writers, though, know better than to trample all over the fragile terrain of puberty like cattle at a watering hole. There are agonies worse than acne, most of them too deeply felt and complex for easy expression or solution, and good fantasy writers approach these mysteries at a tangent.

Grinny by Nicholas Fisk is a genuinely horrifying science fiction tale suitable for children of eleven and up. Fast-moving, colloquial, and utterly accessible, it is exactly the sort of book that can be offered as an alternative to the badly written, shallow "realistic" stories which teachers often insist are the only thing that slower readers will read. True, a story as quiet and strange as a *A Year and a Day* might be savored only by a literate, perceptive reader, but it's hard to imagine any child who wouldn't be riveted by *Grinny*. It's told in lively, almost slangy first person style as the diary of eleven-year-old Tim. Though we are immediately unsettled by the arrival of the sinister Great Aunt Emma, who somehow mesmerizes the adults into thinking they remember her, the tension and mounting spookiness are leavened by Tim's sarcasm and boyish humor—usually at the expense of his maddeningly adorable little sister, Beth, age seven. "Beth was ever the Outstanding Social Success," writes the disgruntled Tim. He takes consolation in banter with his father about the soppy emotionalism of women and the unfair advantages they enjoy.

Great Aunt Emma swiftly turns out not to be quite what she seems, and it is the despised Beth who twigs first. "Pooh," she says, after being forced to kiss GAE good-night. "She doesn't smell. It's all wrong." And then Beth swears that when GAE slipped and fell in the backyard, her hand was dangling from a wrist that was all too genuinely broken: The skin was open in a gash, the bones were showing—and there was no blood. "The bones were made of shiny steel, like little collections of umbrella ribs."

Once Tim is convinced by Beth that "Grinny" (as Beth spitefully calls her) is not a real person, but a visitor from a spaceship, the children are plunged into the real dilemma: The adults are hypnotized. No matter how many inadvertent clues Grinny lets slip that she is a highly sophisticated and malevolent robot, the adults refuse to believe the evidence of their senses.

One of the most disillusioning passages of prepuberty is just this realization that adults are not infallible. And the first and most frustrating revelation of adult frailty, to many children, is the experience of standing by, helplessly, while adults are duped (viz. *Madeline and the Bad Hat*) by a fraud transparent to children.

As Tim begins to realize that the three children—Tim, Beth, and their friend Mac—are utterly alone against this powerful invader, he must gradually shift ground. Only on second reading do you notice how deftly Fisk has planted the hints at Tim's transformation into the developing story. Once the adults have proven impervious to the truth, Tim begins to distance himself from that manly English reticence of which he boasted earlier. Derision for his parents' "hear-no-evil" stance creeps into his tone; he begins to imagine a ghastly scene in which the adults line up, chatting about tea and the price of beef "and being marched off to the slaughter, absently swiping away the screaming, begging children" who know the truth.

In the end, it is precisely by the concentrated power of intuition and emotion—Beth's despised emotionalism has finally roused not only Tim's awareness but also his compassion—that the children conquer Grinny. The last triumphant scene, when the children turn her mysterious electric torch on her (it bites her apart, tears and nibbles with "humped-up scurryings and lunges and tugs like a rat," until Grinny is nothing but a pile of metallic rubbish) is absolutely revolting and superbly satisfying. Fear and horror are familiar emotions to a child; the conquest over nightmare is a legitimate literary experience, particularly when it is so well controlled by the author and so thoroughly exorcized by the young protagonists themselves.

The flip side of horror is, of course, comedy, the celebration of hopefulness in human life, and an apt medium for tales of youthful growing pains. Two excellent examples of comic fantasy spring to mind: Helen Cresswell's *The Bongleweed* and *Alan Mendelsohn, the Boy from Mars* by Daniel M. Pinkwater.

In *The Bongleweed,* we first see Becky in the potting sheds at Pew Gardens with her father, Finch, the head gardener, and in three quick lines of dialogue, their characters and their companionable relationship are established. " 'Oh Dad,' said Becky. 'Polishing spades again!' 'A good workman,' he began, not even lifting his head. 'Oh I know,' she said quickly, 'Don't tell me again. I believe you.' "

Becky loves the garden, perhaps more fiercely than her father does, but she is restlessly poised on the hinge of adolescence: Finch reproaches her for not having enough respect "for the things that really matter." True enough, Becky distrusts the scientific botanical mania shared by Finch and his boss Dr. Harper. Impatient, scornful but curious, she spies on the adult world through a peephole into the dining room of the Harpers' grand house, separated from the Finches' own little house by one thin wall.

In a moment of petulance—annoyed, too, because she is expected to entertain twelve-year-old Jason, a brainy but sickly boy who has come to visit the Harpers—Becky plants a mysterious seed, prized by Dr. Harper, in her mother's kitchen garden. That night, she hears a strange whispering noise under her window—"a hissing like wind in poplars, a conspiracy of leaves . . . bless, bless, bless . . . or was it wish, wish . . . or again us, us . . ."

It is the bongleweed growing, growing phenomenally, magically, and soon the giant plants are rioting in growth, springing to fifteen feet tall overnight, smothering the cemetery next doory in a twining, leaping jungle of greenery. While Finch and his sturdy wife Else are badly rattled by the bongleweed (and their working-class pragmatism, touched with endearing eccentricity, makes them a marvelous creation), Becky and Jason are drawn into the conspiracy of uncontrollable life.

> She wanted to laugh at the sheer nerve of it, the life, the
> cheek of the thing, with its careless lack of consideration for
> walls, boundaries, rules—even for all the laws of nature—
> With a sudden rush of affection, she realized that she *loved* it,
> found it bold and splendid beyond anything she had ever
> known.

Becky and Jason are like a prelapsarian Adam and Eve, sitting under the apple tree lost in wonder at the lush beauty of the bongleweed: When it flowers, the blossoms are apricot colored, of extraordinary sheen and delicacy, like silk umbrellas. This is, however, no passive flower; it has the strength and wiliness of a panther, a lion; its rush to growth is unstoppable, like Becky's own. And Becky learns that she has power over the weed. She created it, she named it, and, at last, she can command it to draw back and make a passage for her through its densest thickets.

The whole of this adventure is written with the most engaging poetic exuberance, always balanced by the gruff realism of Finch and the believably acerbic sparring of Becky and Jason. The bongleweed must die, of course, and it dies not by the hand of the scheming undergardener, but by "nature taking its course"—a spring frost. But Becky has changed. She has experienced not only the exultation of adolescence with its sudden burst of joy when it realizes its own surging power but also "a complicated sadness" at the opening of a subtle gap between her and her parents. But she is most definitely not sorry for having planted that seed. And when the bongleweed dies ("wish ... loss ... miss ..." are the last evocative whispers Becky hears from it) she consoles the grieving Jason. She knows that now there has been one bongleweed, anything—anything desperate, beautiful, and reckless—is possible.

Not one youngster in a thousand may explicitly recognize the images of puberty, the echoes of the Garden of Eden, in this lovely and funny story, but many will respond to its energy without knowing why.

Alan Mendelsohn, the Boy from Mars is a comedy in an entirely different tone. This is the wry, sophisticated, satirical voice of the North American city boy, woefully exiled with his parents to a new home in the suburbs. Portly Leonard Neeble is too short and rumpled to be acceptable at his new school, Bat Masterson Junior High, where all the gleaming tanned youths match each other in their permapress clothes and conspire together to ostracize anyone who doesn't conform.

Pinkwater, as usual, is the tenderhearted champion of every harmless eccentric and hapless outsider in America. But that doesn't stop him from spoofing their nuttiness either: Leonard's grandmother, a health food maniac, who likes to be called the Old One, lives "basically on what grandfather's parrot eats": sunflower seeds and nut cutlets. And Leonard's father, when he is not compulsively barbecuing, is complacently showing off his new electric remote-control garage door opener.

Leonard is more than usually lonely now that the family has moved far from his grandparents and his inner city buddies who don't care what people look like. But he is saved by a new friend at school, the tough and self-sufficient Alan Mendelsohn, a boy who refuses to submerge his individuality.

Together, the two boys stumble on Samuel Klugarsh's shop where they buy his patented mind control system and learn to achieve "mental state 26." Until they run into the biker and folk singer Clarence Yojimbo, a Venusian, all they can do with their "mind control" is to make strangers take off their hats and rub their bellies ... But no synopsis can do justice to the galloping hallucinatory quality of the boys' adventures, spiked all the way through with satirical swipes at contemporary life.

It is part of Pinkwater's comedic skill that he can captivate readers with precisely the foibles he's trying to spoof. Of course, a deepened consciousness of life's complexities is what the boys arrive at, but their journey through the mumbo-jumbo of the occult is rich in lunatic pleasures, like the Bermuda Triangle Chili Parlor (three strengths of chili: regular, H-Bomb, and Green Death), throwback genius chickens, and Nafsulian linguistics (the ancient Nafsulian words, Haya and Doon, survive today in a common American greeting).

Leonard's loyalty to his friend Alan and his bravery in following through the demands of "interplanar existential communications" have their reward. After all the science fictional escapades, Leonard has figured out how to survive in high school, how to cooperate with the system without surrendering. Disguised in antic colors like a court jester, Pinkwater is nevertheless steadily, subversively on the side of human life and sanity.

Science fiction has an innate fascination for boys, compounding electronic gadgetry with cowboy characters. The phallic speed and thrust of missiles and spaceships notwithstanding, there are other forms of fantasy that might prove just as appealing and offer deeper pleasures. Diana Wynne Jones is a British fantasist of astonishing originality and power. She is equally adept at those mind-opening reversals of perceptions (*The Power of Three*) that make *The Borrowers* outstanding, and at wittily elaborate magical farces (*Witch Week* and *The Magicians of Caprona*). Like Joan Aiken, she happily borrows from myth, legend, and folk tale for her basic plot ingredients. But so accomplished is she at sleight-of-hand and bewildering complications that they exist just out of sight, submerged like the concrete underpinnings of a fantastically ornate bridge.

The Homeward Bounders, in fact, is based on the craze for fantasy and war gaming, and is a bracing antidote to the excesses of both. Not till halfway through *The Homeward Bounders* does it become clear that the first-person hero, thirteen-year-old Jamie Hamilton, has been permanently exiled from his nineteenth-century English working-class home by a shadowy group of futuristic gamers who play "The Real and Ancient Game" with real people and overlapping worlds.

Struggling through endless worlds, some more tormented than others, Jamie begins to discover other Homeward Bounders, who, like him, are doomed to walk the boundaries of the worlds forever. Among them are legendary or mythological figures like Prometheus, the Flying Dutchman, the Wandering Jew—all of them plausibly entangled in the complex plot, and all of them springing into a curious new life in Wynne Jones's hands.

Just as *The Homeward Bounders* is tailor-made for the youth who can't be coaxed to read anything but Dungeons and Dragons handbooks or sci-fi, *Dogsbody* may entice a girl who's stuck on animal stories to reach a little further. The story begins when Sirius, the dog star, a hothead among the stellar beings, is exiled by a heavenly court of judgment for an alleged murder and for the accidental loss of a "zoi," an object of supreme magical power. Sirius is cast down to earth in the form of a newborn puppy, an unwanted byblow who turns up (red ears and all) in a pedigree setter's litter.

Sirius grows to dog's estate, and his growing strength and understanding are brilliantly delineated from the dog's eye point of view—albeit a supernatural dog who just happens to be cared for by a lonely orphan girl, Kathleen, living with her unlovable aunt, uncle, and cousins.

Sirius's dawning realization that he is a fallen star on a mysterious earthly mission is perfectly integrated with his clumsy, enthusiastic growth from puppyhood. Somehow, Wynne Jones conveys a doggy nature of wagging optimism that perfectly accords with the boundless energy of an astral lord. Sirius's growth, not coincidentally, parallels a child's development into maturity and skill, and also the progress of the meek, almost Cinderellalike Kathleen toward self-assertion and independence. As in all Wynne Jones's books, the narrative suspense is muscular enough to carry the reader right through mazes of bewildering plot twists. *Dogsbody* is, however, one of her more coherent and accessible fantasies, a sometimes rueful, sometimes lyrical journey toward self-knowledge.

At the pinnacle of all such fantasies stand two trilogies: *A Wizard of Earthsea* by Ursula K. LeGuin, and *The Ice Is Coming* by Australian author Patricia Wrightson. There are remarkable points of similarity in the structure of the two trilogies, and it is this underlying pattern that makes them both so vividly appropriate for adolescent reading. In the first books, a boy goes through trials and crises to emerge in manhood as a powerful magic-user. (Magic as a metaphor for adult potency and knowledge is particularly apt for young readers; these two books are unusual in that it is the boy who attains that power, not a wizardly father figure who has it already). In the second books, the youth helps an enchanted (in the sense of "sung into a spell") girl-woman free herself to become fully sensually alive and self-determining. In the third books of each trilogy, the man accomplishes his lifework—a struggle against evil that lies partly within himself—grapples with death, and passes beyond the active, heroic stage of his life.

The publication of *A Wizard of Earthsea* in 1968 immediately established Ursula LeGuin as the leading writer of fantasy in North America; her invention of a "secondary world" is second only to Tolkien's (if that) in richness, detail, consistency, and fascination. LeGuin's "archipelago" is complete with island nations and tribes, each with its own commerce, language, culture, and religion, and into this lucidly imagined world, on the island of Gont in the storm-racked Northern Sea, is born an impetuous, neglected, dark-skinned boy whose birth name is Duny.

Duny (later he takes the name of Sparrowhawk, with the secret true name of Ged) is reared harshly by an aunt who dabbles in cottage witchcraft. The boy soon shows frightening depths of magic power, and a frightening arrogance in using them carelessly. By the age of twelve he has mastered all the local lore of "finding, binding, mending, unsealing, and revealing, various tricks and pleasantries and spells of illusion" and is taken on as an apprentice by the mild and wise Ogion the Mage.

A fantasy writer, in creating an wholly fabricated world, spins a web of imagination that is easily torn. A clumsy word, an anachronism, an accent of "Poughkeepsie," and our eager belief is fatally torn. LeGuin, however, never puts a word wrong. Her prose is vigorous, precise, clear, and sturdy enough to sustain a whole archipelago; even at her most incantatory (". . . this was the way he was to follow all his life, the way of magery, the way that led him at last to hunt a shadow over land and sea to the lightless coasts of death's kingdom . . .") she does not embarrass her readers with a falsely exalted tone. Her mages speak with the kind of runic simplicity that delights young readers while it illuminates her mode of thought: When Sparrowhawk, impatient for more dazzling feats of magical power, asks Ogion, "When will my apprenticeship begin, sir?" Ogion answers, "It has begun." "But I haven't learned anything yet!" "Because you haven't found out what I am teaching."

What Ogion is teaching is restraint and moderation, the search for the innate Balance and Pattern in all creation. But Sparrowhawk wants more, and rashly uses a spell to raise the dead. "Looking over his shoulder, he saw that something was crouching beside the closed door, a shapeless clot of shadow darker than darkness." Ogion rescues him from the nameless nightmare that Sparrowhawk has summoned, but deeply reproves him: Danger surrounds power as shadow does light, Ogion tells him, and he sends his headstrong pupil at last to the school of wizardry at Roke to learn the High Art.

A school of wizardry offers almost unlimited scope to a gifted writer, and LeGuin makes the most of it; we are shown in fascinating detail what Sparrowhawk learns, and it is the densely realized detail that is enchanting: the lessons in shape changing, the spells over wind and weather taught by Master Windkey, the long hours in the Isolate Tower under the stern tutelage of the Master Namer, who teaches them the thousands of true and hidden names of things in which real magic inheres.

Unlike most fantasy writers, however, LeGuin does not equip her hero with nifty weapons and send him out to defeat evil in one great clanging battle. Sparrowhawk-Ged's true battle is with himself. Time and again, arrogance and ego lead him to rash acts of excess. His enemy is the dark thing, "the shadow," the Archmage tells him, "of your ignorance, the shadow that you cast."

Scarred and humbled, Sparrowhawk leaves the school at the age of nineteen, in a blue cloak and clutching a yew staff, to work as an unassuming neighborhood wizard on the remote sea-washed island of Low Torning, where housewives row across canals to take a cup of rushwash tea with a neighbor. From there he begins the series of voyages and crises—battles with dragons, journeys to far seas with his roughhewn friend Vetch—to "finish what he began," to find, face, and name the shadow he unloosed.

One reason the fantasy never loses its grip on our attention is LeGuin's power to create intensely attractive male heroes. Ged's potency is admirable rather than bellicose and repellent. His maturity is not that of a warrior or conqueror, but the maturity of a man who recognizes and leashes his aggression. His tenderness is the movingly gentle gesture of a man of great power and self-knowledge.

The second story in the trilogy is equally compelling and even more tautly written. In *The Tombs of Atuan,* the scene shifts to a distant, dusty island of the archipelago where an order of priestesses presides over ancient rituals in the place of ancient tombs. Images of ruin, dryness, and emptiness predominate in LeGuin's evocation of this grim place. As usual, details of food, work, materials, and crops, herbs, and songs appear naturally, unforcedly, in the narrative. And this is a convincingly three-dimensional world, in which all these details accord. You always know, with LeGuin, that if the local people eat corn porridge, there will be cornfields, workers who must draw water for the fields, a ritual and a pattern for the watering and harvesting, and a sharp feel for the taste of the thing.

Tenar, the peasant girl chosen in infancy to be Arha, the Eaten One, the high priestess of the Tombs with their dark gods, is the heroine of the story. By the time she reaches the age of fifteen, we

know her fierceness, her somber resolution, and the deeply buried
gleam of defiance in her character that will lead her, with Ged's help,
to shatter the ancient maze of underground tombs and find her freedom. The clutch of a fearful religion on a young soul is shown this
powerfully in only one other children's book that I know of: *The Blue
Hawk,* by Peter Dickinson, in which a boy, Tron, is doomed to priesthood in an equally baleful ancient order. Like Tenar, he, too, is freed
at last with the help of his own questioning mind and of a young
man on a quest of his own.

But as a story of a young womanhood bursting the bonds of
repression, *The Tombs of Atuan* is unique, reverberating with archetypal echoes that LeGuin herself recognized as Jungian only some
years after writing the book. And though Ged is at his prime in this
book—gentle, knowing, profoundly resigned—it is friendship, not
sexual love, which he offers the struggling Tenar. All his magic is
placed at the service of her emergence from the suffocating, imper-
sonal dark. "You told me to show you something worth seeing," says
Ged, imprisoned in the tombs by the priestesses, and ordered by a
hostile Tenar to create a magical illusion. "I show you yourself."
Later, when the two have escaped, Tenar wakes outside the temple
compound on a hillside, filled with sweetness and pleasure. "Living,
being in the world, was a much greater and stranger thing than she
had ever dreamed." Though Tenar naturally is drawn romantically
to her rescuer, Ged, the impulse is unexpressed except for one sentence ("What was in her heart as she looked at him in the firelight
she could never say"). This reserve deepens the impact of the story,
mirroring a truth in the lives of young girls and leaving Tenar as the
center of energy and action in a story that is open-ended.

The last book in the trilogy, *The Farthest Shore,* is the most
complex and least satisfying; perhaps that is inevitable, since its subject is the confrontation of the aging Ged, now Archmage, with death
itself. The sense of confusion in the philosophical underpinnings of
the story is reflected in the first falterings of LeGuin's pristine language: There are more "Aye, lad" slips into strained dialogue, and
the overwhelming aura of moral disorder and decay is disheartening.
But the book is distinguished by the most original and magnificent
dragons in literature, ancient and thunderously immense creatures
whose eyes glitter with a remote and ironic amusement at the doings
of men.

Like LeGuin, Patricia Wrightson places a dark-skinned hero at
the center of a magic-drenched land, but this is not a mythical world—
it is Australia. In a flowing, open voice, the rolling rhythms of the
tale-teller rather than the flat choppy edginess of most contemporary

prose, the narrator begins by showing us the vast landscape set in a tumbling, beating sea. White people are marginal here. Wrightson, in a clever distancing trick, calls them the Happy Folk, and shows us a frantic, cavorting society of consumers scattered along the fringes of the "great open hand" of the continent. We see them rushing about in pursuit of pleasure on beaches and in shopping malls, but we see them as though through the wrong end of a telescope, tiny as puppets and somehow irrelevant to the massive ancient unknown land slumbering behind them.

We see them also through the old eyes of young Wirrun, an aborigine who lives among but not of them, quietly working in gas stations and taverns but keeping his own counsel and listening uneasily to voices from elsewhere. A teenager, he notices first some small newspaper accounts of ice being found, in midsummer, in isolated rock hollows and gullies. Quietly, he begins to collect evidence, unnoticed or dismissed by the Happy Folk, that something is going wrong in the land.

Wrightson draws on aboriginal folklore to create a secret population of earth spirits who have always lived in the land. There is the Mimi, thin and frail rock spirit from the far North, with round frightened eyes like a possum, carried away accidentally to the south by an errant wind, to the desert where "the sun beats down like a gong." There are the Ninya, men of ice in caverns of ice, whose voices creak and grate as they plot to take over the land—the sinister summer frost is their first sly attempt to repossess the country. And there is the Nargun, most ancient and powerful rock spirit of all, whom Wirrun must find in order to stop the ice.

It is Wrightson's extraordinary accomplishment to have found a vigorous, startlingly fresh language for all these ancient spirits. Amid the spate of children's fantasy novels that work and rework the Arthur legend and Celtic history, this is the most original and surprising creation of them all. The whole face of Australia leaps into majestic and secret life.

Wrightson's earth spirits are vibrant, varied, and individual: the sullen Bagini has clawed fingers and sly hard eyes; the faces of the prankster Pot-Kuroks are clownishly woeful; the fierce, angrily buzzing little Wa-tha-gun-darl growl "Very long time not see that Nargun"; and every species has its characteristic speech. One almost believes it possible to buy an airline ticket to Australia and be greeted by a spring-kneed, cantankerous, twiggy-fingered Mimi.

The Mimi accompanies the reluctant hero, Wirrun, on his journey to the country's far corners; it is she who gives him courage, and who watches with old spirit eyes as he engages finally in the battle to save the land: "This, [she] knew, was the curious thing that men were made for: to care." Between these two, there is a beautiful ripening of respect, trust, and friendship, as Wirrun grows in understanding and tolerance.

In *The Dark Bright Water*, another female spirit is lost from her rightful place in the land. This time it is a Yunggamurra, a wild, heartless water spirit of uncanny beauty, one of a tribe of sisters whose sport it is to lure men to their deaths. Wirrun is again called on by his people to save the country, this time from a drought. But already he has been troubled by a mysterious, disembodied song— the enchantment song of the lost Yunggarmurra. If Wirrun is "called" by her, his friend Ularra is obsessed. In the town where they both work, Wirrun is disturbed by his friend's dissolute ways; Ularra drinks too much, boasts, and likes to spend evenings in the pub staring at waitresses—"eyeing off a chick," he calls it. Ularra joins Wirrun on the quest to find the cause of the drought and is destroyed, finally, by his sexual drives; Wirrun, also driven, but more complex and aware, struggles to conquer his lust and grows finally into love.

The love story of Wirrun and the Yunggamurra who chooses mortality to be with him is tense, funny, lyrical, and unabashedly sensuous without ever becoming crudely explicit. It's a splendid accomplishment, given the *Blue Lagoon* perils of writing about teenage eroticism played out against a backdrop of wild nature. And though the passages between the two are written in the highly charged language that Wrightson uses for the spirit world, the aesthetic effect is neatly balanced and anchored by the laconic, earthy, and knowing exchanges between Wirrun and the other aboriginal people.

The relationship of Wirrun and Murra, as he calls her, is elaborated in *Behind the Wind*, the third book of the trilogy. Their marriage ("he taught her tenderness and she taught him laughter") is an arcadian romance. Unable to contemplate bringing his lovely wild wife into the Happy Folk cities of flats and jobs, he has chosen instead to lead the old tribal life with her, nomadic and free. But Wirrun has transgressed in mating with magic, and his intense happiness is short-lived. First he loses Murra, who is lured away from individual freedom and back to immortality by the songs, "sharp and sweet as wild honey," of her sisters. Then he must embark on a long, bitter pursuit of the mysterious enemy, an evil spirit, a thing of death. At the end, when he has lost the battle with the Wulgaru but won a triumph of will and spirit, he dies physically and joins Murra in an immortal spirit life.

Like LeGuin, Wrightson boldly tackles the huge perplexities of adolescence: how to live by guiding principles, to reconcile liberty and responsibility, to know what is truly of value, to learn the nature of love and to accept the fact of death. Like LeGuin, she is most abstract and least comforting in the final volume—but then, the very nature of the question of mortality means that it is most remote to young readers, and that no ultimate answer can be given.

Both create heroes of touching nobility; both carry off persuasive portraits of potent men who are also emotionally vulnerable; both have the courage to depict love and friendship as rigorously challenging as physical prowess. Both have dealt with difficult, rewarding themes that could have fallen as flat as a political tract without the depth and range of their imaginative power to create new worlds, so richly and strangely peopled. It is their lasting achievement to have pushed the fantasy form to its farthest reaches without once straining credibility; their triumph is to have written books that, long after they are closed, go on "waking meanings" in the minds of young readers.

Chapter 8

TRAVELING
IN TIME

Sherwood in the twilight, is Robin Hood awake?
Gray and ghostly shadows are gliding through the brake;
Shadows of the dappled deer, dreaming of the morn,
Dreaming of a shadowy man that winds a shadowy
horn . . .

Oberon, Oberon, rake away the gold,
Rake away the red leaves, roll away the mold,
Rake away the gold leaves, roll away the red,
And wake Will Scarlett from his leafy forest bed . . .

Friar Tuck and Little John are riding down together
With quarter-staff and drinking-can and gray goose
feather;
The dead are coming back again, the years are rolled
away
In Sherwood, in Sherwood, about the break of day.

Alfred Noyes, from "A Song of Sherwood"

Time is the element in which we live, like fish in water, and yet the realization that time flows on and on and never flows backward is one of the most stunning of childhood discoveries. Perhaps the shock of that revelation derives from the way time stands still, like a deep dreaming pond, in our earliest years. Those endless summers, lapped in maternal safety that we never dreamed would end, flecked with sunshine and leaf shadows that we always forgot would turn to decay and frost, gave us the blessing of boredom, a time standing still in the heat of noon.

Tranquil, serious, we could lose ourselves in reverie as we contemplated an ant's minute struggles across the Himalayan sidewalk, a minnow's transparent flicker in the bars of sunlight beneath the dock, the precise parallelogram of cool shade behind the house.

I wonder if modern children, rushed from kindergarten to summer camp, with Flintstone reruns to use up any moments in between, have time for that contented, sad, and solitary boredom in which one's being is lost in, or rather, merged with the fragrance and colors of the perceived world. Do modern children have long afternoons to lie on the Persian carpet, staring at the march and swirl of deep red geometric patterns until they blur, sharpen, blur, and become part of one's inner universe?

If timelessness is the taste of early childhood, the rush and spin of time is the dizzying revelation of later years. It does not surprise me that time-slip fantasies, in which the heroes travel backward and forward in time, are among the most enthralling of all children's books. They arouse, and sometimes satisfy, that intense longing of middle childhood years when a lost golden age seems tantalizingly close and yet forever beyond reach.

Is that golden age the Eden of lost childhood, whose memories lie just too deep for recall? Or is it the confused impression of a child who, born into the ongoing lives of others, begins to piece together the fragments of talk and family reminiscence and to reconstruct in imagination a past time that was fuller, more precious and perfect?

The charm of time travel has less mysterious origins, too. What child has not tried to bring the past to life, or wished desperately that some talisman—an ancient stone, an arrowhead—would unlock the door to vanished worlds? And, of course, once you realize that you are indeed a traveler in time, a traveler to a certain end, time has ceased to be reflecting pool and takes on a momentum that is half dreadful, half exhilarating.

On the edge of adolescence, with the future unimaginable and the present a formless flux, the past is burnished by nostalgia. An adolescent's nostalgia is not the doting over quaint objects or the trivia game it fades into for some adults, but the precise original meaning of the word: Nostalgia is "the ache for home." It is the backward step we take on the brink of adulthood. We are about to reject our parents and the safety they offered us; we are about to set our lives in motion, and our first exciting step into the future is shadowed with regret that it will take us farther and farther from that stillness of stopped time in childhood's garden.

"The dead are coming back again, the years are rolled away"— I memorized these lines when I was twelve or so, and they never failed to wake that pleasurable pang of longing. Part of it, of course, is simply that insatiable childhood curiosity to *know,* to spy like Becky of *The Bongleweed* on the grown-up world of the past, partly as a reassurance about the future. But not all time-slip fantasies take the reader back to a golden age. In fact, had it not been for my oldest daughter's love of *Charlotte Sometimes,* by Penelope Farmer I might have entirely missed another aspect of time travel, which is the chance to find consolation for present sadness, to escape temporarily from the prison of our days and to return with the solace that we, too, will change, that sadness or loneliness will pass.

    Charlotte Sometimes, on the face of it, is a book steeped in melancholy, frustrated affections, missed chances at emotional connection. The motherless Charlotte Mary Makepeace, age twelve or thirteen, is the new girl at boarding school: sober, withdrawn, a girl who worries too much to be able to fit in easily with a crowd of boisterous schoolmates. Arriving at school, she is met by a tall older girl, Sarah Reynolds, who inexplicably helps her to find her room and choose the best bed, the one by the window, before the other girls arrive. "My mother," Sarah later explains, cryptically, "told me that if a girl called Charlotte Makepeace came to school I was to be kind to her."

    Charlotte's first day at school is so confusing (looking for her name on dozens of lists, finding her initials here, her surname there) that she feels herself to be many different people—and half of them she doesn't recognize. When she wakes next morning in a room mysteriously transformed, and is addressed as "Clare" by a little girl in the next bed, her confusion deepens. She looks at her hand, touches her face, wonders if you can recognize your own face just by feel.

    Charlotte, in fact, has slipped back into the school as it was in 1918 and switched places in time with the bed's earlier occupant, a devout and straight-laced thirteen-year-old called Clare Moby. Day by day, Clare and Charlotte switch about. Much of the story has a desperately bleak uneasiness to it as Charlotte struggles to cope with unfamiliar schoolwork, and the scrambled perceptions of her by teachers and schoolmates when she reappears in her own present world after Clare has been in her place. Worse, when she is Clare in 1918 she must cope with Clare's ten-year-old sister Emily, a quick-witted and mercurial child who reminds her of her own little sister Emma at home. (The similarity in names of the two sets of sister is, I confess, somewhat harrassing to the reader.) Most of all, Charlotte is worried by her own wobbly identity—"not by how Emily knew she wasn't Clare, but why and how she seemed so much like Clare that Emily mistook her for several days."

Though the world of 1918 is comfortless, with its horrid wartime food, its air raids and slippery linoleum and difficult deceptions to avoid detection, Charlotte is stabbed with regret whenever she leaves it. It's as though there is something hidden in that past world that she has to find—or something in the present world she wants to avoid.

What she has to find is a surer sense of her own identity. That confusing process begins when Charlotte finally gets stuck in the past; she and Emily are moved out of the school, with its magic bed, and into grim lodgings at Flintstock Lodge. There, stuck with Clare's identity for months, Charlotte begins to lose all sense of her Charlotte self.

Caught up in the drab lives of the Chisel Brown family at Flintlock Lodge, Charlotte begins to brood about the bull-necked Chisel Brown son who has been killed in the war. Playing with his toys, looking at a picture of him as a youth, she is frightened by the awfulness of how people grow up.

This dread of one's grown-up self is a small submerged theme in children's literature. E. Nesbit uses it to great comic effect, and has one character take comfort from the thought that you grow up so gradually that you have time to get used to it. In Charlotte's case, the worries over her identity have no such easy comic release. One of the book's most hallucinatory and upsetting scenes is the celebration of the armistice, when Emily and Charlotte get separated in a wildly buffeting, hooting, surging crowd. The moment of losing her own self is radically dislocating, surrealistically horrible.

All this seems a long way from the time-slip fantasies of a vanished Eden. Farmer is a powerful enough writer to make the smothering little world of school and Flintstock Lodge almost unbearably uncomfortable; rereading it, I wondered what makes this book so popular that it has run through a dozen printings since its appearance in 1969. Only the ache is there. One night, when Emily puts some marbles in a glass of water, Charlotte muses on their transformed beauty, and how they shrink back to their normal size and plainness when taken out of the glass:

> It was like the difference between what you long for and what you find . . . It was like other times, her own proper childhood time, that seem so near to her memory and yet so far away. It was like everything that made you ache because in one sense it was close and in another unobtainable.

Charlotte never meets Clare, the girl with whom she has been switching places, whom she has imagined as a friend; when Charlotte gets back into her present time, Clare is, of course, gone. But now Charlotte finds a new, tentative alliance with another marginal student, the prickly but bright Elizabeth, who has guessed about the time switch. Elizabeth recognizes Charlotte the minute she reappears, even though Clare has been successfully taking Charlotte's place in the present time, undetected by most, all this while. Identity, it seems, is forever elusive, but absolutely unmistakable. This, too, seems chilly comfort.

The last shock is the discovery that Sarah Reynolds' mother (the woman who told Sarah to be kind to a girl called Charlotte if she ever turned up at school) is not a grown-up Clare, as Charlotte had wistfully begun to hope, but Emily, the little sister from 1918, old enough now to be a grandmother, plump and gray, but having "lived a happy life after all." Clare, it seemed, died in the 1918 flu epidemic right after she returned to her own time. And Emily, writing to Charlotte about all this, sends Charlotte the toys they had played with together at Flintlock Lodge. Charlotte puts the marbles in a jar of water on her dresser, and now that she has some small personal ornament, her dresser looks as though she, too, "belongs" at school.

These are the book's rather wan consolations: Emily has told her that it is possible to grow up and have a happy life; Charlotte now realizes that though Clare is gone, her own memory of being Clare will go on mattering in her life just as the war goes on mattering. Charlotte, in our last glimpse of her, is riding on the bus from school and joining in a rowdy song "No more beetles in my tea / Making googly eyes at me/ No more spiders in my bath/ Trying hard to make me laugh." But that is not quite the last word. "She had never seen spiders in a bath in either time, thought Charlotte seriously . . ."

Charlotte, with her stubbornly serious mind, will never be wholeheartedly part of the extroverted crowd. But she is more sure of herself now, less fearful of the future, and so able to enjoy friendship in the present. In the gray and anxious light of the novel's mood, this small illumination has the special radiance of hard-won optimism. For a time-slip fantasy, *Charlotte Sometimes* is a rare displacement: The glimmer of a golden time is not in the fantasy past, but in the real world of the child's barely glimpsed future. No glory, no sunlit gardens, but hope. I believe, partly on the evidence of my own daughter's undimmed memories of the impact the book had on her life, that this unconventional approach to time travel is intuitively inspired, and speaks straight to the heart of an introverted child hovering uneasily on the brink of adolescence.

Much more common is the heroic or pastoral past, the "Sherwood" of the poem and my daydreams, in which a child derives new strength and wisdom from a magical foray into history. *A Traveler in Time* by Alison Uttley is one of the most lyrical of these. A young girl of Edwardian England, Penelope Taberner Cameron, visits Thatchers, the Derbyshire ancestral farm of her mother's family. There, in a manor house that predates Elizabethan time, she has an almost double experience of the past. The old country ways of her affectionate Aunt Tissie and Uncle Barnabas surround the child with warmth, love, and the nostalgic fragrances and tastes of the rural past. And Penelope goes even further back; a quiet, daydreaming, fanciful child, she opens a door in the ancient farmhouse and there are ladies in long brocaded gowns, who look up at her, startled, from their game with ivory counters beside the firelit hearth.

Penelope goes back more and more often into that Elizabethan era, when the house sheltered a warm and lively family that tried to help Mary Stewart, Queen of Scots, escape from imprisonment. She slips back and forth like a ghost from the future, materializing as a niece of the housekeeper in the Thatchers of 1582, an eager participant in the exciting escape plot, though helpless to change history. The time transference is beautifully and naturally handled:

> The fivefold hills were lavender, indigo, violet in the soft light, one behind another, concealing the small villages in their shadowed troughs. Life went on unseen in those misty shallows, and another life moved in the folded layers of time.

The most satisfying aspect of this book is its loving idealization of Elizabethan times; the bustling, kindly aunts (Dame Cecily in the past is an ancestor of present-day Aunt Tissie), their hands always in a basin of plump dough or floured to the elbow from pastry making, the busy domestic hum of the cool dairies, pantries, and kitchen, the scented herb gardens, all are as rosy and appealing as a ripe apple.

Perhaps the wittiest of all time-slip fantasies is *The Ghost of Thomas Kempe* by Penelope Lively, in which the spirit of a seventeenth-century sorcerer and alchemist, the maddeningly high-handed Thomas Kempe, haunts and bedevils eleven-year-old James Harrison, whose family has just moved into the old village cottage where Kempe once practiced his arts. The invisible Kempe, released from a bottle where he was imprisoned like an errant genie by an earlier inhabitant, takes James for his apprentice and issues peremptory orders, in writing, on papers, mirrors, school notebooks, and even blackboards.

The humor, which is sometimes tart, sometimes hilarious to the point of slapstick, comes from Kempe's meddlesome interventions in the busy, modern, quarrelsome life of the Harrison family. "I am glad to see thee at thy studies, though I lyke not thy bookes," Kempe harrumphs when James does his homework. "Where is thy Latin?" Kempe's busybody invisible spirit breaks pots when the family watches weather forecasts on television ("Thy familie shall knowe what the weather will be from me and not from that eville machine or I will breake more pots . . ."), yanks a chair out from under the bottom of a visiting clergyman, and scrawls furious curses on the walls of an old woman next door ("Widdow Verity is a wytche"). Of course, James or his dog Tim usually get the blame for this mayhem, and James frantically tries to lay the unquiet ghost to rest.

Before he succeeds, though, he is brought into contact with all the townspeople who are, in one way or another, trying to delve into the past—and mostly getting it all wrong. The archaeologists busily digging on the town outskirts are oblivious to the real ghost of the past that accompanies James; the teacher, self-satisfiedly lecturing the class on the gullibility of their forebears who invented witchcraft as an explanation for the inexplicable, falls smack into the same fallacy right in the middle of his lecture: "Pick up those papers, would you, Simon, they keep blowing off the desk," he says distractedly, as the invisible Kempe surges around the classroom.

Others are more tuned in: Mrs. Verity next door, who had seemed like just a nosey old lady to James, tells him an impish anecdote about her youth that makes James realize that people are many layered, with the past still alive in them somewhere. Bert, a local workman, matter-of-factly helps to exorcise Thomas Kempe. The local library turns out to be "inexhaustibly surprising," another place where the past is still alive and acknowledged, like "opening a grocery box and finding it full of Christmas presents."

Most of all, James is aided by a diary he finds buried deep in the rubbish heap of old belongings cleared out from the cottage during the Harrisons' renovations. The diary belonged to a good-hearted Fanny Spence, owner of the cottage in 1856, who entertained her visiting nephew Arnold with boating on the river, a new puppy named Palmerston, and sumptuous feasts of homemade desserts. Arnold, too, it turns out, was plagued by Thomas Kempe. But Arnold, unlike the harassed James, was helped by his sympathetic Aunt Fanny to trap and bottle the alchemist.

To James, Arnold and his dog become even more real than his own doubting friends; he spends long hours in their imaginary company. His daydream of playing with Arnold comforts him for the "odd, lonely, deprived feeling" he had when he had finished reading the diary and grieved because "he would never know about the further adventures of Arnold and Palmerston the puppy." But that's not so; the past is still alive in a hundred different ways, and James learns that the school's portrait of a whiskered benefactor is, after all, a picture of the grown-up Arnold—grateful, apparently, for all his happy vacations in the village.

Penelope Lively is fascinated by the theme of time; another of her skillful and amusing novels on the subject is *A Stitch in Time*, about a shy, introspective little girl on seaside holiday who makes the same discoveries as James about the complex ways in which past history doesn't vanish but becomes part of the web of human existence. Both novels are deeply reassuring about the continuity of time (a moot point in our nuclear era), and about the role of the sensitive, alert child whose own developing maturity parallels and enhances the evolution of humanity's history on earth.

As in *The Ghost of Thomas Kempe*, the past unsettlingly invades the present in *Earthfasts* by William Mayne, this time in the person of Nellie Jack John, an eighteenth-century drummer boy who comes marching—rumpatatump rumpatatump—right out of a crack in the earth before the horrified eyes of two boys in a Cumbrian village. *Earthfasts* is more uncanny, confused, and frightening than *The Ghost of Thomas Kempe*, and the plot less controlled, but it is a gripping and sometimes very funny story. It is also typical of many English novels in its powerful sense of places suffused with past life that threatens to break into the present (not always benignly) at any moment. Again, as in Penelope Lively's work, this is a brisk antidote to the prevailing romantic view of history as a tranquil retreat from present perplexities.

Two recent ventures into time change by Canadian authors take their characters back to a time of war and struggle, in which important truths are to be discovered.

The Druid's Tune is the first novel by a young Canadian writer, O.R. Melling, who sends her two heroes—Rosemary, seventeen, and her fifteen-year-old brother Jimmy—on a vacation trip to relatives on an Irish farm. Their father hopes that the trip will shape them up, since Rosemary has become romantically involved with a law-breaking hippie: He wants them to have a summer of "clean air, hard work, and a good simple way of life . . . maybe you'll come back a little wiser."

If that sounds simplistically reactionary, so is the plot of the book. The teenagers are carried back into Celtic prehistory where Jimmy learns to be a charioteer and then a warrior at the side of the legendary hero Cuculann. Rosemary, in the war party of Queen Maeve, falls in love with a flirtatious princeling called Maine. The agent of their time change is a wandering Druid, a brooding and tormented soul drifting through the centuries, who calls himself, in the present time, Peter Murphy.

There are thumping echoes of C.S. Lewis's Narnia cycle in the way the two youngsters go through a baptism of blood, steeling themselves for righteous war as part of their character building, and there are borrowings from John Masefield (*The Midnight Folk*) and T.H. White (*The Sword in the Stone*) in some of their shape-changing adventures.

Worse than the derivativeness, though, is the leadenly modern soap opera tone in which all characters, both ancient and modern, speak. "Fetch me a Druid. I have enough problems without this infernal delay . . ." snaps Queen Maeve, in the very voice of an impatient matron who summons a tardy plumber. The Druid, fetched, is equally up-to-date: "What is it you want, Maeve?" And Finnabar, a Bronze Age princess, languidly drawls to Rosemary, "Don't mind my mother—she thrives on all this war and slaughter and glory."

Nevertheless, the book has proven remarkably popular, thanks to its strong story line. What it lacks in finesse, it makes up in swiftness, urgency, and contemporaneity. It has romance, melodrama, and the eeriness of the occult ("I see it! Blood pours from the knotted trunk of the sacred tree of fire!"), and thoroughly modern ideas about gender roles: Jimmy learns to cook and to be more emotionally responsive, and Rosemary, when not reveling in romance and beautiful gowns, develops muscles and aggression through her training for war.

O.R. Melling's second novel, *The Singing Stones,* is a more complex and rewarding story, and her narrative style has shed most of its earlier clumsiness. Still, it's worth reading *The Druid's Tune* in tandem with another recent Canadian novel, Janet Lunn's *The Root Cellar,* for the sake of contrast, and to see how satisfying the time-shift theme can be in the hands of an author with depth, subtlety, and a real feel for history—not just for historically correct language and customs, but also for the way earlier generations perceived and thought differently from ours.

Like so many heroes of time-slip novels, Lunn's twelve-year-old Rose Larkin is an isolated, precociously prim youngster who has had an unusually solitary childhood. She has been brought up by a cold, wealthy grandmother and now finds herself on threatening new terrain. We meet her as she arrives from New York, wary and resentful, at the dishevelled rural Ontario home of her aunt, uncle, and rowdy boy cousins. As an orphan, Rose is more than usually rootless; she has no memory of her father, and all she has from her mother is a silver rose on a chain, a copy of *The Secret Garden,* and a music box. Part of her task in the novel is to learn to accept her new family on their own terms, and to accept herself through discovering, as the title hints, her own roots.

In fact, she begins by making "a secret garden" of her own in a beautiful glade near the old house, a place of soft autumn colors which she first explores by moonlight. It is in this garden that Rose stumbles, literally, on the way into the welcoming past. Under the leaf mold, she finds a trap door that leads into an abandoned root cellar; she has just pushed her way through the rotting door and is examining the rows of jars on the shelves when somebody—a girl her own age in a long brown dress, boots, and apron, with one long braid and bright black eyes—stands on the steps behind her and blocks her light. "You'd best get out of the root cellar," says the girl, Susan. "Missus will be terrible cross."

It's an interesting phenomenon that, while boys in time-slip novels are often preoccupied with laying the past to rest, girls often rush into the past to be nurtured by a transforming and empowering mother love. Susan, for example, is one of Lunn's best creations, a practical, affectionate, hard-working hired girl, whose friendship with Rose is an education of the heart.

When Rose emerges from the root cellar to find herself outside the same house, but back in 1862, she also shifts seasons, from a damp autumn to a sunlit, basking June. And this, too, is typical of time-shift stories, when children magically find themselves in that longed-for summer of rapt memory.

This "secret garden" is a vision of colonial prosperity, where the sun glitters on Lake Ontario and where the house, neglected and run-down in Rose's own time, is surrounded by bright flower beds and apple orchards in full bloom. The boy of the house, fifteen-year-old Will Morrissay, feels as restless and rootless as Rose: Just across the bay, the American Civil War is raging, and, because his mother came from the American shore, he is itching to be off to fight on the Union side.

The Root Cellar is particularly fine in making the reader feel Rose's real joy and sensuous delight in the rural past, and her grieving sense of loss when she is accidentally whisked back to the uncomfortable, messy, unresolved present. But it goes much further than this. Eventually, Rose takes part in a great adventure which has the welcome effect of making the complicated American-Canadian mingling of history and culture on the shores of eastern Lake Ontario seem resonant, intimate, a significant shaping force in the development of both countries.

Will has run off to join the Union army, and, when the war is over and he fails to return, Rose (who has learned how to use the root cellar to travel in time) urges Susan to join her in a search. In a long, picaresque, and lively episode, the two girls disguise themselves as boys, cross the lake, and search for Will across the eastern United States, working at odd jobs and finally ending up in Washington, tracking Will from one military hospital to the next.

In this section of the book, the past loses its enchantment and becomes menacingly realistic. It's a time of harsh, postwar dislocation and hardship, and a world of dust, heat, ravaged fields, and reeking hospitals crammed with the war wounded. And when they finally find a battle-shocked Will, his stories of war are more like Stephen Crane's *Red Badge of Courage* than the glorified gory exploits of C.S. Lewis or O.R. Melling.

Like the characters in Penelope Lively's books, Rose must eventually leave the past behind her and engage herself with present realities. The story of her reconciliation with her family is believably tentative, touching, and optimistic. Particularly robust and joyful is her grand gesture of appeasement at the end. She cooks (disastrously) a whole Christmas dinner; the shambles is turned into a gloriously savory Christmas feast, evergreen boughs, candles, and all, with the invisible aid of "old Mrs. Morrissay"—the ghost of grown-up Susan, come back into the future to help Rose. Like James in *The Ghost of Thomas Kempe,* Rose has also found contemporary allies whose memories and fidelity to the past are an important source of continuity. In keeping faith with Susan by vowing to help restore the Morrissay house to its former beauty, Rose gives herself a new sense of rooted identity and purpose.

An author who dips into that still pond of timelessness must also deal with the anguish of its loss. Two memories of my childhood still carry the sharpness of such a loss for me. The first was my conviction, when I was five or six years old, that the towering maple tree on our tiny front lawn had blossomed the previous spring. All of one winter, I waited for that lavish, scented, pink and white flowering foam to reappear. My mother told me that I must have dreamed it: Maple trees don't blossom. I stubbornly believed that she was wrong. I knew I had sat under those blossoms and been filled with their sweetness. Every year, I waited. No matter how keen my disappointment, I was never able to feel, in my heart of hearts, that I had been mistaken. Almost to adulthood, some primitive insistence on the realness of that flowering tree persisted underneath my rational understanding that maple trees don't blossom, and I never quite lost the feeling that somehow I had been cheated.

The second memory is even more explicitly arcadian. When I was eight or nine, my mother took me to see the film version of *A Midsummer Night's Dream*. That enchanted forest, with its imps and fairies who made an airy but palpable link between nature and humans, absolutely haunted me. For several years, I dreamed of myself blissfully roaming in that forest. To wake was to be bitterly exiled; I would shut my eyes as quickly as I'd opened them, hoping to dream my way back into Eden. Unless a time-slip story evokes that moment of longed-for paradise fading away right before our tantalized eyes, I know it has not hit the mark.

In *Playing Beatie Bow*, Ruth Park has sidestepped paradise; instead of a rural idyll, her hero, fourteen-year-old Abigail Kirk, stumbles into a squalid, dangerous slum of nineteenth-century Sydney, stinking of "horse manure, tidal flats, wood smoke, human sweat, and an all-pervading smell of sewage." But it is, nevertheless, a kind of emotional paradise for the discontented Abigail. Unlike most such fantasies, where the charm of slipping back and forth through time is an intense element in the story, both worlds in *Playing Beatie Bow* are vividly realistic in detail. Once Abigail has slipped backward, she stays in the world of 1873 for almost a year, always desperate to return to her own time despite her growing attachment to the Bow family: old Trooper Bow, a candy-maker who is half-mad from an old head wound; saintly Dovey; scrappy and ferociously intelligent little Beatie, Granny Tallisker from the Orkney Islands with her deep sureness of right and wrong and her gift of second sight; hateful nine-year-old Gibbie, a self-pitying, morbidly pious invalid; and, above all, the young man Judah, with his "ruddy and snubbed country kind of face."

Abbie has come from the contemporary world where she is a loner, a self-preoccupied teenager who lives with her mother in a modern high-rise, prickly, resentful, and unforgiving of her father's desertion of the family four year earlier. Her only gesture of involvement with the outside world is her kindness to four-year-old Natalie, a neighbor in the apartment building. Sometimes she takes Natalie outside to play, and it is Natalie who shows her "the little furry girl"— the woebegone Beatie, head shaven from a bout with fever, visiting from the past to watch modern children playing an eerie, frightening game of ghosts called "Beatie Bow." Abbie follows the mysterious "furry girl" one day and is lead down a narrow alleyway straight into the past.

Nothing is fudged: the dreariness of housework, the smells, the hideously uncomfortable clothes, the unpleasant sanitary arrangements, the degradation of the poor, including prostitution. In one ghastly scene, Abbie is actually kidnapped to a sleazy gin house and makes her escape from the grotesque inhabitants just in time.

Yet, remarkably, the mutual kindness of the small tradesmen, the warmth and strength of family ties, and the uncomplaining willingness of family members to work hard and help each other convincingly offset all the hardships with an enduring impression of vitality and purpose.

Abbie's purpose in being there, it turns out, is to fulfill an ancient Tallisker family prophecy about "a Stranger" who will save the family from extinction. At first, Abbie is surly and resentful at being kept in the past. Then she schools herself determinedly to recover from her rage and to fit herself into the family's life, hoping to earn her return, one day, to her own time. The many small shocks of Victorian slum life, as well as its unexpected pleasures, begin to do their work on Abbie. She becomes less self-centered, braver, more tolerant.

In all this, Park is at her best, showing us Abbie's changing character through dramatic action and dialogue. Most affecting is the moment when Abbie falls hopelessly in love with Judah. The first delicious, painful infatuation of a fourteen-year-old girl with a much older boy—and Judah is already betrothed to his distant cousin Dovey—could have been embarrassingly banal. But Park makes it both poignant and true. Even better, this infatuation is seen as an invigorating force in Abbie's life. It leads her to an act of bravery and altruism that will, much later, end the book with seventeen-year-old Abbie's unexpected, startling, and completely satisfying romantic fulfillment.

Strong as *Playing Beatie Bow* is, it is still outranked in my mind by the most subtle, moving, and beautifully written time-slip fantasy of them all, *Tom's Midnight Garden* by the consummate English writer Philippa Pearce. Perhaps I am biased by my predilection for enchanted gardens, or perhaps it is the sheer unfaltering authority of Pearce's burnished prose, but this novel, even on second and third reading, never loses its force for me.

Tom Long has been packed off, weeping and angry, to spend his summer holidays with his Aunt Gwen and Uncle Alan in their "stuffy flat" in an old converted house—all because his younger brother has measles. Pearce has a sympathetic genius for portraying young boys, their worries and rebellions and their stubborn mental processes, in a manner so understated it is almost translucent. Tom seems like a perfectly ordinary boy, neither more aggressive or more introverted than others; perhaps just because there is nothing pronounced about his character to set him apart, readers are easily drawn into the magnetic field of his emotions.

Feeling caged up, longing for outdoor play, sleeping badly because of all Aunt Gwen's good cooking, Tom lies awake at night listening with irritated anticipation for the chronically misstriking grandfather clock in the entrance hall of the building. And at last it strikes—and goes on striking to thirteen. Uneasily, Tom feels "that this had made some difference to him. The stillness had become an expectant one; the house seemed to hold its breath; the darkness pressed up to him, pressing him with a question . . ."

Tom has been forbidden by his rigid Uncle Alan to get out of bed on these sleepless nights; now he cleverly argues with his conscience that the clock has struck an extra hour, and so he can spend time out of bed and still have his mandatory ten hours' rest. Throughout the book, we see Tom's mind work in this dogged way, patiently worrying away at puzzles or dilemmas until he arrives at a comforting rationalization or a sensible explanation. It's one of the novel's underpinnings that gives it such lucid plausibility.

Eventually, Tom discovers that the rear door in the downstairs hallway—rusted shut during the days, and giving onto a strip of pavement cluttered with garbage cans—mysteriously opens onto an immense, beautifully intricate garden when the clock strikes midnight. Gradually, he becomes almost obsessed with his stolen hours of play in the garden. He works out a cunning system of adult-evasion to escape into the garden undetected; he whiles away the days in dutiful boredom, impatient for the magical nights. In the garden, however, it is not always night. Almost always it is full summer, and though Tom is uncannily invisible there, one of the garden's inhabitants (a family of three boys, with one small girl cousin tagging pitifully after them) is watching him.

The girl, Hatty, is a poor relation, despised by the cold aunt who has been forced to take her in. It is she, after all, who can see Tom, and who becomes his constant playmate. She loves the garden as passionately as he; it is her refuge from a bitterly lonely and unhappy life.

Pearce's powers of description make the garden and all its delights shimmer with almost surrealist intensity: the geese in the meadow beyond the hedge, the stone walls, the trees, the feathery green tunnels between the asparagus rows, the steamy greenhouse. The garden's strange loveliness is so seductive that we are as impatient as Tom to get back to it, but the forward movement of the plot is delicately restrained by passages in which Tom spends his days worrying away at the garden's mysteries. Why do the seasons switch around so abruptly there? Why does he see the tallest fir tree crash to the ground in a lightning storm one night—and see it standing there, tall and rooted, the next? Why does Abel, the gardener, mutter prayers whenever Tom stands invisibly (or so he thinks) in front of him?

At first, Tom is as impulsive and unobservant as any active, ordinary boy. But his friendship with Hatty changes that. Bit by bit, through excitements, griefs, and crises, he becomes more sensitive. A lovely pattern of imagery throughout the book underlines that almost imperceptible growth in Tom, and the more startling leaps to a maturity of Hatty, who begins to grow older than Tom. It is a series of images of climbing: First they climb the trees, higher and higher, so they can see the meadow beyond; then they scale the towering orchard wall, over which Tom can see the village and the whole countryside. Finally, at the book's intense climax, just when Tom tingles with excitement at the plan he has worked out to elude time altogether and live in both worlds, the grown-up Hatty and still-young Tom skate down the frozen Ouse river and climb the tower of Ely Cathedral to look out over the whole landscape, with its frosted river going down to the sea. (The description of the skating is breathtaking in its icy exhilaration, speed, and dazzling impression of freedom.) At that dizzying summit, Tom looks away from the view and turns to Hatty—and realizes at last that her own time, moving onward, has defeated his plan to foil the clock. She has grown up and grown past him.

It is a haunting and heartwrenching moment. It is the moment of loss and the beginning point of growing up, the moment that lies at the core of all time fantasies and that gives rise to them in the first place, the moment when the passage of time, and the certainty of death, become real.

There are few climaxes in children's literature more affecting than Tom's despair when he knows that the garden and Hatty are lost to him forever. But, like Farmer, Lively, Lunn, and Park, Pearce ends her book on a note of healing optimism, and the conclusion is genuinely thrilling. Tom finds the answer to all the torturing bewilderments of time passing and time past—the mystery of the legend on the clock ("Time No More") and of the strange sequence of events in the garden. And he is consoled, in a surprising and deeply touching new friendship, by the knowledge that though time sweeps on, it does not sweep away everything that we love. The dead do come back again in the lives they have touched, in the gardens they have made, and in their children's children; the years are rolled away in stories and poems, and in the Edens we remember.

Chapter 9

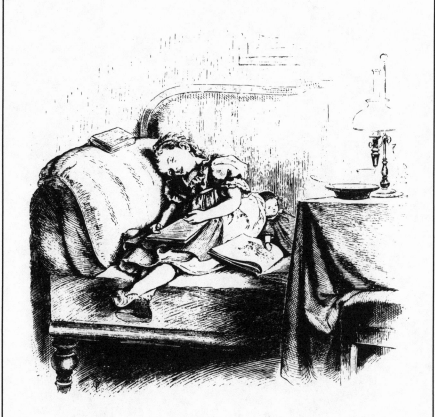

GROWING UP

This is then the real meaning of not being any longer a young one in living, the complete realizing that not any one really can believe what any other one is believing . . .

Gertrude Stein, *The Making of Americans*

The first demand any work of art makes upon us is to surrender. Look. Listen. Receive. Get yourself out of the way.

C.S. Lewis, *An Experiment in Criticism*

Though I think it is possible to learn from works of fiction, I don't think it possible to teach from them . . . One does not rush to give *Anna Karenina* to friends who are committing adultery. Such impertinence is limited to dealings with children.

Jill Paton Walsh, in *Celebrating Children's Books*

Anyone who writes about books for adolescents must do battle with a paradox. The urgent message of literature's most thoughtful critics (and the message, I hope, of this book) is that the reading of good books can work in a mysterious, compelling way to enlarge the reader's life. Vast numbers of books for beginning and middle readers, both the most praised and the most popular, seem to have exactly that effect. On the other hand, a tidal wave of books with an obsessively narrow focus on contemporary teenage preoccupations has inundated the market in the last decade, triumphantly carrying with it the majority of readers in this age group. At precisely the moment when youngsters hesitate on the brink of the larger world, the popular literature for them is totally given over to navel gazing and trendy "problems." In this chapter, I'll try to grapple with the questions posed by the lucrative market in teenage fiction, and to propose some alternatives to what is currently most popular.

The special quality of self-forgetfulness that we cherish in reading the best fiction has been lovingly and painstakingly described by many critics over the years. T.S. Eliot called it the "radical innocence" of the person who is amused and entertained, and thus wonderfully distracted from self-concern. Gertrude Stein wrote about the shocking discovery of immutable otherness which yanks us permanently, disillusioningly but liberatingly, out of our egocentricity. Helen Gardner drew our attention to the mother reading to her child: Both mother and child, she said, have "thrown open the doors of the prison of the present" and the child is temporarily distracted from "the clamant needs and desires of childhood."

Mere distraction is not the goal; rather it's that while the claims of the ego are temporarily stilled, the mind and the imagination can fearlessly explore other ways of being. The unique gift of literature, its priceless contribution to our children's lives, as C.S. Lewis said, is to make us see with other eyes, imagine with other imaginations, feel with other hearts *as well as our own*. Even children can distinguish, if they are pressed to analyze it, the different qualities of reading experiences. The best books demand a depth of involvement that is clearly missing from purely escapist literature, and, in return, they reward us with something that is added to our essential selves; we come back into the real world with a more tantalizing sense of its complexity than we had imagined before. Our sensibilities are stretched and enhanced; our intellect provoked; our apprehension of the world around us changed in some way.

This is the unique purpose and profit in reading good fiction. I'm hard pressed to find any other. For passive escapism and whiling away time, television wins hands down. For instruction, our society brims over with pamphlets, videocassettes, discussion groups, films, hotlines, night courses, and public agencies. For practice in the mere mechanics of reading itself, the backs of cereal boxes are omnipresent. "Bulk reading" has its uses, which I discuss in the next chapter, but most of us hope our children will not stop there.

Why, then, the unparalleled rush on the part of so many adults to press second-rate mass-market books into the hands of preadolescents and teenagers? Sheer availability is one answer. Chain bookstore shelves gleam with fast-selling romance series—guaranteed quick turnover. Parents sigh with relief when their children read anything at all. Overworked teachers may be grateful for undemanding or titillating books that effortlessly "sell themselves" in the students' peer group. Librarians are often powerless to resist the pressure to increase circulation figures by lowering standards. In other words, the adult world shrugs uneasily and accepts the inescapable proliferation of inferior children's books. But that acceptance has nothing to do with the books' intrinsic merit; it springs from a premonition of defeat.

This, I think, goes a long way towards explaining the Judy Blume phenomenon. Blume is such an overwhelming presence in modern prepubescent reading that any book that aspires to serve as a guide for parents must take account of her. Davis Rees, a critic, author, and teacher at the University of Essex, in an essay entitled "Not Even for a One-Night Stand," wonders whether "Perhaps the best thing to do with Ms. Blume would be to ignore her altogether; she is so amazingly trivial and second-rate in every department . . ."

But though Rees complains that reading Blume feels like "a bashing on the head with a blunt instrument," neither he nor I can afford to ignore such a singular success story. Blume's paperbacks have sold more than 30 million copies, a number equivalent to more than half the number of children between the ages of five and seventeen in the United States. No other author even comes close to having such universal access into the minds of North American youth. Yet I would assume that most adults have not actually read her works. For that reason, I feel compelled to devote part of this chapter to a discussion of her style, techniques, and substance, and then to offer a range of valuable alternatives for preteen and teenage reading.

It is revealing, I think, that both Judy Blume and S.E. Hinton, another popular American writer for young teenagers, have both explained their motivation thus in interviews: "When I was young, I could never find any books about kids like me, and that's what I wanted to read about." Their almost identical statements lay bare an almost identical narcissism, as well as an astonishingly limited knowledge of available children's literature.

"Kids like me." Of course children want to be able to "identify" with the characters in books, in the sense of recognizing similarities in emotional experience, if not in precise situation; the finest authors have always been able to show us the universal in the unique. Mary Norton's Arietty and Ursula LeGuin's Ged are quintessentially themselves—they are never described physically but we know them intimately, would recognize their characters at once in a crowd—and yet they share the boldness, impatience, dreams, and fears of all young people.

Hinton and Blume cater to quite a different level of self-knowledge. Without question, puberty brings with it a consuming absorption in the self as a social and sexual being. Normally, however, this is only one aspect of the adolescent's self-awareness. The difficulty arises from the single-mindedness of Blume's focus. For her, it seems, books are only "about kids like me" if they mirror the lives of young North Americans with a constant repetition of brand names, fashionable problems, and current "lifestyles." This facsimile realism, like TV soap opera, has the ultimate effect of shrinking the world to a small, square frame, leaching it of complexity and depth and draining it, finally, of all that is most elusive, pungent, and vital. It is as though we invited youngsters into an art gallery where every frame held only a mirror.

I don't mean to imply that youngsters should be prevented from reading these books (please see the chapter on bad books for a discussion of this conundrum). However, concerned adults have a duty to consider whether badly written "problem novels" are in fact a distortion of reality and whether they may reinforce some of the more questionable values of our culture.

Judy Blume, Paula Danziger, Paul Zindel, and, in Canada, Kevin Major are among the leading exponents of the modern problem novel in which contemporary children, from the ages of eleven to about sixteen (or seventeen, the acceptable problem-novel age for sexual activity), usually tell their stories in the first person in a loosely chronological diary of events. Though the social class of the protagonists ranges from middle-class suburban (Blume) to Newfoundland working-class (Major), all these youngsters see themselves as ill-done-by. They suffer from incomprehensibly repressive teachers, obtuse adults, social dislocation not of their own making (death, divorce, rape, acne, scoliosis, sexual frustration, infuriating siblings, or disgusting classmates) and a vague, discontented sense of meaninglessness in life.

From all that I have been able to observe, Blume and Danziger are read almost obsessively by youngsters from about the age of nine to twelve. At an age when social acceptance by the peer group is the longed-for panacea, when prepubescent anxiety and narcissism are at their peak and when a restless curiosity about sex is linked with personal inadequacy, fear, and excitement, these books become classroom bibles, passed from hand to hand and giggled over at recess. They become almost a talisman of belonging, like the latest style of sneakers or gimmick pencils. Sheila Egoff, in a memorable phrase, called these books "a social glue"; reading them assures one a place in the in-group.

Some of their glamor comes from their naughtiness: Here, in the flat and stumbling language of the prepubescent, mirrored by Blume with uncanny accuracy, are all the "gross" preoccupations—pimples, smells, breast size, wet dreams—given the imprimatur of authority by their sheer presence in print. And the books make no demands: There will be no surprises, no unusual words or feelings, no plots to speak of, no shocking "enlargements of the self" or imaginatively taxing viewpoints of a world seen through other eyes.

Judy Blume is overwhelmingly the most popular, and overwhelmingly, in my opinion, the poorest of all the problem novelists. I am continually amazed when parent groups rise up in protest against Judy Blume because of her *sexually explicit content;* her sexual forthrightness is the least offensive of all her qualities, particularly given that her readers grow up in a society saturated with sexual symbolism and rampant exploitation.

What may indeed corrupt the children (again, see the chapter on bad books) is not Blume's frankness, but her bland and unquestioning acceptance of majority values, of conformity, consumerism, materialism, unbounded narcissism, and flat, sloppy, ungrammatical, inexpressive speech. Her success with youngsters, paradoxically, springs from these very qualities: Unlike more probing authors, who raise uncomfortable questions in the readers' minds, Blume seems to endorse trivial self-centeredness by embodying it in her books. Blume once told an interviewer that she had herself founded a club, at the age eleven, called the Preteen Kittens, and says that long after she began writing she was "a little girl with little-girl dreams." I believe her.

In *Then Again, Maybe I Won't,* Blume tries to give us—in the person of eleven-year-old Tony—a contemporary, working-class version of Holden Caulfield, the sensitive and disillusioned hero of J.D. Salinger's *Catcher in the Rye.* We catch the authentic Blume tone— monosyllabic, surly, cliché-ridden—in the first paragraph: "Who says March is supposed to come in like a lion and go out like a lamb? That's a lot of bull. All it's done this March is rain. I'm sick of it."

Tony belongs to a struggling Italian working-class family which strikes it rich, suddenly and improbably, thanks to the father's invention of "electrical cartridges." As usual, in Blume, we are given a rough sketch of Tony's character, not through action or interaction, but by his interior monologue. He is concerned about being short ("Basketball is my favorite sport. I just wish I was taller. My brother

Ralph says I'll probably sprout up at fourteen like he did. I hope I don't have to wait that long. It's important to be tall when you're playing basketball. You're that much closer to the basket"); he is hostile (he daydreams about shooting Mrs. Gorsky, who wants him to put the newspaper under the mat when it rains); and he is sexually avid ("I wonder what it's like watching ladies try on underwear all day? I'd really like to get a look at that!").

Because the book is narrated by Tony, and because the author uses no ironic or distancing techniques, his character seems as flat, uninflected, and diffuse as his nearly moronic style of speech. Complexity or inner conflict is shown by two limp devices: physical distress whenever Tony is confronted by a problem ("I get real bad stomachaches. My mother says it's gas") and the repeated use of the single phrase that gives the book its title: "Maybe some day I'll marry a girl like Angie. Then again, maybe I won't."

When Tony's family becomes instantly rich and moves to a wealthy suburb, Blume tries to show us how disgusted he is, à la Caulfield, by his family's burgeoning materialism. She fails in this attempt to give Tony a moral dimension, however, because he is just as much a prey to his family's consumerism as they are. Dotingly, Tony describes the floor plan of the new house, complete with five bathrooms. This is a frequent feature of Blume's books, in which room-by-room descriptions of layout and furniture often substitute for the vivacity of daily life.

Tony is ostensibly disapproving when his grandmother is ruthlessly edged out of her central position in the family because she upsets the new maid by insisting on cooking as she has always done. (As Rees points out, the ostracizing of the grandmother seems far-fetched in what is supposed to be a close Italian family.) But Tony is as emotionally passive as the rest of the family, and makes no attempt to mitigate his grandmother's lonely imprisonment.

He despises a girl at school who admires him ("I hate skinny girls"), loathes his baby niece ("Maybe she'll get better looking. Then again, maybe she won't"). He gets stomachaches when his new friend Joel steals apples from the school cafeteria. But what are we to make of this supposed moral scrupulousness when Tony himself participates in the malicious ragging of a waitress, and asks for binoculars for Christmas so he can spy on Joel's sixteen-year-old sister Lisa every night while she undresses? Tony's self-righteous contempt for his parents always seems unfounded. He objects to his piano teacher because she has bad breath, badgers his parents to let him quit, and when they agree, telling him they are only concerned for his happiness, he thinks, "Sometimes they're so full of bull they make me sick."

The secret of the book's success is not that Tony is morally superior to those around him, but that Blume gives an earnestly liberal *carte blanche* to all his own pecadilloes. We are told in painstaking detail how Tony hides his sheets to conceal his nocturnal emissions from his parents; how he carries a raincoat to conceal involuntary erections; how, when he is sent to a psychiatrist because of his stomachaches, the psychiatrist does not disapprove of Tony's voyeurism—and even how, when he is hospitalized, "curvy" Lisa, the unwitting object of his peeping Tom activities, brings him "dirty books" to read.

It is certainly true that Blume has tried to graft some twigs of sprouting conscience onto the main trunk of the story. The harassed waitress Bernice, for example, finally turns on the boorish boys and indignantly tells them she needs their insolent penny tips (usually drowned in the milk shakes) to buy herself bread. The boys' sheepish but limited reaction: They never sit in her section of the restaurant again. But such incidents fall far short of moral revelation; the focus of the book is relentlessly on Tony's self-preoccupation. The author's "nonjudgmental" reportorial style reassures preadolescent boys that peeping, wet dreams, and emotional numbness (Tony can never feel anything about the neighborhood friends he left behind or his brother killed in Vietnam) are normal and okay.

Blume's books, in other words, are intended to offer a therapeutic, not a literary experience. From a literary point of view, her work is a disaster. All her characters, of any social class, speak in the same lowest-common-denominator voice: "Bundle up good," says a middle-class mother, and "I do pretty good in school" says a suburban youngster. Style, it must be emphasized, is not a detachable frill that "fancier" writers tack on like a ruffle on a dress. Style *is* the writer; it is not possible to differentiate the manner of expression from what the author notices, what she values, how she reacts to it, what she thinks is important to mention, the emotional weight and color of her own experiences. Since all Blume's characters speak without subtlety, indirection, metaphor, vitality, originality, or even basic grammatical precision, the very least one can say about the effect of such indifference is that a youngster who reads only Blume will remain unaware of the possibilities of fictional language to create new realities.

In Blume books, there is rarely any natural world outside of shopping malls; there is not even a vestigial political or social awareness; no consciousness of injustice; no soul-searching beyond petulance and spite ("I was making Debbie feel bad and I was glad. Sometimes I am a mean and rotten person" is the farthest reach of self-awareness attained by her characters) and the potential for human action is, to put it mildly, circumscribed: The painfully simple plots are wrapped up neatly at the end of an hour's reading, just like TV drama.

Even as therapy, however, Blume's books are often wide of the mark. She flatters her young readers by mimicking all their most superficial concerns, and proposes to deal with difficult dilemmas, insofar as they are recognized at all, with a spate of practical instruction. In one of her most flat-footed books, *Deenie*, the reader is offered an encyclopedia definition of scoliosis, detailed descriptions of visits to the doctor and medical procedures, and some unbelievably naive ruminations on masturbation from the thirteen-year-old protagonist: "As soon as I got into bed I started touching myself. I have this special place and when I rub it I get a very nice feeling. I don't know what it's called or if anyone else has it . . ."

Undoubtedly Blume conceives of her books as liberating and helpful. My own impression is that her values break through at every turn—values that many alert parents will find questionable. Girls come in three varieties: pretty and popular and boy-obsessed (these are always the heroines); smart and ugly (big or little sisters); and the truly loathsome (always fat). Blume's anorexic writing is a true measure of her anorexic obsessions with personal appearance; not only are her female characters narcissistically obsessed with clothes and appearance, but they are always justified by the author in hating anyone who doesn't measure up to their standards of physical beauty.

Mothers never go out to work in Blume books except in dire emergency, and then they are resented by their children. Fathers are usually more caring than mothers, though equally characterless. No one in Blume ever reads a novel, thinks about any sphere of human congress beyond the classroom or bedroom, or rises above a materialistic self-absorption. Even physical love rarely transcends mere self-infatuation in Blume's books; girls love and pursue boys as they pursue the desirable position of cheerleader, in order to see themselves reflected admiringly in the eyes of others.

This emotional impoverishment is most embarrassingly on view in Blume's controversial book *Forever*, in which seventeen-year-old Katherine and Michael consummate a love affair. Joyce Maynard once reported in the *New York Times Magazine* on the horror expressed by a group of middle-class New Jersey mothers who felt that their thirteen-year-old daughters, all of whom were wild to read the book, should be kept from such explicit sexual knowledge.

Their concern smacks of self-deception: no ten-year-old in our sex-drenched society can be unaware of adult sexuality, and every eleven-year-old I've ever known has secretly riffled through parental copies of *Playboy* or *Lace* to learn what adults do together. Innocence, if it ever existed in the sense of sexual ignorance and/or purity, is a vanished quality. Perhaps it is adult innocence that is threatened here: If statistics can be believed, the vast majority of North American parents prefer not to know that their children masturbate from infancy on and are naturally possessed by ardent sexual curiosity, sharpening in intensity and secrecy at the age of ten or eleven.

Forever follows the patented Blume method of giving the young reader a great deal of mechanical information. There is, for example, instruction on how to masturbate a boy; the highlight of the book for giggling eleven-year-olds is the moment when Michael undoes his pants and tells Katherine "I'd like to introduce you to Ralph," his penis, which, she discovers, "feels like ordinary skin." Blume teaches readers how to wipe up semen with Kleenex; how to make an appointment at a Planned Parenthood clinic ("You wish to make an appointment?" "I guess so."), what it's like to have a gynecological examination ("This is a vaginal speculum . . . Would you like to see your cervix?"), what it's like to put after-shave lotion on a boy's "balls" ("Ralph was small and soft and just hung there" and then "Ralph stuck straight out as if he was watching too"—I don't know which is worse, the lack of grammar or the lack of humor) and how laborious effort is rewarded by mutual orgasm.

The thrill of this for the very young reader is in receiving first-hand sexual information without the unease of listening to a parental lecture or ploughing through a boring technical book. Bearing in mind, though, that seventeen-year-olds do not read Judy Blume's books, one must ask if the depressing banality and crassness of these sexual interactions are a rewarding depiction of teenage erotic life for the prepubescents who do read them. How is it possible to devote an entire novel to teenage love without conveying one tremor of rapture, joy, delight, intensity, sadness, dread, anxiety, or tenderness? Blume's "love" is all fumbling and bra hooks, semen and birth control pamphlets, and the featureless Katherine (all we really know about her is that she weighs 105 pounds and is conscious that cold air gives her becomingly rosy cheeks) moves on from Michael, her "forever" love, to Theo, a green-eyed, twenty-one-year-old tennis instructor.

Children are, perhaps, the best unconscious critics of Blume. They skip over all the mind-numbing conversations that fill the pages between the explicit passages: "Do you by any chance like spinach?" "Ugh, no . . . why, do you?" "It's only my favorite food." "Like Popeye?" "Like Popeye." "In that case, maybe I'll try to develop a taste for it . . . but I can't promise . . ." "Hey, you know tomorrow's Friday?" "I know." "How's 7:30?" "Fine." "Well, see you then." "See you then. Oh Michael . . ." "Yeah?" "I'll be ready."

Blume introduces a few scrawny side-plots. Michael has had V.D. but that's all right; the repulsively fat Sybil who has a high I.Q. "just by luck"(nothing to be jealous of) has an illegitimate baby; a tense boy tries to commit suicide; a grandfather dies . . . it all reads like a laundry list of "okay" adolescent concerns, with no more emotional depth than Katherine displays on achieving orgasm—"I came right before Michael and as I did I made noises, just like my mother."

The indictment against Blume is not that she is too frank, but that her depiction of human beings is so shallow, flat, and limited, so preoccupied with clumsily perceived surfaces, that she reflects back to children, and seems complacently to validate by her unquestioning journalistic style, a repugnant image of the ideal teen: mindless, sullen, ruthlessly self-centered, emotionally stunted.

Preadolescents are desperate to know what teenagers do and how they feel about it; they are preparing themselves for the next exciting stage of life. Adolescents, on the other hand, from the age of thirteen on, rarely read about other teenagers; if they read at all, they most often devour adult mass-market paperbacks like Stephen King's and Judith Krantz's in an attempt to understand, not just the mechanics of adult sex, but how adults feel about their relationships, and what adult life will be like. Their escapist reading leans to Harlequins, westerns, mysteries, and thrillers.

Young Adult books, then, as they are called in the trade, cater to an ambiguous market, much younger than their stated target audience. What purpose is served by *Thirty-Six Exposures,* Kevin Major's Newfoundland novel about a seventeen-year-old boy's coming of age? As a slice of life, it displays the same limited verisimilitude as Blume's efforts: We're shown how Lorne masturbates while reading skin magazines and listening to taped music, squeezes pimples, watches pornographic movies at a stag party ("He felt as if he has just joined in on a great secret"), and, in a repulsively mechanistic scene with his girl friend, tries to arouse her sexually ("His hand curved to enclose her bare breast. His heartbeat quickened. He stroked it, his fingers brushing against the hardness of the nipple. He began to massage it with quick pulsations of his palm and fingers").

Major tries his best to make us see Lorne as a multidimensional character, a boy who distances himself from life through his hobby of photography, reads Yevtushenko's poetry, and struggles to regain a sense of roots by doing a creative local history project. But Major's hard-nosed "realism" about working-class Newfoundland speech patterns ("Jesus, I got a good mind to slip my dick into that one of these nights" says Lorne's friend Trevor, leering at a local bad girl) undercuts the supposed humanity of his characters. Aside from sexual exploration, there are two subplots in the novel, both involving Trevor. A student strike at the high school is organized because Trevor has been unfairly punished by a disliked teacher. At the end of the book, Trevor is killed when he drunkenly drives his car off the end of a dock. The subplot of the student strike is ill-motivated, flimsily described, and somehow irrelevant. When Lorne defiantly shouts "We did it our way!" after the final tragedy, as though to give meaning to Trevor's death, the effect is ridiculous: The car crash had nothing to do with the strike or with adolescent independence. It is as pointless and unmeaningful an event as one can imagine. If the book is read mostly (as seems likely) by thirteen- or fourteen-year-olds, it will cater to their prurience, but give them little else to take back into their lives.

The whole idea of realism in "young adult" novels is problematic anyway. Does an individual child struggling with grief, unpopularity, or parents' divorce really gain fresh insight or consolation from reading about these dilemmas in a novel? When you think back to your childhood reading, what was it that stirred, excited, thrilled you with the unfolding potential drama of life, moved you by hitherto-undreamed-of riches of possible experience, touched you to tears of compassion, relief, or sorrow? Was it Black Beauty, Mowgli at the ceremony of fire, Tarzan discovering his nobility, Alice pertly talking back to the Queen? Or was it "a kid just like you," worrying about gas pains, tomorrow's math test, and Mom's Pap smear?

Richard Peck, one of the most skillful contemporary authors for adolescents who has written some excellent books, nevertheless exemplifies the difficulties of this genre in his book "about" rape, *Are You in the House Alone?* Peck is his usual accomplished self in evoking the terror experienced by sixteen-year-old Gail Osburne as she is followed, harassed, and menaced by an unknown telephone caller. In fact, he has it both ways, like the makers of teenage-mayhem movies: He rivets the reader's attention by playing on the fears of all young girls who babysit alone in other people's houses or answer the telephone to hear hoarse breathing.

But the limits of the "realistic" novels are severe. From the moment of the rape, Peck dare not use his novelistic powers to the full in letting young readers know how Gail must feel; the rage, the sense of violation, the helpless horror would be too devastating. Instead, he retreats to a benumbed clinical documentation of the aftermath: brutish and blaming policemen, detached lawyers, the doctors ("I'm going to check your cervical lumen for traces of sperm . . . Now I'm looking at your posterior fornix"). And the cumulative message of the last half of the book is almost worse than the more imaginative probing would be: The psychotic rapist escapes without even a reprimand because he is the son of the town's most prominent citizen. Neither in law nor in person does Gail ever attain the cathartic relief of confronting the rapist. She is emotionally abandoned by her repressed parents, betrayed by girlfriend and boyfriend, shrugged off by authorities. The last words in the book go to Gail's ineffectual mother: "What could we do?"

The pitfall of the realistic novel, when it is based on a one-dimensional contemporary reality, is that it is by definition too specific to be of much use. In 1976, when Peck wrote the book, the rape victim faced almost unsurmountably hostile and skeptical authorities. Today, that is rarely true. Peck's careful realism is already dated, because he did not explore in any depth the wellsprings of prejudice encountered by a sexual victim.

In fact, the liveliest spark in the book comes from Peck's only truly fictional device, the fading and eccentric film artiste, Madame Malevich, who teaches at Gail's high school and understands what has happened. Fiction, when it reassures, does so not by a factual rendition of problems, but by luring the reader into discovering the possibilities of the imaginative life. Some of the best writers for young people deal in fantasy (Ursula LeGuin, Susan Cooper, Patricia Wrightson) precisely because the power of young sexuality, the urgency of life and death questions, are diminished and shriveled into lifelessness by too direct a representation. Distancing, obliqueness, texture, subtlety, layers of meaning, and complexity of human response are essential elements of good fiction; there are no "problem novelists" writing today who have these qualities in full measure. What they produce is utilitarian at best, squalidly trivial at worst.

Another popular mass-market writer for teens is S.E. Hinton. Both *Tex* and *Rumble Fish* have been made into widely admired movies, and the books are read and reread avidly by young teenage boys—perhaps the only books which can claim such a ready audience among this least-reading-motivated group.

The characters in S.E. Hinton's books have an undeniably forceful presence, preposterous though they may be; the ardent, almost sexually adoring descriptions of her teenage delinquent heroes lend a feverish animation to the fan-magazine prose. The fourteen-year-old first-person narrator of *The Outsiders*, Ponyboy, introduces himself proudly as a "greaser," a wrong-side-of-the-tracks tough kid and orphan who glories in his class warfare with the privileged middle-class kids in town. Two pages into the first chapter, Ponyboy has already boasted about his lovely hair and greenish-gray eyes, his good build, his "high I.Q. and everything," and his unique ability to "dig movies and books." Then Ponyboy describes his sixteen-year-old brother Sodapop in these words: "He's movie-star kind of handsome, with a finely drawn, sensitive face that somehow manages to be reckless and thoughtful at the same time. He's got dark gold hair that he combs back—long and silky and straight—and in the summer the sun bleaches it to a shining wheat gold. His eyes are dark brown, lively, dancing, recklessly laughing eyes that can be gentle and sympathetic one moment and blazing with anger the next . . ."

As the monologue of a tough street kid, and a male one at that, this is simply absurd. So is the weary repetition of stock phrases meant to show the humane decency of the older members of the gang towards the younger ones: On every other page, one of these paragons, affectionate and amused, will "cock an eyebrow and ruffle the hair" of a younger one.

It's easy to see why this burble is swallowed whole, and eagerly, and repeatedly, by young boys. For one thing, the unbridled impulsivity of the delinquent is inherently fascinating to teenagers. I remember the wave of popularity enjoyed by an adult mass market paperback in the 1950s, *The Amboy Dukes*. I read it myself at age eleven for its shock value and for the heady sense it gave of teenagers living in complete defiance of adults. Hinton's work, furthermore, flatters the egos of young male readers with its barely-subliminal sexual praise, and lets them escape into the fantasized glory of attention and approval from an older teenage tough. Adult criticism is neatly fended off by the fact that the delinquent heroes (Tex, Ponyboy) are clever at school, talented readers, disapproving of drugs, good athletes, and invariably develop worthy crushes on middle-class girls with clean hair.

This pattern is followed religiously by Canadian novelist Marilyn Halvorson, whose hard-riding cowboy heroes (in *Cowboys Don't Cry* and *Let It Go*) also speak ungrammatically, are clever students, and combine toughness with sentimentality. Halvorson's heroes, however, are less boastful, and their sentimental attachment to nature less mawkish than Hinton's; she is able to evoke adult characters with sympathy and natural settings with some conviction. Her latest book, *Let It Go,* with its sensitive depiction of relationships between boys and between teenagers and their parents, is a vast improvement on the Hinton model.

What are the alternatives, then, to all this undernourishing popular material? When I was approaching adolescence, there were no Young Adult novels. Once I passed beyond children's fiction, I read whatever novels I happened to stumble across that seemed to illumine adult life. I remember *How Green Was My Valley; Cry, the Beloved Country; A Tree Grows in Brooklyn; Gulliver's Travels; For Whom the Bell Tolls; Tender Is the Night;* and *All Quiet on the Western Front*—a book I had to start again immediately because I couldn't quite believe I was reading about *German* soldiers as real human beings. It was the shock of that moment that remains with me, the feeling of a full and empathetic portrayal of a human reality—without manipulation, without propaganda—but with the power not just to change my opinions but to shift and rearrange my basic assumptions about the world and the way I was in the habit of perceiving it. It led me to question, not to conclude.

Today, aside from the fantasists (who are the most popular among literate teenagers, while the "problem novelists," as Sheila Egoff notes, are the preference of less accomplished readers), there are a number of first-rate novelists who write perceptively and refreshingly about adolescent experience.

Unlike Blume, Danziger *et al,* they reach more deeply into their characters to transform raw experience into something coherent, shapely, and complex. Or they may have a broader reach, setting young heroes in a historic or geographic context that allows them to be seen as members of a wider world and invites the reader to "get the self out of the way," at least temporarily.

In the hands of a talented writer, even the most unpromising material can sink taproots into the unconscious and bloom gloriously. Virginia Hamilton, in *A Little Love,* presents us with a sweet-faced, overweight black girl, Sheema, who lives with her aging grandparents in tract housing in Dayton, Ohio. Sheema is a slow learner, a student in "food services" at the local vocational school; her boyfriend Forrest, who works as a movie usher at night, is a classmate in the same course.

On the surface, it sounds like the dreary stuff of a sociologically correct novel, as appealing as orthopedic shoes. But Hamilton is a gifted writer; the slow, lilting black dialect of Sheema's speech, the drift of her daydreams and fears and yearnings, draw us deeper into a reality we could never have known or loved without Hamilton's art. This is the opposite of a Blume experience: No smug conceit is reflected back on a complacent reader. Instead, she is stretched to comprehend someone else's life, to taste the differences and waken to the common underlying humanity.

Sheema is alive and complex as Hinton's narcisisstic braggarts never are. Her horrified hypnotic daydreams are haunted by mushroom clouds, by her grandparents' gradual decline, by the menace of the erratically hostile heavy-metal dudes at high school. Sheema may be "slow" academically but she is alertly confident, absorbed, delighted by her own skill in the food preparation classes; it is one of the more moving experiences in teenage literature to see through Sheema's eyes as slowly, seriously, she cooks, cleans, and launders in her grandparents' house, staving off their death with her responsibility.

Forrest, too, is an endearing and believable teenager. He is the lean and quick one, tense with the weight of his plans and ambitions for both of them; he knows how to value Sheema and how to keep her anchored. Nearly every night, Sheema tiptoes out of her grandparents' house to drive with Forrest to hidden country lanes where they make love in the car: Their "serene and silky pleasure . . . softening the time around them . . . holding them strongly together" tells a curious teenage reader everything that Blume doesn't. So does their squabbling, when Sheema strains against Forrest's possessiveness, or pressures him to wake up to the dangers that surround black youths in their society.

When Forrest and Sheema finally set out in search of her long-lost father (a glittering fantasy figure of charm and talent to Sheema), their journey is a classic "on the road in America" odyssey, sharply realized in contemporary detail and felt urgency. Sheema and Forrest, who have none of the affluent privileges of Blume's Katherine, and who resist the slick alienation of Hinton's delinquents, exist in a real world of hopes, loves, and responsibilities, not a hermetically sealed bubble of teenage self-obsession. One of the book's strengths is the largely unspoken tenderness of Sheema's relationship with her grandmother; "I know, baby," Grandma whispers when Sheema returns broken-hearted from her search for her father, "I know all about it. Like fallin weather. Life have its hard edges."

A foreign or minority culture can be a freeing framework for both writer and reader; the sense of a shared humanity pierces us most sharply when we have intuited it in a strange setting, or through the experiences of quirkily individualistic characters.

Black American culture has provided us with some exhilarating examples. *Philip Hall Likes Me, I Reckon Maybe* by Bette Greene, a delightful book for prepubescent Blume-readers who need to be weaned to a richer diet, shows us a strong-willed, bright, impetuous sixth-grader in rural Arkansas. Beth is smitten by "sweet, cute" Philip Hall who lives on the neighboring farm. Philip, who sneers at her whenever he's in a group of boys, doesn't hesitate to exploit her crush ("I'll let you clean my dairy barn") but likes her only so long as she tacitly agrees to come second to him in every school subject. Eventually, without relinquishing her admiration for Philip, Beth fights back. While the story is never didactic, it certainly dramatizes a central dilemma for primary school girls: how a young girl can like a boy, and get him to acknowledge their friendship, without sacrificing her own self-definition.

A similar rivalry sparks off the conflict in *Words by Heart* by Ouida Sebestyen, in which twelve-year-old Lena, a black girl in the rural Midwest, competes in a Bible-quoting contest at the local white church. The beauty of the fierce verse-swapping ("I am black but I am comely," quotes a defiant Lena, who knows that the crowd is rooting for white Winslow Starnes) springs from the aptness and poetic lucidity of the biblical quotations, but the freshness of the rest of the novel is Sebestyen's own. This is a novel for more mature readers, movingly depicting a girl's inner struggle with hatred and racism and illuminated by the elemental wisdom of Lena's loving father, Ben.

Teenagers, problem novelists to the contrary, are not insensitive to bigotry, irrationality, or conflict in the wider community. *Across the Barricades* by Joan Lingard, written in bare-bones, utilitarian prose, nevertheless gains authenticity from its setting: Sixteen-year-old Sadie is a Protestant and seventeen-year-old Kevin is Catholic, and they dare to love each other in a strife-torn Belfast seething with religious hatred. The scrimping narrowness and harshness of the lives of both their working-class families is identical, and provides a believable background for the teenagers' growing critical awareness of their parents' limitations, as well as their longing for escape.

One More River by Lynne Reid Banks is not nearly so accomplished as her later *Indian in the Cupboard,* but it is a curiously convincing coming-of-age story about a spoiled Canadian fourteen-year-old Jewish girl who finds herself transplanted to an Israeli kibbutz. The most poignant aspect of Leslie Shelby's "enlargement of self" is her tenuous, fragile, wounded friendship with a Palestinian boy who lives on the other side of the Jordan River. The wound of disillusionment—"the complete realizing that not any one can believe" just what you believe—is delicately probed in this book; it touches not only on Leslie and the Arab boy, but on Leslie's difficulties with the Israeli teenagers and on the many inevitable rifts within her family. The adult task of remaking wounded relationships after the ruptures of disillusionment is one of the book's encouraging themes.

The Village by the Sea offers a distant world made brilliantly alive in the hands of a wonderful writer: Anita Desai uses all the physical senses to make us realize the stark and desperate poverty of a brother and sister, twelve-year-old Hari and his thirteen-year-old sister Lila, who live in an Indian village. The setting is far from bleak, however. Desai, a distinguished novelist for adults, evokes the lush and haunting beauty of the sea and the countryside, ironically as exhausted in nourishment as it is fertile in loveliness. The plot is rich with satirical portraits of local derelicts and tycoons, with the mingled menace and promise of encroaching industrialization, with crippling superstitions and profound faith—and, most of all, with Hari's vivid trials and adventures when he runs away to Bombay to find work to feed the family. Befriended by kindly Mr. Penwallah of the Ding-Dong Watchworks, Hari stoically survives gruelling hardships and learns a trade.

For a privileged western child, there must be something bracing—even enviable—about the struggles of Hari and Lila, freed of middle-class self-consciousness and self-pity by their determined battle to survive. There is vigor, hope, and reconciliation in this fine story, with no sacrifice of honesty about India's overwhelming difficulties.

Fireweed, by Jill Paton Walsh, has some of that same force. Bill, a working-class fifteen-year-old, finds himself on the run and on his own during the worst year of the blitz in wartime London. He meets up with another runaway, the obviously upper-class Julie, and they pool resources and wits to survive—creating, by the end, their own little family—in the midst of one of the most sulphurously luminous and grippingly fearsome descriptions of the blitz that I have ever read.

The friendship is drawn from Bill's point of view, obliquely and delicately. We become aware of his growing love for Julie without its ever being belabored; their one physical encounter, when they huddle together under a shared blanket for warmth, is left ambiguous.

Fireweed has been criticized for its squeamishness about sex, though I think it is both sensitive and accurate for those youngsters in that time and place. But the criticism raises a larger question: Can sexuality between teenagers be written about more frankly without sacrificing literary values or emotional depth?

The evidence is scanty. *Snow Apples,* an unevenly written first novel by Canadian Mary Razzell, is nevertheless overwhelming in its sense of a particular time and place—a British Columbia outport in the 1940s. As in *A Tree Grows in Brooklyn*, one feels the presence of a passionate, sometimes angry, adult sensibility, reliving the bitter injustices as well as the intense yearnings of young womanhood. Razzell re-creates what Richard Peck could not: the frightening, queasy aura of male sexuality that closes in on an attractive young girl who is not protected by her family. Those who grew up in the 1940s and 1950s, and can remember the code of puritannical silence which left girls to fend off molesters and aggressive boyfriends without information or support, will find this a disturbingly accurate portrait. But the book is meant for teenagers and it does achieve what more clinical authors have failed to: Razell forcefully conveys the driving urgency of teenage eroticism and the need for love.

These same themes are present, just as openly, in *The First of Midnight*, a historical novel by Marjorie Darke, which is particularly satisfying for teenage girls with a taste for romance but the intelligence to yearn for something more substantial. Jess is a sparky, defiant poorhouse waif in eighteenth-century Bristol, a British seaport that prospered on the illicit slave trade. Escaping from a brutish employer, the ignorant, filthy Jess dresses in boy's clothes and takes refuge on a ship anchored in Bristol harbor. There her fate becomes entwined with that of Midnight, an improbably noble black slave who has been made literate, even well-educated, by a former owner.

There are overtones of both Joan Aiken and Leon Garfield in the colorful language and pell-mell adventures into which Jess and Midnight are propelled, but there is a serious love story here, too, and a deepening of Jess's understanding as she comes to realize the meanings of slavery and freedom. The scene of their lovemaking does not flinch from "the pressure of thigh on thigh, the honey-mouth taste, the smell of cloves and salt . . . the abandoned animal joy." This may not be the pinnacle of erotic literature, but it is an honest and successful attempt, suffused also with a very real tenderness, to convey the experience of sex from both the male and the female point of view. And Jess and Midnight do not live in a vacuum; despite their mutual love, the cultural chasm between them is too deep, eventually, for them to bridge. Midnight longs to leave his free but brutish life as a sideshow prizefighter; Jess is too limited by her past to be able to visualize a life with him back in Africa. Judy Blume wrote that in *Forever* she wanted to show that teenage sexual love can be transient even if sincere; her effort is one-dimensional and trite, but Darke makes us feel its brief happiness, confusion, loss, and ultimate gain.

Bilgewater by the superbly witty and deft Jane Gardam is a more lighthearted, satirical story. Marigold Daisy Green, who describes herself as "froglike—squat and ugly" with bad eyesight and orange frizzy hair—grows up in sheltered and bizarre circumstances in a boy's school where her gentle, eccentric father is headmaster. Indeed, the characters are a gallery of endearing and sometimes buffoonish eccentrics, and all of them, young and old, reticent or extravagant, act out the various and resplendent follies to which they are driven by love.

"Bilgewater," as she is unkindly nicknamed by the oafish boys in their girl-hating prepubescence, leaps into her own adolescent madnesses. First she lets herself be duped by her adored Jack Rose, the school's "silver spoon boy"; sadder but wiser after a comically ghastly visit with him at his parents' house-cum-dental office, she flees to the romantic arms of the mysterious Terrapin, who had looked "like a small albino ape" to her in his childhood.

As the first person narrator, Bilgewater escapes all the dreary, slovenly mannerisms of her American counterparts. She is a funny, shy, clumsy girl, a whiz at math, a mordantly sharp observer of the adult life around her, and a brooder over books. Her narrative sparkles with self-mockery, keen though often naive perceptions of others, and wonderfully fresh and genuine literary references. We see how stories have fed her daydreams, and how the symbolism of various books is absorbed into her consciousness. Before our eyes, Bilgewater metamorphoses into a bright, engagingly idiosyncratic adolescent who is no more misguided in love than all the adults around her astonishingly reveal themselves to be.

Bilgewater's eventual triumph is tinged with a certain sadness: At the peak of her distinguished career, she looks back briefly on this chronicle and hints that she knows what she gave up when she chose a safe, good man over a treacherous but erotically electrifying scoundrel. Although the novel deals with Bilgewater's childhood and adolescence, the education of her heart and mind—and though the sexual encounters stop short of explicitness—this novel makes few concessions to inexperienced readers. It is written with adult sharpness of insight and hilarity, and yet remains perfectly accessible to a good reader over the age of twelve.

Bilgewater's choice is one that every adolescent must make; the "fool's gold" of misplaced teenage affections is a frequent motif in books for this age group. When the theme is handled well (as it is also in Gardam's *A Long Way from Verona,* in K.M. Peyton's Pennington books, and in *Up a Road Slowly* by Irene Hunt), it is an idea of enduring human interest. When, as in *Bilgewater,* it is illuminated at so many levels, and with so much understanding and gentle irony, it provides far more valuable insights than a mere description of sexual intercourse.

The erotic life in all its dimensions has its rightful place in adolescent literature. The adult writer who is aiming at more than mass sales will take the matter seriously enough to write about sex without crudity, without banality, and will not offend any but the most prudish. The prerequisites seem to be tact, emotional depth, and a sense of the power of the unspoken word. Shakespeare did not have to show us Juliet mopping up semen to make us feel the force of her passion. Such well-intentioned literalness is the kiss of death for the imaginative apprehension of what love might mean.

Wit—polished, ironic, deflating, or heartening—is the special quality of some of the most appealing adolescent literature. Anyone who has heard thirteen-year-old girls lampooning with deadly precision the genteel sado-masochism of Harlequin novels knows that teenagers can hear several tunes at one time: They can be enthralled by romantic daydreams while their intelligence simultaneously plays a sardonic counterpoint. The humorous handling of adolescent tensions is not necessarily belittling. On the contrary; wit can signal the reassuring news that you will live to laugh at your traumas, that adulthood will bring a calming perspective. And laughter is the best defense against that most limiting of all adolescent tendencies, self-pity. To laugh means that you have gained some distance from yourself.

In *Goodnight, Prof, Love, (Goodnight, Prof, Dear* in the United States—another misguided concession to linguistic parochialism) by John Rowe Townsend, it is sixteen-year-old Graham Hollis's wry self-awareness that gives life to a potentially hackneyed story. Graham is a gangly, shy teenager who fantasizes romantically about rescuing pale-faced maidens from cliffs. When his parents leave on a week's vacation, though, it is a very different kind of girl he meets and tries to rescue: a hard-luck, chipper, working-class girl of eighteen, Lynn, who works in a local greasy spoon and is at the mercy of her domineering employer. She calls Graham "Prof" because of his bespectacled schoolboy innocence; teases him fondly ("I've took quite a fancy to you . . ."); and gets him a temporary job washing dishes in the restaurant.

Graham, of course, eventually falls madly in love with Lynn and persuades her to elope with him. Half-tempted by his boyish ardor, she agrees, takes him on the road, initiates him sexually with earthy kindness and sends him home at last. The sex scenes are notable for their discretion. The focus is on the emotional transaction between the characters: his shamefaced failure at first, her cheery tolerance, his eventual exhilaration. The novel gains from the play of Graham's sardonic self-awareness and his innocence; it is swift, funny, collo- quial, and decent, a slender but believable story.

Richard Peck, too, uses wit to convince us of the credibility of his unalienated teenagers; they may have problems, but they are not embittered or cynical. Two of his best are *Representing Superdoll* and *Father Figure,* both of which are distinguished by their sympa- thetic humor and their splendidly fresh settings. *Superdoll* is a satire of the beauty contest mentality, as seen in the rise of Darlene Hoff- meister from Miss Hybrid Seed Corn to Central United States Teen Superdoll. The narrator is the temporarily mousy farm girl, Verna; her style is easily conversational and as polished as a freshly husked cob of corn. Verna has native intelligence on her side, along with the natural grace to be tolerant, though mildly envious, of her beautiful classmate. When she accompanies Darlene on the Superdoll promo- tional trip to New York, Verna comes splendidly into her own. The reader, and Verna, can see that a tantalizing future—uncomplicated by self-conscious beauty—lies just over the horizon for her.

Father Figure lacks the sunniness of *Representing Superdoll;* the seventeen-year-old narrator, Jim Atwater, is a more tormented, more sophisticated and introverted hero whose story of reconciliation with a long-lost father, down on his luck in Florida, is peppered with dry New York witticisms. Jim is a private school boy, a well-behaved and tightly controlled upper-class kid who worries too much about his self-contained little brother Byron. He's given to knowing observa- tions about his grandmother and her wealthy, stiffly respectable Re- publican friends, whom he calls the "Gray Panthers." When one of them pulls strings to arrange a summer job for Jim, Jim remarks to himself "The elderly can't deal with you, but they sure as hell can deal you in."

The novel is at its richest in its depiction of the summer the boys spend—Jim resentfully and Byron expansively—with their estranged father. Their mother has committed suicide after a lengthy struggle with cancer. Jim is beseiged by complicated feelings: He's jealous of his father's growing closeness with Byron, sexually competitive with him for the favors of yet another waitress-with-a-heart-of-gold, and unforgivingly enraged by his father's long neglect of the family. Peck, however, is utterly unlike problem novelists in that he never allows his adult characters to become cardboard villains in order to indulge teenage readers in a pleasant wallow of self-righteousness. Jim's dad, Howard, knows he is a failure, more pathetic than evil. By the end of the summer, Jim has painfully learned to accept both his father and the warm-hearted Marietta as people in their own right, not players in his private drama.

It's a touching and brave novel, with rounded characters who are capable of surprising you, and with Peck's special gift: a devastatingly accurate eye for class distinctions, social styles, and affectation of dress and speech.

Peck, like Townsend and LeGuin, has a talent for drawing male characters who are clearly masculine without being crass, super-athletic, or conceited. If you read enough adolescent novels, you will know this for the rarity it is. Contemporary novelists, like many of their subjects, seem to think they must choose between only two kinds of male characters: brutes and wimps. Because the male hero is rarely admirable in modern teenage novels, I think it worth a special discussion of two books that are wonderful exceptions.

Johnny Tremain is as fresh and compelling now as when it won the Newbery Medal in 1943. It follows the fortunes of Johnny from the time he is a fourteen-year-old silversmith's apprentice in Boston to the emotionally patriotic ending two years later when he plays a part in the American Revolution. This is a vigorously written historical novel, busily populated with rich merchants, tradesmen's daughters, eloquent revolutionaries, dreamers, affable British enlisted men, arrogant officers. But as much as it is a dramatic and lively account of a busy seaport and the conflicts that gave rise to the Revolution, it is also the story of Johnny's coming of age.

When we first meet him, he is as headstrong and domineering as many another precociously gifted boy. A quick-witted orphan who must make his own way, he has grandiose dreams for himself and little patience with the less fortunate. Just as his star is rising (he has been noticed favorably by the famous silversmith, Paul Revere), Johnny suffers a ghastly accident which costs him the use of his right hand. Soon, he knows the bitterness and despair of being without work, a home, or a future. His arrogant assumptions crumble.

It is an old-fashioned plot, the proud brought low, but youngsters read it as ardently now as they ever did. Whatever the current fashions in teenage cynicism, the elemental challenges of youth—to make something of yourself, to learn the art of friendship, to make sense of the adult world, to discard false idols—remain unchanged. Johnny's transformations take place through dramatic action. He rebuilds his life, wins friends, abandons false pride, discovers love. It's a sturdy, extroverted story, with a wide enough slice of life (Johnny becomes a courier for the rebels and practices one-handed axe wielding so he can take part in the Boston Tea Party) to make the reader experience history as a series of human actions.

If the amplitude of *Johnny Tremain* is daunting to a less-motivated reader, then there is, last but never least, Pennington, rebellious hero of K.M. Peyton's *Pennington's Seventeenth Summer,* a delinquent whose surging energies make Hinton's self-conscious male models seem like a parcel of poseurs.

Pennington is an overgrown schoolboy from the north of England, a working-class hulk, whose antics are the despair of his teachers. "May God forgive the boy for abusing so unusual a talent," rages Mr. Crocker, Penn's maddened music teacher, on the report card. For Pennington is not just massive and physically gifted, the pride of his school's soccer team; he also has huge hands that stretch easily across the octaves. And his mother, an argumentative, erratic shrew who works in a trousers factory and gambles away her earnings, has nagged him since he was three to stick to his piano lessons.

Pennington is sublimely indifferent to his musical talent; what he likes to do is to noodle on the harmonica whenever his buddy Bates, the cowman's son, gets drunk enough to sing plaintive ballads in a sweet tenor voice. Pennington is the kind of teenager who makes respectable adults yell "Hooligan!" after him in the street. Irreverent, laconic, a thoughtless prankster, he is nevertheless enormously sympathetic. He may provoke fistfights with his arch enemy, Smeeton; he may have swiped some Easter eggs and ten cigarettes from a local store, but Pennington is not a bully and not mean-spirited. All he really wants is to be left alone.

But Pennington's life is a series of pratfalls and choking injustices; his own thoughtlessness leads him into a tumultuous series of scrapes in which he is constantly running afoul of adult authority, usually through some utterly plausible misunderstanding. Rueful, harassed, saved from mournfulness by his own animal high spirits, Pennington cannot fail to endear himself to the reader. It's the sheer dash, humor and energy of the writing that serve to enlist our sympathies on Pennington's side; somehow, Peyton makes us believe wholeheartedly in the way the hapless Pennington constantly trips over the rules.

The dialogue helps: Peyton has a perfect ear for Penn's surliness as well as shaggy-dog aimiability with friends, and for the characteristic speech of all the adults, too—the mother who makes the house reverberate as though it's "wired up for canned invective"; the father who alternately thumps Penn and slyly incites him to rebellion; the avuncular local constable, always chastising Penn more in sorrow than in anger; the frustrated but decent Crocker, who believes in Penn; and Penn's spiteful and sadistic nemesis, the teacher Mr. Marsh, appropriately nicknamed "Soggy" by the boys.

What transforms Pennington's chaotic life is that Mr. Crocker has entered him for a piano competition, and arranges for an enforced three hours of practice at school every day. Despite himself, Pennington begins to be drawn into the music he had despised. Part of music's new appeal for him is that he has been inarticulately, helplessly smitten by a silvery apparition of a girl, a folk singer seen at a distance. ("All the girls he knew were busty and thrusty and strong, all private giggles and shrieks, nudging and daring and passing notes.") From the moment when he slumps resentfully on the piano bench, "resistance setting in like arthritis," as Crocker sets him to work, until the suspenseful climax at the music competition, Pennington is unwillingly discovering the rewards of hard work.

The plot is dazzling for its physical impetuosity, its inventiveness, and the inevitability with which all the incidents are drawn together in a comic chain of overlapping cause-and-effect. Peyton triumphs at graphically clear descriptions of physical feats, whether it's Pennington taking a reckless fifteen-foot dive into shallow water, or his friend Bates, drunkenly and hilariously uncoordinated, turning pages for him at a stuffy school concert. The pace during the last few chapters is absolutely breathless. So relentless are the complications, so frantic is Pennington as he tries both to elude the police and to accommodate a dozen conflicting adult demands on him, that the reader is almost as exhausted by tension as the hero.

But Peyton is not just a whiz at physical action, slapstick and offhanded satire of the way adults are always getting things wrong. In this, her best book, she can also make you feel the plangent sweetness of Bates's voice coming across the water from a wrecked old fishing boat (followed, of course, by muffled curses and the splash of a can being hurled into the water); she can make you *hear* the way Pennington plays Mendelssohn, hands raw from a school strapping, but doggedly thinking of "Mendelssohn's flaming fairies."

Best of all, I think is the way Peyton keeps Pennington's character true to itself. He simply never thinks about his affect on others; he doesn't give a damn for adult opinion, not even when it might be approving for once: After he risks his life and the piano competition to save old Crocker's life out at sea, and then the town wrongheadedly gives the credit to Bates who was a mere bystander, Pennington just shrugs. He cares about Crocker, but never does anything about expressing it verbally. He accepts a piano scholarship to London from a distinguished teacher—whom he mistakes for a bothersome vicar—because he fancies having a room of his own.

The modulations in Pennington's attitudes towards the end are beautifully underplayed. Music has begun to mean something to him, he has begun—perhaps through sheer force of exhaustion—to stop and *think* before he acts recklessly, but Peyton never spoils her portrait of Pennington by sentimentality. Never once does she dilute or fudge the impact of Pennington's character by descending into the kind of maudlin self-dramatization that makes Hinton's characters glow with a sickly phosphorescence, like "a bad lobster in a dark cellar," to use Dickens's phrase.

Two sequels, *The Beethoven Medal* and *Pennington's Heir,* are told sympathetically from the point of view of Ruth, the girl who loves Pennington helplessly and whom he eventually marries. Both are notably competent portraits of the pains and pleasures of young love and a musician's life. Peyton seems always to be warmly on the side of her young protagonists, inarticulate though they may be, wrongheaded as they often seem to be to the adults around them. She can empathize with their energies and their willful passions without condescending, and without ever being, like Blume, a mere conduit for their egocentricity and banality.

It would be a shame to leave this chapter on alternatives in teenage reading without mentioning two fictional works with strong elements of autobiography, a genre that is particularly attractive to adolescents. Both *A Bird in the House* by Margaret Laurence, and *Lives of Girls and Women* by Alice Munro, are series of linked stories that share a precision and sharpness of insight, a luminous imagery and a scrupulous honesty about girlhood that goes several layers deeper than almost any other fictional work that comes to mind. This is the kind of writing that helps a young person to "set the self aside" for a moment, only to regain it more profoundly when the story has been absorbed. That—and not problem solving, not sexual instruction—is what teenage fiction is most deeply concerned with.

Chapter 10

GIRLS' BOOKS,
BOYS' BOOKS,
BAD BOOKS,
AND BIAS

> Whatever my children read, I have faith—indeed, I would say that I know—that they are resting for a while in the recesses of their souls, in places where I will never know them, can never know them, am not supposed to know them.
>
> Julius Lester, *Horn Book,* April 1984

> It is sad that childhood is only one-seventh of one's life, and only five years of one's reading life.
>
> Gilliam Avery, in *Writers, Critics, and Children,* 1976

> Junk books can dull the hunger of a child's mind, stuff it with unearned certainties . . .
>
> Paula Fox, in *Celebrating Children's Books,* 1981

I respond with visceral and instant agreement to all three of the above statements; I suspect that most parents would find themselves on the horns of the same dilemma. If we care what our children read, if we know what a wealth of literature is available to them for those too-short years of reading intensity—what shall we do about the junk?

The first thing, I suppose, is to know about it. Recently I met a friend with her two children at the theater. She is energetic, independent, and talented, a university professor and published author. Her son and daughter, about eleven and nine years old, are sensitive and highly intelligent. The little girl was carrying a paperback copy of a Judy Blume novel. "Oh, horrible!" burst out my own fourteen-year-old daughter. And there I was, embarrassingly stuck with explaining our aversion while trying not to seem overbearingly critical.

As it happened, my friend was interested rather than defensive. She had thought (being a feminist) that these modern novels might as least be contemporary in tone and without the sexism of older children's works. She wanted to hear more.

It is for her and other adults like her, who have not had the time or perhaps the inclination to read children's books for themselves, that I have taken pains to point out what I feel is shoddy and meretricious in authors like Blume. I know that I risk flaming indignation from her loyalists, who are legion: When I wrote about Blume in my newspaper column, I was attacked by some teachers and librarians for my supposed "elitism." Children found freshness and insight into their own current problems in these books, I was told, and I had no right to try to suppress them.

But I do not want to suppress them. If my own children had loved Blume's books (or Hinton's or any of the legion of their imitators) I would have respected their choices while tactfully offering others—or at least keeping the door open to other rooms, other voices. As the English reading expert Margaret Meek has stressed, children do seem to need "bulk reading," which, by its very nature, is undemanding and often of very low literary quality. My own observation is that at crucial moments of change and growth, children often need to fall back temporarily, as though to test the firmness of their former ground before stepping forward into the unknown.

At the age of seven or eight, when reading skills have recently been integrated, a bright child will gobble endless junk books, such as Enid Blyton's *Noddy,* or recycled pap from movies such as *Star Wars.* Comics are another familiar form of transitional reading, still using some of the easy picture-book format while introducing more sophisticated vocabulary and either slapstick humor or exaggerated violence. Speed, comfort, familiarity, a reassuring simplicity, devotion to surface actions and conventional behavior, a complete absence of introspection—these are the ingredients of bulk reading. The "bulk" is not a total loss; as Meek and others point out, the child is learning the shape of stories—episode, climax, resolution, even rough outlines of such archetypes as heroes and villains—in privacy and independence. No teachers correct mistakes; no parents hover over the page to reprove. The freedom to choose one's own books is in some ways the most bracing and dramatic taste of liberty a child can know: At five or six or seven, browsing in the library or bookstore and then reading at home, the child is suddenly free to enter other worlds, spy from within on a thousand lives, leap oceans with a single bound.

Safely and with the undiluted pleasure of pure pastime, the child unwittingly practices the recently acquired skills of reading until they become smoothly unconscious. There may also be the spice of naughtiness in "bulk reading"; intelligent children know very well that they are skimming along with the merest surface involvement, and they even know that this is a tiny betrayal of that more complex demand made by real books. I distinctly remember the headiness of this reading libertinism when I was six years old and reading *The Bobbsey Twins*. Series books, of course, offer the most simple enjoyment: You don't even have to bother becoming acquainted with the characters. You can go on and on, like skating up a frozen creek, the characters and incidents blurring past you.

Good books, though, can spoil the sheer mindlessness of bulk reading for you. By the time I was ten or eleven, and a friend begged me to read her complete set of Nancy Drew, I was bored stiff by the stilted writing and cartoonish characters. Without realizing it, I had already become addicted to the more intricate rewards of good prose; from then on, when I wanted bulk reading, I had to resort to magazines. A book that didn't give me the total absorption I craved was not a distraction but an irritation and a fraud.

Though every age group has its cherished forms of private reading indulgence, it is especially at puberty that junk books reassert their claim. Rapid change is frightening. A twelve-year-old's development may be drastically slower or faster than that of her friends; the known safety of the primary grades has been exchanged for the threatening gauntlet of junior or senior high school; the future rushes in and the past drops away. Romances, mysteries, thrillers, and westerns provide a haven of completely reliable escape structures. The tough-jawed cowboy will never break down and grovel before the bully; the heroine of the romance will never be rejected by all the men in her life; if change or death have roles in the drama, they will never stab the reader with real anguish. Furthermore, the youngster who relies on these predictable stories is at least gaining pleasure and distraction from the reading of fiction, and this may be a base to build on for more satisfying reading in the future.

Bad books, the mindless-but-benign as well as the insidious, have their own distribution system. The child who needs them finds them as though by magic; they are pervasive, unnoticed, and disposable as Kleenex. My local libraries—and that includes the libraries in primary and second schools—have shelves full of Blume, Harlequins, and Louis L'Amour. So we don't have to worry about young people getting their fill of junk reading.

We do have to worry, however, if those five or six years of childhood reading time speed past, crammed with television, sports, and Care Bears, and presto—a young adult emerges who has never been deeply moved by a book, who has never had experience transfigured into art through reading, and who, consequently, may never again think of books as a serious adjunct to life. A priceless opportunity will have been lost forever, and one of the most humanizing and profound resources available to us as parents and teachers will have been abandoned without a second thought.

Yet it is so easy to take the other route. The child may read Little Golden Books on the living room rug, but hear Joan Aiken, Ted Hughes, Clive King, or E.L. Konigsburg read aloud at bedtime. (And if the child insists on hearing Care Bears stories read aloud, read them, but follow up with something as vibrant as William Steig.) It is as easy, and nutritionally more sound, to take a five-year-old child to the library every week as it is to make an outing to McDonald's part of the family routine.

The problem of preadolescent reading is admittedly more difficult. No eleven-year-old wants to have mummy or daddy peering over her shoulder at the library and recommending books, and the most heartfelt urgings from a parent or teacher may have a stubbornly contrary effect.

Still, with hundreds of children's bookstores in every major town and city, it is as easy to buy a paperback version of *A Bridge to Terabithia* or *Anne of Green Gables* as it is to head for the shelves of teen romances. Gift certificates to children's bookstores may yield surprising results; a young shopper on his own may be astonishingly receptive to guidance from knowledgeable sales staff. It's the same principle by which your churlish young heel-dragger, who cannot be persuaded to pick up his socks from the middle of the living room, will gladly, gallantly mow the lawn and wash the storm windows at his friend's house. The sheer independent generosity of the act, free of all compulsion, has a propulsive glamor of its own.

I've had concerned, literate parents beg me to tell them how to wean their children from trash reading. Alas, there is no easy answer, although a parent who reads and enthusiastically enjoys a sprinkling of the most highly recommended children's books is a vital example for any youngster. Though I would never attack a young person's choice of a book, good or bad, I would never pretend to a false approval, either, any more than I would feign a rapt delight in those boring recitals of television plots to which some children are so given. The "mm-hmmm" response is one I have polished to a high gloss. It signifies an interest in the child and his feelings, while withholding an ecstatic approval of the subject matter: it might be of keen significance to me that a child is wildly excited by a police shoot-out on television, for example, while the program itself is interesting only as an example of cultural aberration. And the child gets the message: He is left with an uneasy question in his mind about what exactly the adult *thinks* of all this. Our reticence can provoke a wholesome uncertainty; all understanding begins in questions.

Reading aloud is a more offbeat tactic at this age, but perfectly plausible: Consult Jim Trelease's *Read-Aloud Handbook* for a down-to-earth description of his practice of reading aloud while his teen-aged son washed dishes.

"Problem" novels, as I argued in the previous chapter, present a particular challenge. Our streak of North American utilitarianism predisposes us to think of books as medicine; one whole school of reading experts wholeheartedly endorses something called "bibliotherapy." For anyone who has experienced reading as one of life's most intense aesthetic pleasures, the very word "bibliotherapy" must sound thumpingly perverse. The thinking behind it seems inexpressibly crude: Child is in pain from parents' divorce, give child a cheerful novel about divorce, child will feel better. The child is not a questioning mind and seeking heart but a patient. The book is a commodity, like a patent drug.

My entire life as a reader rebels against this prescription. As a sheltered little girl in tranquil Toronto—far more sheltered than my brothers—I read, with palpitating excitement, stories of adventures in which brothers and sisters shared alike. I would have loathed books about sheltered little girls who lived in rented duplexes in Toronto and argued with their parents for permission to play outside after dark.

As a clunky twelve-year-old, I read Japanese haiku with chills of discovery chasing down my spine: They had all the compression, coherence, delicacy, and purity of design and intention that my life did not. Furthermore, they had an artistic existence of their own, quite apart from my immediate personal needs. On and on through my life, they would still be there, offering new facets of themselves, new depths, with each rereading. They meant many things—remember George MacDonald's observation on the multiple meanings yielded by each work of art—and each time I came back to a poem, I brought new worlds of experience to it, enriched by my history of conversation with each particular poem. No one can have that ongoing intimacy with a "problem novel"; it is by definition static, chained to particularity, a throwaway designed to handle one problem and then be discarded.

Even more to the point, perhaps, was my experience of agony in adult form. When I was broken-hearted after my mother died in a horrible accident, I went, after a few days, blindly and instinctively, to a bookstore to buy some Swedish detective stories. I did not want to read—could not have borne to read—about middle-aged women in mourning. Neither realistic contemporary novels about common problems nor the consolations of high art could offer me anything in that state of crisis. (Critic Lissa Paul has pointed out to me, too, that murder mysteries deal at a comfortably cool remove with the ultimate puzzle of death.) At first it was hard even to focus my swollen eyes on the detective stories. After a while, though, they served to blot out the world, and blot out myself, so I could fall asleep at night. Five months later, vacationing where I could hear the sea and the wind at night, I found myself rereading *To the Lighthouse* with an almost unbearable sharpness of response. After that, my life began to go on again.

I think those two poles of experience illustrate what anyone— child or adult, the pain is the same—may seek in books: obliteration or transcendence from the bottom of one's soul. I would have been enraged, insulted, or baffled by anyone who had tried to press into my hands a trite little novel about overcoming the pain of loss of one's mother.

Art "works" by tangents and imaginative leaps, and it is both arrogant and tactless to assume that we can supply machine-made books to heal a child's wounds. It is far more likely that the child well supplied with good books that range widely in style and substance will find the needed consolation on his or her own in the most unforeseeable ways, out of the richness and multiplicity of art.

The greater danger in junk books is the "mind-stuffing" referred to by Paula Fox. A Canadian study a few years ago revealed that one of the prime sources of advice and moral guidance for teenagers is the television soap opera. Soap operas are a kind of open-ended storytelling, in familiar settings and with stereotyped roles, in which problems of family, sex, morality, and relationships are taken seriously by all the characters. Talk is their main ingredient. Who has ever heard a male character on a police drama stop to discuss his emotional life in leisurely intimacy? Where in our society are adult men as openly, loquaciously, obsessed by gossip and love relationships as they are on the daily soaps? I can imagine that this openness is of absorbing interest to young people yearning to plumb the secrets of adult life. There may be more frank conversation on one episode of a soap opera than they would hear in a month of dinnertimes at home.

The shortcoming of this form of public continuous storytelling, as I need not stress, is that it is so shallow. It shares the penchant of prime-time dramas for glib transformations of character, swift and unequivocal justice, cheap moral certainties. Devotees of soap operas are often given to a watery version of Freudian insight; for each wayward or harmful action, there is an "explanation" which excuses all.

Very well, but is there any harm in it? Can "unearned certainties" gleaned from sociological teenage novels really hurt anyone? The answer is complex. There is lasting harm, certainly, if a young person becomes accustomed to lazy, self-indulgent reading and never learns what more may be gained from books. Literature, however, works at a different level from movies and television, and, unlike graphic, violent pornography, it is rare for a book to stimulate imitative action. Because they appeal to the imaginative life, good books in particular may provide children with patterns of play—but usually children are well aware that this is the realm of fantasy. I may have sailed the South China Sea with Arthur Ransome's Missee Lee, but I knew better than to save my allowance to buy a junk.

Confusion arises when a book pretends to offer a mechanical representation of "real life," implicitly justifying all the destructive impulses of childhood but raising no questions of moral perplexity. I apologize to my forbearing readers for returning once more to this particular bogyperson, but I'm constrained to say that Judy Blume's *Blubber* is the one children's book I know of that, to my personal knowledge, has provoked many incidents of classroom viciousness. I think it is worth dwelling for a moment on the kind of writing that has this unfortunate potential.

Blubber has one main plot and one subplot; both deal with incidents of group spite against isolated individuals who are perceived as being different. Both victims are disagreeable in appearance: The grumpy neighbor has "eyes that turn down at the corners," and the victimized classmate is fat. The heroine, Jill, participates in both campaigns and is justified, both in her own mind and in the tone of the story, in her actions.

The main plot shows the permanently aggrieved narrator, Jill, ganging up with the classroom leaders, Wendy and Caroline, to bully a girl named Linda Fischer. Linda's crimes are that she is fat, has a gray tooth, and "lets people walk all over her." In a mounting campaign of excited cruelty, the girls not only call her "Blubber" but force her to say "My name will always be Blubber"; they tease her for bringing cupcakes in her lunch and taunt her all the more cruelly when she tries to go on a diet.

Jill participates willingly in all the most disturbing sequences: The girls accost Blubber in the girls' bathroom, rip the buttons off her blouse while threatening to strip her, force her to curtsy to "Queen Wendy," and even to kneel and kiss Wendy's shoe. They hold her arms behind her back while lifting her skirt to expose her to the boys and finally bully her into eating what she supposes to be a chocolate-covered ant. Linda vomits the chocolate all over her desk, but even then the girls are unrepentant and unpunished: The teacher and the principal are easily duped by Wendy's smooth lies, which manage to humiliate and turn the blame back on Linda for the whole episode.

Though there is no introspection in Blume's books, we are meant to understand, from one brief dialogue, that Jill is bothered by the Blubber campaign—bothered not by the cruelty, but by Linda's acquiescence. She talks to her mother about a girl "who lets other people walk all over her." The best strategy, says mother, is to laugh off any teasing. Then people will respect you. Anyway, says Jill defiantly, "I could never be in her place!"

Jill does become a victim, though. Predictably enough, Wendy turns on her, incites the class to call her names, isolates her and seeks to humiliate her. Jill fights back. She laughs off the jokes at first, then defies the bullies. At home, she weeps tears of self-pity. But her abasement is short-lived. She quickly makes friends with a new girl in school, and as we leave her at the end of the book, we see her wholehearted again, merrily joining in the group teasing of yet another victim on the school bus.

Contrast this story with *The Hundred Dresses* by Eleanor Estes, discussed earlier in this book. *The Hundred Dresses* also shows the prettiest and most popular girl in class bullying a girl who is different—Wanda Petronski with her ragged clothes and funny name. The main character, like Jill, is a sidekick to the leader of the girls. There is the same feverish impetus to the teasing: The children are caught up in the daring game of aggression against a victim who can't fight back. But there is a world of difference in the tone of the two books; Maddie, the heroine, is vividly observant. Through her eyes, we not only follow the classroom events, but share the delights of friendship, activity, the changing season, and the excitement of holidays. Jill, Blume's modern heroine, is too neurotically self-obsessed to take such natural pleasure in life. She sees everything in her world through lemon-colored glasses. Her voice is one of perpetual sour disgruntlement with everyone and everything; adults, except for a few idolized men, earn nothing but contempt; holidays, like Halloween, yield pleasure only in the opportunities they present to torment victims or win contests. Nothing is good and rewarding in itself.

From the beginning of the persecution of Wanda in *The Hundred Dresses,* the reader's pleasure is clouded by the tiny shadow of Maddie's uneasiness. Through her dialogue and actions, we see that she is torn: She furtively identifies with Wanda's poverty, yet is loyal to her friend Peggy, the ringleader, and afraid of her scorn.

Because Maddie's response is so much more complex than Jill's, it is more true to life; it draws the reader into the heart of the conflict. Even an adult reader is smitten by sheepish memories of the price paid for membership in the gang; Estes evokes this inward dismay with needle-sharp delicacy. In the end, even though victim Wanda is seen to be triumphing in a new school, though she has made a lovely gesture which would seem to pardon them all, though ringleader Peggy has leaped at the reconciliation without a pang, Maddie's relief—and ours—is tinged with sadness. Not even forgiveness and good resolutions can totally absolve you from the consciousness of the wrong you have done. This is infinitely more thought-provoking, rounded, vivid, and touching than Blume's morally lobotomized Jill, and its effect is profoundly different too. The reader emerges from the book a changed person: She has not been *taught* about cruelty and guilt, but has experienced it, in bearable doses, through the flow of feelings of a child very like herself.

Blubber's amorality leaves the reader confused. I have known of three classrooms, and heard about others, where readers of *Blubber* have been so keyed up by the book's apparent acceptance of viciousness that they have actually instigated a "Blubber" crusade against the nearest fat classmate. There is something more that is troubling. No child is free of vengefulness and spite, and a kind of blithe, willful unconsciousness of the sufferings of others. But the torment of Blubber has sado-masochistic overtones that seem to go beyond the normal hit-and-run meanness of children. Would fifth-graders really revel in the systematic debasement of another? Would they think of making a classmate grovel publicly and kiss the feet of the tormentor?

My friend who thought that Blume was "at least modern" was worried about sexist stereotypes in children's fiction. It seems to me that although Blume avoids overtly sexist remarks, her fixed loathing of physical ugliness, usually directed at females, is even more insinuatingly deprecating. Not all Blume's readers, after all, are as naturally skinny or pretty as her heroines always are. A bright-eyed, attractive but plump nine-year-old once slapped down a copy of *Blubber* on her desk and said, choking with emotion, "I can't see why anyone who isn't fat would even be interested in this nasty book, and a fat kid reading it would just feel terrible!"

Sexist and racist stereotypes are an immensely difficult question. My friend was right, in one way, to be wary of the literature of an earlier time; much of it is riddled with casual contempt for the feminine and with offhand slurs of different racial groups. So, however, is some of the most modern writing for youth. It's no use simply dismissing anything that smacks of bias, because, provokingly enough, some of the best-written books carry traces of thoughtless stereotyping—and some of the worst-written stuff available is conscientiously liberated and free from every trace of prejudice against women, blacks, homosexuals, the aged, the disabled—the list goes on to include every worthy cause known to the aroused conscience. Some of this determinedly progressive fiction for youth has an eerily Victorian ring to it: Didacticism clangs on every page like an iron bell, heavy, clumsy, reverberant with good intentions.

We can't always have it both ways. Art springs from the anarchic spirit of the artist, and, if we are lucky, if the artist is possessed of a humane and capacious spirit, the work of art will transcend pettiness and narrow prejudice. Worthy motives and a raised consciousness do not an artist make, and novels which are calculated to exalt our levels of tolerance rarely emerge as more than earnest tracts. All ulterior motives tend to undermine a work of art: C.S. Lewis's Narnia cycle, which he said he wrote to make children aware of "the suffering of Christ," has been called forced and unconvincing by more than one critic.

By their sheer abundance of perception, the most gifted writers for children can endow both male and female characters with fully realized humanity. When Eleanor Estes wrote *The Hundred Dresses* in 1942, she certainly depicted boys and girls in the narrow gender roles of the time (the class art contest: Boys draw motorboats and girls draw dresses), and yet this book is indispensable and humanly liberating. Both Edith Nesbit and Arthur Ransome cast some of their girls in anxiously mothering roles; both also created girls of spirit, daring, imagination, and resource.

And what of the most rebelliously modern authors, those pioneers of new forms and subjects of fiction for youth? The works of Ivan Southall, Robert Westall, and Robert Cormier all smack of misogyny. They have a single-mindedly male outlook in which girls are referred to by their breast size, sex appeal, or relative sexual repulsiveness; Southall is at his worst in a recent book, *A City Out of Sight*, in which he strives to depict a girl finding liberation from her sex-object style when she is stranded on a desert island. The strain shows: He reverts, time and again, to the crudest male dismissal of girls as either rapaciously boy-crazed or dreaded potential wives who are homely, shrill nags.

Westall is even more disturbing, since he's a powerful writer with an urgent, compelling style. *The Machine Gunners* is an extraordinarily tough book about a group of boys in wartime England who steal a machine-gun from a downed Nazi plane and create their own foxhole on the edge of town. Their ingenious, stubborn physical effort; their mounting war hysteria; their unconscious parodying of fascist behavior as they set up their own military unit; and their final, strange bonding with an escaped German flier whom they take prisoner and who becomes their ally against their own parents—all make for a gripping and brilliantly told story. Yet there is no denying that Chas, the fifteen-year-old central character, is a sexual bigot: Girls to him are "silly cows," "bossy females." He flies into a rage of disgust with a neighbor woman who comes into his family's air-raid shelter one night; he hates her because she sits with her knees apart. His own mother "nags and whines"; Nicky's mother is hated for being upper crust and sleeping with sailors billeted in her mansion. She gets her just deserts in an air raid one concupiscent night, but all the boys see her promiscuity as having been unforgivably damaging to her son.

Audrey, the one girl who is allowed to join the group, automatically takes a submissive role as "quartermaster" in the dugout and does the cooking and cleaning for the boys. Chas hates her voice and her "bulging hockey muscles," and takes a grim relish in seeing her reduced to "all eyes and a woman for once" when she is shocked at the sight of a rotting corpse.

I assume that Westall meant us to see that this panicky revulsion against female sexuality is part of Chas's pathology. Nevertheless, I remember too well what it was like to read this constant male harping on female loathsomeness when I was a child. It hit me like a physical blow in the stomach; I fought it, but it deeply shook my sense of self. The authority of print carried great weight with me and I certainly internalized and accepted, however protestingly, however unhappily, the relentless stereotyping of girls as sweet, pretty, passive, and inferior—and sly, bitchy, envious schemers, too—at least until the age of twelve when I became a conscious feminist. Even female authors, and even contemporary ones—especially the British—frequently make casual reference to girls as barely tolerated inferiors to boys. "She was all right for a girl" is a commonplace of children's fiction; worse is the accepted convention that normal, lovable boys in fiction will naturally prefer the company of other boys and will usually harbor real spite against girls.

Soup by Robert Newton Peck, for example, is a high-spirited and perennially popular story of boyhood, written in 1974. The prose is crisp and vivid, the humor racy, unsentimental. It is, in other words, a superior book. Yet it is laced with vignettes depicting women as repressive, prudish, religion-prating authoritarians. Should we quietly remove this unpleasant distortion of reality from the shelves? What about the splendidly written, moving coming-of-age novel, *And Now Miguel* by Joseph Krumgold, a recently reissued Newbery Medal winner? I would want every boy to read this excellent novel for intermediate readers, and yet there's no gainsaying the fact that the women in Miguel's family are little better than slaves—no doubt the reality of that time and place—and that Miguel exults once or twice too often in his superiority as a male.

The answer, I believe, is to make sure that we express our nonsexist and antiracist values to children in every area of their lives and to ensure that *both* boys and girls have a balanced exposure to books which feature both sexes in leading, admirable roles. In choosing books for children, we should select those works that offer a depth in characterization that will compensate for any lapses into gender bias. There is no reason to endorse (though we can't prevent) the reading of teenage romances, such as the *Sweet Dreams* series, or detective thrillers, which deliberately trade in extremes of gender stereotypes: tough macho heroes and love-sodden girls. Well-read youngsters, who are sensitive in their family lives to questions of fairness and equality, will soon be alerted to biases in books, and perhaps there is something salutary in having to come to grips with recognizable prejudice in the writings of those who give us pleasure. It is a dilemma our young people will face often enough in the course of their lives.

I'll return to this theme of books for girls and boys after a look at another frequent problem in children's literature: racial prejudice. As an Anglophile Jew who grew up ardently reading English literature, I am an expert in the subject. It would be hard to name an English writer for adults—from Shakespeare to Agatha Christie, Dickens to Chesterton—who did not include anti-Semitic stereotypes as part of the writer's stock-in-trade.

I can't say that it wasn't wounding. Nevertheless, the mere presence of anti-Semitism could not spoil an otherwise good book for me. As I've noted elsewhere, E. Nesbit's *The Story of the Amulet* moved me profoundly by its vision of a utopian society. I chose to ignore, sturdily, the fact that the same book has three extraneous, jarring caricatures of a grossly anti-Semitic nature. I was able to preserve my mood of rapt enchantment, however, because *I knew she was wrong*—we just weren't like that. Note that I was far more vulnerable to slurs against girls because I was growing up in a society which reinforced my inferior position at every turn. This leads me to wonder if a girl today, growing up in just the kind of enlightened family that would bridle at sexism in books, would be nearly as afflicted by these stereotypes as I was. Perhaps she would be proof against them as I was against anti-Semitism.

What about other, less sensitized children? What about boys and girls of Anglo-Saxon background reading, for example, Enid Blyton, whose hundreds of books still maintain their worldwide popularity? I chose a few of her books to read, at random, because I had never read her as a child (my library, I'm glad to say, didn't carry them), and I felt I should know why she is loathed by every intelligent critic in the world and adored by so many children.

The adoration was instantly explained: These are hilariously awful books, exactly parallel to lurid adult thrillers of the Mickey Spillane type. It's pop literature at its most page-turning, breathless, utterly predictable extreme. *The Circus of Adventure*, for example, stars four British children, Jack and Lucy-Ann and their friends Philip and Dinah, all of whom live with Philip and Dinah's mother, Mrs. Mannering, who is married to secret service agent Bill Cunningham. One summer this unlikely family must play host to a mysterious eleven-year-old foreign boy, Gussy. The British children are uproariously bloody-minded, aided and abetted by their mother: They are disgusted by timid little Gussy's polite manners, the way he helps carry the bags for Mrs. Mannering, and by his "greasy" black curls and silk pajamas. They tease, harass, and brutalize him in the most unfair and cruel ways, and all with the blithe approval of the adults: "I think you can quite safely make young Gustavus toe the line. That won't do him any harm at all," Mrs. Mannering says smugly. "He seems like quite a spoilt little crybaby to me." This, after they have abused him till he, a homeless fugitive, is ready to weep.

British fair play is stunningly absent from these various torments: They trick him, terrify him, and then laugh riotously when he is upset. Poor Gussy never learns how he has been duped, but is always slavishly admiring of these true British boys. Only when it turns out that Gussy is the crown prince of Tauri-Hessia do the children complacently change their minds: When Gussy welcomes them as his royal guests to his royal palace at home, "it seems quite all right somehow" that he should bow to them and kiss their hands.

The anti-foreign bias is staggering. (Not to mention the homo-phobia: The worst thing about Gussy's curls is that they make him look like a girl. "We have enough poofers here," says bully-boy Jack.) Gussy is made to speak in a grotesque parody of immigrant English, and the police in Tauri-Hessia are spluttering idiots who wear "comic flower-pot hats." Indeed, all the Tauri-Hessians are either greasy vil-lains or greasy fools, and it is up to the invincibly energetic, resource-ful, clever, manly Brits to save the whole country. At last, when order is restored, and the British educated king is on the throne, all look forward to Gussy's eventual rule. "Gussy was just a silly little boy at present—but perhaps, when he had learnt all that the British people had to teach him, at lessons and at games, he would be as fine a king as his uncle," Blyton writes.

Needless to say, the gender stereotyping and the scorn for any-thing girlish is as extreme as the xenophobia. But children read these books as they read comics, for the sheer preposterous adventure; the physical action; the glorious deeds done by the children themselves; the trying on, in fantasy, of various roles, which may actually be facilitated by the crude exaggeration of the characters.

Blyton books are "bulk reading"; they would not be likely to satisfy a sophisticated reader any more than *Nancy Drew* would, but they may provide a moment of relaxing escapism even for those who are accustomed to better fare. If parents are aware of the far-fetched chauvinism (of both male and British varieties), they can perhaps defuse their silliness. But it would be a phlegmatic parent indeed who would willingly *buy* these books for children, knowing what's in them. If children beg for them, however, there is not much sense in an outright ban. In that situation, I would consider the Blyton (or what-ever) as just one rung on what has been called "the reading ladder"; buy the Blyton if you must, but sandwich it between two or three more highly recommended books with strong reader appeal.

A far more contentious issue arises when books that are deemed racist turn up in school libraries and in school curricula. I loved *Little Black Sambo* when I was a child; that African family seemed as won-derfully warm, endearing, and admirable to me as the family of Peter Rabbit. I can still see, in my mind's eye, that delicious moment when the tigers melted into butter; I can still see the enviably radiant colors of Little Black Sambo's clothes. Nevertheless, we have the word of black children that the book can lead to humiliation for them; that when it is read aloud in kindergarten, they are singled out on the playground and called "Sambo"—not affectionately. No sensitive teacher would insist on reading this book in a class with black chil-dren present unless she had some malicious motive. There are too many wonderful alternatives—think of Ezra Jack Keats's *The Snowy Day* or *Why Mosquitoes Buzz in People's Ears* by Verna Aardema—which have the same warmth, but implicitly affirm the dignity of black people and do not inadvertently lend themselves to ridicule by schoolyard bullies.

That's true, also, of *Huckleberry Finn;* of course it is a classic, a great and wonderful book, and it grieves me to think that many black parents think it is racist when it is, in fact, the opposite. Nevertheless, why would a school insist on using it as a text in the early years of secondary school in big city schools heavily populated with blacks who protest its use? With so much to choose from, why be rigid about using the one book that hurts and humiliates these vulnerable youngsters who are struggling for a sense of their own worth in an alien school system?

We can never have a sterilized literature, free from all offensive racist and sexist references, but we can use common sense in choosing which books to put on school curricula and which to reserve for the privacy of home, where parents can counteract any mistaken impressions.

Books are powerful; even illiterates acknowledge the power of the printed word when they demand the banning of such fine novels as Margaret Laurence's *The Diviners.* Their power is not the same as the direct impact of visual images, however, and they work in strange and oblique ways: I cite my own experience with Nesbit to show how unforeseen their influence can be. We cannot predict and control the ways in which books will affect our children. Art bursts free of our grasp or it is not art, and those who seek to censor their child's reading will either fail, or deprive their child of the riches of literature altogether by poisoning the intellectual freedom without which reading is a stifling mechanical chore.

Even the most enlightened, progressive parents can fall into the trap of thinking of children's books as just another dose of moral cod liver oil. There may even be a danger that some dedicated parents would consider each book another investment in the careful grooming of their little achiever. Undoubtedly, they would make sure to avoid stories tainted with sexism. I have noticed, though, that some feminist mothers are more scrupulously liberated about daughters than sons. Mothers are still wary about that tender male ego and the possible damage it may suffer from too much dish washing or doll playing. Perhaps they are made nervous, too, by the chorus of masculine voices insisting on the basic male need for aggressive play, sports fanaticism, and male bonding. How can we women really know if these traits are inherent in boys or just the product of conditioning?

I've been particularly perplexed, in writing this book, about the fictional portrayal of boys in modern novels. As a feminist, I am repelled by the crudely aggressive heroes of Cormier, Major, Westall, and Southall. It is true that we are long past the age of idealism; Nesbit's boys could try to model themselves on highly principled men of action, but that conscious nobility would seem idiotic in the post-Hitler, post-Vietnam world. It is also true that novels about alienated youth win an automatic response from literate teenage males; a certain veneer of tough cynicism, a determined anti-sentimentality, is the uniform of the modern hero. That leaves me with a gnawing self-doubt; could my criticism of these novels be unduly influenced by my female bias?

My conclusion, after much soul searching, is that a critic is entitled to demand more of a novel than a one-dimensional portrait of masculinity. Literature, from its beginning, is filled with virile heroes who nevertheless have space in their lives for more than aggression or sex obsession. Only the most emotionally limited teenage boy is as callously contemptuous of girls and as single-mindedly bent on macho aggression as the heroes of some of the teenage novels I've discussed. This stereotype, in other words, is as unfair to boys as its opposite is to girls.

Browsing in a bookstore one day, I met a woman who complained bitterly to me that "there are no books for boys." She insisted that even in Toronto's Children's Book Store, the largest such store in the world, "all the books" had girls on the cover and "boys just won't read a book with a girl on the cover." Her own husband, she told me proudly, had solved the problem by encouraging their son to read the hockey scores in the newspaper every night.

Anyone who haunts an excellent bookstore looking for good fiction for herself, but assumes that a child's reading is so mechanical a business that hockey scores will do as well as a novel, has just not taken children seriously. Nor has she done battle against the ghettoization of her son's mind; she seems to concur with the perverse idea that boys should not be forced to read about anything but boys.

The opposite is true. I wish that woman had read *We've All Got Scars*, by Raphaela Best, a stunning expose of the kind of macho conditioning which ordinary primary school boys enforce upon each other. Best stayed with a class of children for five years, minutely recording their daily interactions. By grade two, the boys had established a clear-cut in-group. To belong, a boy had to be willing to fight—physically and painfully; had to defy female authority; refuse to be seen obeying mother's orders; avoid the company of girls at all costs; insist, in the face of all evidence to the contrary, that boys were physically and mentally superior to girls. It's a hideous picture of boyhood, violent, brutish, narrow, egotistical, and frighteningly lonely. In their constant jockeying among themselves for supremacy ("Me first! I'm boss!" was their constant cry), these boys missed out on affection, curiosity, cooperation, and many special moments in the classroom which the girls, more relaxed, were able to share and enjoy to the full.

Nothing—not argument, persuasion, example, or the teacher's interference—affected the boys' image of themselves as two-fisted warriors or shook their rigid power hierarchy. By grade one the boys refused to help clean blackboards or wash paintbrushes; they denied that they would ever do housework, insisting that their wives would do all that dumb stuff. They would rather die of starvation, they said, than cook for themselves. They were adamant that girls could never be strong enough to be police officers. Confronted with evidence of real live female police, they nevertheless refused to change their fixated ideas.

Not only were these stereotypes repugnant in themselves but they were, Best revealed, devastating to the boys who were not accepted into the macho in-group. One of her most surprising findings was that school achievement for boys in this school (a typical middle-class suburban school in the eastern United States) was linked chiefly to membership in the macho group. Boys who were excluded were so crushed that they simply lost heart; they had no will to learn, gave up ambition, and fell behind irrevocably.

What Best discovered was that the friendship of girls finally broke down some of the boys' defenses and allowed them to be less aggressive, more cooperative, and open to all kinds of experience. It did not happen automatically. Best intervened, when the boys were in grade five, to set up a coeducational discussion group. For the first time, the fanatical, self-imposed sex segregation of the classroom was breached. The girls began to blossom into independence and less feminine-stereotyped ambitions, and the boys became more human.

When I investigated the local situation for a radio series based on Best's book, I found that the same conditions, the same ferocious taboos and rigidities, were duplicated in most classrooms. I checked with teachers at homogeneous middle-class schools in affluent neighborhoods, at downtown schools, and at suburban schools with many immigrant children. All confirmed, to a greater or lesser extent, Best's observations. Only one teacher, at a very mixed inner-city school, saw a different pattern: Many of her students had attended a progressive, kindly day-care center together from the age of two or three. These children were able to be friends across the gender barrier and had far fewer stereotypes and prejudices about one another. The boys were able to be openly affectionate, to play with girls, and to enjoy books and stories that did not always focus on male activities.

It seems to me that books can play an important role in the humanizing of little boys. Publishing insiders, teachers, and writers have always asserted that boys will read only about boys, but that girls will read anything. Researching this book, racking my memories, quizzing my daughters, I unearthed a slightly different truth: Girls do read more widely than boys, but their deepest allegiance, their fondest memories, are always of books about girls in a vigorous, independent central role.

It seems natural to both genders to want an affirmation of their own possibilities in their books. Girls have been better served in this than boys: Though modern "realistic" novelists, paradoxically, have propagated an image of girls as narcissistic, shallow, and manipulative, the predominating tone of earlier popular books has often been a liberating one, all the way back to the first half of *Little Women*. Not only are girls depicted in active roles, but boys are welcome participants in the action, warmly and acceptingly portrayed. I don't think I've ever read a girls' book that indulges in the heartless deprecation of the opposite sex that seems so routine in boys' books, even those written by women.

Could it be that the indoctrination of boys, through their literature as well as through movies, popular music, television, and schools which put such a heavy emphasis on sports, has continued unabated right through the sexual revolution? Having examined my own conscience, I've concluded that most of those books are wrong: The boys I've known are as interested and involved in family relationships, friendships, nature, cooking, music, or canoeing, as they are in their admittedly overpowering fascination with sex. They brood, they worry about nuclear war, they plan for the future, they have serious questions about the meaning of life. If we accept the narrow portrait of boys as hardened sexual exploiters that is offered in so many novels, we are acquiescing in that battle-scarred and joyless male ghettoization so shockingly recorded by Best.

It would certainly be futile as well as pointless to try to prevent boys from reading boys' books, but it is well within the realm of possibility to search out and provide for young boys of primary school age a wide range of stories, involving girls as well as boys, that will be just as satisfying to them as the hockey scores.

Books that celebrate the range of life's possibilities, books that acknowledge and delight in the variety of human experience, books that by their virtuosity of language make the reader share in that curiosity and excitement—these are the books that enhance children's lives, that give them food for thought, pique their imaginations and sensibilities, and arouse their sense of wonder.

The adult who takes the time to learn something of children's books and to pass them on with enthusiasm and care gives something precious to the child—and gives something priceless to the world: A child deep-rooted in language and story, a child with an educated heart.

A GUIDE
TO CHILDREN'S
BOOKS

A word of explanation is in order about the use of the book guide. For the readers' convenience, I've divided the books into age categories, but these are very rough guidelines. A six-year-old may enjoy reading something from the Beginning Readers list, for example, but may listen with equal pleasure and comprehension to a book from the Middle Readers category if it is read aloud. Your understanding of the child's reading skills and emotional level is the best guide of all.

The books listed under Young Fluent Readers (a handy title which I have borrowed from Taylor and Braithwaite's *Good Book Guide*) are appropriate both for talented youngsters reading ahead of themselves, and for older readers of eight or nine who are just honing their reading skills, but who need interesting content along with simplicity and brevity.

Please note that many books in the Middle Readers section are challenging both in content and style. They can certainly be relished by youngsters as old as twelve or thirteen. There is a conscious overlap between Middle, Preteenage, and Teenage books; the latter two categories have more to do with emotional than reading or age levels and generally have been chosen as apt for the special social and moral concerns of those going through puberty. Many, though not all, of the Teenage books, for example, focus on male-female relationships and are sexually explicit.

When in some cases, a book is suited for a narrower age range than others in that section, this is noted (Ages 4–6).

At the end of each book description, you will find an entry giving the author's nationality. Availability as part of a series (S) or in hardcover (H) or paperback (P) is also noted. The sad designation of OP (out-of-print) is not the final word. Many out-of-print works can be found in libraries or used bookstores, or may suddenly become available again. Keep looking.

Most of the authors are represented here by only one or two of their works. If you enjoy one book, search out the others by that author; you are bound to make some wonderful discoveries.

Many outstanding, irreplaceable British, Canadian, and antipodean books described in this guide are simply not published in the United States. Most may be ordered, quite easily, from Canadian bookstores, which carry a large stock of British books. Two excellent sources are:

The Children's Book Centre,
229 College St, Fifth Floor,
Toronto, Ontario
Canada M5T 1R4
Phone: 416-597-1331

This nonprofit information center will provide a complete list of Canadian retailers and wholesalers who sell by mail.

The Chidren's Book Store
605 Markham St,
Toronto, Ontario
Canada M6G 2LB
Phone: 416-535-7011

The world's largest children's bookstore, it offers catalogs for schools and general readers, retail to the public, and wholesale to stores, libraries, and schools.

Beginning Readers: Ages 4 through 8

These picture books and stories are chosen for their special qualities of stimulating and helping children to want to learn to read.

Alexander and the Terrible, Horrible, No Good, Very Bad Day by Judith Viorst. A perennial favorite because of the hip-urban tone in which Alexander tells of his all-too-familiar middle-class aggravations on a day in which he trips on his skateboard, the store is all out of snazzy sneakers, and there's kissing on television. (Ages 5–8, American, P)

Anno's Journey by Mitsumaso Anno. An adventure in close reading of a richly detailed "text" without words. A man travels across a Europe peopled by famous fairy tale, contemporary, artistic, and musical characters; the reader can follow a dozen interwoven wordless narratives as well as spotting familiar references. (American, H and P)

Applebet, an ABC by Clyde Watson. A rollicking, affectionate alphabet that tells a story of a little girl's day at a country fair, in lilting rhyme and richly sensuous language. Appropriately glowing pictures by Wendy Watson. (Ages 4–6, American, P)

Are You My Mother? by P.D. Eastman. A classic of separation anxiety and its soothing resolution, as a cartoony little bird tries to find his mother. Very simple, repetitive text. (Ages 4–6, American, P)

Arthur's Prize Reader by Lillian Hoban. Not just one of the excellent I-Can-Read series for beginners, but one of the very few stories in which reading is depicted in the plot as a natural and interesting part of children's lives. (Ages 5–7, American, S, P)

The Baron's Booty by Virginia Kahl. A deliciously absurd reworking of the old rueful-kidnapper story; this time it's a Baron who kidnaps thirteen boisterous little girls. Told in irresistible, linguistically rewarding rhyme, with sprightly drawings. (OP)

Ben's Trumpet by Rachel Isadora. A little black city boy yearns for a trumpet so he can play like the jazz musicians at the Zig Zag Club. Music practically sizzles out of the elegant, black-and-white art deco illustrations. (Ages 6–8, American, H)

Bonnie McSmithers You're Driving Me Dithers by Sue Ann Alderson. Appealing red, inky black, and creamy white book, with a catchy refrain, about a rambunctious girl and her distracted exasperated mother . . . who later repents. (Canadian, S, P)

Brave Irene by William Steig. Irene struggles through the snowstorm to deliver the dress her seamstress mother has made for the duchess. This is Steig's newest book, his only one with an active heroine, and among his most radiant and tender. He captures Irene's predicament—her courage, her uncertainty, her loneliness and loyalty—with his usual uncanny emotional precision, lending satisfying depth to a simple tale of overcoming. (American, H)

Bread and Jam for Frances by Russell Hoban, with pencil drawings by Lillian Hoban. Witty verses enliven the sympathetic story about a little girl badger who will eat only bread and jam . . . until her family finds a clever solution. (American, S, H and P)

Brenda and Edward by Maryann Kovalski. Two happily married dogs who live in a cozy crate behind a French restaurant are parted by an accident, only to reunite years later in their old age. A small, offbeat story with appealing illustrations. (Canadian, H and P)

The Bunyip of Berkeley's Creek by Jenny Wagner. Huge, homely and engagingly vulnerable, the bunyip searches for his identity and finds the true answers in love. Wonderful, rich, and humorous drawings by Ron Brooks. (Australian, H)

Cannonball Simp by John Burningham. A homely, forlorn little dog survives abandonment and danger to find a warmly lit, thrilling new home in the circus. A tale of courage and survival by a wonderfully gifted artist whose pictures are a marvel of subtle color and suggestion. (British, H)

Cat on the Mat by Brian Wildsmith. The artist turns this elemental "cat on the mat" text into a charming visual joke with his usual deep, tantalizing colors. (Ages 4–5, British, S, P)

CDB! by William Steig. A piquant word game for those who are firmly in control of the alphabet. (Ages 7–8, American, P)

Cherries and Cherry Pits by Vera B. Williams. Bidemmi, a little black girl, visits the artist and draws these enchanting stories-within-a-story. Her impromptu fantasies achieve a remarkable blend of nature and urban life: Cherries sprout everywhere! The watercolor and felt-marker illustrations, as juicily color-drenched as the cherries themselves, ought to inspire a host of young artists in word and color. (Amercian, H)

Chin Chiang and the Dragon's Dance by Ian Wallace. Brilliant and delicate paintings of Vancouver's Chinatown add to the realism of this story about a shy boy's nervousness at participating in the Dragon Dance, and the unexpected encouragement he gets from an old woman. (Canadian, H)

Clams Can't Sing by James Stevenson. Lots of funny sound effects in this encouraging story about two derided clams, Benny and Beatrice, who prove that they can participate (clap, fooosh, oosh, ba-loop) in the beach concert. (Ages 4–6, American, H)

Come Away from the Water, Shirley by John Burningham. While Shirley's parents absent-mindedly nag at her from their beach chairs, Shirley's full-color piratical daydreams are dramatically but word-lessly illustrated on the facing pages. A delightful exercise in reading between the lines. (Ages 5–7, British, S, P)

Corduroy by Don Freeman. A much-loved, optimistic, and tender picture book about how a little black girl and a department store teddy bear find each other. (American, S, H and P)

Could Be Worse! by James Stevenson. A deadpan tall tale, told by a sleepily imperturbable grandpa. Sparkles with the wry, laconic wit and laugh-out-loud visual humor of an accomplished *New Yorker* car-toonist. Despite his sophisticated style, Stevenson's books have a warm undercurrent of sympathetic acknowledgment of childhood emotions. (American, S, H and P)

Curious George by H.A. Rey. Children never tire (though adults do) of the antics of this harum-scarum monkey. Simple prose and fresh, lively illustrations. (American, S, H and P)

Dionsyos and the Pirates by Penelope Proddow. Barbara Cooney's translucently lovely painting, with the authentic light and colors of Mediterranean Greece, are the extraordinary backdrop for the equally fascinating translations of Homeric hymns. A lyrical and dra-matic retelling of Greek myths. (Ages 6–8, American, S, OP)

Do Not Open by Brinton Turkle. Intrepid old Miss Moody, a beach-comber, and her cat, Captain Kidd, find a terrifying genie in a bottle. Superbly told story, full of surprises, sly humor, quiet courage. Out-standing illustrations. (Ages 6–8, American, H and P)

Don't You Remember? by Lucille Clifton. An appealing story about a little black girl in a working-class family. Desire Mary Tate is afraid that her busy family is going to forget her birthday cake. Told with verve and sensitivity, and strongly illustrated by Evaline Ness. (Amer-ican, OP)

Duffy and the Devil by Harve and Margot Zemach. Duffy, a feckless Cornish girl, makes a Rapunzel-type pact with the devil. With the help of witchy old Jone, she wins out in the end. Exuberant, dazzling language, Zemach's most appealing pudgy dogs and gnarled faces, and a robustly life-affirming story. (American, H and P)

Each Peach Pear Plum by Janet and Allen Ahlberg. Familiar nursery characters are slyly hidden in each sunny pastel picture, with a rhyming couplet on every page. Quickly becoming a classic of "lap books." (Ages 4–6, British, H and P)

Ellen's Lion by Crockett Johnson. These twelve tender but unsentimental stories about Ellen's imaginary dialogues with her fond, grumpy stuffed lion sensitively illustrate the quality of play which is superior to mechanical amusements. (Ages 6–8, American, P)

Everyone Knows What a Dragon Looks Like by Jay Williams. A small boy (like the one who saw that the Emperor had no clothes) saves his mountain village from destruction by the Wild Horsemen while the pompous elders panic. Surprise ending and gorgeously Chinese illustrations by Mercer Mayer. (American, H and P)

The First Books by M.B. Goffstein. A collection of artfully simple tiny stories, with astonishingly laconic and expressive small line drawings. The exceptional spareness and evocativeness of the first five stories ("Brookie and Her Lamb," "A Little Squirrel Went Walking," "Across the Sea," "The Gats!" and "Sleepy People") make them perfect for beginners. (Ages 5–8, American, OP, but several stories available in separate hardback editions)

The 500 Hats of Batholomew Cubbin by Dr. Seuss. An offbeat masterpiece. An imperious king is taught a sharp lesson by a polite small boy whose shabby hat assumes a mysterious multiplicatory life of its own. Other deservedly loved Dr. Seuss classics for beginning readers are *Fox in Socks* and *Green Eggs and Ham*. (Ages 6–8, American, H)

The Fool of the World and the Flying Ship by Arthur Ransome. A classic Russian folk tale about the foolish younger son who triumphs against the odds. An ample, lively retelling by Ransome and richly illustrated by Uri Shulevitz. (Ages 6–8, British, H)

The Funny Little Woman by Arlene Mosel. A Japanese tale about a little old woman who pursues a roll-away dumpling into the land of demons, and outwits her captors. The many-layered drawings by Blair Lent are a tantalizing addition to an enduringly fine story. (American, H and P)

George and Martha by James Marshall. Five simple but funny and pertinent stories about the friendship of two endearingly childlike hippos. Marshall has a gimlet eye for the small conflicts that lead to wounded feelings between friends, and for the affectionate honesty that can heal the hurt. The drawings amplify the plot with broad comic details. (Ages 4–7, American, S, H and P)

Go, Dog, Go by P.D. Eastman. Basic vocabulary, but riotously funny, with energetic cartoonlike illustrations and a captivatingly nonsensical series of events. Perfect for learning to read. (Ages 4–7, American, H)

Goggles! by Ezra Jack Keats. A sympathetic and realistic story of two little boys who outwit the bullies in a vacant lot, enhanced by Keats's impressionistic collages and his characteristic intuitive feel for children's vulnerability and resilience. (Ages 5–7). Of course, no child should miss Keats's other immortal picture books, *Whistle for Willy* and *The Snowy Day*, both from Viking Penguin. (American, H and P)

Harquin, the Fox Who Went Down to the Valley by John Burningham. Harquin is too daring, and brings his family into danger, but after a cinematically thrilling chase scene, he leads them out again. Burningham at his most vibrant. (British, H)

Harry the Dirty Dog by Gene Zion. Harry is alarmed when his owners don't recognize him under a layer of dirt, but all comes right in the wash. A deceptively simple, reassuring, and much loved story about identity. (Ages 4–6, American, S, H and P)

Herman the Helper by Robert Kraus. Irrepressibly perky Herman the octopus finds more than eight ways of helping. Humanely supportive of a child's need to feel useful, without preachiness. Lively, colorful, and humorously detailed pictures by Jose Aruego and Ariane Dewey. (Ages 4–6, American, S, H)

Hey, Al by Arthur Yorinks, illustrated with witty panache by Richard Egielski. Al is a New York janitor. When he and his dog Eddie are transported to a faintly eerie bird-inhabited paradise, they learn that "ripe fruit soon spoils" and there's something rotten about this avian nirvana. Sharp young readers will spot, in the picture of the dodo, an early clue to the goings-on. The acclaimed wit and modern edge of this award-winning duo are anchored by strong and humane feelings. (American, H)

Hey Diddle Diddle illustrated by Randolph Caldecott. A reissue of the first, never surpassed children's illustrator. Caldecott's endlessly inventive interpretation of familiar nursery rhymes are a delightful education for the eye. (British, P)

The House on East 88th Street by Bernard Waber. "Every home should have a crocodile," conclude the Primms, who moved into a brownstone to find lovable Lyle in the bathtub. Wryly uproarious, with enchantingly witty drawings by the author. (American, S, H and P)

How Tom Beat Captain Najork and His Hired Sportsmen by Russell Hoban. The glorious victory of Tom, that fidgety, fool-around boy, over the smarmy "sportsmen" sicked on him by his grim Aunt Fidget Wonkham-Strong. Wickedly funny language, hilarious pictures by Quentin Blake, and balm for the soul of every child who's been scolded for idleness. (Ages 5–8, British, H and P)

The Island of the Skog by Steven Kellogg. A band of mice cast away on an island find that the mysterious monster, Skog, is a timorous, rumpled, little animal who was afraid of them. Boisterous humor, intricate drawings, and a gentle message. (American, H and P)

Johnny Crow's Party by Leslie L. Brooke. A Victorian classic, newly reissued and still fresh, crammed with fascinating details in superb pen-and-ink drawings of Johnny Crow, who is the amiable host of an animal garden party that sometimes threatens to get out of control. With brisk and engagingly odd rhyming couplets that stick in the mind. (British, S, H)

The Judge by Harve Zemach. A cumulative story with bubbling language, in rhyme and breathless rhythms, about an imperious judge who gets his comeuppance in a marvelous visual surprise. Margot Zemach's sketchy pastel drawings are as swift, comic, and as rich in observation as ever. (American, H)

Little Bear by Else Holmelund Minarik. The first, and among the best of all the excellent I-Can-Read books, these affectionate, insightful stories of a small bear, his family, and animal friends are illustrated by Maurice Sendak at his most tenderly expressive. The economical but richly evocative text is an artistic triumph. (Ages 4–7, American, S, H and P)

Madeline by Ludwig Bemelmans. Urbane and delightful drawings of Paris and an irresistible rhymed story about the youngest (and naughtiest) little girl in the orphanage. (Ages 6–8, American, S, P)

Mary Alice, Operator Number Nine by Jeffrey Allen. A seemingly simple story about a duck who stays home sick and turns out to be irreplaceable. Reassuring and hilarious, with drawings by James Marshall. (American, P)

Meg and Mog by Helen Nicoll. Meg is an amiable witch whose amusing spells ... frog in a bog, bat in a hat ... make reading practice fun. Jan Pienkowski's black stick-figures on vibrant colored backgrounds add to the allure. (Ages 4–6, British, S, P)

Millions of Cats by Wanda Gag. Hundreds of cats, thousands of cats, millions and billions and trillions of cats, in Gag's unforgettable bold black-and-white woodcuts and equally memorable rhythmic text. (American, H and P)

Mister Rabbit and the Lovely Present by Charlotte Zolotow. A rabbit helps a little girl find a lovely present of fruit in every color for her mother's birthday. Dreamy, luminous illustrations by Maurice Sendak. (Ages 4–6, American, H and P)

Moonlight by Jam Ormerod. A remarkable, beautiful wordless picture book tells an uncannily subtle and perceptive story of a little girl's bedtime rituals in a warm family setting. These pictures may well spark a thousand words. By the same author, about the same child, *Sunshine*. (British, H and P)

The Most Amazing Hide-and-Seek Alphabet Book by Robert Crowther. Every big, black lowercase letter hides a pop-up matching animal. Unsurpassed for wit and inventiveness. (Ages 4–6, British, H)

The Napping House by Audrey Wood. A rainy day, and everyone's napping . . . granny, boy, dog, and car. Alert lap-sitters will spot a hidden mouse and a flea who will create uproarious chaos in this delicious cumulative rhyming story. Gentle, light-drenched illustrations by Don Wood create a magical atmosphere, moving from drowsy coziness to wide-awake energy. (American, H)

Noisy Nora by Rosemary Wells. Nora is the neglected middle child who feels left out as father plays chess with big sister and mother fusses over baby brother. Her revenge: noise, and lots of it. An amusing, small-size book, with the simple story told in fluid and appealing rhyme. (American, H)

One Monday Morning by Uri Shulevitz. A comic juxtaposition of urban reality and make-believe, with a spare, cumulative text. Gorgeously arrayed playing-card royalty come to visit a daydreaming boy in a tenement. (Ages 5–7, American, H and P)

Our Snowman by M.B. Goffstein. The soft, evocative pastel illustrations are a triumphant new departure for Goffstein. In an understated but richly nuanced story of family life, a brother and sister celebrate the first snowfall by building a snowman. The deceptively simple plot has true fictional impact: Every image and every sentence resonates with sensory perception and emotional insight. (American, H)

Papagayo, the Mischief-maker by Gerald McDermott. Sizzling hot, almost fluorescent colors make the jungle spring alive in this story about a naughty parrot who is vindicated when he turns his energies to leadership against a common enemy. (American, OP)

The Paperbag Princess by Robert Munsch. Elizabeth is a modern princess who rescues her preppy prince from a dragon and concludes that he is a "bum" when he objects to her untidy appearance in this broadly farcical fairy tale update. (Canadian, P)

Rosie's Walk by Pat Hutchins. A hen takes a nonchalant walk through a bright Pennsylvania Dutch landscape, slyly followed by a fox who comes to grief in a series of pratfalls. The child "reads" the pictures as well as the text to get the joke. (Ages 4–6, American, H and P)

Sally Go Round the Sun by Edith Fowke. Three hundred skipping rhymes, singing games, finger plays, and familiar chants and jingles, with music and bright decorations. A wonderful aid to active play. (Canadian, H)

Shadow by Blaise Cendrars. An eerie, imaginatively provocative African prose-poem for stalwart readers, with startlingly brilliant collages by Marcia Brown that reward long moments of mesmerized scrutiny. (Ages 7–8, French, H)

Sid and Sol by Arthur Yorinks. Startling closeups, zoom, and distance "shots" in black-and-white make this one of the most convincing (and contemporary) portraits of a giant in picture books. Sol, the boastful giant in a cardigan, towers over the skyscrapers. But Sid, "a short guy," as archetypal as the "youngest son" of fairy tales, triumphs over the giant. Richard Egielski's mordantly modern illustrations are stunning. (American, H)

Six Darn Cows by Margaret Laurence. A sturdy story of family responsibility and mutual warmth by one of Canada's outstanding novelists; simple, resonant text with real chapter headings; watercolors by Ann Blades. (Ages 6–8, Canadian, H)

The Story about Ping by Marjorie Flack. A Chinese duck's first adventures in independence include friendship, loneliness, and a welcome retreat to his huge family at the end. Kurt Wiese's glowing and sensitive pictures are masterful and ensure this story's status as a classic. (American, H and P)

The Story of Ferdinand by Munro Leaf. This book celebrates its fiftieth birthday this year, and is still going strong, thanks to its gentle, life-affirming story and the charmingly funny black-and-white drawings by Robert Lawson. Ferdinand is a bull who refuses to participate in bullfights, despite the rip-snorting enthusiasm of his peers. His mother worries, but she understands that Ferdinand "just likes to sit quietly under the cork tree and smell the flowers." (American, P)

Sylvester and the Magic Pebble by William Steig. A poignant and beautifully illustrated story about a donkey child who gets turned into a stone, to the grief of his parents . . . until they are reunited. By one of the great, humane picture book artists of our time, whose language is always as rich as his art. (American, P)

The Tale of Peter Rabbit by Beatrix Potter. An indispensable hand-size classic, with suspense, vigorous prose, exquisitely precise and memorable watercolors. Read the whole series aloud. Like most adults, you'll probably most cherish *The Tailor of Gloucester*. (British, S, H and P)

Tell Me a Mitzi by Lore Segal. Warm but chaotic family life, in which the parents are as realistically depicted as the competent little girl and her brother Jacob. A funny, wise, and wonderful "shaggy dog" story, with equally wonderful homely illustrations by Harriet Pincus. Also, *Tell Me a Trudy*. (American, H and P)

Three Big Hogs by Manus Pinkwater. Three big hogs lose their cozy home, but overcome their fears to survive happily as "tough, hairy, regular forest hogs." An invigorating modern twist on the old *Three Little Pigs* tale. Wittily illustrated by the author, written in his usual jaunty and endearing style. (American, OP)

Three Strong Women by Claus Stamm. A charming tall tale from Japan about an impish girl, her mother, and her grandmother, who secretly coach a sumo wrestler. An unusually unforced and liberated folk tale, brilliantly and good-naturedly illustrated by Kazue Mizumura. (American, OP)

Tikki Tikki Tembo by Arlene Mosel. The story of how a too-favored older brother nearly comes to grief because of his inflated name, which just happens to be a favorite, rollicking tongue-twister. A classic; perfectly illustrated by Blair Lent. (American, P)

The Trek by Ann Jonas. A little girl turns her morning walk to school into a fantastic safari of the imagination. Every shrub, grocer's display, and shadow on the way hides a lurking and possibly dangerous jungle beast . . . but her "amazing skill" as a pretend-trekker "saves her day after day." Some of the hidden animals are a miracle of witty artistry; discovery and triumphant laughter will accompany each rereading. Best of all, the text acknowledges a young child's fears while helping to transcend them. (American, H)

The Vingananee and the Tree Toad by Verna Aardema. A vivid and exciting Liberian tale about how tiny Tree Toad saves her bigger friends from the hairy monster. Satisfying sound effects for the reader-aloud, a suspenseful cumulative plot, and charming illustrations by Ellen Weiss. (American, H)

Where the Wild Things Are by Maurice Sendak. Every word is perfect in this justly famous and reassuring story of a small boy conquering his own aggressions in the wild monster-kingdom of his mind. Sendak's full-page art work is dazzling. (American, H and P)

Whose Mouse Are You? by Robert Kraus. A splendidly swift, evocative story of a little mouse's anger (and reconciliation) when a baby brother is born, with bold, brilliant pictures by Jose Aruego. (Ages 4–5, American, H and P)

Why Mosquitoes Buzz in People's Ears by Verna Aardema. A familiar nuisance amusingly accounted for in a West African chain-reaction tale, rich in onomatopoeia. Vivid, stylized illustrations by Leo and Diane Dillon. (Ages 4–7, American, H and P)

The Wild Washerwomen by John Yeoman. A good-natured tall tale, proletarian style, about some washerwomen who rebel against drudgery, marry seven woodsmen, and share the work. Spiked with quirky, eccentric, hyperactive drawings by Quentin Blake. (British, P)

Would You Rather? by John Burningham. Would you rather be covered in jam, soaked with water, or pulled through the mud by a dog? Riotous and sometimes fiendish alternatives (as well as large illustrations) encourage readers to engage in conversation with the book or the reading-aloud parent. (Ages 4–6, British, H)

Zoom at Sea, by Tim Wynne-Jones. Soft full-page pencil drawings by Ken Nutt add tender humor and mystery to this enchanting, evocative story of Zoom, the kitten who longs to go to sea. His dream is thrillingly fulfilled by the mysterious, maternal Maria. (Canandian, H)

Young Fluent Readers:
Ages 5 through 8

These stories and picture books have ample text. They are good for skillful young readers or older children who need stimulating content with which to hone their reading skills.

Alligator Pie by Dennis Lee. These fresh, contemporary Canadian variants on old nursery rhymes are already on their way to becoming "classics," thanks to the infectious rhythms and inspired word play. The humor is less aggressive than in the two sequels, *Jelly Belly* and *Garbage Delight.* Illustrated by Frank Newfield. (Canadian, H)

The Amazing Bone by William Steig. Pearl the pig is befriended by a magic bone with the gift of tongues. Steig's pictures are drenched with color and his language alive with wit, invention, and variety. A picture book for readers. (American, H and P)

Arabel's Raven by Joan Aiken. Wildly funny and verbally inventive adventures of Mortimer, the raven, adopted by Arabel's unsuspecting working-class family. His escapades lead them into Monty Python-esque lunacies that are irresistible. Slapstick, satirical, deadpan, ironic . . . Aiken is a genius of every kind of humor. (Ages 6–8, British, S, H)

Aurora and the Little Blue Car by Anne-Catharina Vestly. Aurora's father, a Ph.D. student, looks after her and baby Socrates while mother works. The small storms, anxieties, and gaieties of contemporary family life are seen with marvelous accuracy through the eyes of Aurora, a resourceful preschooler, who helps her father learn to drive. (Norwegian, S, H)

The Bat-Poet by Randall Jarrell. A little brown bat stays in the outside world when his relatives go to hibernate; he turns his dazzled perceptions of the world's beauty into poems, but "the trouble's finding somebody that will listen to them." An unusually literate, charming allegory about making and listening to poetry, with wonderfully soft, mysterious drawings by Maurice Sendak. Ages 7–8, American, H and P)

The Bee-Man of Orn by Frank Stockton. This turn-of-the-century fable about an eccentric old beekeeper who wants to find out what he was "transformed" from has its *longueurs* in the middle, but is redeemed by its gentle integrity, surprise ending, and Maurice Sendak's ugly-hilarious illustrations. (American, H)

Blue Moose by Manus Pinkwater. A quirkily charming short novel about an urbane talking moose who emerges from the north woods to serve as headwaiter at the isolated restaurant of flustered little Mr. Breton. The story and pictures are among Pinkwater's wittiest and most endearing. (Ages 7–8, American, S, H)

The Brave Little Toaster by Thomas M. Disch. Five "minor appliances" run away from their dear little cottage near the forest to find their master in the big city. This comic updating of a folk tale follows the adventures of a vacuum cleaner, an electric blanket, an AM radio, and a lamp, led by a stout-hearted two-slice Sunbeam toaster. Delightfully tongue-in-cheek without spoiling the suspense of the story. With drawings by Karen Lee Schmidt. (American, H)

Bridget and William by Jane Gardam. Two short, simple, large-print stories about horses and girls. One is Bridget, who gets a pony that later saves a life; the other is Susan, age six, who cares about the local hillside chalk horse, grown over and threatened by a government fir tree plantation. The stories are lively, swift, and told mostly in dialogue. (British, P)

A Candle for Christmas by Jean Speare. Tomas lives on a northern Indian reserve and the whole texture of life there is felt through Tomas's perceptions in this simple, satisfying story. He anxiously waits for his parents to return from a journey in time for Christmas; his yearning and joy are warmly conveyed in lovely full-page paintings by Ann Blades. (Canadian, H)

The Castle of Yew by Lucy Boston. Joseph finds his way into a magic garden where he becomes page to an older boy playing knight, lives in a castle carved from a yew tree, and yearns to ride Emerald, the chess-piece horse. Despite the poetic nature of the fantasy, the language is crisp, clear, and forceful and the emotions—especially the jockeying for position between the two friends—strongly delineated. (Ages 7–8, British, H and P)

The Cat's Elbow and Other Secret Languages by Alvin Schwartz. Not fiction, but unique and desirable: a handsome compendium of secret languages, most of them variants on English that will mystify eavesdroppers. With exercises, word lists, illustrations by Margo Zemach, and lots of stimulus to play with language. (Ages 7 plus, American, H and P)

Charlotte's Web by E.B. White. Wilbur is the runt of the litter, but he is saved from death first by the girl, Fern, and later by Charlotte, the remarkable spider. Rightly considered a classic of elegantly precise, moving prose and luminous insights. And it's the single most popular children's book in America. (American, H and P)

Clever Gretchen and Other Forgotten Folk Tales retold by Alison Lurie. Fifteen authentic old folk tales in which the girls are as clever, brave, and active as the boys . . . including a Spanish role-reversal version of *The Sleeping Beauty*. Illustrated in pen and ink by Margot Tomes. (American, H)

Clever Polly and the Stupid Wolf by Catherine Storr. Twelve slyly hilarious stories in which calm, composed Polly outwits the scheming, childish wolf. An added pleasure is that many of the episodes are modern twists on favorite stories and nursery rhymes. Great fun to read aloud. (British, S, H)

Cliptail by Gabrielle Roy. Cliptail is a cozily purring stove-cat in Berthe's old farm house until she realizes that a certain rural ruthlessness is intended toward her kittens. Her adventures in saving her next litter from a winter storm emphasize her fierce courage rather than her motherliness. A distinctively French-Canadian style of folk narrative gives this book a special flavor. Illustrated by Frances Olivier. (Canadian, P)

D'Aulaire's Book of Greek Myths by Ingri and Edgar D'Aulaire. For ambitious readers, this is a handsome, large format, forthright retelling of fifty-six essential Greek myths, with many color illustrations. (Ages 8 plus, American, H and P)

Dawn by Molly Bang. The little girl, Dawn, unravels the mystery of her mother's disappearance in this poetic, haunting refashioning of the Japanese folk tale, *The Crane Wife*. Extraordinarily beautiful and evocative full-page illustrations by Bang, which reward close and sensitive observation. (Ages 6–8, American, H)

The Devil's Storybook by Natalie Babbitt. Ten original and vigorously told stories about the Devil and his plans to cause mischief in the world. They read like folk tales, swift, wise, illuminating, and sly. (Ages 6–8, American, P)

The Fairy Tale Treasury by Virginia Haviland. Wonderful for browsing—here are thirty-two world favorites, with their verses and incantations intact, from "The Gingerbread Man" to "Molly Whuppie." Splendidly humorous, robust color or black-and-white illustrations by Raymond Briggs on every page. (American, H)

Fanny and the Monsters by Penelope Lively. Three excellent stories about nine-year-old Fanny, the oldest of eight children in a Victorian family. She wishes that God might take back the newest baby, and then makes a desperate, comical atonement when she fears God might oblige. She longs to be a paleontologist, and actually discovers dinosaur bones. And she takes part in a rip-snorting play battle against the family next door. Artful, funny, with sophisticated vocabulary and delightful line drawings by John Laurence. (Ages 7–8, British, P)

Five O'clock Charlie by Marguerite Henry. One of those old-fashioned mass-market books that deservedly find a niche in young readers' hearts—a bookstore clerk recommended it to me with tears of remembered passion in her eyes! Charlie is an old work horse who breaks out of his lonely retirement pasture to reclaim the friendships and pleasures he used to know. Spacious watercolors and black-and-white drawings by Wesley Dennis add immensely to the good-hearted charm of the story. (American, H)

Flat Stanley by Jeff Brown. Stanley Lambchop has been flattened by a bulletin board falling off his wall, a convenient catastrophe: Now his parents can mail him to California, his brother can fly him like a kite, and he can prove his mettle in solving an art theft. Simple enough for the youngest reader; funny enough for all. Engaging drawings by Tomi Ungerer. (American, H)

The Fools of Chelm and Their History by Isaac Bashevis Singer. Eight exuberantly funny and universally appealing folk stories about the "shmendricks" (idiots) who live in the legendary town of Chelm. Outstanding illustrations by Uri Shulevitz. (American, H)

Freddy the Detective by Walter R. Brooks. This prewar series of books about a self-impressed pig and his barnyard friends is still popular because of its dry New England humor and genial inventiveness, and despite its leisurely pace and sometimes smugly reactionary tone. Illustrated splendidly by Kurt Wiese. (Ages 7–8, American, S, P)

Goodbye, Sarah by Geoffrey Bilson. The Wright family suffers hardship during the Winnipeg General Strike, and Mary has a painful parting of the ways with her closest friend. The best part of the story is the way the two children struggle to make sense of adult disputes, take sides, quarrel, and yet realize the value of what they are losing. Illustrated by Ron Berg. (Canadian, P)

The Happy Orpheline by Natalie Savage Carlson. The gentle adventures of a group of little girls in Paris emanate a cozy quaintness and a real tang of Paris life. Orphan stories satisfy an old-fashioned but not outmoded thirst among young readers; those about girls are relatively rare. Illustrated by Garth Williams. (American, S, H)

Harald and the Giant Knight by Donald Carrick. Harald admired the baron's fierce, leather-clad knights (who bear an uncanny resemblance to a modern motorcycle gang) until they ravaged his own father's farm. Then Harald had to come up with a plan to oust them. A richly illustrated picture book with a strong story. (British, H)

Higglety Piggelty Pop: Or, There Must Be More to Life by Maurice Sendak. Jenny, the dog, thinks there must be more to life than having everything, so she leaves home on a quest that leads her to strange, frightening, and mystical experiences. Both the superb pictures and the gripping narrative show Sendak's genius for teasing eeriness and humor that tingles with elusive meanings. (Ages 6–8, American, H and P)

The Hoboken Chicken Emergency by D. Manus Pinkwater. Arthur's immigrant family is startled when he buys a 280 pound hen (with a tenor cluck) from Professor Mazzocchi, inventor of the Chicken System. A favorite among the fans of Pinkwater's good-hearted spoofs of American clichés, con men, and cops-and-robbers conventions. (Ages 7–8, American, H and P)

Hugo and Josephine by Maria Gripe. First-grader Josephine is lonely at first, but discovers friendship with the help of Hugo, a woodsy free spirit. A sensitive, amusing, and warm-hearted story, with an intriguing taste of strangeness and a fine understanding of children's concerns and misconceptions. (Ages 6–8, Swedish, S, OP)

The Hundred Dresses by Eleanor Estes. A lovely, sensitive story about a crisis of conscience. Maddie reluctantly joins in the teasing of an outsider in class . . . but what can she do when her conscience needles her too late, after Wanda has moved away? Not a "problem novel" with prefab conclusions, but a real novel, delicately exploring profound questions of mischief, guilt, and reparation. Finely illustrated by Louis Slobodkin. (Ages 8 plus, American, H and P)

The Iron Man: A Story in Five Nights by Ted Hughes. The boy, Hogarth, makes friends with the terrifying huge robot that comes out of the sea, and learns how to tame the giant's powers. In one of these linked stories, the robot saves the world from an outer-space threat. A scary, amusing, gripping story, told with hair-raising poetic intensity and powerful imagery. An absolutely sure-fire read-aloud. (Ages 7–8, British, H and P)

Jacob Two-Two Meets the Hooded Fang by Mordecai Richler. Jacob is the youngest of five brothers and sisters, some of whom help to rescue him after he is convicted of rudeness to adults (his lawyer is named Louis Loser) and sentenced to prison on Slimer's Isle, where he finds the wit and courage to unmask the Hooded Fang as a big softie. (Canadian, H)

Just So Stories by Rudyard Kipling. The cat who walked by his wild lone and Yellow-dog Dingo are still bywords in many families. Read these hypnotically cadenced stories aloud; they are the prototype, and still the best, of modern "how things came to be" fables. (British, P)

Little House in the Big Woods by Laura Ingalls Wilder. A sturdy favorite. We feel the rhythm of the year, the beauty of the wilderness, and the purposefulness of pioneer life, its excitements, fears, and family love, through the sensibilities of lively five-year-old Laura. Detailed, informative line drawings by Garth Williams. (Ages 6–8, American, S, H and P)

Little Tim and the Brave Sea Captain by Edward Ardizzone. Tim runs away to sea, where he overcomes fear, is competent and brave when the ship goes down in a raging storm, and returns a hero. The charm of Ardizzone's busy, sketchy drawings is undying, and Tim's fantasy of grown-up risks is lightened by humorous daily details and cocoa comforts. (British, S, H and P)

Lost and Found by Jean Little. Lucy is lonely in her new neighborhood until she finds a fluffy little lost dog. She yearns to keep him, but a new friend, Nan, maddeningly persists in trying to find the dog's true owners. A touching story written with extreme simplicity and emotional honesty. (Canadian, H)

The Lost Umbrella of Kim Chu by Eleanor Estes. The not-to-be missed adventure, told with delicate observation and wit, of how a desperate but ever-ingenious Kim Chu tracks her father's missing prize umbrella from New York's Chinatown to Staten Island. (Ages 7–9, American, OP)

Louhi, the Witch of North Farm by Toni de Gerez. Louhi, more puckish than fearsome, steals the sun and the moon, plunging the world into darkness, in this splendidly lively retelling of an ancient Finnish epic. Barbara Cooney's magnificent pictures glow with snow-light and firelight and the fresh spring beauty of the Finnish landscape. Rarely has a folk tale been revived with such magical immediacy of detail in both languages and picture. (American, H)

Mary of Mile 18 by Ann Blades. The author's light-washed watercolors of the bleak, dramatic northern landscape are an integral part of this touching story about a Mennonite girl who yearns to adopt a homeless pup. (Ages 7–9, Canadian, P)

Maurice's Room by Paula Fox. The grown-ups don't understand that eight-year-old Maurice doesn't want a dog or trumpet lessons; he just wants to collect bedsprings, stuffed bears, and other junkyard treasures in his already-crammed bedroom. A wryly funny portrait of a curious, self-contained, and interesting boy and his baffled, if kindly parents. (Ages 7–9, American, H)

McBroom Tells a Lie by Sid Fleischman. A rollicking tall tale about a world champion liar; with narrative and dialogue in the hillbilly idiom and humor based on zany exaggeration. (American, S, H and P)

The Moffats by Eleanor Estes. Intense, imaginative Jane, age nine, is the central figure in this enduringly popular series about prewar family life in a small town. Rufus, Joel, and Sylvie also have lively, sympathetic roles. Estes's assured and intimate understanding of children's feelings lend a unique warmth and veracity to the series. (American, S, H and P)

Mountain Rose by Patti Stren. Rose, daughter of the Flying Flushmans, was so big the other kids said she needed her own zip code. Stren decorates every page with her appealing, wittily captioned cartoons that add to the story of how Rose, a wrestler, wins the world championship and finds her long-lost brother. The tone is urban-hip, funny, and sweet. (Canadian, H)

Mrs. Dunphy's Dog by Catharine O'Neill. A hilarious, captivating picture book that tells a fine tale and also celebrates the joys of reading. Mrs. Dunphy always reads the newspaper, and James, her dog, always shreds the discarded pages. One night, he stops long enough to read a headline ("Giant Flying Cat Terrifies Tots") and is hooked. The watercolor illustrations are rosy with wit, charm, and merriment. All are choc-a-bloc with funny headlines to tantalize the young reader, and all add visual amplification of the amazing things James reads about. James progresses from enthrallment with the sensational press, to disillusionment, to the discovery of the joys of fiction. But he always keeps a soft spot for junk reading. This accomplished first book radiates a generous, amused spirit, and, for sheer pleasure, is not to be missed by anyone. (Canadian, P)

Mr. Popper's Penguins by Richard and Florence Atwater. Mr. Popper, with his little-boy fascination with explorers and the Arctic, has a dream come true: Admiral Drake sends him some penguins. The story is as bouncily good-hearted and uproarious today as it ever was; what seems dated to adults is merely fresh to new readers. Illustrated by Robert Lawson. (Ages 7–8, American, P)

The New Golden Land Anthology edited by Judith Elkin. A banquet of very well and widely chosen poems and stories, both old and very new, from a brief page's length to the more leisurely, from Greek myths and Wordsworth to Ogden Nash and Shel Silverstein. Delicious for browsing or bedtime. (British, P)

The New Wind Has Wings: Poems from Canada by Mary Alice Downie and Barbara Robertson. An ample and fascinating collection, from Bliss Carman to Jay McPherson and many others. With vivid collages by the distinguished Elizabeth Cleaver on every page. (Ages 8 plus, Canadian, P)

The Olden Days Coat by Margaret Laurence. A simple but affecting time-shift story, by one of Canada's greatest novelists, about ten-year-old Sal, who slips into her grandmother's past to discover a wonderful Christmas present—and a memory of snowy woods and sleigh bells—they can share. Warm and richly colored naturalistic illustrations by Muriel Wood. (Ages 6–8, Canadian, H)

Outside by André Norton. A simply written but very popular future-fantasy for the young, about nine-year-old Kristie who finds the secret way out of the ruined, domed city where survivors of a polluted world live in resigned misery. Bravely venturing outside, she discovers the world has been reborn. (Ages 8 plus, American, P)

Penny Candy by Edward Fenton. Little Paul can't quite keep up with his bossy big sister Lily and her gang . . . but he gets his revenge in the Widder Shinn's candy store, where the delicious penny treats mysteriously give you magical fantasies. The writing is superb, the whiff of misogyny less so, and Edward Gorey's drawings are among his most forgiving. (American, OP)

The Piemakers by Helen Cresswell. Set in a rural English past of the imagination, this is a funny, exciting story about Gravella Roller, a rebellious member of a family of piemakers, who nevertheless gets caught up in the excitement of baking a giant pie to win a royal contest. (British, P)

Pippi Longstocking by Astrid Lindgren. She's the strongest girl in the world, and lives in a house of her own where she rolls cookie dough on the floor and keeps her horse on the porch. Pippi is a classic figure of childhood's anarchic energy and imaginative spirit; her self-confidence, tomfoolishness, and fertile inventiveness at play are liberating for both boys and girls. (Swedish, S, H and P)

Ramona the Pest by Beverly Cleary. A warmly amusing and sympathetic story about a rambunctious little girl's difficult and sometimes embarrassing first experience of school. Though it reads quickly and easily, it is filled with incident, humor, and intimate perception of a child's feelings. (American, S, H and P)

The Real Thief by William Steig. Gawain the Goose is falsely accused by his beloved monarch of theft from the royal treasury. Gawain undergoes bitter exile before the surprising culprit confesses. A richly told and complex story of human emotion, with a glorious, convincing reconciliation at the end. (Ages 7–8, American, H and P)

The Rocking Horse Secret by Rumer Godden. The housekeeper's six-year-old daughter, Tibby, finds a lost will in the rocking horse and saves Pomeroy Place from auction. An exciting adventure for young horselovers. (Ages 6–8, British, H)

Saturday by Seven by Penelope Farmer. Peter hasn't saved the money for his school camp outing, and now he has to earn it all in one day. The story is simple but perfect; we follow Peter's anxious busy day and the flux of his emotions, as he is by turns humiliated and triumphant. Unusual in its unflinching assumption of a small child's responsibility and capability. (British, P)

The Secret Language by Ursula Nordstrom. Rebellious, prickly Victoria, age eight, a new girl at boarding school, slowly discovers the rewards (and torn loyalties) of friendship. The secret language, the secret hideout, the "playing house" games of two best friends are very convincing and freshly conveyed, though the smarmy house mother is hard to take. (Ages 7–8, American, H and P)

The Shrinking of Treehorn by Florence Parry Heide. A mordantly witty satire on the banalities and inattention with which adults treat children's problems. Treehorn is shrinking; his parents exhort him to sit up straighter at the table; his teacher tells him "We don't shrink in this class." Drawings by Edward Gorey. (Ages 7 plus, American, P)

Song of the Trees by Mildred Taylor. Eight-year-old Cassie's first person story, lyrical and suspenseful, of a black family's battle to save the trees on their Mississippi farm from the schemes of white racists. (Ages 7–8, American, H)

Stig of the Dump by Clive King. Barney is eight and lonely when he discovers a stone-age man living in a chalk quarry. The lively story of their shared adventures is particularly rich in graphic descriptions of their ingenious inventions and hair-raising escapades. Illustrated by Edward Ardizzone. (Ages 7 plus, British, H and P)

Stone Fox by John Reynolds Gardiner. A gaspingly tense, terse, exciting story about Willy, age ten, who tries to save his ailing grandpa and his threatened farm by winning the cash prize in a dogsled race. His chief competitor is a giant, unspeaking Indian. Exhilaration, surprise, and sadness go hand in hand. Illustrated by Marcia Sewall. (Ages 7–10, American, H and P)

Thing by Robin Klein. A funny story about a girl who lives in a flat and can't have pets. When Emily accidentally hatches a baby stegosaurus from a round "stone," she has to invent all sorts of subterfuges (abetted by Thing's own genius for disguise) to hide his presence from the landlady. (Australian, S. P)

The Tin-Lined Trunk by Mary Hamilton. Polly and Jack are wretched London street urchins who are "rescued"—a bit of a mixed blessing—by Dr. Barnardo and sent off to Canada, where their endurance, courage, and fierce determination slowly win them the friendship of dour Ontario farmers. An orphan story anchored in reality. (Ages 7–8, Canadian, P)

Very Last First Time by Jan Andrews. A haunting yet reassuring picture book with a unique story. Eva, a contemporary Inuit girl, tries, for the first time, an annual rite in her village: going beneath the sea ice, when the tide is out, to harvest mussels. Danger, mystery, and triumph are reflected in full-page, evocative paintings by Ian Wallace. (Canadian, H)

The Violin by Robert Thomas Allen. Misty full-page photographs by George Pastic and Andrew Welsh dramatize the story of two boys who live on Toronto Island. They become friends with a gentle, crumple-faced old man (the real-life violinist Maurice Solway) and one of them satisfies his heart's desire: to learn to play the violin. The ending of this dreamy, mysterious story is particularly poignant. (Canadian, P)

Walter the Lazy Mouse by Marjorie Flack. Walter is so lazy that he gets left behind when his family moves, and has to survive by himself on an island in the woods for a year. Comic-rueful adventures in independence. Amusing drawings by Cyndy Szekeres. (American, P)

Wingman by Manus Pinkwater. The author's heavy-black-ink cartoon illustrations are the perfect witty complement to this superbly told story about a Chinese boy in New York who skips school every day to climb the George Washington Bridge and dream about a Chinese superman. It's one of those stories with layers and layers of felt life and deep emotion behind them; a classic. (Ages 6–8, American, OP)

The Yellow Airplane by William Mayne. Rodney finds a wonderful model airplane that flies into his grandparents' garden, discovers a tree fort, joins a gang called the Three Bad Eggs, and wins over Maureen, the local bully. Mayne is an artist in prose, able to see the world through the child's eyes and re-create it with elegant precision. A perfect story for a young, accomplished reader. (British, OP)

Zlateh the Goat and Other Stories by Isaac Bashevis Singer. Seven wonderful stories, some about Chelm, the mythical village of fools, all told with the economy, eccentric detail, and humor of a masterful storyteller. The title story is particularly touching. Fine illustrations by Maurice Sendak. (American, H and P)

Middle Readers: Ages 8 through 12

The Adventures of Robin Hood by Roger Lancelyn Green. The most straightforward and comprehensive retelling of the indispensable Robin Hood legend, free of forsoothery, and with excerpts of old ballads to head the chapters. (British, P)

All-of-a-Kind Family by Sidney Taylor. The sympathetic story of five Jewish sisters (ages four to twelve) who live on the Lower East Side, with lovingly realistic descriptions of the library, Papa's rag business, school, the street peddlers, family hardships and feasts, and a wonderfully romantic grown-up love story seen through the children's eyes. (American, S, P)

Angel Square by Brian Doyle. Angel Square is where the kids from the Jewish, Catholic, and Protestant schools meet to fight every day in this high-spirited, tough-talking, tolerant, and nostalgic farce about Ottawa's Lowertown after the war. But the kids all get together to track down the real anti-Semite who beat up Sammy's father. Doyle's most accomplished book yet. (Canadian, H)

Anne of Green Gables by L.M. Montgomery. Anne is an unconventional orphan, much given to self-dramatization. But the tart humor and reticence of the adults, Matthew and Marilla, save the book from mawkishness. Anne's unusual character and the author's palpable, sensuous love of the Prince Edward Island landscape have made the book a worldwide favorite. (Canadian, S, H and P)

The Baby Project by Sarah Ellis. Jessica, eleven years old and the youngest of three, is elated when her parents announce that a new baby is expected. This is an unflaggingly funny, warm, and insightful story about a contemporary family in which all the characters—spunky friend Margaret, the hip hairdresser who lives downstairs, Aunt Eileen who sends stocks to the new baby ("Nothing gives a woman more confidence than her own financial portfolio")—are vivid, complex, yet lovable. The tragedy at the book's climax is heartbreakingly poignant, but the resolution is both touching and optimistic. This is a perfect book to tempt readers of "problem novels" because it is swift, accessible, and realistic without any sacrifice of depth. (Canadian, P)

The Battle of Bubble and Squeak by Philippa Pearce. The battle is really between unhappy Sid and his resented though affable stepfather. Sid's mother, Peggy, who doesn't want him to have gerbils, is another combatant. A sympathetic and piercingly intuitive story about the feelings of a working-class family as they move towards a resolution. On the surface, delighted attention is paid to the gerbils' antics and crises. (British, H and P)

Beowulf by Kevin Crossley-Holland. In this electrifying translation of the Anglo-Saxon epic, young Beowulf sails over the whale's way to fight the clawed monster Grendel and his mother the sea-wolf. The harsh northern background springs to life in marvelous imagery, and Charles Keeping's full-page black-and-white drawings are appropriately sinister. (British, H and P)

Black Hearts in Battersea by Joan Aiken. When Simon comes to nineteenth-century London to be an artist, he meets Dido Twite, the most appealing guttersnipe in fiction, and the two of them are dragged into a wildly complicated and comic "Hanoverian" plot. The story joyfully spoofs all the clichés of missing heirs, meaningful tapestries, and royal jewels. Don't miss the wonderful sequels, up to and including the most recent, *Dido and Pa.* (British, S, P)

Blue Willow by Doris Gates. An exceptionally sensitive and evocative story of a too-thin, lonely, guarded child, ten-year-old Janey Larkin, the daughter of dustbowl migrant farm workers. Bible phrases are woven into the story with great poetic force. Janey survives, and believably saves her family and wins them a home, by her defiant courage and one great act of generosity. (American, H and P)

The Bongleweed by Helen Cresswell. Rebellious Becky Finch plants a mysterious seed in the manicured Pew Gardens where her father is head gardener. The analogy with Eden is no mistake; while the Bongleweed takes over the gardens, Becky is bursting with new intimations of creativity and freedom. A perfectly written, poetic, and humorous fantasy. (British, H and P)

The Borrowers by Mary Norton. Pod and Homily Clock and their thirteen-year-old daughter Arietty are "borrowers," those little people who live hidden in houses and whisk away useful small things such as thimbles. Their miniature world is worked out with great imaginative vigor, and the clash of their world with the larger one, when a Boy intervenes, is not only comic and wise about the energies of youth but filled with perceptions about the nature of reality. (British, S, H and P)

Bows Against the Barons by Geoffrey Trease. A romantically radical version of Robin Hood, in which the struggle is not so much Saxons against Normans but peasants against overlords. The political idealism gives new vigor to the story. (British, H)

Charlotte Sometimes by Penelope Farmer. Charlotte, a lonely thirteen-year-old at boarding school, shifts back in time to 1918; the tone is somber and often haunting, but this is a subtle, provocative, and touching book about finding one's identity. (British, P)

Come Sing, Jimmy Jo by Katharine Paterson. Eleven-year-old James struggles to cope with the strains in his family and with his own frightening new fame as a TV country singing star. His strong relationship with his Appalachian grandmother helps him to deal with complexities in this fresh, funny, and touching story. (American, H)

The Cremation of Sam McGee by Robert Service. The bold, brilliant, rainbow-hued paintings by famed Yukon artist Ted Harrison are a perfect complement to the irresistible rhythms of the poem; there's a spirit of vigor to the point of excess here, both in the poem's comic exaggeration and the vibrant paintings, that make it ideal for the restless or reluctant "middle" reader. (Canadian, H)

The Cricket in Times Square by George Selden. A cheerfully urbane story about Chester, the cricket, who makes a fortune for the Bellini family's subway newsstand by playing classical music. But fame isn't enough; Chester is homesick for the country, so his streetwise pals, Tucker Mouse and Harry Cat, help him escape. (American, S, H and P)

The Dark Is Rising by Susan Cooper. This five-book series, beginning with *Over Sea, Under Stone,* in which children battle against the forces of darkness, is a gripping, complex fantasy based on Welsh legend. For excellent writing and imaginative depth, this cycle is head and shoulders above most of the fantasy genre. (American, H and P)

Dawn of Fear by Susan Cooper. Seven days in the life of Derek, a young boy in suburban London during the Blitz. The fort he and his friends build, and their own war with a gang of bullies, is more real to him than the nightly bombardment . . . until the heartrending end. Stunningly vivid evocation of the Blitz, and superb perceptions of childhood feelings. (American, H)

The Devil's Children by Peter Dickinson. One of Dickinson's three excellent novels about the Changes (a future time when all the English turn against machinery and revert to a kind of chaotic medievalism), this story features twelve-year-old Nicky and a band of wandering Sikhs with whom she finds sanctuary. Dickinson is an outstanding storyteller, whose swift, engrossing narratives are always as intellectually stimulating as they are exciting. (British, S, H)

The Diamond in the Window by Jane Langton. Edward and Eleanor, who live in a "Gothico-Byzantine" house in Concord, Massachusetts, solve an old mystery involving their lost aunt and uncle, Prince Krishna, a magic mirror, a secret code, and a fabulous treasure. This book has everything, including rich literary allusiveness and a naturalistic family background, that makes an enthralling read. (American, S, H and P)

The Disappearance of Sister Perfect by Jill Pinkwater. Sherelee Holmes, girl detective (and, she's convinced, a direct descendant of Sherlock), is sardonic, tough-talking, smart, and absolutely nothing like Nancy Drew. When her older sister Myra disappears into a sappy cult, the Temple of Perfection, and her parents seem too distracted to notice, Sherelee takes direct action. She's helped by an extraordinary cast of characters, including Aunt Irene, who wears paratrooper pants and has been living in Tibet; George, a butler who is a master of thieves' cant; and Clara, an undaunted bag lady. The action is swift and original, the dialogue funny, and the whole tone suffused with satiric intelligence. An enticing choice for children addicted to series action stories. Pinkwater's gripping first novel, *Cloud Horse,* a time-leap story about a Viking girl and her extraordinary horse, is also worth searching out. (American, H)

A Dog So Small by Philippa Pearce. What happens when you finally get your heart's desire . . . and reality falls short of the dream? Ben Blewitt, the middle child in a large working-class family in London, yearns passionately for a dog of his own. Of all yearning-for-a-pet stories, this one ranks with *The Yearling* in sheer intensity. The drama of the plot is matched by the subtlety of Ben's inward struggle to relinquish a dream and take pleasure in reality. (British, H)

Dominic by William Steig. Dominic is an anthropomorphic dog who sets out to satisfy his need for adventure. Filled with the ardor, restlessness, and reckless generosity of youth, he befriends hapless animals, conquers the ruthless Doomsday Gang and finds his true love. A romantic, exuberant, satisfying story, crackling with energy, love of life, and Steig's dazzling breadth of both vision and vocabulary. (American, H and P)

The Egypt Game by Zilpha Keatley Snyder. An imaginative game of Egyptian queens, priests, and oracles, that takes place in a junkshop yard, turns into something spookier and more exciting than even the gang of eleven-year-old players could have dreamed up. (American, H and P)

The Eighteenth Emergency by Betsy Byars. Benjie, nicknamed "Mouse," is pursued by an angered Marv Hammerman, the Neanderthal of the sixth grade. Wry and wisecracking, this short novel perfectly captures the fear and hopelessness—and eventual relief—of anyone hounded by a bully. (American, P)

Emil and the Detectives by Erich Kästner. A rousing and delightful story about how Emil is robbed of his mother's hard-earned money while on his first solo train trip to visit relatives in Berlin. Quick-witted Emil follows the thief, and is aided by a friendly gang of city kids. Together they form a clever plan to get the money back. Swift action and warmly believable characters and settings have made this an enduring favorite. (German, P)

Emily Upham's Revenge by Avi. Prim little Emily, age seven, ends up as the bank-robbing accomplice of Seth Marple, alias Deadwood Dick, age eleven, in this fast-moving, plot-twisting, good-natured Massachusetts version of the Wild West. (American, H)

The Empty Schoolhouse by Natalie Savage Carlson. A simple but affecting story about clever, ten-year-old Lullah's passionate desire to attend a white school, as told by her teenage sister. The children struggle against southern racism and win . . . though the book itself is not entirely free of some racial stereotypes. (American, H)

Five Children and It by E. Nesbit. The five children are a triumph of affectionate observation: Decent, funny, quarrelsome, and occasionally grubby. Their dialogue, written at the turn of the century, still crackles with spontaneity. Nor can age wither the fresh inventiveness and satirical snap of their adventures with the cranky sand fairy who grants wishes. All the sequels are as good or better. (British, S, P)

From Anna by Jean Little. Anna is the clumsy, ten-year-old outsider in her warm but sometimes insensitive family. When her idealistic father insists that they flee from Hitler to Toronto in 1933, Anna resists—but in Canada she comes into her own. When it's discovered that she is nearly blind, a special class is found for her and we see her begin to bloom. A moving, honest, and strong story. (Canada, S, P)

From the Mixed-up Files of Mrs. Basil E. Frankweiler by E.L. Konigsburg. When twelve-year-old Claudia and her younger brother, James, run away from home to live in the Metropolitan Museum of Art, they not only survive with great ingenuity but also solve a museum mystery. Sophisticated, fun, and convincing. (American, H and P)

Gaffer Sampson's Luck by Jill Paton Walsh. When James's family moves from familiar Yorkshire to the strange, watery flatness of the Fens, he feels stranded—and at school, he *is* stranded between the rival cliques of tough villagers and snobbish suburbanites. Worse, in his attempt to help a marvelously crotchety old neighbor to find a long-lost lucky charm, James runs afoul of the local bully and has to accept a hair-raising dare. Walsh's swift, polished, and drily humorous prose make this an immensely evocative story for a skilled reader who will relish the strangeness of British landscape and mores. At the same time, the realistic scrapes and adventures of boyhood provide a lively read for the action oriented. (British, H)

The Ghost of Thomas Kempe by Penelope Lively. Ten-year-old James is uproariously and maddeningly haunted by the ghost of a cantankerous seventeenth-century apothecary. A wonderfully funny and intelligent many-layered story about a boy's perception of time. (British, H)

Ginger Pye by Eleanor Estes. Jerry and Rachel Pye, ages ten and nine, live in a small town in prewar America. The story of their amazing dog, Ginger, how he was lost, and how he was finally recovered, is full of warm family feeling, telling detail, humor, suspense, and the leisurely, incident-filled childhood of other times. (American, S, H and P)

Goldie the Dollmaker by M.B. Goffstein. A touching and original story about a girl who lives alone in the forest, making wonderful dolls, who comes to realize that her craft and independence are more precious that a disappointing boy friend. The author's wiry line drawings add a folk tale atmosphere and are an expression of distilled tenderness. (Ages 6–10, American, H and P)

Gone-Away Lake by Elizabeth Enright. Portia and her cousin, Julian, discover a long-abandoned summer village at the edge of a swamp, and learn that some old people are secretly living there. A lovely, sympathetic, and believable family story of exploration. (American, S, P)

A Handful of Thieves by Nina Bawden. Fred tells how he and his gang track down the lodger—a sanctimonious fraud artist—who stole Granny's life savings from her teapot. An exciting and often funny "detective" story, with understated and tolerant affection among working-class friends and relatives. (British, P)

Harriet the Spy by Louise Fitzhugh. A colloquial and still disturbingly funny story about a headstrong eleven-year-old, Harriet, who lives in Manhattan with her parents and Ole Golly, her eccentric governess. Harriet records in her notebook her devastating observations about schoolmates and neighbors . . . until her scathing honesty backfires. (American, H and P)

The Haunting by Margaret Mahy. Eight-year-old Barney fears that he has inherited the Scholar family magical powers when he begins to be haunted by a missing uncle. But his silent twelve-year-old sister Troy is guarding a secret. A tense psychological thriller with a background of family affection. (New Zealand, H and P)

Heidi by Johanna Spyri. Like Anne of Green Gables, this little free spirit wins over a crotchety old man; the sensual beauty of life on the Swiss Alps—the wildflowers, sunsets, beds of sweet hay, bowls of milk, and toasted cheese—is still captivating. (Swiss, H and P)

Hey World, Here I Am! by Jean Little. Warm, funny, unsentimental poems and musings by the fictional eleven-year-old poet, Kate Bloomfield, who was the central character in *Kate,* another excellent novel by Jean Little. Kate is an ebullient, willful, spontaneous, and thoroughly believable preadolescent. In the sensitive and satisfying novel, she struggles to sort out her half-Jewish identity. This separate collection of "her" poems is recommended not just for its uncanny perceptiveness, but also as a model of fresh, unforced writing that might stimulate other young poets to equally original and honest efforts. (Canadian, P)

The Hobbit by J.R.R. Tolkien. Bilbo Baggins sets out, at the urgings of the wizard Gandalf, to help the dwarfs recover their lost treasure from the dragon Smaug. A much-loved tale told in an avuncular, fireside tone. (British, H)

The House of Sixty Fathers by Meindert DeJong. A richly imagined, touching, and powerful World War II story about a Chinese boy and his pet pig, Glory-of-the-Republic, who make a frightening, desperate journey to find the boy's family while eluding the advancing Japanese troops. Danger, hunger, and anxiety are offset by Tien Pao's resilience, courage, and love. (American, P)

The House with a Clock in Its Walls by John Bellairs. Lewis Barnavelt, a chubby ten-year-old orphan, goes to live with his jaunty Uncle Jonathan in a strange mansion haunted by the ghost of a warlock. It turns out that Jonathan and his friend, Mrs. Florence Zimmerman, are magicians too. Spooky, exciting, funny, and sweet. Coziness and cocoa always balance the ghoulishness. (American, H and P)

How Many Miles to Babylon? by Paula Fox. A bleakly convincing but ultimately optimistic story of how ten-year-old James, a black boy in Brooklyn, is kidnapped and terrorized by a teenage gang in an abandoned fun-house, and manages to escape. (American, H)

Hurry Home, Candy by Meindert DeJong. The suspenseful, empathetic story of an abused puppy who becomes a stray, his year-long hardships on the loose, and his eventual happy homecoming to a retired sea captain who understands him. Illustrated by Maurice Sendak. (American, H and P)

The Indian in the Cupboard by Lynne Reid Banks. An extraordinary book, exciting and thought-provoking, about Omri, whose plastic Indian comes alive when it is shut in a special cupboard. Both the thrill and the growing burden, physical and moral, of caring for living, miniature, recalcitrant people are astonishingly well conveyed. The newly published sequel, *The Return of the Indian,* is just as tense, thrilling, and provocative, as Omri is tempted to travel through time to provide "his" Indians with modern weapons. (British, H and P)

Into the Dream by William Sleator. Paul and Francine, twelve-year-old classmates, learn they have telepathic powers and are reluctantly drawn into a nightmarish CIA plot to kidnap a four-year-old with even greater psychic gifts. This popular, easy-to-read thriller is written with urgency and conviction. (American, H and P)

Jasmin by Jan Truss. Jasmin, defiant and depressed by her chaotic rural-slum family and her imminent failing of sixth grade, runs away into the Alberta bush where she survives alone in a cave, is swept away by floods, and is rescued by new friends who show her a way to independence and happiness. (Canadian, P)

Jennifer, Hecate, Macbeth, William McKinley, and Me, Elizabeth by E.L. Konigsburg. Elizabeth is lonely in her new suburban apartment until she meets Jennifer, a tall, skinny, fierce, and imaginative black girl who claims to be a witch. An air of mystery hangs over Jennifer's amazing feats, and much ghoulish humor attends Elizabeth's apprenticeship in make-believe witchcraft, but the real story is of their growing friendship and confidence. (American, H and P)

The Juniper Tree and Other Tales from Grimm translated by Lore Segal and Randall Jarrell. An indispensable collection of the eeriest and most powerful Grimm stories, translated with riveting clarity and illustrated with haunting strangeness by Maurice Sendak. (German, OP)

A Lemon and a Star by E.C. Spykman. An unusually vibrant depiction of a high-spirited, wealthy New England family at the turn of the century. The motherless children have uncommon freedom, and Edie, the youngest (at five) is the boldest and most interesting, though most vulnerable to her brothers' teasing. In a sequel, *Edie on the Warpath,*

Edie at eleven rebels against "ladylike" restriction and joins the suffragettes. Funny and wonderfully perceptive. (American, S, P)

The Lion, the Witch and the Wardrobe by C.S. Lewis. The best of the popular Narnia series (the symbolism does not weigh too heavily on the plot), this is the story of how Lucy, her brothers, and her sisters go through the back of the wardrobe in the old professor's house and into a kingdom where, because of a spell cast by the White Witch, it is "always winter but never Christmas." (British, S, H and P)

Lisa and Lottie by Erich Kästner. There is something uniquely satisfying about the reunion of twins who have been separated from birth: Perhaps we all long for a double, a perfect soul-sister? This charming and lighthearted novel is emphatically a girls' book, and almost quaint, but still imperishably delicious. The nine-year-olds discover each other's existence accidentally, at a summer camp, and contrive to reunite their divorced parents by secretly switching places. Despite the lively pace and sustained suspense, the atmosphere is sunny and loving. (German, P)

The Little Bookroom by Eleanor Farjeon. Hosannas to David Godine, publisher, for reissuing this award-winning collection of fairy tale-style short stories by the unusually imaginative, humorous, and lyrical Farjeon. "And I Dance My Own Child" and "The Connemara Donkey" are particularly touching and splendid, as are the lovely drawings by Edward Ardizzone. (British, P)

The Magic Adventures of Pretty Pearl by Virginia Hamilton. A stunning book, perhaps even an indispensable one: I don't know any other children's book that lends such mythic force to the black experience in America. Pretty Pearl is a "god chile" who comes down from Mount Kenya to help the black people during the painful persecutions of Reconstruction times. She finds a clan of "inside people," hidden away in a magically self-sufficient and beautiful secret world in a huge forest in Georgia, and her fate becomes intertwined with theirs. Hamilton renders black speech so lyrically that it mesmerizes the reader; she makes folk tale tricksters and heroes vibrant with life. There is strangeness, "otherness," here for the white reader unfamiliar with African lore; Hamilton makes it glorious, with great emotional warmth and depth. The book is beautifully produced, with a Romare Bearden painting on the cover and elegant African decorations throughout. (Ages 11 plus, American, H and P)

Marianne Dreams by Catherine Storr. Two convalescent children, a ten-year-old girl and a teenage boy, who have never met, come together in a terrifying dream from which they gradually free themselves. An eerie, sometimes frightening, psychologically convincing, and ultimately reassuring story. (British, H and P)

Me and My Million by Clive King. A gimlet-eyed illiterate urchin, Ringo, is led into crime by his older brother, Elvis, and ends up on the lam in London with a priceless Pestalozzi painting of the Madonna ("some mum and her kid"). Ringo is unexpectedly aided by an amiable art forger who lives on a canal boat. Suspenseful, satirical, funny, and fine, puncturing the pretentions of everyone from art experts to animal liberationists, and posing some subtle questions about art and truth. (British, H)

The Midnight Fox by Betsy Byars. Twelve-year-old Tommy looks back on the extraordinary summer when he was eight and stayed at his aunt and uncle's farm, where he formed a mysterious bond with a black fox and its cub. Tommy's ironic fantasies provide a witty commentary on the often tense, humane, and subtle story of how he saves the fox from death. Moving and funny. (American, P)

The Mouse and His Child by Russell Hoban. This poignant and absorbing story of a clockwork mouse and his father—their journeys, perils, and adventures, rich in symbolism—has become something of a cult favorite among adults. Teenagers will also appreciate its philosophical, humanistic underpinnings. (American, H and P)

Mrs. Frisby and the Rats of NIMH by Robert C. O'Brien. Some superintelligent rats escape from an experimental lab and, with the help of a courageous mother mouse, attempt to found a new rat civilization based on self-sufficienty instead of stealing. An absorbing and ingeniously worked out fantasy. (American, S, H and P)

The Mysterious Disappearance of Leon (I mean Noel) by Ellen Raskin. Mrs. Carillon seeks her long-lost husband with the help of adopted twins Tony and Tina. A widely loved, funny, and satisfying detective adventure, complete with puzzles, riddles, codes, and visual clues, it also resonates with meaning: The mystery is solved when everyone's true name is known and false roles and identities discarded. (American, P)

The Night Watchmen by Helen Cresswell. Henry meets two strange tramps, Josh and Caleb, who come from There by the mysterious night train. But the Green Eyes, a frightening enemy, appear, and Henry begins to realize the world is filled with infinite possibility. (British, P)

Ninny's Boat by Clive King. "Bat bee iroo low"—that scrap of a forgotten language is Ninny's only clue to his identity. He is a thrall to a primitive Anglish tribe, a funny, shaggy, kindhearted, and resourceful boy. It's a marvel how thoroughly King makes us see and hear everything through Ninny's sensibility. The saga of his quest is exciting, uproarious, and linguistically rich; just unmissable. (British, H and P)

No Way of Telling by Emma Smith. Amy and her grandmother are isolated by a blizzard in their remote Welsh farmhouse when a frighteningly huge, wounded stranger blunders in. Whom should they help: the fugitive or the smooth-talking men on skis who pursue him? An extraordinarily believable and superbly written heart-thumping tale of tension, character, intuition, and courage. (British, H)

Nurse Matilda by Christianna Brand. Nurse Matilda, with a nose like two potatoes, is brought in to teach seven mysterious, magical lessons to the completely unruly Brown children, an innumerable Victorian family. It accurately captures both the anarchic fun and ultimate misery of being out of control. A wonderfully strange and memorable fantasy. Illustrated by Edward Ardizzone. (British, S, P)

Ordinary Jack by Helen Cresswell. Jack is eleven, the only "ordinary" member of the wildly competitive, overachieving Bagthorpe family, which is mercilessly and hilariously spoofed. The slapstick, fast-paced comedy is up-to-date and Pythonesque, though it always stops short of the grotesque. (British, S, H and P)

Owls in the Family by Farley Mowat. A lovable and funny memoir of boyhood in Saskatoon and the boys' unusual pets. Mowat, who also immortalized his comical dog in *The Dog Who Wouldn't Be,* here describes the antics of two owls, Wol and Weeps. Abounds in physical comedy and affection. (Canadian, P)

The Peppermint Pig by Nina Bawden. Nine-year-old Poll has an amusing pet, a riotously disruptive pig, to console her during a difficult year in her family's life. Through this unconventional family— strong-willed aunts, a mother who loves to tell ghoulish stories, a hysterical younger brother—themes of betrayal, family trust, loss, and reaffirmation are touched on with vivacity and wit. (British, H)

The Phantom Tollbooth by Norton Juster. The picaresque adventures of Milo, tootling through Dictionopolis in his electric car to rescue the "fair" princesses, Rhyme and Reason. The whole story is a light, airy juggling of wordplay and witty abstractions, with some luminous moments of imagery, as when an orchestra "plays" the sunset. (American, H and P)

The Pinballs by Betsy Byars. Written with extraordinary simplicity, directness, and wisecracking humor, this story of how three preteen-age foster children come to terms with their hurts nevertheless avoids slickness and rings true emotionally. (American, H and P)

A Pocket Full of Seeds by Marilyn Sachs. A strongly moving and emotionally honest fictionalized account of a real girl, Nicole, age thirteen, who is left behind in a French town when her parents and sister are deported by the Nazis. The moral confusion of the times is vividly conveyed, and the sometimes stormy but deeply loving relationship between Nicole and her mother is heartbreakingly real. Illustrations by Ben Stahl. (American, H)

The Princess and the Goblin by George MacDonald. A wonderful, large-spirited and vigorous Victorian fairy tale that remains in the memory for years. Gallant Curdie, a miner's son, fights back against the sinister underground goblins; at one point, his life is saved by the king's little daughter Irene, helped by her magical great-great-grandmother. The children's tender friendship and some delicate issues of trust and belief are beautifully conveyed. (British, S, P)

The Riverside Anthology of Children's Literature edited by Judith Saltman. A remarkable collection, of nearly 1,400 pages: international folk and fairy tales, myths, legends, hundreds of poems, excepts from the finest children's novels and picture books, colored illustrations, riddles, singing games, poetry by children, science fiction, and even a large selection of excerpts from biography, history, and science writing for children. A unique resource for parents, and one of the best rainy day browsing books I can imagine for the middle reader. (American, H)

Sadako and the Thousand Paper Cranes by Eleanor Coerr. A very simply written, somber but sensitive and honestly told true story of a twelve-year-old Japanese girl who died from the aftereffects of Hiroshima. Her courage and faith during her illness endeared her to Japanese schoolchildren and these qualities shine though this unaffected account. Gentle black-and-white paintings by Ronald Himler. (American, H)

The Saga of Erik the Viking by Terry Jones. Sea demons, mischievous trolls, islands of bleak rock, and dog-headed warriors—this series of new stories seems to capture all the fantastic magic and rugged conflict of Norse legend in swift, gripping prose. A perfect read for superhero addicts, and a civilizing one, too: These heroes are capable of fear, tenderness, and foolishness as well as great boldness. Abounding invention and superb full-color illustrations by Michael Forman. (British, P)

The Sea Egg by Lucy Boston. Two boys on a seaside holiday find a mysterious rock that hatches into a "triton," a sort of youthful merman who leads them on exhilarating magical adventures in the sea. Intensely poetic and beautiful writing. (British, H)

The Secret Garden by Frances Hodgson Burnett. Mary, a sickly, self-centered orphan, discovers a locked garden on her uncle's Yorkshire estate, where she finds emotional and physical healing through her closeness to nature and through her friendship with Dickon and Colin. Despite some religiose posturing at the end, this book has never lost its power to enchant. (British, H and P)

Shadow of a Bull by Maia Wojciechowska. Manolo, at twelve, must face his first bullfight, and all because his father was Spain's most famous torero. Secretly, Manolo is torn by doubts and fears. A vivid, convincing, and dramatic story of a boy's difficult choices. (American, H and P)

Smith by Leon Garfield. Smith, a grubby eighteenth-century urchin and pickpocket, witnesses a murder, befriends a blind Justice, unravels a mystery, and finds a treasure in this brilliant novel. Garfield dazzles with his speed, sardonic wit, Gothic plots, and mastery of the language, but beneath the dazzle there is also irony and subtle moral discrimination. (British, H and P)

Smoky, the Cow Horse by Will James. A rambling, old-fashioned narrative about the birth, adventures, and misadventures of a cow pony who is adopted by Clint, a cowboy, on the cattle ranges of the old West. The story is told in cowboy lingo, and tinged with the casual racism of its day (the villian is a "half-breed"), but the narrator's impassioned empathy with the horse, and the authentic, unromanticized details of rodeo and range life make this 1926 tale a sturdy old favorite, particularly for young horse lovers. (American, H)

Snow Treasure by Marie McSwigan. Despite its somewhat simplistic style, this true action story has been loved by generations of schoolchildren. Sledding right under the noses of Nazi occupation troops, Norwegian children smuggle $9 million of Norwegian gold bullion to a waiting ship for transport to America. Their courage and steadfastness, and the swift, suspenseful plot, make the story almost cinematically gripping. (American, P)

Soup by Robert Newton Peck. A classic "boys' book" about a New England boyhood, complete with fistfights, escapades, moral revelations. The prose is crisp, wryly observant, unsentimental. (American, H and P)

The Stone Book by Alan Garner. Mary's father is a stonemason in a Cheshire village; he takes her to the dizzying top of the steeple on a church he has helped build, and deep into a hidden underground cave where he shows her a family secret: a prehistoric painting. This is the first of four very short, intense, and poetically powerful novels in which different generations of craftsmen and their children in Garner's family are glimpsed in a mesh of criss-crossing relationships and tasks. They are beautiful, demanding, and unique. (British, S, H and P)

The Story of the Treasure Seekers by E. Nesbit. An unforgettably funny and charming book about the struggles of the Victorian Bastable children—all of them distinct characters in their own right—to restore "the fallen fortunes" of their motherless family. Part of the delight is the tone of the supposedly anonymous narrator, Oswald, who can't resist giving away his identity through some not-so-discreet boasting. (British, S, P)

The Summer of the Swans by Betsy Byars. A down-to-earth and affecting story about a summer in the life of a fourteen-year-old American girl who worries about her looks, loves her retarded brother Charlie, and makes some important discoveries on the heart-stopping day when Charlie gets lost. (American, H and P)

Swallows and Amazons by Arthur Ransome. This series about two families of children who sail their dinghies and camp out on an island on Lake Windemere were the first and forever the best of the "children on holiday" books. The novels are about the developing character, spirited independence, and imaginative play of the Walker and Blackett children; Ransome tells their story with a journalist's feel for humor, dialogue, and concrete detail. At their best *(Missee Lee* and *We Didn't Mean to Go to Sea),* they are exciting, dramatic, and liberating. (British, S, H and P)

That Scatterbrain Booky by Bernice Thurman Hunter. A warmhearted, fictionalized account of a skinny, spirited little girl growing up in a real Depression in Toronto. Rich in recollected details of city life, hardship, family struggle, and improvised fun. (Canadian, S, P)

Tom Tiddler's Ground by John Rowe Townsend. A straightforward "summer adventure" story in a modern industrial setting of unusual charm. Victor and Brian live beside an old, unused canal where, tagged after by some pesky girls and an unpopular boy, all of whom soon become valued members of the gang, they discover a half-sunken barge. There's treasure, warfare with crooks, and an old family mystery to unravel in this lively, naturalistic, and appealing story. (British, H)

The Three and Many Wishes of Jason Reid by H.J. Hutchins. Eleven-year-old Jason tricks an "elster"—a kind of elf—into giving him unlimited wishes, but all the magical toys (a homework machine, a dinosaur book with living pictures) begin to pale. Jason and his friend Penny try to invent a really worthwhile wish and end up saving the local park from development. (Canadian, H and P)

Three Royal Monkeys by Walter de la Mare. The immense odyssey of the three monkeys, Thumb, Thimble, and Nod, to the secret kingdom of Tishmar has been called "one of the most imaginative and poetic stories ever written for children." Rich, strange, and wonderful, it is a rewarding challenge for good readers. (British, OP)

Thunder and Lightnings by Jan Mark. Two boys of very different backgrounds, living in Norfolk, form a friendship around a fascination with airplanes from a local base. Andrew, the middle-class boy, learns some subtle lessons of friendship. Sharply observant, verbally inventive, and emotionally rewarding. (British, H)

Tikta'Liktak: An Eskimo Legend by James Houston. Adrift on an ice floe, and then marooned on a barren island, the young Inuit hunter Tikta'liktak resigns himself to death—and then resolves to live. His ingenuity, skill, and daring, and eventual reunion with his family, make a realistically detailed and exciting story of survival. Excellent drawings by the author. (Canadian, H)

Tom's Midnight Garden by Philippa Pearce. Tom is bored at his aunt and uncle's flat until he discovers a door to an enchanted garden whenever the hall clock strikes thirteen. The story gains unusual emotional depth from the superb imagery and from the evolving friendship between Tom and the mysterious Hatty, a girl who lives in another time. The resolution of the story is uniquely satisfying.

This is widely regarded as the finest, most poignant, and exhilarating time-shift fantasy ever. (British, H and P)

Tuck Everlasting by Natalie Babbit. A beautifully written fable about overprotected Winnie Foster, age ten, who stumbles on the Tuck family's secret: a fountain of eternal youth. Winnie rebels, discovers the joys of freedom, and has to make a profound choice. (American, H and P)

The Twelve and the Genii by Pauline Clark. Under a loose board in the attic of the farmhouse, eight-year-old Max finds twelve faded wooden soldiers. And then they come to life, under the leadership of their "patriarch," Butter Crashey. They are, in fact, the famous lost soldiers of the Bronte children. The engagingly intense Max and his sister Jane must negotiate perilously between the "real" adult world and the fascinating miniature one they are trying to protect and preserve. The story is written with crackling vitality, mesmerizing drama, and a vigorous moral dimension. (British, P)

Two Piano Tuners by M.B. Goffstein. Debbie wants to be a piano tuner like her grandfather; he wants her to be a concert pianist. An empathetic story about love and individuality, with Goffstein's characteristic vividness of homey details. (American, H)

Warrior Scarlet by Rosemary Sutcliff. Drem, a nine-year-old boy in a Bronze Age village, grows to manhood but fails his crucial "wolf-slaying" test because of his withered arm. Heady, Kiplingesque language and a powerful, emotional evocation of a distant time. (British, H and P)

We Couldn't Leave Dinah by Mary Treadgold. A fast-moving, exciting adventure story about a brother and sister who are accidentally left behind when a Channel island is evacuated as the Nazis invade. The children engage in a daring plot to rescue their beloved pony from the Nazi occupiers before they flee. Believable and tense, and a favorite of horse-lovers. (British, P)

The Way to Sattin Shore by Philippa Pearce. Nine-year-old Kate Tranter's family has too many secrets. Brooding and reserved, she puzzles over her missing . . . dead? . . . father. In solving the mystery, Kate begins to move out of childhood's self-centeredness. This is a subtle, splendidly written story of family relationships and reconciliation; unsentimental, lucid, and challenging. (British, H and P)

Wildcat under Glass by Alki Zei. Two little girls in a Greek village are caught up in wrenching political controversies as fascism poisons prewar Greece. The younger, Melia, influenced by her sagelike grandfather, chooses democracy, and helps to hide her fugitive freedom-fighter cousin, Niko. A rounded and fascinating portrait of both child and adult characters; play and friendship go on during the tense excitements and moral dilemmas of the times. (Greek, H and P)

The Wind in the Willows by Kenneth Grahame. This arcadian reverie is not only a wonderfully well-written celebration of rural bliss, but is peopled with endearing, comic childlike characters (Mole, Ratty, and Toad of Toad Hall) whose affections and escapades are unforgettable. With the familiar E.H. Shepard drawings, far preferable to most later versions. (British, H and P)

Witch Week by Diana Wynne Jones. In a world where witchcraft is common but absolutely illegal, two students in a boarding school are persecuted for their suspected witchery. As usual in Wynne Jones, there is spirited comedy, a plot filled with twists and surprises, vigorous action, and a deeper, unstated, and valuable message: In this case, it's that growing to adult power is all the revenge you need for childhood injustices. (British, S, H)

The Yearling by Marjorie Kinnan Rawlings. The story of a lonely backwoods boy, Jody, and his pet deer, Flag, won a Pulitzer Prize in 1939, and retains all its power to seize the reader by the imagination and the heartstrings. This is an unparalleled re-creation of the primitive, beautiful Florida wilderness and the hard-scrabble lives of its inhabitants. Jody's intense, sometimes heartbreaking, relationships with his father, his fawn, and his crippled friend, Fodder-wing, are drawn with compelling force. A recent Charles Scribner's Sons edition has the original N.C. Wyeth color illustrations. (American, H and P)

Preteenage Readers: Ages 10 through 12

Reading levels of the books in this section overlap with those of older "middle readers," but the content tends more toward the introspective and social concerns of the prepubescent.

Alan and Naomi by Myron Levoy. When thirteen-year-old Alan is asked to befriend a disturbed girl who is a refugee from Nazi-occupied France, he is afraid of losing his street-smart best buddy, Shaun Kelly. Levoy brilliantly captures the conversation, games, and complex feelings of the three youngsters and the atmosphere of wartime New York. (American, H)

Alan Mendelsohn, the Boy from Mars by Daniel M. Pinkwater. When portly Leonard Neeble goes to Bat Masterson Junior High, he is definitely odd man out—until he meets Alan and the two of them embark on a zany exploration of the occult, including a solemn study of Samuel Klugarsh's Mind Control Method. The story is thickly populated with Pinkwater's most inspired eccentrics, and riotous with his off-the-wall deadpan humor. Humane values underlie this lovable spoof-cum-fantasy. (American, H)

And Now Miguel by Joseph Krumgold. A remarkably fresh, realistic, and sympathetic first person account of Miguel, the middle son in a large New Mexico sheepherding family. Miguel is impatient for adulthood to arrive, so he can be allowed to join the men who drive the sheep up into the Sangre de Cristo Mountains for the summer grazing. The setting of a warm, traditional family structure and Spanish culture is intensely particular; the tumult and the longings are universal. (American, H and P)

Ask Me No Questions by Ann Schlee. Stifled by the Victorian respectability of her aunt's village house, Laura is unable to make anyone listen to the truth about the ghastly conditions she has observed in the "baby farm," or paupers' orphanage, next door. At last she takes desperate action to deal with the moral dilemma herself. (British, H)

The Baitchopper by Silver Donald Cameron. The liveliest part of this boys' story, about a fishermen's strike in Nova Scotia and the rancorous divisions among the townspeople, comes at the climax when two boys, sons of strikers, rescue a fishing boat that has been set adrift in a storm. (Canadian, H and P)

The Book of Three by Lloyd Alexander. Taran is an assistant pigkeeper who finds himself helping a prince to save the land of Prydain from the Horned King and the forces of evil. The sturdy, open honesty of Taran's youthful character, the humor, and the natural dialogue save this Welsh-legend-based five-volume fantasy from seeming derivative. (American, S, H and P)

Bridge to Terabithia by Katherine Paterson. Eleven-year-old Jess's family is rural, poor, and harsh. But his life changes forever when Leslie, a bright, independent city girl, moves nearby. Together they create an imaginary kingdom where Jess absorbs enough of Leslie's courage to enable him to deal with the tragedy that ends their idyll. An intensely moving and widely loved book. (American, H and P)

Carrie's War by Nina Bawden. Carrie, now grown up, brings her own children back to the Welsh village to which she was evacuated as a twelve-year-old during the war. The novel is a flashback to dramatic events and powerful emotional ties which have haunted Carrie ever since. The ending, back in Carrie's adult present, provides a deeply satisfying conclusion to the story of a lost friendship. (British, H and P)

A Chance Child by Jill Paton Walsh. An especially gripping time-shift fantasy in which Creep, an abused child, escapes down a northern England canal and slips back a century, to a time in which seven- and eight-year-old children drudged in mines and smithies. Creep, a shivering, bewildered ghost, can be seen only by children as hungry as he is—and they befriend him despite their own horrifically convincing misery. Poignant and memorable. (British, P)

The Court of the Stone Children by Eleanor Cameron. Nina, new to San Francisco, spends her time daydreaming in the French Museum, and finds that her life overlaps with that of a mysterious French girl from another century. Together, they help the museum curator unravel a romantic mystery from the past. A love story and time fantasy expertly woven together. (American, H and P)

Dear Mr. Henshaw by Beverly Cleary. A lightly and skillfully written epistolary novel. Leigh Botts, age ten, writes a series of letters to the author of his favorite book, *Ways to Amuse a Dog.* Obliquely, through their correspondence, we watch Leigh come to terms with his distress about his divorced and negligent truck driver father. (9 plus, American, H and P)

Death over Montreal by Geoffrey Bilson. A Scots immigrant boy, teenaged Jamie Douglas, finds himself in the midst of a cholera epidemic in the new country. A vivid story of the confusion, the squalor, and the riff-raff who preyed on new immigrants—and of Jamie's growing courage and competence. (Canadian, P)

Dogsbody by Diana Wynne Jones. An astonishingly original account of how hotheaded Sirius, the dog star, is cast down to earth in the shape of an Irish setter puppy and adopted by the lonely daughter of an imprisoned I.R.A. member. The entire story of Sirius's search for a lost "Zoi," or magical power, and his eventual return to his status as a heavenly luminary, is told from inside his doggy persona. Parallel to the exciting fantasy is the touching story of the girl's affection for Sirius and her growth to independence. (British, OP)

Drift by William Mayne. An extraordinarily believable adventure, in which Rafe, an American boy of early settler times, is lost in the wilderness when he follows an Indian girl to see a bear. We see Rafe's frightening odyssey through his own baffled eyes and then through the eyes of Tawena, the resourceful Indian girl, who helps him to save himself. The clash of cultures and the strange bond between them is beautifully evoked through the youngsters' reactions to each other and to crisis. (British, H)

Earthfasts by William Mayne. When Nellie Jack John, drummer boy, comes marching out of a crack in a Cumbrian hillside before the astonished eyes of two contemporary schoolboys, he opens a "leak" in time: Soon the neighboring farms are beseiged by walking stones, giants, boggarts, wild boars, and the clatter of King Arthur's troops. Told with hallucinatory clarity by a master of English prose. (British, OP)

The Eight Days of Luke by Diana Wynne Jones. Twelve-year-old David has to live with ghastly relatives until he accidentally conjures up a mysterious boy, Luke, who has strange powers—and powerful enemies. A suspenseful, comedic fantasy with elements of Norse legend. (British, P)

The Emperor's Winding Sheet by Jill Paton Walsh. Young Piers is kidnapped from a British merchant ship by Turkish pirates, escapes, and ends up as a sullen captive mascot to the Emperor Constantine in the exotic, doomed city of Byzantium. As the Turkish seige tightens around the city and the gruesome last battle begins, Piers learns to see the world through changed eyes. A subtle, intelligent, and highly charged historical novel. (British, P)

The Endless Steppe: A Girl in Exile by Esther Hautzig. Like *The Diary of Anne Frank,* only less tragic, this true story of a Jewish girl and her family who are deported to Siberia during World War II is inspiriting, rather than gloomy. Despite overwhelming hardship, Esther approaches her experiences with the buoyancy, freshness, and optimism of youth; her concerns and triumphs are those of adolescence, not those of a starving refugee. (American, H)

Fireweed by Jill Paton Walsh. Runaway teenagers Bill and Julie meet during the London Blitz and try to survive together in a bombed house. The Blitz is evoked with eerie sensual power, and the tensions, the growing bond, and the eventual heartbreaking gulf between the young people is handled with moving delicacy. (12 plus, British, P)

A Flute in Mayberry Street by Eileen Dunlop. A teenage brother and his sickly sister in Edinburgh stumble on a family mystery. The solution, with fantasy elements, is gripping, and the character development is strongly integrated with the plot. (British, H)

Freaky Friday by Mary Rodgers. Annabel Andrews, thirteen, "metal-mouthed killer ghoul of Central Park" wakes up one morning to find herself in her mother's body. All set to savor the delights of adulthood, she runs into a Marx Brothers kind of mayhem. Spying on her own life, however, she finds out some ego-bolstering truths. Hilarious. (American, H and P)

Frozen Fire by James Houston. Matthew Fraser, thirteen, and his Inuit friend Kayak, get lost in the Arctic winter in a search for Matthew's missing father. The story is strong on information and excitement; the style is the usual brisk journalism of all these Canadian-boy-and-native-friend adventures. (Canadian, H and P)

The Ghost Belonged to Me by Richard Peck. Thirteen-year-old Alexander, living in a midwestern town in 1913, gets a crackerbarrel, folksy, funny education in the interesting subject of girls—via a ghost of a southern belle with whom he falls romantically in love, and also via the all-too-real, skinny, snap-eyed Blossom Culp, his unwanted but tenacious accomplice in solving the mystery. (American, H and P)

The Great Gilly Hopkins by Katharine Paterson. Gilly, the eleven-year-old abandoned daughter of a flower child, is tough, smart, and hostile. Too late, she realizes that the freakish foster home she has rejected is a loving haven. Though the ingredients are the familiar ones of contemporary "problem novels," Paterson writes with such skill and sensitivity that her characters are alive with stubborn complexity; they are both moving and memorable. (American, H and P)

The Hand of Robin Squires by Joan Clark. An eighteenth-century English boy is brought to Oak Island, off Nova Scotia, by his piratical uncle. The boy is forced to work with pitiful black slaves to dig the shafts where treasure is to be buried, and escapes only with the help of a Micmac Indian friend. This is an ingenious fictional explanation for the real Oak Island diggings. (Canadian, H and P)

Handles by Jan Mark. The deliciously funny story of eleven-year-old

Erica's holiday with sluglike country relatives. Erica, miserably exiled from town life, consoles herself with imaginative stream-of-consciousness private jokes. Then she discovers the motorcycle garage in the village. Erica, mad for motorcycles and determined to be a mechanic, finds a kindred soul in "Elsie," who owns the garage and who bestows witty "handles," or nicknames, on everyone and everything. Jan Mark creates a vivid private world in the life of the garage. For good readers only: English slang and comic turns ("high strikes" for "hysterics") can be daunting for North Americans. But absolutely worth the effort. (British, P)

Harpoon of the Hunter by Markoosie. Canada's most thrilling, poignant, and poetically intense story of Inuit life. Kamik, sixteen, must survive alone in the wilderness after his father's hunting party is wiped out. We see how Inuit resourcefulness and courage are born of desperation and fear. There are convincing portraits of the women's strength, too, and a touching but tragic love story. Illustrated by Germaine Arnaktauyok. (Canadian, H)

The Hill of the Red Fox by Allan Campbell McLean. Alasdair, twelve, is a big-city bookworm and daydreamer when he visits his dead father's former home on the Isle of Skye, where he forms a strong and heartening bond with his father's rugged friend, Duncan Mor. This is a wonderful, suspenseful spy thriller, with lively Scots background and affecting relationships worthy of R.L. Stevenson. (British, P)

Homecoming by Cynthia Voigt. A long, naturalistic, and very compelling novel about strong-minded, resilient thirteen-year-old Dicey. She shepherds her younger brothers and sisters from Cape Cod to Maryland, mostly by foot and mostly hungry, to find a relative who will take them in after their confused mother deserts them. Vivid, believable characters, a suspenseful quest, and a deep feeling for the contemporary landscape. (American, S, H)

Homesick: My Own Story by Jean Fritz. A memoir of Fritz's missionary childhood beside the Yangtze River in turbulent prerevolutionary China. Fritz's account of colorful experiences, fascinating people, and dramatic events are told so freshly from within a lively child's keen sensibility that the memoir reads like fiction. (American, H and P)

The Homeward Bounders by Diana Wynne Jones. A dazzlingly complex and suspenseful fantasy about Jamie, age twelve, who is doomed to be an exile from his own time after he becomes a Random Factor in a world-dominating war game played by shadowy evil figures. Especially thought provoking for Dungeons and Dragons devotees.

Strands of mythology (Prometheus, the Flying Dutchman), and original characters like Joris the Demon-hunter enrich this mysterious and surprising story. (Ages 12 plus, British, H)

I, Juan De Pareja by Elizabeth Borton de Trevino. A strange, fascinating fictionalized "autobiography," by turns stoic and lushly exotic, of a black slave in seventeenth-century Spain, who became an apprentice to the great painter Velasquez. (A famous portrait of De Pareja exists.) Only in middle age, when he goes to Italy, does De Pareja realize his dream of becoming a painter himself, since Spain forbade slaves to practice any art. (American, H and P)

I Own the Racecourse by Patricia Wrightson. Andy, who is slightly retarded, is like the mascot of a good-hearted gang of working-class boys in Sydney. When a tramp "sells" the local racecourse to the gullible Andy, they are indignant on his behalf and finally confused about just what is real and what isn't. An extremely unusual, rounded, and luminously written story. (Australian, H and P)

Island of the Blue Dolphins by Scott O'Dell. A poignant and dramatic story, restrained in tone but powerful in impact, about the resilience of the human spirit. Karana is only twelve when she is accidentally abandoned on a wind-scoured Pacific island by her departing tribe. Her lonely survival into womanhood is both heartbreaking and triumphant. (American, H and P)

Jeremy Visick by David Wiseman. Matthew, twelve, works on a "boring" history assignment and finds himself caught up in a Cornish mining tragedy of a century before, in which another twelve-year-old boy was buried in a lost mine shaft. A tense, adventuresome time-shift story. (British, H)

Johnny Tremain by Esther Forbes. An enduringly spacious, detailed, and lively historical novel about an arrogant and talented silversmith's apprentice in Boston just before the Revolution. Johnny becomes an outcast after a crippling accident, but it is the making of his character, and he goes on to become an idealistic young acolyte of the Revolutionaries. (American, H and P)

Journey of the Shadow Bairns by Margaret J. Anderson. Elspeth, suddenly orphaned in a Glasgow slum, is only twelve, but she manages to bring her four-year-old brother all the way to Canada, following a charismatic leader who takes a group to the North Saskatchewan territory. An added dimension is the way Elspeth stubbornly works out for herself whether to continue to follow the group's leader after the other settlers become disillusioned with him. A believable and dramatic story of pioneer days. (American, OP)

Julie of the Wolves by Jean Craighead George. An implausible yet convincing and touching story of a thirteen-year-old Inuit girl who runs away from an arranged marriage in Port Barrow. She is lost on the tundra, survives with the help of a wolf pack and the memory of her father's lore, only to arrive at safety in a bittersweet conclusion as she realizes "the day of the wolf and the Eskimo is gone." (American, H and P)

The Keeper of the Isis Light by Monica Hughes. Sixteen-year-old Olwen has kept the lighthouse on the planet Isis for years, alone with her mysterious Guardian, just in order to guide Earth refugees to a haven. But when fellow humans do arrive, her happiness is shattered as they recoil from the strange adaptations she has been forced to make to live there. Easy-to-read science fiction, but thought provoking, with much more scope for emotional empathy than is usual in sci-fi. (Canadian, H and P)

Kim by Rudyard Kipling. The great adventure of Kim, the Irish-Indian bazaar urchin who speaks a dozen dialects, goes on a pilgrimage with a Tibetan Lama, is master of a thousand disguises, lives by his wits, and is trained to be a spy, is told in the rolling, rhythmic, highly colored language that makes it irresistible. (British, H and P)

The Lantern Bearers by Rosemary Sutcliff. In a time of wrenching dislocation in Britain's history—brutal pillaging by Saxon "sea wolves" and the departure of the last Roman troops—Aquila and his younger sister make painful decisions about their destiny. Aquila, after escaping from Saxon slavery, takes arms under Artos, British warlord. His sister marries a Saxon. Sutcliff gives a human face to history in this and her other fine novels, such as *The Eagle of the Ninth*. (British, H and P)

Let It Go by Marilyn Halvorson. Fifteen-year-old Jared and his Métis friend, Lance, are buddies, but they each hide one secret. Jared has a brother in a drug overdose coma, and Lance's absent mother is a country singing star who has reappeared suddenly, threatening Lance's happy life with his father. A "problem novel" that is saved from being a S.E. Hinton clone by a strong evocation of adolescent emotions and of Alberta wilderness living. (Canada, H)

Little Women by Louisa M. Alcott. The adolescent sisters and their "Marmee" (Smarmee, as one biting critic called her) still hold fascination, mostly by virtue of their moral ambition—their ongoing game is to act out Pilgrim's Progress—and the rebellious character of Jo. The eventual "taming" of Jo into ladylike behavior is a letdown but central to the purposes of antifeminist Alcott. (American, S, H and P)

Mama's Going to Buy You a Mockingbird by Jean Little. After his father's lingering death from cancer, Jeremy, age eleven, must cope with repressed rage and grief, his mother's new life, and the tall, embarrassingly unconventional girl his father wanted him to befriend. A touching, naturalistic novel. (Canadian, H and P)

Midnight Is a Place by Joan Aiken. Cruel child labor in a nineteenth-century carpet mill is the extraordinarily vivid background to this lively gothic adventure, in which two orphans, Lucas, thirteen, and waiflike Anne-Marie, are cast down from cold privilege to hard times. Independence, comradeship, and an enlightened conscience are their reward for their determined survival in the slums. Aiken can infuse the grimmest situation with humor, and her characters are always warmly appealing. (British, H and P)

The Moves Make the Man by Bruce Brooks. Jerome is witty, endearing, a brilliant student, a basketball whiz, a thirteen-year-old who unabashedly takes cooking lessons at school so he can feed his older brothers while Momma is ill. He is also hearteningly impervious to the crude racism he meets at his all-white school. But he's completely convincing, partly because Brooks can write about Jerome's solitary basketball practice in a way that makes the reader feel the exhilaration of physical mastery. Jerome, whose wily trickster "moves" in basketball are a metaphor for methods of black survival, befriends a white athlete, Bix, who is neurotically fixated on an ideal of "truth," however narrowly defined and destructive. Their strange friendship illuminates the black-white culture gap, while the story never loses momentum. (American, H)

My Side of the Mountain by Jean George. Sam, a teenager, lives a modern Robinson Crusoe dream for a year, alone in a Catskill mountain tree house, eating wild foods, training a wild falcon, and even making his own deerskin clothes. Abundant naturalist details smooth over the implausibility of the story. (American, H and P)

Nkwala by Edith Lambert Sharp. Nkwala is a Salish Indian boy of twelve who must undergo a lonely manhood vigil on the Canadian prairies. His trials of endurance and skill are fascinating, and the story of his tribe's trek into danger is both dramatic and touching. (Canadian, P)

Nobody's Family Is Going to Change by Louise Fitzhugh. Eleven-year-old Emma is a "fat brown girl" determined to be a lawyer like her father; her little brother Willie is equally determined to be a dancer. Her tough-minded rebellion against her parents' stereotyped expectations leads her at last to an understanding that time and hope are on her side. An unsentimental, vigorously written and optimistic story. (American, H and P)

The One-Eyed Cat by Paula Fox. Ned is haunted by guilt: Did he shoot the one-eyed cat that night in the dark with his forbidden Daisy air rifle? A subtle, controlled, and moving story about a boy's conscience and expiation. Comic relief is provided by a savage satiric portrait of a repulsive housekeeper. (American, H and P)

Pat of Silver Bush by L.M. Montgomery. Another thick, sweet fudge of a Montgomery book, filled with stage Irish, ardent innocent girlhood, and rural nostalgia, still a potent (and reactionary) mixture. Pat grows from a tradition-loving seven-year-old to a tradition-loving young woman who is taken in by several different meretricious styles of manhood before she settles for her childhood chum. (Canadian, S, P)

Philip Hall Likes Me, I Reckon Maybe by Bette Greene. Beth, a black sixth-grader in rural Arkansas, has a crush on the boy next door, but has to let him win every contest to keep his friendship—until she gets fed up. A short, jaunty, and good-humored novel of budding boy-girl relationships. (American, S, H and P)

Playing Beatie Bow by Ruth Park. Spiky and resentful Abigail, age fourteen, quarrels with her divorced parents just before she is led into the past by a mysterious little girl. Her year with the Bow family in nineteenth-century Sydney is an amazingly vivid and poignant recreation of the hardships of working-class life in the slums. An extremely absorbing, exciting, and touching account of growing maturity and first love. (Ages 12 plus, Australian, H and P)

Roll of Thunder, Hear My Cry by Mildred D. Taylor. Cassie is the middle child in a proudly independent black family that struggles to hold on to its own land in Depression-era Mississippi. This is a richly detailed, powerful, and unflinching family drama of a girl's confrontation with brutal racism. (American, S, H)

The Root Cellar by Janet Lunn. An unusually fine time-shift fantasy about Rose Larkin, a lonely thirteen-year-old orphan, who slips back in time to Upper Canada where she is befriended by a warmhearted servant girl and a restless, sensitive boy, Will. During a graphically realistic search for Will, lost somewhere in the American Civil War, Rose discovers compassion, roots, and the warmth of friendship. (Canadian, H and P)

Runaway to Freedom by Barbara Smucker. (Originally *Underground to Canada*) Tall, strong Julilly, twelve, and thirteen-year-old Liza, who is crippled from cruel beatings, escape from slavery in Mississippi and travel to safety to Canada by the underground railway. This immensely strong story is told with honest simplicity and real emotion. The girls have dignity and resourcefulness, and those who hinder or help them along the way are sharply drawn. (Canadian, P)

The Sign of the Beaver by Elizabeth George Speare. Twelve-year-old Matthew is left to fend for himself in a Maine cabin when his pioneer father unaccountably doesn't return from a trip to town. How he copes with difficulties—and his dawning awareness of injustice as he forms a prickly, tentative friendship with Attian, a Penobscot Indian boy—make a strong and provocative story. (American, H and P)

The Slave Dancer by Paula Fox. A horrific and illuminating story of Jesse, a twelve-year-old boy who is kidnapped from New Orleans to serve as a fife player on a slave ship. Perfectly pitched to the understanding of young readers without shirking or exploiting the gruesome reality and moral horror of the slave trade. (American, H)

Soumchi by Amoz Oz. An ancient quarter of postwar Jerusalem, crowded with exotic cultures and political passions, is the colorful background for this lovely, funny story of a day in the life of eleven-year-old Soumchi. He trades his new-old bike for an electric train, acquires and loses a dog, runs away from home, falls in love, and tastes the first nostalgia for swiftly passing childhood. Superbly translated from the Hebrew by Penelope Farmer. (Israeli, H)

A Stranger Came Ashore by Mollie Hunter. Robbie, twelve, is suspicious when handsome Finn Lerson is washed ashore on their Shetland island and courts his pretty sister, Elspeth. Hunter, a vigorous and compelling storyteller, draws on Scottish legend for this swift-moving, suspenseful story. (British, P)

Summer of My German Soldier by Bette Greene. Patty, an abused twelve-year-old Jewish girl in a racist Arkansas town, daringly hides an escaped German prisoner-of-war. The unmitigated cruelty of her parents and the unbelievable nobility of the prisoner make this story into a melodrama, but it is undeniably powerful, especially in the relationship of Patty and Ruth, the family's black servant. (American, H and P)

A Summer's Lease by Marilyn Sachs. Gloria, fifteen, is mercurial, prickly, and gnawingly competitive; she is determined to overcome her bleak and limiting home life to become a great writer. A summer with a group of youngsters at the country home of her English teacher takes her through some alternately blissful and agonizing steps to maturity. A compelling insight into the abrasive egotism and wounding vulnerability of adolescence. (American, H and P)

The Sword in the Stone by T.H. White. The first book in the *The Once and Future King* trilogy, and by far the best; the sequels are marred by White's bitter misogyny. The Wart (to rhyme with Art) is just a scruffy orphan, fated to be squire to the arrogant young knight Kay, when a scraggly, wise, mysterious Merlin singles him out for a magical education. This comic, fantastic, and capacious re-creation of the King Arthur legend is not just a classic but also a deserved favorite. (British, S, P)

Tex by S.E. Hinton. This immensely popular story of two brothers in Oklahoma is a sort of Harlequin for boys; beneath their tough, macho swagger and narcissism, the boys are sensitive, loyal, and have well-scrubbed middle-class values. No prizes for the Rebel-without-a-Cause prose, but the emotional bond of the brothers and the reconciliation with their father is strongly evoked. (Ages 12 plus, American, H and P)

A Traveller in Time by Alison Uttley. Penelope Taberner steps through a door in an old farmhouse and finds herself in Tudor times, in the midst of a plot to save Mary, Queen of Scots. A dreamy, romantic time-travel story, drenched in pastoral colors and fragrances, combining the sturdy domestic comforts, affections, and intrigues of a prosperous Elizabethan farmhouse with a shimmering kind of time-magic. (British, H)

Treasure Island by R.L. Stevenson. Blind Pew, Long John Silver, Dr. Livesey, Squire Trelawney—and yo-ho-ho and a bottle of rum!—who can forget any of these provokingly ambiguous characters, or the magnificent story of piracy, the sea, buried treasure, and the disillusionment of its pursuit? An essential book, especially in the facsimile edition with superb N.C. Wyeth oil painting. (British, H)

Up a Road Slowly by Irene Hunt. The great strength of this story about Julie, who goes to live with her austere Aunt Cordelia in New

England when she is seven and stays until she graduates from high school, is the sensitive observation of both adult and teenage male-female relationships in all their variety, and the sometimes agonizing struggle of a strong-willed, talented girl to conform to the expectations of male society. The tone is restrained, adult, and optimistic. (Ages 12 plus, American, H and P)

Up to Low by Brian Doyle. A rollicking story of pubescent love in the Ottawa Valley, told with an Irish lilt, genuinely funny grotty humor and an economy and freshness of language and imagery that distinguishes this writer among his contemporaries. (Canadian, P)

The Village by the Sea by Anita Desai. A superbly written novel about an Indian brother and sister who struggle to keep their family alive in an impoverished but heartbreakingly beautiful village near Bombay. Hari, twelve, runs away to the city where he endures cruel deprivation but does find work and learn a trade. This novel has all the texture and drama of Indian life and the believable emotion and yearnings of youth. (Ages 12 plus, British, H and P)

Walkabout by James Vance Marshall. The prose is too didactic, but this is a taut, tense, and provocative story of how Mary, a prudish thirteen-year-old from South Carolina, and her more free-spirited six-year-old brother, are rescued by an aboriginal boy when their plane crashes in the Australian desert. Mary's inability to overcome her racism and passive conditioning leads to doom for the boy who saves them. (Australian, H and P)

Where the Lilies Bloom by Vera and Bill Cleaver. Mary Call, age fourteen, struggles with all her ferocious determination to keep her Tennessee mountain family together after their father dies, and to prevent her "cloudy-minded" older sister from marrying a boorish neighbor. By teaching her brothers and sisters to wildcraft—gather local herbs and roots—she keeps a roof over their heads despite all odds. (Ages 12 plus, American, H)

The White Mountains by John Christopher. Europe has been returned to a kind of ruined feudalism by the mysterious, menacing Tripods from outer space, who keep people ignorant and docile by the "capping" ceremony. Will Parker, thirteen, flees with a friend to join a group of rebels. Effective, stripped-down prose and dramatic action for young science fiction addicts. (British, S, H and P)

Words by Heart by Ouida Sebestyen. Lena's fierce pride is tempered by her father's gentle dignity in this well-written, moving story of a black family's struggle to establish themselves in the rural Midwest. (American, H and P)

Teenage Readers: Ages 13 Plus

The emphasis in these books is on relationships of all kinds, some explicitly sexual, and on the spiritual and moral struggles of adolescence.

Across Five Aprils by Irene Hunt. Jethro, an Illinois farm boy, is only nine when the American Civil War begins. Over the next five years, his large, affectionate family is wrenched and buffeted by the strains of war, brought home to the reader in an intensely personal way. A growing-to-manhood story of unusual depth and solidity. (American, P)

Across the Barricades by Joan Lingard. The working-class families, Belfast streets, and constant poisonous pressure of religious hatreds add interest to the simple story of a Protestant girl who dares to love a Catholic boy. (British, S, P)

The Adventures of Huckleberry Finn by Mark Twain. Around the basic adventure story of two runaways rafting down the Mississippi— a boy and an escaped slave—Twain exuberantly weaves this high-spirited, satirical, complex story of growing up. Twain exposes every variety of hypocrisy and human self-deception, and shows us how Huck learns to choose between good and evil, truth and lie, cruelty and compassion. His innate decency constantly bursts through the smokescreen of his learned "morals." Unforgettable. (American, H and P)

The Apprentices by Leon Garfield. These twelve stories sparkle with scintillating imagery, much of it drawn from the Garden of Eden and Song of Songs, as they follow the linked destinies of twelve variously grimy, wretched, but chipper London apprentices through the cycle of the year and the cycles of adolescent love and hope. Only Garfield could combine so much tenderness with so much glittering wit and verbal dash. (British, H and P)

Bilgewater by Jane Gardam. As sophisticatedly satirical and insightful as—and certainly better written than—most adult novels, this is the funny, oblique, and many-layered story of Bilgewater's education of the heart. A pudgy, bespectacled, eccentric child growing up in the boys' boarding school where her father teaches, Bilgewater barely notices when she turns into a leggy adolescent. And she's just as myopic in her choice of boyfriends, falling for a handsome lout and then a poetic cheat while sturdy, unnoticed Boakes trots loyally at her heels. Meanwhile, the adults around her—from aging profs to the wonderful matron—are engaging in their own foolish, wrongheaded or downright peculiar affairs of the heart. Bilgewater makes the right choices at last, but, years later, her backward look at her youth is tinged with the inevitable regrets. (British, H)

A Bird in the House by Margaret Laurence. Eight beautifully written, resonant stories about the young Vanessa MacLeod and her tough, wry, domineering or defiant relatives—especially some wonderful aunts—in Manawaka, Manitoba. Through layers of the narrator's memory and Vanessa's growing awareness, we taste the irreducibility of early experience and the moral complexity that haunts us in the best fiction. (Canadian, P)

The Blue Hawk by Peter Dickinson. The remarkably convincing and vivid story of a priestly culture resembling ancient Egypt. Tron, a boy marked for the priesthood, begins to doubt, and is gradually moved to a daring rebellion. Dickinson makes the desert air crackle, the temples echo with hidden menace, and his characters live and breathe in an atmosphere charged with tension and awe. (British, H)

The Book Lovers by Leon Garfield. A shy young man woos a pretty librarian by offering her this glorious compendium of love scenes from famous literature—Turgenev, Dickens, Balzac, Tolstoy, Austen, and more. The playful intertwining of the nameless young couple's courtship with apposite selections from literature makes this a double treat. (British, OP)

Dance on My Grave by Aidan Chambers. A first person story of homosexual love and tragedy, in which sixteen-year-old Hal confides to his journal (in a brittle, defensively cynical tone) the course of his shattered love affair with Barry, and why he had to keep the bizarre vow he had made to dance on Barry's grave. Through scraps of news reports, social workers' notes, court records, and Hal's flashbacks, we watch him come to terms, painfully but with growing strength, with his own character. (British, H)

Dragonsong by Ann McCaffrey. On a planet menaced by deadly spores, where society is highly structured, a young girl, Menolly, breaks through taboos because she is the only one talented enough to take up the duties of Harper. One of the strongest of a very popular series of dragons and space fantasies. (American, S, H)

The Druid's Tune by O.R. Melling. A melodramatic but effective first novel by a young Canadian in which a Toronto brother and sister, Rosemary, seventeen, and Jimmy, fifteen, visit Ireland and are taken into a battle in prehistory at the side of the legendary hero Cuculann, through the medium of a hired hand who turns out to be a wandering Druid. (Canadian, P)

The Ennead by Jan Mark. Isaac, a fifteen-year-old house steward on the bleakly authoritarian planet Erato, is a scrawny, nervous boy, as self-seeking and pettily corrupt as those he serves. Two immigrants—the silent, prophetic Moshe and a gangly, defiant artist, Eleanor—shake him out of his complacency and force him to make a desperate choice. Crisp, challenging prose and a thought-provoking story. (British, H and P)

A Fabulous Creature by Zilpha Keatley Snyder. Vacationing in the Sierra Nevada mountains, fifteen-year-old James falls in love with a dazzling bikini-clad flirt, daughter of a trophy hunter, and, from the basest of motives, betrays to her the secret that only he and the imaginative thirteen-year-old Griffin know: An incredible twelve-point stag is living nearby in a secret valley. An honest and sensitive look at teenage infatuation. (American, H)

Far from Shore by Kevin Major. It's a bad year for fifteen-year-old Chris. Dad is out of work and drinking, his older sister does well in school while he is failing, and Chris drifts into bad company with disastrous results. The story of his troubles—and recovery—is believably and sympathetically told through the interior monologues of each family member, with an earthy and amusing use of Newfoundland dialect and humor. (Canadian, P)

Father Figure by Richard Peck. Upper-class New Yorker Jim Atwater, seventeen, is too controlled, too sardonically defensive, to grieve openly over his mother's death. But when he and his precocious little brother Byron are forced to spend a summer in Florida with their shabby, estranged father (and his father's friend, the warmhearted downhome Marietta), Jim learns some hard lessons about his own sexual uncertainty, rivalry, and defensiveness. Peck is at his urbane, witty, and compassionate best in this excellent novel. (American, H and P)

The First of Midnight by Marjorie Darke. Jess is a truculent, benighted poorhouse urchin in eighteenth-century Bristol; her growth into some kind of personal freedom is accomplished when she helps and then falls in love with an educated runaway Ibo slave. Dickensian settings, lively prose, and believable, sensitive though explicit rendering of Jess and Midnight's delighted discovery of sexual joy. (British, S, P)

Frost in May by Antonia White. An adult work of art perfect for adolescent reading, this is the story of Nanda Grey, who arrives at a rigorously authoritarian English convent boarding school at the age of nine. Through restrained, elegantly precise yet quiveringly intense prose, we relive the passionate desire of childhood to belong utterly. A riveting study of atmosphere and character. (British, S, P)

A Game of Dark by William Mayne. Donald Jackson, fourteen, leads a disturbing double life: In his cold, rigid family, he struggles against his mother's sternness and his father's hysterical fundamentalism; in his fantasy, he is a beleaguered medieval squire doomed to fight the loathsome giant Worm, or monster, who threatens a town. Gradually, Donald integrates his conflicting yearning for and rage against the different father figures in his life. A strange, surreal, and powerful novel. (British, OP)

Gentlehands by M.E. Kerr. Buddy Boyle, a working-class local in a wealthy resort town, tries to impress the glittering Skye Pennington with his only social asset: his remote, elegant German grandfather. The fantasy begins to falter when a reporter unearths the truth that grandfather Trenker was the vicious "Gentlehands," an S.S. officer at Auschwitz. Kerr is an excellent contemporary writer with an ear for dialogue that makes all the characters of every age and social class thoroughly believable. (American, H)

Goldengrove by Jill Paton Walsh. Goldengrove is Gran's house in Cornwall, where Madge and Paul, who think they are cousins, spend every summer together. Walsh's finely controlled yet sensuous, color-washed prose is the perfect translucent medium for this delicate novel about childhood's last summer and the misguided passions of adolescence. The sequel, *Unleaving,* is equally strong. (British, S, H)

Goodnight, Prof, Dear by John Rowe Townsend. Graham Hollis, the sardonic but well-behaved son of an accountant, dreams of rescuing pale maidens—and ends up rescuing and running away with a good-hearted tart of a waitress from the local cafe. With wry wit and dead-on dialogue, Townsend moves his awkward hero from blushing daydreams through a tender and funny first sexual encounter to a more mature self-awareness. (British, H)

Howl's Moving Castle by Diana Wynne Jones. Jones can wrap a light-hearted love story in such a dazzle of mystification, magic, and swift-moving plot that young romantics, fantasy-lovers, and adventure addicts will all be captivated. Her characters and settings always have strong appeal. In this story, timid Sophie is cast under a spell by the Witch of the Waste, and is changed into an ancient crone, in which guise she seeks work in the moving castle of the fearsome wizard Howl ... who is not what he seems, either. Hidden in her ancient body, young Sophie finds herself becoming stubborn, tough, and tart-tongued. Irresistibly funny and charming. (British, H)

The Ice Is Coming by Patricia Wrightson. A remarkably original fantasy trilogy about Wirrun, an aborigine youth who is called upon to save the land from the conspiracy of ice. Wrightson's free-flowing prose compels our utter belief in the spring-kneed possum-eyed Mimi, a rock spirit who helps Wirrun on his quest; the creaking Ninya, men of ice, and dozens of other fresh and fascinating earth spirits bred of Australian aboriginal folk-lore. *Dark Bright Water,* the second in the trilogy, is a fine work about the complexities of passion and love. Humor, imagination, suspense, depth, and beauty. (Australian, S, P)

In Summer Light by Zibby Oneal. A beautifully crafted story about seventeen-year-old Kate, whose artistic talent has been strangled by rage at her domineering father, a famous painter. Shimmeringly evocative landscapes of summer on a New England island are the backdrop for Kate's growing self-awareness. Best of all is the way in which Kate's musings on Shakespeare's *The Tempest* obliquely illuminate her working out of the Oedipal struggle. (American, H and P)

The Islanders by John Rowe Townsend. A tiny community clings to life on a windswept South Pacific island, reinforced by rigid, if half-understood, traditional laws and customs. One iron rule says that all newcomers must be killed. But when two young strangers are swept ashore, apocalyptic changes come with them. Molly, a teenager who rebels against the restrictive laws of the colony, is a key figure, along with her brother Thomas. A gripping adventure that poses thorny but essential questions about the nature of society and change. (British, P)

The Jersey Shore by William Mayne. A strange, dreamy, quiet book, filled with submerged emotion and slanting drama like fish glimpsed in an aquarium. Arthur, a black American boy, visits his grandfather on the sandy New Jersey coast, and shares visions of his English past—some real and some dream memories of the farther past—that he can carry on into his future life when, as an American pilot in World War II, he will visit the ancestral English Fen district, joining the generations. Mystifyingly, Arthur's blackness was deleted from the American edition. (British, OP)

John Diamond by Leon Garfield. William Jones is a twelve-year-old middle-class country innocent when he goes to London to right a family wrong and falls into a wildly complex mystery in the city's menacing slums. Garfield's careless abundance of sparkling imagery and entrancing characters—notably Liverguts, the hook-handed villain, and Shot-in-the-Head, a roof-dwelling urchin who lives by "snick-an-lurk" (pickpocketing)—build an atmosphere of ghoulish hilarity. But underneath is an unmistakably sober conclusion: "Boys and fools dream of treasure." (British, H and P)

The King's Daughter by Suzanne Martel. High-spirited Jeanne Chatel, an eighteen-year-old French orphan, is chosen to join the "King's daughters," the brides for Quebec's first settlers. Though her marriage is unpromising at first, Jeanne's stoicism, audacity, and intelligence at last overcome incredible hardships in the wilderness and she and Simon achieve an affectionate, fruitful marriage. A naturalistic and lively novel. (Canadian, H and P)

The Lark and the Laurel by Barbara Willard. Cecily, sixteen, is a mincing, conventional Tudor aristocrat who is suddenly dumped in the remote forest home of her strong-willed aunt, Dame Elizabeth, who runs an iron foundry. Cecily's liberation and her love for Lewis Mallory are vigorously and believably written. The Mantlemass series follows the intertwining fates of subsequent generations in the Ashdown Forest. Willard usually weaves a spirited story of romance into her exciting historical settings. (British, S, H)

Let the Circle Be Unbroken by Mildred D. Taylor. A continuation of the powerfully told story of Cassie Logan and her family *(Roll of Thunder)*. This richly textured narrative of black life in Mississippi gives a vivid fictional background to the roots of the civil rights movement, from the organizing of tenant farmers to voter registration drives. (American, S, H and P)

A Little Love by Virginia Hamilton. Sheema and Forrest are black teenagers in a vocational high school, but this is no sociological tract. Instead, it is a sensitive, complex, and touching exploration of their hopes, daydreams, fears, and sexual tenderness, by one of America's finest writers. (American, H)

A Long Way from Verona by Jane Gardam. A witty, perceptive, and finely written novel about Jessica Vye, a teenager on England's north coast during the war. Her intelligence and literary talent don't protect her from hasty misjudgments, the small betrayals of adolescence, and the rueful experience of falling in love with a handsome but shallow boy. (British, P)

The Lord of the Rings by J.R.R. Tolkien. By now a rite of passage, the reading of this massive trilogy about the hobbits and dwarfs who fight the forces of evil is bound to be thoroughly engrossing. It's like an immense, magical compendium of fairy tales, enriched with wonderful folkloric names, poems, battles, and unforgettable archetypal characters. (British, H and P)

The Machine Gunners by Robert Westall. Chas, fifteen, steals a machine gun from a downed Nazi plane and builds a hidden bunker with his friends. Gradually, the boys are caught up in the hysteria of war; their confused adolescent hatred is directed against the adults who have failed to protect them rather than against the German enemy. This is an accomplished, overpoweringly effective novel, marred by the boys' panicky misogyny from which the author never dissociates himself. (British, H)

Moses Beech by Ian Strachan. A strong, forthright novel about teenage Peter, who runs away from a slovenly home and finds refuge with an eccentric old hermit, Moses. Their developing friendship—not to mention Peter's love affair with a local farmer's daughter—brings down catastrophe on Moses, but both of the young people are left with a legacy of self-reliance and saner values. (British, H)

One More River by Lynne Reid Banks. Leslie Shelby is a spoiled, petulant Canadian fourteen-year-old who sulks when her family moves to an Israeli kibbutz. There, her prickly relationships with her peer group, her tentative distant friendship with an Arab boy on the West Bank, and her observation of the Six Day War, help her to grow in valor, resilience, and tolerance. (British, H and P)

A Parcel of Patterns by Jill Paton Walsh. The grim true story of Eeyam, a lovely English village of 350 people that was almost entirely wiped out by the plague in 1665, is told here in a graphic and

moving fictionalized account of love, tragedy, and survival by sixteen-year-old Mall Percival. Such courage and moral perseverance in
the face of doom have a particular relevance for today's teenagers.
(British, H and P)

Pennington's Seventeenth Summer by K.M. Peyton. He's a hulking,
working-class thug, a tornado of reckless energy, a thoughtless
prankster, loathed by his teachers—and he's a brilliant pianist. This
trilogy is a *tour de force:* hectically funny, written with a flair for
dialogue and pell-mell physical action but just as good at evoking the
sound of classical music, and the most sympathetic and believable
portrait in print of an inarticulate delinquent with genius in his hands.
Less breathless but equally unsentimental are the sequels about his
jail sentence, marriage, fatherhood, and musical career. (British, S, H
and P)

A Pistol in Greenyards by Molly Hunter. Connal Ross is a hotheaded
fifteen-year-old whose family is shattered by the brutal Highland
clearances of the 1850s. A vivid, fast-moving historical drama with
romantic interest. (British, H and P)

Raisins and Almonds by Fredelle Maynard. Sharp and sweet as wild
berries are these memories—in twelve short stories—of a Jewish girl
growing up in a series of tiny Prairie towns where coyotes howled
at the icy moon outside the bedroom window. The Canadian experience seems more vividly real here, in its harshness, beauty, and bigotries, than in much fiction. (Canadian, P)

Representing Superdoll by Richard Peck. Verna, sixteen, is an ordinary Indiana farm girl who can't help but feel that her life is a little
flat—especially compared to that of her voluptuous classmate, Darlene Hoffmeister, Miss Hybrid Seed Corn. But the future begins to
look more expansive than Verna had suspected when she is chosen
as Darlene's chaperone on her prize trip to New York. Peck is at his
suave, satirical, observant best in this story of Verna's growing self-
awareness and triumphant good sense. (American, P)

*The Secret Diary of Adrian Mole, Aged 13³/₄ by Sue Townsend. The
satire is aimed at the priggish, self-absorbed diarist himself, would-be
intellectual Adrian Mole, the kind of klutz whose nose sticks to his
model airplane when he tries to sniff glue. Adrian's parents are engaged in a chaotic variety of extramarital dalliances which he is too
naive to notice; by the end, Adrian has become more human and his
family has settled down. (British, P)*

Shadow in Hawthorn Bay by Janet Lunn. Mary is a spitfire: a fifteen-year-old Highland Scot, gifted (and, she thinks, cursed) with "second sight." When she hears her beloved cousin Duncan calling her from the New World, she sets out on her own to join him, only to find, after a stubborn, arduous journey, that he is dead. Lunn brings alive the clash of cultures between brooding, aloof Mary, with her other-worldly beliefs, and the friendly, practical Yankee settlers with whom she must make a new life on the shores of Lake Ontario. Before she can find new love, she must throw off the shadow of her morbid attachment to Duncan. This is an exhilaratingly many-faceted novel, strongly and unsentimentally written, with a fine feel for the dailiness of colonial life. (Canadian, H)

The Singing Stone by O.R. Melling. A vigorous, action-filled fantasy about a contemporary eighteen-year-old orphan who is unaware of her secret powers as a Mage. Kay Warrick's lonely life is disrupted by a mysterious anonymous present: a package of ancient Celtic tomes. They galvanize her to search for her Irish roots—and she is soon caught up in a terrifying quest for four lost treasures of power. Kay is accompanied by a strange waif of a girl, Aherne, who grows to be an unexpected heroine. This is one of these rare quest novels that turn received conventions on their heads: There are lots of pitched battles and action scenes, but, in the end, it is through betrayal and love, not war, that a people is saved. The contemporary love story that frames the time journey is also appealingly handled. (Canadian, H)

Snow Apples by Mary Razzell. A grittily honest and compassionate novel about what it was like to be a bright and pretty sixteen-year-old girl in the 1940s, growing up in a west coast outport. Sheila's embittered, begrudging mother and her chauvinist brothers do nothing to protect her from the cruel sexual double standard of the times, and only Helga, an old Norwegian woman, comes to Sheila's aid after a horrifying illegal abortion. The tone of working-class realism is reminiscent of *A Tree Grows in Brooklyn*. (Canadian, P)

A Sound of Chariots by Mollie Hunter. This incandescent and powerfully emotional autobiographical novel traces the life of Bridie McShane from the age of nine to her teens. Bridie, passionate, brave, and defiant, with a Celtic sense of the richness of words, is her father's favorite, and her life is shattered—and only slowly remade—when he dies suddenly. (British, H)

Them That Glitter and Them That Don't by Bette Greene. Half gypsy, half Irish, with a derelict family living in a trailer, Carol Ann is an outcast in her Arkansas town, ferociously determined to achieve fame as a country and western star. The local color, clever characterizations, humor, and deft colloquialism lift this novel above the ranks of the merely predictable. (American, H and P)

This Strange New Feeling by Julius Lester. Three love stories based on true accounts of slavery days: vivid, direct, easy-to-read and yet with the sharp flavor of a heartbreaking reality. Though the characters are young, theirs is an adult love, and the heroes and heroines have the courage, dignity, and bluntness of survivors. (American, P)

Two's Company by Catherine Storr. Kathy, fifteen, is envious of her beautiful older sister's success with boys, and resentful of her father's infidelity. On a family holiday in southern France, she falls in love with the broodingly handsome Val, only to discover too late that he is homosexual. This is an intelligent, sympathetic, and humane story that captures the temporary frenzy of infatuation and puts it into perspective. (British, H)

Very Far Away from Anywhere Else by Ursula K. LeGuin. A sharply perceptive novel about Owen Griffiths, a seventeen-year-old introvert, who finds himself falling in love with another nonconformist, the fiercely dedicated musician Natalie. Too late, Owen realizes that he has warped their relationship by a knee-jerk insistence that love must lead at once to sex. A thoughtful and honest look at teenage relationships. (American, H)

What About Tomorrow? by Ivan Southall. Sam is fourteen, an impoverished Melbourne schoolboy during the Depression, when he smashes his bicycle and decides to run away. This picaresque story of his startling encounters, the people who befriend him, the girls with whom he falls in love, is told with tenderness and insight through Sam's own vulnerable, optimistic, and endearing sensibility. A dimension at once somber, exciting, and satisfying is added by virtue of the flash-forward scenes to his life and death as a World War II pilot. (Australian, H and P)

A Wizard of Earthsea by Ursula K. LeGuin. The education, spiritual and magical, of the young wizard, Ged. This magnificent, powerfully imagined trilogy (the second book, *The Tombs of Atuan*, deals with the emergence to womanhood of a young captive priestess) is more sensitive, intense, and original—and certainly more egalitarian—than *The Lord of the Rings*, and its prose is at once more muscular and polished. (American, S, H, and P)

Books about Children's Reading

Babies Need Books by Dorothy Butler. A trail-blazing and completely accessible book, written with charm and vivacity and detailed, helpful advice. (H and P)

The Child and the Book: A Psychological and Literary Exploration by Nicholas Tucker. A wonderfully sensitive and sensible exploration of the connection between children's psychological development and the literature they need and enjoy. (P)

Cushla and Her Books by Dorothy Butler. A dramatic, true and detailed account of how the life of a multiply handicapped child was transformed through picture books. Indispensible for parents and teachers of handicapped children. (P)

The Marble in the Water: Essays on Contemporary Writers of Fiction for Children and Young Adults edited by David Rees. Fascinating essays about some of the leading British and American children's authors of today. (P)

Read-Aloud Handbook by Jim Trelease. Useful and persuasive guide to reading aloud to all age groups, with 300 suggested books. (P)

Thursday's Child: Trends and Patterns in Contemporary Children's Literature by Sheila Egoff. A comprehensive, densely packed historical survey and analysis of all forms of children's literature, by Canada's leading critic in the field. (H)

We've All Got Scars: What Boys and Girls Learn in Elementary School by Raphaela Best. A unique, riveting account, filled with startling and illuminating anecdotes, about sexist conditioning boys impose on each other in primary school, and its effect not only on their play and character but also on their reading ability. (H)

Written for Children by John Rowe Townsend. A sane, knowledgeable and thorough history and critique of children's literature up to the 1970s, gracefully written. (P)

Index

INDEX

Illustration Credits